Medieval
$5.40d.

Medieval
Merchant Venturers

THE EARL OF WARWICK LOADING ENGLISH CLOTH

"Here shewes howe good provision made of Englissh clothe and other thynges necessary, and licence hadde of the kyng, Erle Richard sailed towardes the holy londe, and specially to the holy Cite of Jerusalem, where our lorde Jhesu Criste wilfully suffered his bitter passion for the redempcion of al man kynde."

(See *Introduction* p. xvii)

Medieval
Merchant Venturers

COLLECTED STUDIES

by

E. M. CARUS-WILSON

*Professor of Economic History in
the University of London*

METHUEN & CO LTD, LONDON
36 Essex Street, Strand; WC 2

First published in 1954

CATALOGUE NO. 5465/U

PRINTED IN GREAT BRITAIN BY THE RIVERSIDE PRESS
AND BOUND BY HUNTER AND FOULIS, LTD, EDINBURGH

CONTENTS

	PAGE
Preface	ix
Introduction	xi

CHAPTER

I. The Overseas Trade of Bristol in the Fifteenth Century	1
II. The Iceland Venture	98
III. The Origins and Early Development of the Merchant Adventurers' Organization in London	143
IV. An Industrial Revolution of the Thirteenth Century	183
V. The English Cloth Industry in the Twelfth and Thirteenth Centuries	211
VI. Trends in the Export of English Woollens in the Fourteenth Century	239
VII. The Effects of the Acquisition and of the Loss of Gascony on the English Wine Trade	265
VIII. The Aulnage Accounts: a Criticism	279
Subject Index	293
Index of Persons, Places and Ships	300

FRONTISPIECE

The Earl of Warwick loading English Cloth

MAPS AND CHARTS

1. The Rise of the Merchant Adventurers: England's Exports of Raw Wool and Woollen Cloth, 1347–1544   *facing p.* xviii

2. Bristol's Overseas Trade at the Close of the Middle Ages   *page* 1

3. Bristol *circa* 1480   3

4. The Regional Trade of Bristol   6

5. Bristol's Imports of Wine and Exports of Cloth, 1399–1485   42

6. England's Exports of Woollen Cloth, 1347–99   245

7. South-west France   278

vii

PREFACE

THE essays here collected are reproduced virtually in their original form; a few misprints and errors of detail have been corrected and a few statements slightly modified, but beyond this no attempt has been made to incorporate the results of later research or to amend what is amiss. Many records consulted in manuscript are now available in print, as for instance the Southampton Brokage Book of 1439–40,[1] the Great Red Book of Bristol,[2] and the first volume of the Mercers' Acts of Court,[3] while a number of customs accounts and miscellaneous documents illustrating Bristol's trade have been brought together in *The Overseas Trade of Bristol in the Later Middle Ages*.[4] References to such records have, however, been left unchanged, since they can easily be followed up, if desired, in the published volumes.

It is a pleasant duty to acknowledge the kindness of the many owners and custodians of manuscripts who have allowed me to consult records in their keeping and have made my researches both easy and agreeable. Thanks are due in particular to the Town Clerks and Archivists of Bristol, Gloucester, Southampton, Exeter, Hull, Beverley, Lynn, Yarmouth, Norwich, Ipswich, Leicester and elsewhere; to the Rector of Christ Church with St. Ewen's and to the Vicar of St. Nicholas at Bristol; to Miss Fox of Yate House; to the officers of the Mercers' Company, the Skinners' Company, and the Ironmongers' Company; to Mr. A. H. Thomas, late Deputy-Keeper of the Records of the City of London; and to Mr. V. B. Redstone who generously allowed me to consult his transcripts of various

[1] *The Brokage Book of Southampton, 1439–40*, ed. Barbara M. Bunyard (Southampton Record Society Publications, 40, 1941).

[2] *The Great Red Book of Bristol*, ed. E. W. W. Veale (Bristol Record Society Publications, II, IV, VIII, XVI, XVIII, 1931, 1933, 1937, 1950, 1953).

[3] *Acts of Court of the Mercers' Company, 1453–1527*, ed. L. Lyell and F. D. Watney (Cambridge, 1936).

[4] *The Overseas Trade of Bristol in the Later Middle Ages*, ed. E. M. Carus-Wilson (Bristol Record Society Publications, VII, 1936).

Ipswich records. I should like especially to acknowledge the constant helpfulness of Miss Dermott Harding, Miss Nott, and Miss Ralph, the three successive Archivists of the City of Bristol, where my earliest researches were pursued to a lively accompaniment of hammers as the walls of their strong room gradually rose. My debt to the officials of the British Museum, the Bodleian, Somerset House, and, above all, the Public Record Office, is, it need hardly be said, a heavy one.

Dr. M. K. James, Dr. A. R. Bridbury, and Miss Olive Coleman have ably assisted in the burdensome and intricate tasks of collection and calculation necessary for the construction of the new chart which accompanies the Introduction, while Mr. Peter Ramsey has kindly put at my disposal his tables of cloth exports for the reign of Henry VII. Miss Olive Coleman has also given expert and ungrudging help in the preparation of the volume for the press and in the correction of the proofs, and she has compiled the Index.

I should like here to express my great gratitude to the Leverhulme Trustees, whose award of a Fellowship in 1936 gave me for the first time the luxury of leisure for the uninterrupted pursuit of research, and to the Economic Research Division of the London School of Economics and Political Science, whose provision of assistance, especially towards the work involved in making the chart, has been invaluable.

Acknowledgments are due to Messrs. Routledge & Kegan Paul Ltd. for permission to reprint Chapters I and II, which first appeared in 1933 in *English Trade in the Fifteenth Century* (ed. Eileen Power and M. M. Postan), and to the Economic History Society and the Institute of Historical Research for permission to reprint the remaining chapters, first published in the *Economic History Review* and in the *Bulletin of the Institute of Historical Research*.

London School of Economics   E. M. C.-W.
March 1954.

INTRODUCTION

THE essays that make up this volume, disconnected though they may at first sight appear, have in fact a common origin and a common theme. They arose out of an enquiry into the condition of Bristol's trade in the fifteenth century and the circumstances that prompted the Bristol Merchant Venturers at the close of the century to sponsor the voyages of the Cabots in search of the New World. This enquiry, embarked upon many years ago when the study of medieval customs accounts was in its infancy, revealed at once that the basis of Bristol's trade was the export of manufactured woollens; the export of wool, which then played so prominent a part in the trade of most English ports, as it has since in writings on English economic history, was never of any significance there. The enquiry revealed Bristol, further, as a port where the influence of English merchants was paramount, unchallenged by that of the Italians or the Germans, whose activities then dominated the trade of many another city in England. It led therefore inevitably to further investigations into the expansion of England's woollen industry and into the evolution of that "wealthy and well experimented body of English merchants", known as the Merchant Adventurers, which marketed its products. English enterprise in English woollens is the prevailing theme of this book, as it is one of the prevailing themes of England's economic development in the later Middle Ages. The essays here collected cannot claim to be more than an interim report on work that is still in progress, but it is hoped that they may make some small contribution towards elucidating the history of a branch of England's commerce not less important than the trade in raw wool, which indeed it was wholly to supersede.

The epithet "merchant venturer" or "merchant adventurer" came into use only towards the end of the fifteenth century. But the conception of a merchant venturer, or at

least of a merchant venture, goes back far beyond this. A
venture (*aventure, auenture*, or *auntre*, in Middle English [1])
was a risk. To venture was to take a chance, to hazard one's
life or one's goods in an enterprise that might bring a worth-
while reward. So Chaucer's rascally canon urged the
necessity of taking a risk, putting one's goods "in aventure",
if profits were to be made:

> "Us moste putte oure good in áventúre.
> A marchaunt, truly, may not ay endure,
> Truste me wel, in his prosperitee,
> Som tyme his good is drownèd in the see,
> And som tyme cometh it sauf unto the londe." [2]

Was not God Himself an adventurer when He ventured His
own person for the salvation of the world as related in the
story of the Nativity? As Langland wrote of it in *Piers
Plowman*: "And after auntrede god hymself, and tok
Adams kynde." [3] If all merchants were, in a sense, adventurers, more particularly so were those who braved the
perils of the ocean, seeking markets for their goods in lands
across the sea. No doubt England had her merchants
venturing overseas to foreign parts from the very dawn of her
history. Such was Lunaris of York who in 237 A.D. gave
thanks to the gods on his safe arrival in Bordeaux.[4] Such,
too, was the Saxon merchant of Aelfric's *Colloquy* who,
having sailed across the sea to sell his merchandise and
acquire precious things not to be had in England, would
return "*cum magno periculo*", perhaps even suffering shipwreck with the loss of all his cargo, "*vix vivus evadens*".[5]
And such was the twelfth-century saint, Godric, whose
overseas trading enterprises are so vividly described in the
biography written by a devoted disciple of his old age,

[1] Latinized later as "adventure".
[2] Chaucer, "The Canones Yeoman's Tale", ll. 393–7, *Chaucer's Canterbury Tales* (Everyman's Library), 428.
[3] *The Vision of Piers the Plowman*, ed. W. Skeat, I, 585 (Passus XXI,
l. 232).
[4] *An Economic Survey of Ancient Rome*, ed. Tenney Frank, III (Baltimore,
1937), R. G. Collingwood, "Roman Britain", 114.
[5] *Aelfric's Colloquy*, ed. G. N. Garmonsway, 32–4.

when the saint had abandoned merchandise for meditation. Coulton indeed gives the title of "Merchant Adventurer" to St. Godric.[1] Yet the actual term "merchant adventurer" seems nowhere to have been applied, either to an individual or to a specific body of merchants, in Godric's time or even in the time of Langland or Chaucer; it was not, in fact, so applied until it had acquired a more specialized and restricted meaning than that which Coulton had in mind. What then is its significance, and what were the historical developments that gave rise to its adoption?

It was a very usual practice in the Middle Ages for merchants from one city, or from a group of cities, doing business in some foreign mart, to form a "fellowship" or "hanse" to further their common interests. Thus associated, they could jointly negotiate concessions which would ensure them favourable conditions for trade, such as freedom from vexatious restrictions, permission to set up an authority of their own to order their affairs and settle disputes among themselves, and power to exclude from the trade any of their fellow townsmen who were not of their fellowship. In thirteenth-century London, for instance, merchants from certain Flemish cities, buying wool and selling cloth, were at one time united in "la hanse c'on apiele hanse de Londres",[2] while merchants of certain German towns were joined in the hanse of the "Easterlings", and Picardy woad merchants in the "hanse of Corby, Amyas and Nelle".[3] One of the first known fellowships of English merchants on the continent was that which secured concessions from the Duke of Brabant at the moment when England's wool exports were being directed by Edward I to the Brabant port

[1] G. G. Coulton, *Social Life in Britain from the Conquest to the Reformation* (1918), 415.

[2] *Bulletin de la Commission Royale d'Histoire*, t. CXVIII (Brussels, 1953). H. van Werveke, "Les 'Statuts' Latins et les 'Statuts' Français de la Hanse Flamande de Londres", 316. A paper, as yet unpublished, by Professor Perroy throws further light on the still obscure history of this hanse.

[3] *Calendar of Letter Books of the City of London, Letter Book B*, ed. R. R. Sharpe (1900), 77.

of Antwerp. By the Duke's charter of 1296 the "merchants of the realm of England" were granted, amongst many other privileges, the right to hold courts and assemblies of their fellowship ("*compaignie*") and of those whom they wished to admit to it. By a subsequent charter of 1305 they were allowed to elect among themselves their own "mayor, captain or consul".[1] Some half-century later, when England's wool was being directed to Bruges, we can discern a very similar fellowship there, privileged by charter from the Count of Flanders in 1359 to have its own courts and assemblies and its own "governor".[2]

In the early and mid-fourteenth century the members of these fellowships of English merchants in the Low Countries may possibly have been selling some English cloth, for this was then being exported in small though not altogether insignificant quantities, as it had been during the two previous centuries.[3] But their primary concern, as the charters make abundantly clear, was the sale of the English wool that was then being shipped across the Channel in vast quantities—a business far more important to England and far more welcome to the Flemings, whose thriving industrial cities, beside which those of England were puny indeed, lived by the manufacture of cloth made from English wool. England was still, as she had been in Roman times, an exporter first and foremost of food-stuffs and raw materials, and the chief of these was wool. Indeed it was doubtless the direction of England's wool to one particular mart in the Low Countries—whether in Flanders, Brabant, Holland, or Zeeland, according to the diplomatic exigencies of the moment—that prompted the organization of the

---

[1] *Bulletin de la Commission Royale d'Histoire*, t. LXXX (Brussels, 1911). H. Obreen, "Une charte brabançonne inédite de 1296 en faveur des marchands anglais", 528–557; J. de Sturler, *Les relations politiques et les échanges commerciaux entre le duché de Brabant et l'Angleterre au moyen âge* (Paris, 1936), 212 *et seq.*

[2] E. Varenbergh, *Relations diplomatiques entre le comté de Flandre et l'Angleterre au moyen âge* (Brussels, 1874), 447.

[3] See *infra*, Ch. V.

merchants there and made them strong enough to secure wide franchises from local rulers. In the later fourteenth century, however, when England's exports of wool were canalized compulsorily through Calais, her newly-conquered outpost across the Channel,[1] English merchants doing business in the foreign towns of the Low Countries ceased to be concerned with wool. From then until the loss of Calais in the mid-sixteenth century there were two clearly differentiated groups of Englishmen trading across the English Channel—the "Merchant Staplers" shipping wool and other "staple" wares to the English staple town of Calais, and the merchants shipping cloth and other miscellaneous wares to the foreign marts of the Low Countries.[2] It was these cloth exporters, continuing to transact their business in old-established marts under alien rule, who now became the "community of the English nation" there, eagerly cherishing the privileges they had inherited. How closely they treasured them is shown by the fact that copies or ratifications of early charters, like those of 1296 and 1359, were carefully preserved among their archives and were later included in an inventory made by the Merchant Adventurers Company in 1547 of privileges kept at the Company's headquarters.[3]

In one sense, then, we may discover the origin of the Merchant Adventurers in these early fellowships in the Low Countries (as did the Elizabethan secretary and historian of the Merchant Adventurers Company),[4] and in the transformation of these communities in the later fourteenth century by the separation from them of the merchants dealing in wool. Little more, however, would probably have been heard of the fellowships had there not come about at that very time a yet more important transformation. It was

[1] E. Power, *The Wool Trade in English Medieval History*, 97 *et seq.*
[2] Other exports were of little significance compared with wool and cloth.
[3] G. Schanz, *Englische Handelspolitik* (Leipzig, 1881), II, 577–8.
[4] J. Wheeler, *A Treatise of Commerce* (1601), ed. G. B. Hotchkiss (New York 1931), 320–1, 325–6, 333.

then that a decisive impetus was given to the expansion of England's cloth industry by war and war taxation. Embargoes on exports of wool and, still more, the imposition of increasingly heavy duties upon it, gave every incentive to Englishmen to make up their wool at home, and to market it on the Continent as manufactured cloth—cloth which could compete favourably with that of Flanders on account of its lower raw material costs. During the second half of the fourteenth century England's wool exports shrank by nearly half—from an average of 32 thousand sacks per annum in 1350–60 to an average of 19 thousand in 1390–1399. Meanwhile her cloth exports increased more than sevenfold —from an average of 5 thousand cloths per annum in 1350–60 to an average of 37 thousand in 1390–1399. By the close of the century England's cloth was well on the way to superseding wool as her principal export; it was invading even the markets of the Low Countries, where for the first time it seriously competed with the cloth of Flanders.[1]

Thus during the late fourteenth century the "English Nation" in the Low Countries became a community primarily concerned with selling cloth, and a thriving community too, whose prospects seemed bright with the sudden expansion of its business. Its growing importance is shown by the Letters Patent of Henry IV in 1407 empowering the English merchants in Holland, Zeeland, Brabant, Flanders, and in certain other parts overseas, to meet when and where they would to elect certain persons as their Governors in those parts and to make ordinances by the common assent of the merchants.[2]

By this time English cloth was also invading the Baltic in force, carried thither not only by the Germans but also by the English themselves: at Danzig, by 1391, there was a community of the English nation, electing its own Governor and ordering its own affairs according to privileges granted

---

[1] *Infra*, Ch. VI, *passim*. Wool exports during the *early* fourteenth century (1305–35) averaged 31 thousand sacks per annum.

[2] Rymer, *Foedera* (1709), VIII, 464.

by the Grand Master of the Teutonic Order. English merchants trading in Norway, Sweden, and Denmark were very similarly privileged by 1408, and shortly afterwards another market for England's cloth was being developed by English venturers in Iceland.[1] The Baltic and Scandinavia, together with the Low Countries, now provided an outlet even more important than Gascony, chief mart for England's manufactures in the mid-fourteenth century.[2]

In the Mediterranean as well as in northern seas there was now a growing demand for English cloth. Here the trade was mainly in the hands of the Italians. But an occasional Englishman ventured thither, sometimes combining business with pleasure and a pilgrimage, as did Richard Beauchamp, Earl of Warwick, when he set out in 1408 for the Holy Land, loading his ship, *inter alia*, with "Englissh clothe"; some of this he bestowed in gifts at Jerusalem upon the Sultan's lieutenant and his men, to whom he "gave largely of englissh cloth to array them in his livere after their degrees, bothe scarlet and other cloth of colour ".[3]

The transformation of England's trade, by which she became an exporter not of wool but of cloth, inaugurated in the fourteenth century, was completed in the fifteenth. The stages by which it was effected are shown graphically in the accompanying chart, which is based upon the annual customs returns compiled by the Exchequer, where exports of wool and exports of woollen cloth are separately listed, each being subject to a specific duty. The chart covers two centuries, beginning in 1347, when for the first time all cloth exports were taxed, as all wool exports had been since 1275, and continuing into the early sixteenth century to the end of

---

[1] Rymer, *Foedera*, (1709), VII, 693; VIII, 511; *infra*, Ch. II, *passim*.
[2] *Infra*, 246, 259.
[3] B. M. Cott. MS.   Julius E. IV, art. 6, Pageants of the Life of Richard Beauchamp Earl of Warwick, ff. 5 and 10b. For folio 5 see Frontispiece. The date of the MS. is unknown, but the drawings are probably English, of the late fifteenth century. (*Pageant of the birth, life and death of Richard Beauchamp, Earl of Warwick, K.G., 1389–1439*, ed. Viscount Dillon and W. H. St. John Hope, 1914. This reproduces both text and illustrations.)

NOTE ON CHART OF ENGLAND'S EXPORTS OF WOOL AND CLOTH, 1347–1544.

This chart is based on the Exchequer L.T.R. Enrolled Customs Accounts, which record, port by port, the totals of customs paid on wool and cloth for each Exchequer year running from Michaelmas to Michaelmas; here and there use has also been made of the Exchequer K.R. Customs Accounts, i.e. of the detailed particulars sent up from individual ports. Under each port, for both wool and cloth, the accounts give separate totals for customs paid by (*a*) native, (*b*) Hanseatic, and (*c*) other alien merchants, since the rates in each case differed. Quantities of wool are given in sacks (each of 365 lbs.); exports of woolfells are separately accounted for, but for the purposes of this chart they have been converted into sacks of wool, at the rate used by customs officials after 1368, viz. 240 woolfells to the sack. Cloths were reckoned by the customs officials in terms of the statutory whole "cloth of assise" (*pannus integrus de assisa*), 26 or 28 yards long by 6½ or 6 quarters wide before fulling, and 24 yards long by 2 yards wide after fulling (*Statutes of the Realm*, I, 260, 395; II, 60, 153, 403, 485); larger or smaller cloths paid customs proportionally (*Calendar Patent Rolls*, 1345–8, 276). Worsteds were separately accounted for; they have not been included in the chart.

Some of the detailed figures from which the chart has been compiled are already available in print. The wool totals for 1350–77 have been taken from A. Beardwood, *Alien Merchants in England, 1350–1377* (Medieval Academy of America, Cambridge, Mass., 1931), Appendix C. For both the cloth and the wool totals for 1399–1482 use has been made of the figures already extracted, port by port, by the present writer and others, and published in *English Trade in the Fifteenth Century* (ed. Eileen Power and M. Postan, 1933). Cloth figures for each port for 1485–1509 have kindly been supplied by Mr. Peter Ramsey, but the totals shown on the chart differ in some cases from his "consolidated totals" published in the *Economic History Review* (2nd Series, VI, 2, 1953); those for 1485–6, 1486–7, and 1487–8, for instance, have been adjusted to take account of the fact that the London returns for those years cover not a precise year but fifteen, seven and fourteen months respectively (giving fictitiously the appearance of a startling slump in 1486–7), while a gap has been left for 1494–6 since no figures whatever are then available for London, and London at that time was carrying some two-thirds of the whole cloth trade of the country. Wool and cloth figures for 1509–44 have been taken from the pioneer work of G. Schanz, *Englische Handelspolitik gegen Ende des Mittelalters* (Leipzig, 1881), but have been adjusted, port by port, in the many cases where they do not cover an exact year, as have those taken from *English Trade in the Fifteenth Century*; until this adjustment has been made their addition into annual totals for the country as a whole is apt to be meaningless.

Such adjustments have been made throughout, wherever the account for any one port does not cover exactly an Exchequer year from Michaelmas to Michaelmas. In all such cases annual totals for the port concerned have been estimated (unless they can be discovered from Particular Accounts) by taking the monthly average over the longer of two adjacent accounts and using it to adjust both accounts; the adjusted totals have then been used in computing export figures for the country as a whole.

Where the account for a port is missing, an annual total has been arbitrarily determined, except as noted below, by taking into account the average percentage of England's total cloth or wool exports carried by that port in the years immediately before and after the gap. No attempt has, however, been made to fill any gap in the case of *London* (e.g. Cloth, 1395–6, 1399–1401, 1470–1, 1494–6; Wool, 1376–8, 1470–1), since London was carrying throughout so high a proportion both of the wool and of the cloth trade. Gaps have also been left unfilled in the case of other ports which were carrying relatively large percentages of the total export, e.g. *Bristol* (Cloth, 1471–7, 1484–5), *Exeter and Melcombe* (Cloth, 1483–5); and in cases where accounts for all or a large number of ports are missing (e.g. Cloth, 1373–7; Wool, 1347–50, 1482–5, 1508–9). Such quantities as have thus been arbitrarily determined seldom, if ever, amount to more than 8 per cent. of the total export for the whole country in any one year.

For some other problems concerning the interpretation and use of the data see Note to Chart of England's Exports of Woollen Cloth 1347–99, *infra*, p. 264 (iv); see also *ibid*. (i) for the taxation of *Kerseys*, *infra*, p. 263. Only those who have themselves worked on the customs accounts can fully appreciate their complexity, especially in the earlier period, and, at the same time, their astonishing thoroughness and attention to detail.

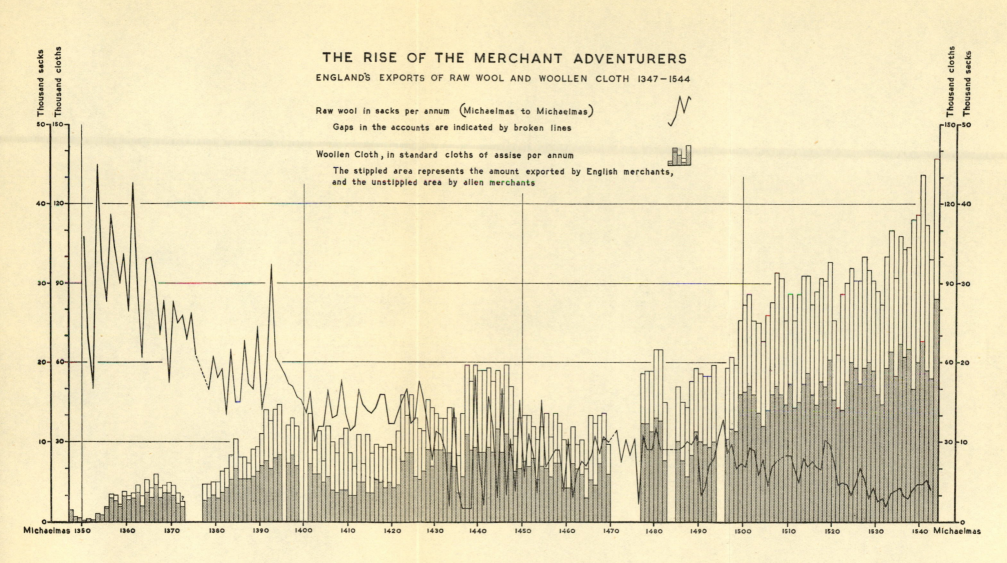

THE RISE OF THE MERCHANT ADVENTURERS

ENGLAND'S EXPORTS OF RAW WOOL AND WOOLLEN CLOTH 1347–1544

Raw wool in sacks per annum (Michaelmas to Michaelmas)

Gaps in the accounts are indicated by broken lines

Woollen Cloth, in standard cloths of assise per annum

The stippled area represents the amount exported by English merchants, and the unstippled area by alien merchants

Thousand sacks
Thousand cloths

Thousand cloths
Thousand sacks

Michaelmas 1350   1360   1370   1380   1390   1400   1410   1420   1430   1440   1450   1460   1470   1480   1490   1500   1510   1520   1530   1540   Michaelmas

[To face p. xviii

Henry VIII's reign.[1] In it there may be seen both the year to year fluctuations in the export of these two commodities, which between them contributed the great bulk of England's exports, and also the long term trends of trade, declining exports of wool being shown against rising exports of cloth. Two periods of rapid advance for English cloth exports in the second half of the fourteenth century, accompanied by a sharp contraction of wool exports,[2] were succeeded, after a slight depression early in the fifteenth century, by a further striking advance towards the middle of this century, accompanied by a further contraction of wool exports. Cloth exports in 1438–48 averaged 55 thousand cloths per annum —half as much again as during the boom at the end of Richard II's reign, and twice as much as during the reign of Richard II taken as a whole; wool exports had fallen to an average of only 9 thousand sacks per annum. A severe depression in the two following decades,[3] when cloth exports were at a markedly lower level and wool exports remained much as before, was succeeded by a further advance. By the end of Edward IV's reign cloth exports had recovered and even exceeded their mid-century level, averaging 60 thousand cloths per annum for 1477–82. The advance continued in the first half-century of Tudor rule, gathering momentum after a slight initial setback. Cloth exports mounted, reaching an average of 82 thousand per annum in the last six years of Henry VII's reign and, towards the end of Henry VIII's reign (1538–44), 118 thousand per annum. Wool exports meanwhile, after a slight increase in the reign of Edward IV, fell to half what

---

[1] P.R.O., Exchequer L.T.R. Customs Accounts. For the first three years (1347–50) the returns for wool are missing, and for the last three years (1544–47) those for both wool and cloth, while there are also some gaps in the course of the centuries, see Note to Chart (p. xviii).

[2] *Infra*, Ch. VI.

[3] Certain aspects of this depression are discussed below in Chapters I, II and VII; see also M. Postan, "The Economic and Political Relations of England and the Hanse", *English Trade in the Fifteenth Century*, ed. E. Power and M. Postan (1933), 150 *et seq.*

they had been in the mid-fifteenth century, averaging only
4·5 thousand sacks for 1538–43.

Thus in the later Middle Ages England became an
exporter of manufactured textiles rather than of raw
materials. If we may assume that approximately $4\frac{1}{3}$ of the
standard cloths of assize in terms of which the customs were
reckoned could, on an average, be made from one sack of
wool,[1] then in the mid-fourteenth century only some 4 per
cent. of the wool that England exported was going out as
manufactured cloth. By the end of the century the proportion had risen to over 30 per cent. By the mid-fifteenth
century it was well over 50 per cent.; England had at this
point become an exporter of cloth rather than of wool. By
the end of Henry VIII's reign it had reached some 86 per
cent. In terms of value rather than of weight the share of
manufactured cloth in England's overseas trade must
obviously be rated more highly. No precise comparison can,
or should, be attempted, if only because prices of cloth vary
even more widely than prices of wool, but it seems that the
price of a sack of wool in this country would purchase, on an
average, certainly not more than three cloths of assize, and
very probably only two.[2] Assuming only two cloths to be the
equivalent in value to one sack of wool, then the relative
importance of raw wool and manufactured cloth would seem
to have been exactly reversed between the mid-fourteenth
and the mid-sixteenth centuries; in 1350–60 cloth accounted
for 8 per cent. of the trade and wool for 92 per cent., whereas

---

[1] *Infra*, 250, n. 2.

[2] Cf. Schanz, *op. cit.*, II, 31, n. 1, and 32, n. 2; H. L. Gray, "English
Foreign Trade, 1446–1482", *English Trade in the Fifteenth Century, ut
supra*, 12–3; P. Ramsey, "Overseas Trade in the Reign of Henry VII",
Economic History Review, 2nd Series, VI (1953), 179, n. 4. Investigation of
production costs shows that if $4\frac{1}{3}$ cloths were made from one sack of wool
costing £6, the cost per cloth of raw material and manufacture, allowing no
profit margin, would amount in the fifteenth century to some £2, 10s. not
including dyeing or finishing. Taking into account the maker's profit
margin and the fact that much cloth was exported dyed and finished, the
estimate of two cloths of assize as equivalent in value to one sack of wool seems
the more reasonable one.

in 1538–44 cloth accounted for 92 per cent. and wool for 8 per cent. The pattern of English trade had been transformed. Manufactured cloth had taken the place of raw wool; the Merchant Staplers had been eclipsed by the merchants exporting cloth. At the same time the value of England's exports had notably increased: though at the end of Henry VIII's reign the total quantity of wool exported, raw and manufactured, was probably not much greater than that exported in the early or mid-fourteenth century, its total value was probably nearly twice as great, because of the substitution of cloth for wool.[1]

The later Middle Ages witnessed the triumph in English commerce not only of English cloth but also of English merchants. At the close of the thirteenth century, when England was primarily an exporter of raw materials, the bulk of her trade was in the hands of foreigners. Flemings had long been coming to this country seeking the wool so eagerly desired by the clothmakers of the Low Countries, until towards the end of the century they were being supplanted by Italians, who travelled the length and breadth of the land collecting the taxes due to the Pope and buying up with them the clip of the religious houses, great and small, before it was even shorn from the sheep's back. And though the English themselves were by no means inactive, yet in the latter part of the century, when the wool trade was probably at its zenith, they handled scarcely more than a third of it.[2] Foreigners also dominated many branches of the import trade. That in wine, chief of them all and then also at its zenith, was very largely in their hands. England at that time imported some 20 thousand tuns of wine a year, and at least two-thirds of this she bought from Gascon importers, who not only shipped their own wines to English ports, but also

[1] No precise comparison can be made for the early fourteenth century, since there is no record of the amount of cloth then exported. For wool exported at that time see p. xvi, note 1.

[2] E. Power, "The Wool Trade in the Fifteenth Century", *English Trade in the Fifteenth Century, ut supra*, 39.

travelled up and down the country, selling them far inland.[1] So, too, Flemish merchants came over selling the much-coveted Flemish cloth not only at the fairs but to English drapers in many parts, while Picard merchants, firmly entrenched with privileges in all the principal ports, pushed the sale of Picard woad even to customers across the Pennines.[2] German merchants likewise had established their privileged settlements in every port of any consequence in East Anglia from Newcastle to London, just as Italian merchants were planted in the principal ports of the south from London to Southampton. And when English kings were in need of money it was Flemish, French, German, and, above all, Italian merchants to whom they turned, pledging to them their estates, the profits of the customs, and even, on the outbreak of the Hundred Years' War, the Crown of England. But from this moment there came about a striking change, already discernible in the thirties and forties of the fourteenth century. Nowhere is the progress of England more apparent than in the advance of her merchants. By the end of the fourteenth century the wool and the wine trade had passed almost entirely into their hands, and though both were much diminished in volume, the share of the English in each was greater not only relatively but also absolutely than at the opening of the century.[3] Picard woad merchants were fast disappearing, while Flemish merchants, like Flemish cloth, were seldom to be seen. Only the Italians and the Germans remained serious rivals of the English, and financially England was no longer dependent upon them;

[1] M. K. James, "Les activités commerciales des négociants en vins gascons en Angleterre durant la fin du moyen âge", *Annales du Midi*, t. LXV, no. 21 (Toulouse, 1953), 35 *et seq.*; "The Fluctuations of the Anglo-Gascon Wine Trade during the Fourteenth Century", *Econ. Hist. Review*, 2nd Series, IV (1951), 176.

[2] E. M. Carus-Wilson, "La guède française en Angleterre: un grand commerce du moyen âge", *Revue du Nord*, t. XXXV, no. 138 (1953), 93 *et seq.*, 97.

[3] E. Power, "The Wool Trade in the Fifteenth Century", *ut supra*, 40; M. K. James, *ut supra*, and unpublished D.Phil. thesis (Oxford, 1952); P.R.O., Exchequer L.T.R. Customs Accounts.

many great Italian banking houses had been ruined by the war, and such loans as English kings could now procure were smaller and supplied as much by Englishmen as by aliens. Foreign merchants still did a considerable business in England, but their ascendancy in England's trade had once and for all been brought to an end.

The growing trade in the export of English cloth had from early in the fourteenth century been predominantly the affair of the English themselves. In the first period of advance which can be quantitatively measured, in the fifties and sixties of this century, some 80 per cent. of the whole trade was in their hands. English cloth, unlike English wool, was not then in such demand as to attract many foreign buyers to this land, and it was doubtless English pioneers who built up a market for it on the Continent. By the end of the century, however, German and Italian merchants were intervening in force; the increasing amounts of English cloth going to the Mediterranean were shipped almost wholly by Italians, and active though the English were in Danzig and Bergen, much of the cloth destined for the Baltic and Scandinavia was being carried by Germans. Yet still, as the chart makes plain, half or more of the cloth trade remained in the hands of the English, and since these were now taking four-fifths of the wool trade, they were then controlling some two-thirds of the whole export trade in these commodities, while their total investment therein must have been about twice as much as early in the century, when they handled only some third of the wool trade and the trade in English cloth was virtually non-existent. In the course of the fifteenth century, though aliens at first shipped slightly more cloth than Englishmen, later the English regained the ascendancy, shipping slightly more cloth than the aliens, while all that remained of the much-diminished wool trade came also into their hands. By the early sixteenth century they controlled rather more than half the whole export trade in wool and cloth, a smaller share of the whole than at the end of the fourteenth century, but no less, and probably slightly more, in value. By the end of Henry VIII's reign, when they handled over half of a much-expanded cloth trade, their total export trade must have been worth about three times what it had been in the early fourteenth century.

Thus the expansion of England's woollen exports was accompanied by a considerable expansion in the activities of her native merchants—an expansion most marked in the fourteenth century and, to a lesser extent, in the early sixteenth. The dominant interest of the English merchants had changed meanwhile from wool to cloth. While at the end of the first period of expansion, in the fourteenth century, their investment in wool must have been twice that in cloth, by the middle of the fifteenth century, after the cloth boom of the forties, the position was very nearly reversed. And though a little later they tended to ship somewhat increased quantities of wool, by the opening of the sixteenth century their investment in cloth was quite twice as great as that in wool, and by the end of Henry VIII's reign seven times as great.

The steady growth in the business of English cloth exporters between 1347 and 1544 may be traced in the accompanying chart, where native are distinguished from alien exports of cloth. By 1400 the business of English cloth exporters had increased fourfold, by the middle of the fifteenth century sixfold, by the early sixteenth century tenfold, and by the end of Henry VIII's reign fourteenfold. At the same time the business of English wool exporters, after expanding in the fourteenth century, shrank to a mere third of what it had been at the beginning of that century, amounting only to about one-seventh of the business of the cloth exporters. If the growth in the trade of native exporters as a whole had been considerable, that of native exporters of cloth had been spectacular. English merchants marketing English woollens were from the middle of the fifteenth century the most substantial men of affairs in the country, of more consequence than the merchants of the

Staple, of more consequence even than the Germans and Italians together.

The increasing volume of overseas trade handled by English men of affairs was reflected in the growing import-ance in English society of merchants specializing in foreign commerce, particularly in the marketing of cloth. The wholesale export trade became a career no less reputable than the church or the law, with prospects no less attractive and a training no less strict, first as apprentice and then as factor.[1] Those who professed it tended to draw apart from those lesser folk—mere shopkeepers, artisans, or small wholesale dealers—who were still enrolled in many a com-prehensive "merchant" gild and in the various gilds and companies of London and the greater provincial cities. For they were an aristocracy of merchants, with problems all their own, making or losing on the markets of Europe fortunes small no doubt compared with those of some continental merchants, but greater than any which could be won at home. As exporters they were concerned primarily with wool or cloth, and sometimes with both, while not disdaining to handle, as occasion offered, those miscellaneous wares—like tin, lead, hides, fish, or pewter vessels—which made up the sum of England's exports. As shippers of wool they were "Merchant Staplers", statutorily bound to be members of the Company of the Staple and to ship (with certain exceptions) only to Calais, where they were assured of a ready sale for their wool and a safe sojourn for them-selves, under the protection of the English garrison. As shippers of cloth they were bound to no one company and to no one port, nor were they assured of a sale for their wares. Despatching them north, south, east and west, wherever they could find an opening, they strove to capture from foreign manufacturers markets which at any moment might be closed against them by war or diplomacy; hazarding their goods, and sometimes their persons, on voyages

[1] *Infra*, 81; cf. Sylvia Thrupp, *The Merchant Class of Medieval London*, 29, etc.

to alien and not always welcoming lands. Venturers in fact, they became venturers in name. As "venturers" or "adventurers" they became individually distinguished both from the Merchant Staplers and from the stay-at-home traders who, though they might occasionally ship a parcel or two, did business primarily in England. And as "fellowships of adventurers", drawn together by common interests, they associated into groups both at home and abroad, inheriting, in the Low Countries at least, privileges obtained long since by their predecessors.

How early the epithet "adventurer" was applied to wholesale exporters of cloth, and how early they came to form fellowships among themselves, it is impossible to say. The earliest indication of such a use of the term that has so far come to light is in the oldest surviving account book of the Mercers' Company of London. Here, just at the time when England's exports of cloth had first outstripped her exports of wool, there is mention of a levy in 1443–4 on all the "adventurers of the Mercery". Before long, in the oldest surviving Acts of Court of the company, there appears a "Fellowship of Adventurers". This was holding assemblies apart from the rest of the company at any rate by 1465. It was also corresponding with William Caxton, himself a Mercer and "Governor of the English nation" in the Low Countries, and it was coming together with similar "fellow-ships of Adventurers" from other London companies to discuss common problems about the shipping of cloth. The great international marts of the Low Countries, focal point to which flocked merchants from all parts of Europe, had now become the principal outlet for England's cloth. Thither the London Adventurers directed most of their cargoes. Hence when Henry VII came to the throne the London merchants who petitioned him for privileges described themselves as "the Merchants adventurers, citizens of the city of London, into the parts of Holland, Zeeland, Brabant and Flanders", and it was they who received privileges from the City and were thereafter referred to in the City's books simply as "the Merchants Adventurers".[1]

But it was not only in London that "Merchant Adventurers" were being spoken of in the late fifteenth century, nor were all adventurers concentrating on the Low Countries. The very expression "adventurers into Flanders"[2] or "into the parts of Holland, Zeeland, Brabant and Flanders" suggests that there were others, even in London, venturing farther afield. Sir William Haryot, Lord Mayor of London in 1481–2, was described by the chronicler Fabyan as "a marchaunte of wonderous aventures into many and sondry countres",[3] and Sir John Crosby, whose beautiful house (built in 1466) still in part survives, transported from Bishopsgate to Chelsea, was talked of after his death as "ane of the first that adventurid into Spayn", Spain being then regarded as a "farre adventure", as it evidently was not later on.[4] Still more adventurers to Spain were to be found in the west of England. Bristol, second seaport in the land, had long been a stronghold of English merchants. Little concerned with the Low Countries or with the Baltic, by reason of its situation, it had never attracted the attention of the Germans, nor had the Italians ever sought or gained a footing there. Almost the whole of its cloth export business was handled by native merchants, and it was apparently problems of trade with the south-west that prompted their first organization as a "Fellowship". Thus when in 1467 the Common Council of the city made provision for the

[1] *Infra*, Ch. III, *passim*, and London, Guildhall, Journal of the Proceedings of the Court of Common Council, 9, f. 102b; 10, f. 154b; Repertories, I, 52b, 55b. It was, of course, not uncommon for a merchant to belong both to the Merchant Adventurers and to the Merchant Staplers.

[2] C. L. Kingsford, *Chronicles of London* (1905) 193: "In this yere (1485) was greate varyaunce bitwene the marchauntes of this Cite, adventurers into fflaunders, for their maister of the ffelishippys in fflaunders."

[3] R. Fabyan, *The New Chronicles of England and France*, ed. H. Ellis (1811), 667.

[4] "A Treatise concerninge the Staple and the commodities of this realme" (*circa* 1519–35), R. Pauli, *Drei volkswirthschaftliche Denkschriften aus der Zeit Heinrichs VIII von England* (1878), 17.

choosing each year of a "master of the fellowship of merchants", with wardens, beadles and brokers to assist him,
giving them the house of the famous pioneer Sturmy in
which to meet, their immediate task was to fix the wholesale
prices of oil, iron, and wax—three of the principal commodities imported from Spain.[1] The first actual mention of
"merchant adventurers" at Bristol seems to be in a petition
to the Common Council in 1477 about the parlous state
of the ancient and noble trade in Toulouse woad, made by
the "Merchaunts Adventurers, with others byers and sillers
of the towne of Bristowe".[2] By the end of the century, if not
earlier, we may clearly speak of a Company or Fellowship of
Merchant Adventurers of Bristol, for detailed statutes drawn
up in 1500 by the Common Council for the "Company or
Fellowship of Marchauntes" purport to be for the good of
"the said marchaunts adventurers". The statutes reveal these
adventurers as exporting cloths each "atte his adventure" to
France, Spain, and Portugal, as well as to Ireland and Iceland,
while the wares whose traffic they specially regulated were
those coming "from beyond the South See", in particular
oil, iron, wax, wine, woad, salt, and the scarlet dyestuff—
grain. Trade with Ireland and Iceland was open freely to all,
but ships bound for other regions could only be freighted by
licence from the Fellowship.[3]

[1] J. Latimer, *History of the Society of Merchant Venturers of the City of
Bristol* (Bristol, 1903), 16–8, gives a more correct version of this clause on
f. 210 of the Great Red Book than that recently published in *The Great Red
Book of Bristol*, ed. E. W. W. Veale, Text Part III (Bristol Record Society
Publications, Vol. XVI, 1951), 82–4, where "yren" is given as "Tren".
The ordinance distinguishes two qualities of oil: edible oil ("meat oil") and
oil used in the woollen industry ("wool oil").
[2] *The Great Red Book, ut supra,* 120–2.
[3] Latimer, *ut supra,* 26–35; cf. *Records relating to the Society of Merchant
Venturers of the City of Bristol in the Seventeenth Century,* ed. P. McGrath
(Bristol Record Society Publications, XVII, 1952), xi. The royal charter
of 1552 speaks of the "marchant adventurers (called marchaunts venturers)"
of the city of Bristol, and provides that their privileges are not to prejudice
those of the company of merchant adventurers frequenting the Low
Countries. The Exeter Merchant Adventurers, as incorporated by royal
charter in 1560, were particularly concerned with France.

York, like Bristol, had its "Fellowship of Merchants" in the fifteenth century, as intimately associated with the York Mercers as were the London Adventurers with the London Mercers. Here again the term "Merchant Adventurer" does not seem to have been formally used in its title until at least the middle of the sixteenth century. Yet by 1478 there was much talk of the "northern adventurers", particularly of how their trade in the Low Countries was being injured by the high-handed action of the Londoners, and it was being urged that though "the aventures made furth of the north contree" were "not lyke in value, ne substance of riches, as been the aventures made forthe of the southe countree into the landes of Braband, Holland, Seeland and Flaunders", yet "right many aventures theer been". Clearly the Fellowship was one primarily, at least, concerned with the export of cloth to the Low Countries, for the discussions at its meetings were mostly about the freighting of ships; buying and selling "beyond the sea"; the fees paid in the Low Countries "for their hansing"; the streets where they might sell their cloth there; the "outrageous contrebucyons" extorted there by the Governor "for the Citee of London"; and the difficult position, in consequence, of the Governor "for the north partes".[1] Hull, too, had its adventurers, and its Gild of St. George, determined to prevent mere artisans from meddling in trade, decreed in 1499 that it would admit only those making

[1] *The York Mercers and Merchant Adventurers 1356–1917*, ed. Maud Sellers, Surtees Society, CXXIX (1917), 64–5, 75–9, 87–8, etc. The term "Merchants Adventurers" appears in the royal charter of 1580 to the Society of Merchant Adventurers of York, but it seems to have been used somewhat earlier, see, e.g., letters from Antwerp in 1549 to the master of the "feolaship of merchants adventurers resydent within the citie of Yorke", Sellers, 140, 143, 199. At Newcastle a royal charter of incorporation was granted in 1547 to the "Merchants Adventurers inhabitinge within the sayd Towne . . . who are now of the Fellowshipp of Merchants Venturers in Brabante in the parts of beyond the seas ", *Records of the Merchant Adventurers of Newcastle-upon-Tyne*, ed. F. W. Dendy (Surtees Society, XCIII), I (1895), 282.

their living "by the way and means of bying and sellyng and by grete aventour".[1]

Thus the expansion of the English cloth industry and the growing importance of English merchants marketing its products, together with the canalizing of wool exports through the staple port of Calais, caused a new phrase to be coined, that of "Merchant Adventurer", in sharp antithesis to "Merchant Stapler". And if English Merchant Adventurers were to be found in many lands, the narrowing of the northern market, so that in the later fifteenth century it became concentrated to a great extent in the Low Countries, gave a peculiar importance to the old-established "community of the English nation" there, with its venerable pedigree and privileges; so much so that its members virtually arrogated to themselves the title of "The Merchant Adventurers of England", frequently omitting the qualifying words "into the parts of Holland, Zeeland, Brabant and Flanders". At the same time the tendency for the export trade to the Low Countries to be concentrated in London, to the detriment of many a provincial city, gave the London Adventurers a supremacy in the councils of this community which, though not undisputed, was yet inescapable. In wealth and influence they increasingly dominated the scene, thrusting both Staplers and provincial Adventurers into the background. London was the nerve centre where matters of high policy were discussed and determined. There the Adventurers to the Low Countries foregathered—the Londoners first and foremost, the provincials joining from time to time in their debate. And greatest among them all were the Mercers, their greatness commemorated by the use of the Mercers' Hall in London as the meeting-place and headquarters of the Merchant Adventurers' Company.

[1] J. M. Lambert, *Two Thousand Years of Gild Life* (1891), 158.

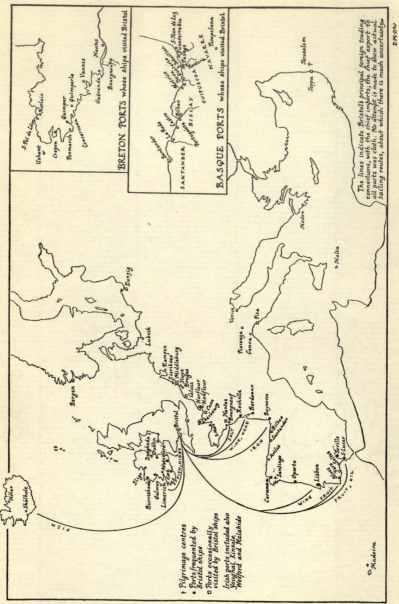

2. Bristol's Overseas Trade at the Close of the Middle Ages

I

THE OVERSEAS TRADE OF BRISTOL IN THE FIFTEENTH CENTURY

§ I

THE PORT OF BRISTOL

"There are scarcely any towns of importance in the kingdom excepting these two: Bristol, a seaport to the West, and Boraco, otherwise York, which is on the borders of Scotland; besides London to the South."

The Italian Relation, 1500.[1]

Fifteenth century Bristol, according to a shrewd Italian, was one of the three most important towns in England, and of the three, it may well be studied as the typical trading city; for York was not a port, though it traded far afield through Hull, and London, though a port, was so much else that its story is very complex. Moreover Bristol is of peculiar interest as a centre of English enterprise, for the principal southern and eastern ports were strongholds of foreign influence, from which Bristol was singularly free. Looking out westwards, she concerned herself little with the spheres of the powerful Hanseatic or Italian merchants, but carved out routes of her own, neither in the North Sea nor in the Mediterranean, but on the eastern shores of the Atlantic Ocean. This independent outlook, foreshadowing a new orientation of trade in the future, gives her yet further interest, for it was her seamen who, intimately acquainted with the eastern coasts of the Atlantic from Iceland to Gibraltar, were the first to venture forth from England across the ocean towards its western shores.

The silver ship freighted with incense which swung to and fro in one of its oldest churches, the banner bearing a ship under which its soldiers fought at Towton, the ship on the city's seal and on the bells from its foundry, all proclaim that the greatness of Bristol was built on its commerce. It boasted no ancient reputation as a cathedral see, as a military station, or as a shire town, but from its geographical position it had unique advantages as a centre for overseas trade.

[1] *Italian Relation of England: A Relation or rather a True Account of the Island of England*, ed. C. A. Sneyd (Camden Society Publications, No. 37, 1847), 41.

"Bristow," as Speed wrote later, "is not so ancient as it is fair and wel seated." The great waterways of the Severn, close to which Bristol lay, flowed through one of the richest agricultural regions of England, rivalled only by the wide river basin drained by the Humber. And the Humber had no such port as the Severn, for the harbour of Hull on its exposed estuary was never so secure as that of Bristol. Here the encircling Avon and the "lusty Frome" gave protection from attack by land, while the seven miles of narrow gorge through which the Avon winds its way to the Bristol Channel guarded against violation by sea; Southampton and the Cinque ports must often have envied Bristol its immunity from foreign invasion and constant assaults by pirates. Just as the Avon gorge has not its like in England, so the long fiord-like estuary of the Severn has no parallel on England's softer eastern and southern coasts of smoothly rounded outline. This also has been of great service to Bristol. For the sudden contraction of the long estuary where the Avon joins it causes exceptional tides, rising to a height of thirty or forty feet, and by these sailing vessels, after waiting at low tide at Kingrode, were swiftly carried up as far as Bristol.

The junction of the Avon and the Frome thus provided a sheltered tidal harbour, capable of defence, where great inland waterways converged, and gave to Bristol a unique opportunity of commanding the commerce of a district noted for its fertility. Already in the days of King Stephen it was characterized as "nearly the richest of all cities of the country, receiving merchandise by sailing vessels from foreign countries; placed in the most fruitful part of England, and by the very situation of the place the best defended of all the cities of England". Not many years later the charter of John (1188) enumerated cloth, wool, leather, and corn as among the articles in which it dealt.[1] To its river defences Bristol now added a turreted wall, almost circular in plan, pierced by

<hr>

[1] *Chronicles of the reigns of Stephen, Henry II and Richard I*, III, Pt. i; *Gesta Stephani Regis Anglorum* (Rolls Series 1886), 36; *Bristol Charters*, ed. N. Dermott Harding (Bristol Record Society Publications, I, 1930), 11, cf. 31.

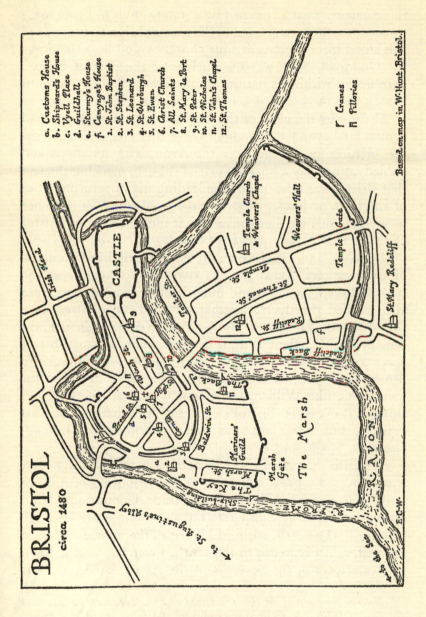

BRISTOL
circa 1480

a. Customs House
b. Shipward's House
c. Vyell Place
d. Guildhall
e. Sturmy's House
f. Canynge's House
1. St. John Baptist
2. St. Stephen
3. St. Leonard
4. St. Werburgh
5. St. Ewen
6. Christ Church
7. All Saints
8. St. Mary la Port
9. St. Peter
10. St. Nicholas
11. St. John's Chapel
12. St. Thomas

Γ Cranes
Π Pillories

Based on map in Wᵐ Hunt, Bristol.

Irish Mead

CASTLE

Tower St.

Temple Church & Weavers' Chapel

Weavers' Hall

Temple St.

St. Thomas St.

Temple Gate

Redcliff St.

St. Mary Redcliff

Redcliff Back

Winch St.

High St.

The Back

Broad St.

Corn St.

Baldwin St.

Mariners' Guild

Marsh St.

The Key

Marsh Gate

Ship-building

The Marsh

R. AVON

R. FROME

to St. Augustine's Abbey

to the Sea

E.C.W.

three gateways each crowned by a stately church. From these three gates, three streets led to the central High Cross; round this stood three more venerable churches, and near them was the Guildhall. Such was the nucleus of the port of Bristol, entrenched within its natural moat, and destined in years to come to be the business centre of an ever widening city.

Already by the close of the fourteenth century Bristol had grown far beyond the circle of these first city walls. Across the picturesque bridge over the Avon, with its shops and gabled houses, lay a busy industrial suburb, marking the fact that Bristol was now one of the leading manufacturing cities of England, no longer exporting the wool which came to her in such abundance, but converting it into the famous Bristol cloth. In this second quarter of the city, sheltered in a curve of the Avon, and with its own protecting wall, lived numbers of clothworkers. Down by the river in Touker Street the tuckers fulled the cloth and hung it on tenters to dry; there also worked the dyers. Further off in Temple Street rose the Weavers' Hall; near by the new Weavers' Chapel was built on to the ancient Temple Church; in St. Thomas' Street was a colony of linen workers.[1] Fronting the river in Redcliffe Street, spacious houses with lofty halls were designed for merchants, like William Canynges, who dealt in cloth and shipped it overseas. Bristol's export of wool had now ceased entirely, but her cloth was being marketed in Ireland, Gascony, Spain, and Portugal.

Fifteenth century Bristol, port and manufacturing city, was therefore a great collecting and distributing centre not only for overseas but also for inland trade. Goods poured into its market from a wide circle on whose circumference lay Chester to the north, Milford Haven to the west, London to the east, and Plymouth to the south. From the north, down the waterways of the Severn and the Avon, came rivercraft

---

[1] *Notes or Abstracts of the Wills contained in* . . . *The Great Orphan Book and Book of Wills*, ed. T. P. Wadley (Bristol and Gloucestershire Archaeological Society, Nos. I–V, 1886), *passim*; The Great White Book, f. 80 (Archives of the Corporation of Bristol); see map opposite p. 2.

with all manner of produce from the heart of England. Cloth was brought from Coventry, where many Bristol citizens were members of the Holy Trinity Guild, and Coventry merchants were free of toll in Bristol, whence they must have procured woad for making the famous "Coventry blue". From Coventry also, or from Nottingham, came the sculptured alabaster for which English craftsmen were then famed throughout Europe; this provided a reredos for St. Ewen's in Bristol, and for many churches abroad, from Iceland to Portugal.[1] The Forest of Dean sent quantities of iron, timber, and coal; the larger timber, called "Berkeley wood", was discharged in Bristol at the Quay, and the smaller wood at the Back, where there were supposed always to be pennyworths for sale. Down the Severn from Worcester, Tewkesbury, and Gloucester, came trowes and other craft laden with wheat, malt, and barley to feed the industrial population in and around Bristol, and for shipment abroad. Yet further north in Shrewsbury Bristol merchants had their agents; some of the cloth they exported came no doubt from the many drapers of Ludlow, and the road from Bristol to Chester with its five stone bridges was evidently a well frequented one.[2] Supplies of wool for the clothmakers were brought by carrier from places as distant as Buckingham;

[1] *The Coventry Leet Book* 1420–1555, ed. M. D. Harris (Early English Text Society, Original Series, Nos. 134, 135, 138, 146, 1907–13), pt. 2, 549–50 Churchwardens' Account Book, Church of St. Ewen, Bristol, f. 1; W. St. John Hope, *On the Early Working of Alabaster in England* (*Archaeological Journal* Second Series, II, 1904), 239; cf. L. F. Salzman, *English Industries in the Middle Ages* (1928), 96–7; Great White Book, *ut supra*, f. 38.
[2] The Great Red Book, ff. 18, 23, 210 (Archives of the Corporation of Bristol); *Victoria History of the County of Gloucester*, ed. W. Page, II (1907), 219–23; *The Maire of Bristowe is Kalendar*, by Robert Ricart, ed. L. Toulmin Smith (Camden Society Publications, New Series, V, 1872), 82–3; *Rotuli Parliamentorum* (Record Commission, 1767–77), IV, 346, and cf. *ibid.*, 332, 351, III, 665; cf. *Calendar of Patent Rolls*, 1361–4, 909, and *Calendar of Close Rolls*, 1374–7, 324; *Eighth Report of the Royal Commission on Historical Manuscripts, Report and Appendix* (1881), pt. I, 367; *Itineraria Symonis Simeonis et Willelmi de Worcestre*, ed. J. Nasmith (1778), 263; *Abstracts of Wills*, *ut supra*, 138, 149, 169; Tolsey Court Books, *passim* (Archives of the Corporation of Bristol).

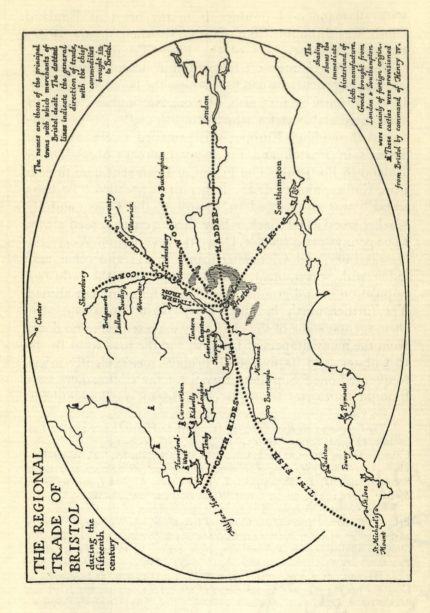

THE REGIONAL
TRADE OF
BRISTOL
during the
fifteenth
century

The names are those of the principal
towns with which merchants of
Bristol dealt. The dotted
lines indicate the general
direction of trade,
with the chief
commodities
brought in
to Bristol.

The
shading
shows the
immediate
hinterland of
cloth manufacture.
Goods brought from
London & Southampton
were mainly of foreign origin.
¶ These castles were provisioned
from Bristol by command of Henry IV.

Chester

Shrewsbury

Bridgnorth

Ludlow

Bewdley

Worcester

Coventry

Warwick

Tewkesbury

Gloucester

Buckingham

London

Southampton

CLOTH

CORN

TIMBER

IRON

MADDER

SILK

Bristol

Tintern

Chepstow

Newport

Barry

Minehead

Barnstaple

Plymouth

Fowey

Padstow

St. Ives

St. Michael's
Mount

Haverford-
West

Carmarthen

Kidwelly

Tinby

Loughor

Milford Haven

CLOTH, HIDES

TIN, FISH

from Coventry, where William Meryell, woolman, had constant dealings with Bristol, and probably from Hereford, near which at Leominster was some of the best wool of all England.[1] From the west, Wales and Monmouth sent up the Bristol Channel wool, hides, and cloth, in innumerable boats of Milford Haven, Tenby, Haverford West, "Lawgher Havyn" (Laugharne?), Llanstephan, Kidwelly, Newport, Usk, Caerleon, Chepstow, and Tintern. The Abbot of Tintern was himself a member of the Staple in Bristol, where he and his monks were exempted from tolls, as were the men of Tenby who carried on quite a flourishing trade of their own with the continent. Wool came from Carmarthen, and hides from Tenby and elsewhere, some of them perhaps for the Bristol parchment-maker who had dealings with Cardiff. Welsh cattle were indeed an indispensable source of raw material to the many tanners, whittawers, pouchmakers, pointmakers, girdlers, glovers, corvesers, and curriers who did a thriving business in Bristol, shipping much of their produce abroad. "Welsh cloth" from Kidwelly and elsewhere was a cheap frieze and provided russet gowns for poor folk in Bristol, whence it was also exported.[2] From the south, from the coasts of Devon and Cornwall, came tin, and also great quantities of fish, mainly for home consumption. The fish arrived mostly in boats belonging to Padstow, St. Ives, and Ilfracombe, but also in those from further afield, from Plymouth to the south to the Isle of Man ("Insula Humana") in the north. Packs of cloth came also up the Channel, especially from Barnstaple, and occasionally from as far as Kendal.[3]

[1] P.R.O., Early Chancery Proceedings, 61/499, 27/201; Tolsey Court Book, *ut supra*, 1480–1, f. 32 *et seq.*

[2] P.R.O., K.R. Escheators' Accounts, 238/2; *Antiquities of Bristow in the Middle Centuries*, ed. J. Dallaway (1834), 111; *The Little Red Book of Bristol*, ed. F. B. Bickley (1900), II, 199; P.R.O., K.R. Memoranda Roll, Mich. 12 Hen. VI, m. 34; Tolsey Court Books and *Abstracts of Wills*, *ut supra, passim; Rotuli Parliamentorum, ut supra*, II, 437, 541.

[3] P.R.O., K.R. Escheators' Accounts, 238/2; P.R.O., Early Chancery Proceedings, 18/189; *Antiquities of Bristow, ut supra*, 111; cf. Great Red Book, *ut supra*, f. 96; see map for summary of regional trade.

All these districts received through Bristol merchants a variety of foodstuffs, raw materials, and luxuries. A Welsh boat, for instance, which brought in fish, was reladen with iron, and corn was sent to the people of Wales as well as to the English garrisons there. The Cornishmen who arrived with fish or tin left with frieze and other cheap cloth; Barnstaple, itself a flourishing cloth manufacturing town, took woad for its dyers, with wax and wine. Much fish was sent inland up the Severn, with coal, wax, and iron, perhaps for Birmingham's nascent industry, and the rich regions in the heart of England depended largely on Bristol for their supplies of luxuries from the South of Europe. Wine, for instance, travelled constantly by river to Gloucester, Worcester, and Bewdley; thence it went on into Shropshire, and one Ludlow merchant, who shipped his cloth through Bristol to Portugal, himself imported both fruit and wine. From Worcester it was taken on, probably in carts, as a century earlier, up the Avon valley to Warwick and Coventry. So much was it in demand for the banquets at Warwick Castle, that the enterprising earl, Richard Beauchamp, once had a scheme for making the Avon navigable as far as his own gates. Coventry also bought iron and manufactured metal goods from Bristol, such as guns from the famous foundry which more than once supplied cannon to the king, besides wax, and, no doubt, raw materials such as alum and woad; and though Coventry merchants, situated in the very centre of England, naturally had some dealings with the East Coast, they often collaborated with Bristol. Thus while they once sent a ship to Iceland apparently from Boston, they sent several ships thither in partnership with Bristol merchants.[1]

---

[1] *Calendar of Patent Rolls*, 1405–8, 163; P.R.O., K.R. Escheators' Accounts, 238/2; P.R.O., Early Chancery Proceedings, 61/489, 45/58; *The Charters and Letters Patent . . . of Bristol*, ed. S. Seyer (1812), 220; P.R.O., K.R. Customs Accounts 19/3, 19/4; *Victoria History of the County of Warwick*, ed. W. Page, II (1908), 138; *Coventry Leet Book, ut supra*, pt. 3, 594,260, cf. *Issue Roll of Thomas de Brantingham*, translated by F. Devon (Record Commission, 1835), 332; P.R.O., K.R. Memoranda Roll, Mich. 9 Hen. VI, m. 19; P.R.O., Chancery Enrolments, Treaty Roll, 1 Edw. IV, m. 10.

With her immediate hinterland Bristol carried on a lively business, for she was in the midst of one of the most vigorous cloth producing regions of England. Innumerable villages at the foot of the Cotswolds and the Mendips and along the valleys of the Somerset Avon and its tributaries had their organized groups of weavers, dyers, and tuckers, making ample use of the water power from the hills to drive their fulling mills. These districts naturally marketed much of their cloth at Bristol and took thence much of their raw material, though in wool they were well provided locally from their steadily increasing flocks of sheep. A Somerset clothier of Shirburn, for instance, in payment for cloth sold to a Bristol merchant, received partly money and partly woad.[1] From the wealth thus accumulated, such villages were beautified with spacious churches, and these reveal for us incidentally not only which were the most prosperous clothing districts, but also with which of them Bristol had the closest connections. For their lofty towers were furnished with bells, many of which bear the mark of the Bristol foundry, then, next to that of London, perhaps the most important in the kingdom. These bells may still be found in large numbers in Gloucestershire, East Somerset, and North Wilts, as also in South Wales, Devon, and Cornwall.[2]

But it must not be supposed that Bristol dealt only with the West of England, Wales, and the Midlands. She was in constant communication also with both London and Southampton. The list of tolls paid at Southampton inscribed on the first page of Bristol's Great Red Book shows how close was the connection between the two, and merchants seem often to have passed to and fro. Bristol sent cloth thither to be laden on the Italian galleys when they called there on their way up

[1] P.R.O., Early Chancery Proceedings, 48/85; cf. ibid., 49/33.
[2] H. B. Walters, *The Church Bells of Wiltshire, their Inscriptions and History*, *passim* (3 pts., issued with the *Wiltshire Archaeological and Natural History Magazine*, vol. 44, Nos. 147, 149 and 151, December 1927, 1928 and 1929); *Church Bells of England*, 179 *et seq.*; *Abstracts of Wills, ut supra*, 133, for will of a Bristol bell-founder.

channel, and received in return some of the luxuries they brought, such as silk for the attire of her wealthy burgesses.[1] Still closer was the link with London, whose Lord Mayor is said to have presented to Bristol a rich sword "embroidered with pearls". Carriers plied between the two cities, and the journey, by way of Chippenham and Newbury, could be done on horseback in rather less than three days. Much Bristol cloth, therefore, went to the capital. A Bristol tucker once stated that he commissioned a weaver to take thither for him a violet and a plunket cloth, and John Henlove and Alice Richards of Bristol both sold broadcloths there to the "Easterlings". Indeed, Bristol men seem to have carried on a lively business in London with these Hanse merchants who, so they said, offered them more favourable terms than did the English merchants there. The Acts of Court of the Mercers' Company in London record an interesting discussion on this subject in 1486, at an "Assembly of the Fellowship of Adventurers". It was reported that the men of Bristol had complained to the king's council that if the Easterlings were banished from London they would be utterly undone. For while the Easterlings bought their cloth for ready money, the merchants of London "buy not but for days, and therefore do make payment in Cardes, tenys balles, fish hooks, bristills, tassells, and such other simple wares". More useful than the tennis balls was the madder for dyeing, which Bristol merchants brought often from London, imported probably from Flanders. London merchants sometimes came themselves to Bristol to purchase cloth, and London ships called sometimes at Bristol to collect cloth on their way to Bordeaux, just as Bristol ships called at London on their occasional trips to Eastern Europe. At least one London fishmonger co-operated with Bristol. "Stephen Forster, citizen and fishmonger of London", was probably the same as he who owned the *Mary Redcliffe* and the

---

[1] P.R.O., K.R. Customs Accounts, 19/11 and 13; P.R.O., Early Chancery Proceedings, 67/187; Great Red Book, *ut supra*, f. 1; Brokage Book, 1439–40, 26 (Archives of the Corporation of Southampton).

Katherine with William Canynges and traded with them to Iceland for fish. At any rate he named William Canynges as one of his executors, and gave generous bequests to several Bristol churches, including St. Mary Redcliffe, and it was in his house in London that one of Canynges' sons died.[1]

Goods thus came into Bristol's market from all quarters for redistribution—by the Severn and its tributaries, up the Bristol Channel, and by road from south and east. On the "Welsh Back", close to the bridge over the Avon, were unloaded fish and tin, cloth, wool, and hides from Wales and the southern coasts of England, while coal, timber, and other goods that came down the Severn were landed on the "Key" by the Frome.[2] Many a greater port must have been put to shame by both these quays. For while every tide left a muddy deposit on the irregular and unpaved quay of Bordeaux, Bristol had not only paved its streets and piled its strands, but had bound its Key and its Back with freestone.[3] Truly might Drayton praise this city as one of the healthiest and most delectable of its day:—

> "The prospect of which place
> To her fair building adds an admirable grace;
> Well fashioned as the best, and with a double wall,
> As brave as any town; but yet excelling all
> For easement, that to health is requisite and meet;
> Her piled shores, to keep her delicate and sweet;
> Hereto, she hath her tides; that when she is opprest
> With heat or drought, still pour their floods upon her breast."[4]

---

[1] Bodleian MSS. Gough, Somerset, 2, App. 33; Archives of the Corporation of Bristol 08153 (1); P.R.O., Early Chancery Proceedings, 32/314, 60/251, 66/354, 64/435; Acts of Court of the Mercers' Company, I, f. 151; P.R.O., K.R. Customs Accounts, 19/1, 19/2, 73/10, 73/20; Register of Wills proved in the Prerogative Court of Canterbury, Stokton, 14, 15; *Calendar of Patent Rolls*, 1441–6, 81.

[2] *Antiquities of Bristow, ut supra*, 69, 111; *Ricart's Kalendar, ut supra*, 83–4; Great Red Book, *ut supra*, f. 18.

[3] *Adam's Chronicle of Bristol*, ed. F. F. Fox (1910), 66; *Calendar of Patent Rolls*, 1429–36, 497; Ricart's Kalendar, *ut supra*, 40, 47; contrast T. Malvézin, *Histoire du commerce de Bordeaux* (Bordeaux, 1892), II, 184.

[4] M. Drayton, *Polyolbion*, Third Song, ll. 241–8.

Bristol's "double wall" was by the fifteenth century ornamental rather than useful, and the city spent more on its quays than on its fortifications, though one burgess left money for their repair. For its life was centred at the quays and the adjoining customs house. There, outside the small circle of the ancient town, distinct also from the wide industrial suburb with its fashionable residential quarter, had grown up a third distinctive district, that of the mariners. In the low-lying region between the two rivers, the Avon with its "Back" and the Frome with its "Key", seamen lived in Baldwin Street, and nearby in Marsh Street the Fraternity for Mariners was formed in 1445.[1] This was supported by a levy from each master mariner, who, on arrival in port, had to pay 4d. a tun on his cargo within two days of receiving his hire. Two wardens were elected by the "craft", and the Fraternity maintained a priest and twelve poor sailors whose duty it was to pray for all merchants and mariners "passing or labouring" on the sea, either outwards or homewards. These seamen who brought fame to Bristol have left little record behind them. From time to time they appeared in the Tolsey Court, and there the clerk on one occasion relieved his feelings by inscribing, in the midst of a monotonous record of debts claimed, a fragment of one of their shanties:—

> "Hale and howe Rumbylowe
> Stire well the gode ship and lete the wynde blowe.
> Here commethe the Pryor of Prikkingham and his Convent
> But ye kepe þe ordoure well, ye shull be shent,
> With hale and howe etc." [2]

It was for men thus in peril on the sea, whether from the Prior or from the sea-bishops, sea-unicorns and the like who enliven medieval maps and bestiaries, that yet another institution was founded in this century, also in the mariners' quarter. On the Welsh Back was the chapel of St. John the Evangelist, and here Thomas Knappe appointed a priest

[1] *The Little Red Book, ut supra,* II, 186–9.
[2] Tolsey Court Book, *ut supra,* 1487–97, 158; no other extant shanty apparently throws any light on the identity of the Prior.

to say mass for all merchants and mariners every morning at five o'clock.[1]

While the Welsh Back received the goods which were brought into Bristol from Wales and the southern coasts of England, it was at the larger quay by the Frome that Bristol's great sea-faring ships were built and loaded. Thence they were dispatched with English cloth and other merchandise, down the Severn and far away to north, south and west. Thither they returned to drop anchor, freighted with rich and varied produce from other lands to be stored in roomy cellars beneath the houses on the quay. Some had sailed simply to Ireland and home again. Others had voyaged on a long and complex course, visiting first Bordeaux or Lisbon, and then Ireland; sailing via Ireland and Brittany to Flanders, and returning by London and Southampton; crossing the ocean to Iceland and back in the summer, and then setting out for Bordeaux in the winter; or penetrating the Baltic to Danzig, and calling on the way home at Grimsby, Hull, and Sandwich. But three main routes were habitually followed, each of about equal importance in the volume of trade which it brought to Bristol. These led to Ireland, to Gascony, and to the Iberian peninsula, and it was on them that the fortunes of the city were founded. All three led away from the traditional centres of European commerce, the Baltic and the Mediterranean, for Bristol looked out on the Atlantic, then to all appearance the utmost bound of the earth, and on its shores her merchants marketed their goods, faring forth as yet unknowingly upon the future great highway of nations.

§ 2

IRELAND

Spenser, describing the beauties of Ireland, her "excellent comodityes", her ports and havens "opening upon England and Scotland as inviting us to come to them", wrote at the

---

[1] *Antiquities of Bristow, ut supra,* 111; *Abstracts of Wills, ut supra,* 68.

close of a century which had brought her many hardships; his words seem even more applicable to what was, for her, the prosperous fifteenth century. With her "havens, great and goodly bays" and her land "plenteous and rich above most", she was a country offering abundant spoil to the foreigner; merchants from far-off Lucca came to her spacious harbours; in them lay ships from Iceland, from Spain, from Lübeck, from Bordeaux, and above all from England's two great western ports on the Severn and the Dee.[1]

Bristol, of all English ports, was then the one most favoured for traffic to Ireland, just as in Hakluyt's day it was well known as "a commodious and safe receptacle" for all ships directing their course thither. It was through a Bristol merchant that the Prior of Christ Church Canterbury once sent his letters to Ireland; while Sir Stephen Scrope, going as deputy thither in 1406, accompanied by fifty men at arms and 300 archers, arranged for their transport from Bristol, Liverpool, and Chester.[2] But if Chester and its less important neighbour were well situated for trade with the more anglicized north, Bristol's position fitted her pre-eminently for intercourse with the more numerous and wealthier Irish ports of the south. Thence ships sailed frequently for Waterford, "Harbour of the Sun". Alongside its extensive quay of half a mile no less than sixty vessels could anchor, and to them river boats brought the wealth of the interior, at small expense, down three great rivers which watered seven counties. There in 1398 the *Trinity* of Bristol unloaded a cargo of wine, and thence cargoes of fish were dispatched constantly to Bristol. Close were the connections between ships and merchants of the two cities. The *John* of Waterford, attacked in her own harbour by a notorious Falmouth

---

[1] A. S. Green, *The Making of Ireland and its Undoing, 1200–1600* (1908), 13, 25; *The Statutes at Large, passed in the Parliaments held in Ireland*, I (Dublin, 1765), 697 (1459–60); *The Reign of Henry VII from contemporary sources*, ed. A. F. Pollard (1913–14), III, 279; P.R.O., Early Chancery Proceedings, 24/211, 24/217.

[2] *Fifth Report of the Royal Commission on Historical Manuscripts* (1876), pt. 1, Appendix, 446; *Calendar of Patent Rolls*, 1405–8, 237.

pirate, was said to be the property of a Bristol merchant; and when the militant Prior of Kilmainham, with 200 horsemen and 300 foot, had sailed from Waterford to serve under Henry V in France, Bristol masters and mariners received £91 for conveying them thither. Waterford merchants were free of toll in Bristol, and were apparently as friendly to its merchants as they were to Edward IV, who recognized their services by letters patent, conferring on them special franchises and liberties. So great was their confidence in a certain Bristol merchant, who had sometimes transacted business for them, that they left these letters in his hands, until on his death they were found to have been mislaid, and the Mayor of Waterford was moved to sue the merchant's executors in Chancery. Thus Waterford, nearest of all large Irish ports to Bristol, and "urbs intacta" that was never captured in the later Middle Ages by Irish chief or Norman earl, naturally absorbed much of the Irish trade. During one winter Bristol shipped more cloth in her merchantmen than in those of any other Irish port.[1]

But Southern Ireland abounds in "great and goodly bays", and along the rugged shores of Munster there was many another sheltered harbour where vessels from Bristol and the Continent found refuge. Ships of Cork and of Kinsale, of Ross and of Youghal, all visited Bristol, and Kinsale bade fair to rival Waterford both in the number of its boats and in the amount of cloth they shipped. Its record is not, however, altogether creditable. Freebooting made it notorious rather than famous. In 1449–50, for instance, the *Mary* of Bristol, with her master, mariners, and fishers, "in fishing fare" on the high seas, captured a ship of Spain, the *Carveule* of Vermewe of 55 tuns, freighted with wine, iron, and salt, to the value of £160. Then Philip Martyn, Patrick Martyn, Thomas (?) Hanyagh, and Patrick Galwey of

---

[1] Green, *op. cit.*, 10, 28; *Select Cases in the Chancery*, A.D. *1364–1471*, ed. W. P. Baildon (Selden Society, X, 1896), No. 34; *Calendar of Patent Rolls*, 1452–62, 119; *Issue Roll of Thomas de Brantingham, ut supra*, 356; P.R.O., Early Chancery Proceedings, 65/215, cf. *ibid.*, 65/242; P.R.O., K.R. Customs Accounts, 17/8–12.

Kinsale, with many others of the same town, manned divers vessels, overcame the *Mary*, killed three of her men, and "divers moo of them hurted and grevousely bet", and led the Spanish ship triumphantly into Kinsale. Thus John Wyche, owner of the *Mary*, told the tale, when later on Thomas Hanyagh turned up in Bristol with a skiff of Kinsale and 6,000 hake of other Kinsale merchants. Hanyagh, the skiff and the hake were all promptly "arrested" and Wyche had the effrontery to claim £200 damages in the Court of Admiralty. The Mayor, evidently suspicious, dismissed the case and cancelled the jury list of eighteen men, but Wyche took the matter into Chancery, asking for a subpœna against the Mayor, and secured a commission to arrest and bring before the king seven of the Kinsale men.[1]

Far away to the west, remote from England, but in a more direct line for Lisbon and Seville than was Bristol, were flourishing ports whose traffic with England was probably but a fraction of their total trade in Europe. There lay Limerick, "a wonderous prosperous city; it may be called Little London for the situation and the plenty". Ships of 200 tuns could shelter in its secluded harbour on the Shannon, and it had ships of its own as large as that which in one voyage took from Bristol as much cloth as seven Kinsale boats took in six months, besides iron and salt. Its church of St. Mary was enriched by merchants of Bristol such as John Bannebury, who bequeathed to it and to the Friars Minor there 33s. 4d. and eight marks of silver, and to his wife two water-mills and other landed property in and near the city.[2] Yet further north, beyond "Munster of the swift ships", stood Galway, centre of the Irish pilgrim traffic to Compostella. Girt about with lakes, her streets lined with houses all of hewed stone, garnished with fair battlements in a uniform course as if the whole town were built upon one model, she was indeed a noble city. Loudly the Irish be-

[1] P.R.O., *Early Chancery Proceedings*, 19/122, 24/221; *Calendar of Patent Rolls*, 1452–61, 60.
[2] *Abstracts of Wills, ut supra*, 70.

wailed that they were in continual peril from their own countrymen and from English rebels who extorted ruinous tolls outside their city gates; and by such laments they sometimes contrived to evade their taxes, as did Limerick for fifteen years. Yet some among them must have amassed considerable fortunes thus to beautify their cities, and trade with the Continent evidently throve. Galway, Burrishoole, and Sligo had constant dealings with Spain and Portugal, and the ships which brought them southern luxuries for sale in Ireland reloaded with Irish produce for the markets of England or the Low Countries. For these three ports "or any one of them" John Heyton, merchant of Bristol, arranged that the *Julian* of Bristol should be freighted in Lisbon with wine, honey, and salt, and that, when she had delivered her burden, she should be reloaded with hides and sail on to Plymouth and thence to Normandy, Brittany, or the Low Countries. Commercial intercourse led to other speculative English enterprises in Galway. When the city was seized in 1400 by the rebel Sir William de Burgh, one "loyal Englishman" came over to Bristol and persuaded four adventurers to take their ships and help him to recover the town; they went at their own expense, but the king, who had little time or money to give to Ireland, and who only maintained troops there by quartering them on the country, gave them permission to recoup themselves with all the goods of the rebels.[1]

In contrast to South and West Ireland, Ulster, with its ports opening upon Scotland and Northern England, had little connection with Bristol, though ships from Carrickfergus sometimes came thither.[2] Their arrival was imperilled by the diligence of those inveterate tormentors of England,

---

[1] E. Curtis, *A History of Medieval Ireland from 1110 to 1513* (1923), 362–3; A. K. Longfield, *Anglo-Irish Trade in the Sixteenth Century* (1929), 25; Green, *op. cit.*, 19–22; P.R.O., Early Chancery Proceedings, 24/211 and 217; J. H. Wylie, *History of England under Henry the Fourth* (1884–98), I, 226; *Calendar of Patent Rolls*, 1399–1401, 254, cf. R. Dunlop, *Ireland from the Earliest Times* (1922), 51.

[2] P.R.O., K.R. Escheators Accounts, 238/2.

the Scots, who preyed constantly upon ships venturing through the North Channel—a passage more dangerously narrow than the Straits of Dover. In 1482, for instance, Richard Chapman, fishmonger, and John Quyrke, mariner, were sailing the seas in the *Flowre* of Minehead when there came upon them two Scottish ships commanded by John de Rumpyll (thus did the Englishmen distort their captor's name Dalrymple). He seized the *Flowre*, took her into Ayr, and then, being a man of business, proposed to sell both ship and cargo to her crew. But how could the £70 he demanded be produced in ready money in a barren land seldom visited by English merchants? At last it was agreed that the *Flowre* must be sent to Minehead with her merchandise and her tragic tale, while Chapman and Quyrke must remain with de Rumpyll to be ransomed. Accordingly the trapped Englishmen decided that one of their "fellowship", William Porter, should be master of the ship and her cargo, should take her to Minehead, and should sell as much as was necessary to pay the £70 and the "costs and other losses" sustained by Chapman and Quyrke during their imprisonment: "which to do the seid William Porter faythfully promysed and agreed in all goodly haste". But Porter's promises were apparently better than his practices, for the £70 was not forthcoming, and Chapman and Quyrke, languishing in the Scottish prison, were moved to send a petition to the Chancellor.[1]

Bristol men certainly visited Ulster less often than the Pale, that ever-dwindling place, scarce thirty miles in length, into which the English were now penned and "out of which they durst not peep". Thence Drogheda sometimes sent ships to Bristol and bought from Bristol merchants, though it was probably in more constant touch with the nearer port of Chester. One Drogheda merchant, for instance, owing 20 marks to Clement Bagot of Bristol, sent to Chester six butts of salmon, which were sold at Shrewsbury for Bagot's benefit. Dublin also must have been more closely connected

[1] P.R.O., Early Chancery Proceedings, 59/88.

with Chester. Henry II's charter had granted to Bristol men all the privileges which they enjoyed in their own city, and men of Bristol origin, perhaps the descendants of early settlers, were still living there. But the men who took a prominent part in founding, in 1479, the Guild of English merchants trading in Ireland, with its chapel on the bridge in Dublin, were none of them well-known citizens of Bristol. And though some business was carried on between the two cities, Dublin ships scarcely ever arrived in Bristol.[1] It was the ships of South Ireland, above all, which had dealings with Bristol, carrying many a cargo for prominent merchants there, and trafficking no doubt also with other Irish ports than their own.

Irish vessels, indeed, took a far larger share in the business than did those of Bristol, which concerned themselves mainly with more distant traffic. Sixteen Irish ships were engaged in it during the winter of 1403–4, as compared with six Bristol ones. Even Bristol's smaller neighbours, especially Minehead, were sometimes more actively engaged than Bristol itself. Nine Minehead vessels went to Ireland in 1465–6 (November to May), and the towns of Berkeley and Walton took a share, as did also Welsh ports such as Milford and Chepstow.

Irish merchants as well as Irish ships busied themselves in the trade, though a part of their own continental commerce was in the hands of Bristol merchants.[2] Many of them must have been to and fro in Bristol, some of them men of doubtful reputations among the English; John Bullok was said to be a common withdrawer of the king's custom and a deceiver of his liege people, and was sued in Chancery by John Bonyfaunt who had stood surety for the payment of his dues.

---

[1] *Eighth Report of the Royal Commission on Historical Manuscripts* (1881), Reports and Appendix, pt. I, 367–8; cf. *ibid.*, 372, for Chester's trade with Ireland; J. T. Gilbert, *History of Dublin* (Dublin, 1854–9), II, 1, 240; *Register of Wills and Inventories of the Diocese of Dublin, 1457–83*, ed. H. F. Berry (1898), 28, 83, 175; D. A. Chart, *An Economic History of Ireland* (Dublin, 1920), 19; P.R.O., K.R. Customs Accounts, 17/8 and 10, 19/14.

[2] P.R.O., Early Chancery Proceedings, 26/474, 24/211 and 217.

The "Irish Mead" on the outskirts of Bristol indicates that Irishmen must also have settled in the city; certainly the Bristol merchants Patrick Irishman and Henry May (perhaps a member of the well-known Waterford family) were Irish at least in origin, as were Patrick Lawless and John Gough, masters of Bristol ships. An interesting light is thrown on Bristol's Irish immigrants by the decree of 1413. In that year, "for quiet and peace within this realm of England and for the increase and filling of the realm of Ireland", all the "wylde" Irish, except those who had an honourable position as burgesses, men of law, and so forth, were ordered to leave England. Amongst those permitted to remain were Nicholas Devenysh, a merchant, Philip Faunt, a master tanner, John Stone and John Ayleward, all of Bristol. When in 1430 the exclusion decree was repeated, exemption was granted to Robert Londe, priest, who is depicted with paten and chalice on a brass dated 1460 in St. Peter's Church at Bristol. Complaint had already been made that the Bristol weavers were taking as apprentices children and young men born in Ireland who were taught for only one, two, or three years and then departed. A decree of 1439 imposed a penalty of £20 on any Mayor of Bristol who admitted to his Council a man born in Ireland of an Irish father and mother. The inference that these immigrants were both numerous and unacceptable is confirmed by a quaint entry in Ricart's Calendar. He records, under the date 1456, that the Irish burgesses began a suit against the mayor and council before the Lord Chancellor, Harry May being "vaunt parloure and chief labourer"; for which he and all his fellows were deprived of their freedom "til they bought it ayen with the blodde of theyre purses, and with weping Ien, knelyng on their knees, besought the Maire and his brothern of their grace".[1]

But if Irish people were not always welcome in Bristol,

[1] *Ibid.*, 15/237 and 238. For names cf. *Wills and Inventories, ut supra*, 38, 144; Curtis, *op. cit.*, 330; *Calendar of Patent Rolls*, 1413–6, 122; *Little Red Book, ut supra*, II, 110, 123; P.R.O., K.R. Customs Accounts, 17/37; *Calendar of Patent Rolls*, 1429–36, 64; *Ricart's Kalendar, ut supra*, 41.

Irish merchandise, on which its fortunes had originally been founded, was eagerly sought after as one of its chief sources of wealth. "Heryng of Slegothe and salmon of Bame heis made in Brystowe many a ryche man." Thus ran a common proverb, quoted for the merchant's instruction in a fifteenth century commercial handbook, and fish was probably the product of Ireland that Bristol men valued most. They caught it themselves off her shores, though an Act of 1465 forbade any stranger to fish without a licence; they chaffered for it in Ireland with fishermen, who sometimes promised to send it at least as far as Kingrode, where the Bristol men might receive it and "convey it at their pleasure and liberty". John Mold, fisherman of Malahide, died in debt to a prominent Bristol merchant who exported fish to Spain; John Jonet owed 5s. to a Lusk fisherman's wife who possessed (besides sheep, cows, pigs, and a cart horse) one boat and fourteen sea-nets.[1]

Of the salt-water fish sent from Ireland the herring came first in quantity. For as the East of England supplied itself with herring from Norfolk and Suffolk, so "as for the west party of Ynglond, thei have ther herynge howe of Yrland". Herring was one of the fish most in demand among house-wives of the period. As Margaret Paston's bailiff wrote to her one autumn: "Mastres, it were good to remember your stuffe of heryng nough this fisshyng tyme"; and in the regulations of the baronial breakfasts of the Percy family throughout Lent it is ordained that my lord Percy (aged 11) and master Thomas Percy shall breakfast daily on three white herrings or a dish of sprats besides a piece of salt-fish, bread and butter, and beer; similarly for the two younger folk in the "Nurcy" there is to be "a Manchet, a Quart of Bere, a Dysch of Butter, a Pece of Saltfisch, a Dysch of Sproitts or iij White Herryng". The same provision of sprats or herring

---

[1] *The Noumbre of Weyghtes* (B.M.MS. Cotton, Vespasian E. ix), f. 100d; P.R.O., Early Chancery Proceedings, 19/122, 64/591; Green, *op. cit.*, 46; Tolsey Court Book, *ut supra*, 1480–1, f. 93; *Wills and Inventories, ut supra*, 83, 144.

is made for all, from my lady to her "Gentyllwomen". These white herrings (fresh or salted as contrasted with smoked herrings) are priced in the Bristol customs accounts at £3 the last of 12,000 fish, and the same customs valuation is given to red herrings, that is herrings salted for about twenty-four hours and hung up to smoke. The Pastons expected to purchase half a last from the North Sea Fisheries for £2 in the fishing season of autumn, when the wise housewife replenished her stock for the following Lent, and it was at this time that boats came from Ireland with as much as £100 worth of herrings, whereas in the spring and summer they brought not more than two or three lasts. So the Paston's bailiff wrote, "Ye shal do more nough with xls. then ye shal do at Cristemes with v marke."[1]

"Pecys of Saltfisch" similar to those provided for the Percy breakfasts came also to Bristol from Ireland in many varieties, chiefly of the cod family. Among these large fish (gadoids), the most highly priced were hake, pollack, scalpin (whiting), and milwell (cod). Inferior qualities of these and other species of the same family, such as haburden (cod used especially for salting) and ling, called grenefish when fresh, very likely went to make up the bulk of the unspecified "fish" and "dry fish". A diminutive shark, the hound fish, was also imported. More rarely seen in Bristol were seals, valued in the customs at 2s. 6d. each and reputed as fit only for the digestions of mariners; the royal fish, whale, at 2s. the barrel; and porpoise at 5s. the barrel—the "sea pig" whose tongue was considered such a delicacy that Henry I, in giving the Bishop of London the right to all those taken on his land, had excepted "the tongue, which I have retained for myself". Some of the fish certainly arrived fresh, for when in 1488 the old records of the town were searched at the request of the water-bailiff, it was found that the king was entitled to a

[1] *The Noumbre of Weyghtes, ut supra*, f. 94; *Paston Letters*, ed. J. Gairdner (1900–8), No. 839; *The Northumberland Household Book*, quoted in *Social Life in Britain from the Conquest to the Reformation*, ed. G. G. Coulton (1918), 383; P.R.O., K.R. Customs Accounts, *passim*.

prise of six fish from every boat with thirty or more fresh milwell, ling, hake, ray, conger, and of twelve fish from every boat with thirty or more fresh gurnard, haddock, whiting, bream, mackerel, plaice, or other small fresh fish. The king had also the right to a hundred fish from every boat with fresh herring not belonging to a Bristol burgess, but for fresh-water fish and fresh salmon there was no prise. Much of the fish must, however, have been cured since, even when it arrived in autumn, it was needed especially for Lent. Ling, indeed, would keep not only until Lent but for two years, if it were put into thick straw and covered with mats "close and dry". Salt was therefore much in demand. For a barrel of salt a man might have "a Barrell fylled full of new herynge nott a day"; and many boats left Bristol for Ireland with salt and cloth, to buy salmon or herring there, salt them, and bring them back to England. Salmon was more highly priced than the salt-water fish, and was frequently imported. Bristol men often secured licences either to buy it or to catch it themselves. Perhaps the Bristol burgess with water-mills in Limerick set traps for it in the Shannon; at any rate it came often from those parts, and sometimes from merchants of Kilkenny, as well as from the river Bann in the north.[1]

Next in amount and value to fish came the hides exported in great quantities as the fishing season waned. For Ireland with its moist climate, "greate mountaynes and wast desartes full of grasse", nourished many thousands of cattle "for the good of the whole realm". Being only fed and not fattened, however, their value was in their hides. These provided shoes and gloves, saddle and harness, coffer and purses, girdles and jerkins, trimmings for the rich, writing materials for the scribe, and rugs for rich and poor alike. Almost every vessel arriving in Bristol brought its quota; shiploads also went in Bristol boats direct from Ireland to the

[1] *The Babees Book*, 171, in *Manners and Meals in Olden Times*, ed. F. J. Furnivall (Early English Text Society, No. 32, 1868); *The Noumbre of Weyghtes, ut supra*, f. 94; cf. the inventory of Sir John Fastolf's goods, *Paston Letters, ut supra*, No. 336; *Calendar of Patent Rolls*, 1399–1401, 248; P.R.O., K.R. Escheators Accounts, 238/2 and Customs Accounts, *passim*.

ports of Southern England, France, and to Flanders, where they could be sold more profitably than anywhere else for £18 the last.[1] Skins of sheep, lambs and kids were very common, and the unspecified hides and salted hides must have included the ox-, cow-, and calf-hides, which are seldom entered separately. In the fastnesses of Irish bogs and mountains wild animals abounded, and from their skins the skilful hunter must have made good profit. Deer skins and rabbit skins were the most common. Less often appear hares, martens, foxes, otters, goats, and squirrels. Wolves also lurked in the forests, and toll was once paid in Bristol for three dozen of their skins. The skins usually arrived raw in Bristol, where they were then worked up, often for re-export, by the many tanners, curriers, whittawers, and corvesers who did business there. Besides the skins of the animals there came tallow, lard, wax, and occasionally butter. But six "bacons" from Carrickfergus, and twelve carcases in a Drogheda boat are unique mentions of "beasts' flesh", in striking contrast to present-day statistics of Irish produce. Other live-stock, however, appear in the accounts, for Ireland was even then famed for her horses, especially for those "gentyll horsys that be callyd hobbeys of Irelond". Merchants of Drogheda once freighted a Flemish ship for Brittany with hides and thirty-four unfortunate horses which were driven by tempests into Dartmouth, and there, so the owner averred, distributed by the bailiff.[2] The needs of sportsmen were further ministered to by the export of hawks, male and female, valued at 2s. 6d. each.

The "goodly woodes fitt for building of howses and shippes" proved also a valuable source of wealth. Irish timber, used freely in Ireland for herring casks, was even more prized abroad, as in England, where Irish oak beauti-fied many a church during the golden age of English wood-work, and in France, where it was considered specially fit

[1] *The Noumbre of Weyghtes, ut supra*, f. 101; P.R.O., Early Chancery Proceedings, 24/211 and 217, and Customs Accounts, *passim*.
[2] P.R.O. Early Chancery Proceedings, 71/54.

for furniture, painting, and sculpture.[1] Ship-boards came constantly to Bristol, as did oars and occasionally bow-staves.

But Ireland was no mere cattle-run interspersed with forests. By the thirteenth century more land had been brought under the plough than was necessary to supply her own needs, especially in the east midlands, and the export of corn was a profitable business. In the early fifteenth century she was still known as a possible source of grain, and Bristol merchants shipped corn thence direct to the Continent. Later on, however, her supplies began to run short. By 1437 Bristol was shipping corn to Ireland; in 1475 the export of corn from Ireland was forbidden[2]; and in the last quarter of the century there were constant shipments from Bristol.

Skilled manufactures were now developing in Ireland, especially that of linen from her unrivalled flax, known in the fifteenth century as far afield as the Netherlands and Italy.[3] Its abundance was graphically demonstrated by the Irishman's thick folded saffron shirt, his smock of thirty yards or more wound about him, with sleeves falling to the knees, and by the great linen rolls upon the women's heads. In vain the English passed laws, "impertinent and unnecessary," forbidding such "barbarous" Irish customs as these and the entertaining of bards and pipers, and setting a limit of seven yards to the shirt; the traditional Irish apparel was still in vogue in Elizabethan days. Consignments of this linen and of linen yarn reached Bristol constantly, and the industry evidently flourished in the fifteenth century, particularly towards its close. During one year the import of over 20,000 cloths was recorded, and the activity of Kilkenny merchants may perhaps indicate a manufacturing centre in that neighbourhood. According to the customs valuation the worth of the linen was $1\frac{1}{4}d$. a yard. This linen manufacture, for which the

[1] Green, op. cit., 46.
[2] Chart, op. cit., 16; Calendar of Patent Rolls, 1413–16, 94; P.R.O., K.R. Customs Accounts, 18/39; cf. N. S. B. Gras, The Evolution of the English Corn Market from the Twelfth to the Eighteenth Century (Cambridge, Mass., 1926), 111; Green, op. cit., 94.
[3] Green, op. cit., 50.

Irish soil and climate was peculiarly fitted, tended to overtake the manufacture of low-priced Irish woollens which were, however, always popular in England. "Drap d'Irland" was one of the cheap cloths which Parliament asked might be exempted from the payment of cocket, provided the dozen (half a cloth) did not exceed in value 10s.[1] Forty yards of Irish frieze were valued in the customs at 20s., and both this and faldynges (rough-napped cloth) were exported in considerable quantities to Bristol. Even more popular seem to have been the capacious ready-made mantles; these, for a cost of something over 3s. 4d., could serve as garment, bed, or even tent when necessary and, as Spenser picturesquely paraphrased it, were "a fitt howse for an outlaw, a meete bedd for a rebell, and an apt cloke for a theif". Whittles also (shaggy blankets) were sent by the Irish at half the price, and also rugs. Finally, they shipped some of their wool as flock, suitable for bedding, at 5d. the stone. Amongst other manufactured articles are now and again exports of "oldware" and "newware"—a foreshadowing of the extensive trade in old pewter and brass of the following century.

Amply supplied for almost all ordinary needs, Ireland asked but two necessaries from outside—salt and iron. Salt often came to her direct from the Continent, sometimes in foreign ships *via* Bristol, and sometimes in Bristol ships, either for sale or for salting their own return cargo of fish. Shipments of salt from Bristol came almost invariably between January and October, so as to be in readiness for the autumn deep-sea fisheries, and for the salmon fishing which took place mainly from January to March and from July to August; it is in February and July that the largest imports of salmon are usually recorded. Iron went throughout the year in small quantities, but manufactured metal goods were still more acceptable—knives, nails, hauberks, basinets, gorgets, with tools of the clothmaking trade like cards, combs, or teasels. Leather goods, too, found a sale, for the tanning industry was further advanced in England than in

---

[1] *Rotuli Parliamentorum, ut supra*, III, 643.

Ireland—tanned hides, girdles, and points; also pots and pans ("battery") and pedlary ware. Alum, invaluable in the dyeing of cloth and the tanning of leather, was frequently sent. This was a re-export, as were pitch, oil, anise, soap, almonds, fruit, and wine. Ireland evidently depended for spices on Bristol as well as on her extensive direct trade with the Continent. Most of her wine, however, she probably received direct. At any rate that shipped from Bristol was usually labelled "corrupt", "old and undrinkable", or at least "not drinkable in England".[1] Possibly this sour wine was not even drinkable by the Irish, but was used for the extensive business of pickling fish. Drinks more usually exported from England to Ireland were perry and beer.

Salt and iron had in the thirteenth century, according to Higden, been the chief goods sought from England by the Irish. But by the fifteenth century neither these nor the luxuries of the south were Bristol's principal export. English woollen cloth now held the premier place in the list, cloth more costly than that of Ireland, for prosperous Ireland, with her superfluity of necessaries, was able to purchase luxuries. Coverlets of worsted, ordinary dyed broadcloth (cloth "without grain"), and even the rich scarlet cloth (cloth "in grain") were sent, and during one winter Bristol's export of cloth to Ireland amounted to one-third of her whole cloth export for that period. Yet even this, with the salt, iron, and other goods shipped, did not nearly equal in value the imports from Ireland, and the balance of trade seems to have been clearly in Ireland's favour.[2]

During this period Ireland, though "miserably tossed and turmoyled", enjoyed virtual independence. After Richard II's visit in 1394 no English sovereign set foot there until

---

[1] P.R.O., Early Chancery Proceedings, 71/54; Salzman, *op. cit.*, 272; P.R.O., K.R. Customs Accounts, *passim*; *Calendar of Patent Rolls*, 1399–1401, 425, 503.

[2] *Polychronicon Ranulphi Higden*, quoted in Coulton, *op. cit.*, 2: "Flaundres loveth the wolle of this lond . . . Irlond the ore and the salt"; P.R.O., K.R. Memoranda Roll, Mich. 12 Hen. VI, m. 22; Customs Accounts, *passim*.

the fugitive James II arrived, and the general policy of her
nominal rulers at the close of the Middle Ages was neglect
rather than interference. Little but the ports and the restricted
Pale remained steadfast in their allegiance, and the rest of
Ireland was left to its own internecine feuds and private wars,
with no firm central authority to keep the peace. Yet, despite
the "tumultuous broyles" which the English delight to
record, there can be no doubt that, left to herself, Ireland was
more prosperous than in most subsequent periods. Her
dealings with Bristol alone, and her constant intercourse
with the Continent, are an eloquent testimony to her
flourishing trade and industry and to her great potential
commercial value, which even to the present day has remained
unrealized.

§ 3

GASCONY

Bristol's close connection with Gascony had its origin in
the wine trade, and on this trade her prosperity was in large
measure based. Wine was then the one article of large daily
consumption which England could not supply to the well-to-
do Englishman. So, said the Italian Salimbene, "We must
forgive the English if they are glad to drink good wine when
they can, for they have but little wine in their own country."
Naturally it was to Gascony that they turned in their need.
This sunny province, with its sheltered valleys peculiarly
suited to the vine, had been part of the king of England's
realm ever since Henry II married Eleanor of Aquitaine,
and on its vineyards its very existence depended. From the
fertile dunes at the estuary of the Gironde to the eastern
extremities of the great valleys which there converged, the
rivers were fringed with vines which penetrated even into
the heart of at least one large city. All ranks of society, from
the mighty prelate to the humble shoemaker, possessed their

vineyards; for the mass of the population their cultivation was the dominant interest in life; a bad harvest was a calamity to the community duly recorded in local annals.[1] To have sent their wines overland for sale would have been a task fraught with difficulty. Roads were so rudimentary and roving bands of freebooters so menacing that land transport was tedious and perilous; it was also costly because of the inordinate exactions of covetous seigneurs. They therefore shipped them to other shores by the two convenient natural outlets of the Gironde and the Adour—to Normandy and Brittany, to the Low Countries, to Spain, to Portugal, but above all to England; for with England, then part of the same realm, trade was assured, and England not only made the biggest demand but had the most to offer in return in her cloth and hides, corn and fish. "How," as a fourteenth century Bordeaux merchant remarked, "could our poor people subsist when they could not sell their wines or procure English merchandise?"

Thus ports owing their prosperity mainly to the wine trade had grown up at the river estuaries, and among them Bordeaux and Bayonne had gained the pre-eminence. At the opening of the fifteenth century these two cities were the customary resort of the English merchants, and in both Bristol merchants were domiciled.

Bayonne's reputation as a port was the more transient. By the latter half of the century her decline was marked, and less than a quarter of the wine imported to Bristol from Gascony came from Bayonne. One reason for this decay was very probably the silting up of the Adour. Choked with sand swept thither by wind and sea, it was driven to seek new and ever-shifting channels along the low-lying coast. The obstacles to navigation became therefore almost insurmountable. Further, Bayonne's position as a southern outpost of the English territory exposed her to attack not only from Frenchmen but also from Spaniards, who on more than one occasion

[1] *Inventaire sommaire des archives départementales antérieures à 1790. Gironde.* Série E supplément, II, 3.

laid waste the surrounding country, leaving ruin and desolation behind them.[1] Yet in spite of her decay as a port, the seafaring enterprise of her shipmen continued, and Bristol sometimes received more than half as many tuns of wine in Bayonne ships as in ships of her own.

In situation alone Bordeaux had extraordinary advantages. Protected seaward, unlike Bayonne, by wide landes and lagoons, this was the effective meeting-place of five great river valleys, built at a point where the tide might still be felt. So the city had unrivalled opportunities of monopolising the commerce of an extensive and highly productive area wherein the vine throve exceedingly. Through the great wealth they accumulated her citizens gained influence, and this they used to win for themselves special privileges, so that it was with these ambitious burghers that English merchants could most effectively deal. They strove, for example, to draw to their own city for export all the wines of the rich river valleys round about, to concentrate trade there, and to strangle all possible rivals. And so anxious were English kings to conciliate the leading towns of Gascony and to simplify the control of trade, that they frequently granted exclusive rights of trade to Bordeaux and Bayonne, even forbidding their English subjects to bargain for wines elsewhere in Gascony. Bordeaux also took advantage of being on the route by which most wine for export must reach the sea to enrich herself by levying heavy tolls on passing vessels. Such was the Issak or Petty Custom on all wines brought from the Haut Pays, except on those from vineyards owned by Bordeaux citizens. She further handicapped the wines of the Haut Pays by forbidding their import before St. Martin's day, so that by the time they arrived the Bordelais had already gathered his harvest and monopolized the first sale. Moreover, for her own citizens she secured exemption from the Great Custom due on all exported wines; this privilege was recognized by all English sovereigns, and confirmed in

[1] E.g. J. Balasque, *Etudes historiques sur la ville de Bayonne* (Bayonne, 1862–75), III, 480.

1401, 1420 and 1441. Thus the wines from the estates of Bordeaux citizens—though not the wines bought by them from Gascons—could be brought to and dispatched from Bordeaux free of any tax. Further, the Bordelais gained immunity from virtually all river tolls, including the multi-tudinous dues extorted by covetous seigneurs who were fortunate enough to live on the banks of the Gironde. These exactions had caused tedious delay and a serious addition to the expense of the voyage, and their remission benefited not only the Bordelais but also English and aliens, for their goods too could now sail unchecked down the Gironde and out into the open sea. One such toll had been paid to the lord of Cypressat, a small domain opposite Bordeaux, and in sign of payment a cypress branch used to be delivered to the captain of each ship. This due survived, but the branch was now delivered at the castle of l'Ombrière in Bordeaux by the Constable, who handed over part of the money to Cypressat, keeping part for the king. Finally, after an intense and pro-longed conflict, and in spite of the hostility of the Londoners, the citizens of Bordeaux secured in 1388 complete freedom to come and go in England.[1]

Such comprehensive privileges raised Bordeaux to the rank of a commercial suzerain on the Gironde, and naturally evoked strong opposition from her neighbours, who succeeded to some extent in modifying them. Such river ports as could claim special consideration, on account of their strategic value as well as of their wealth, made frequent complaint to the king against the arrogant encroachments of Bordeaux. Some of their petitions, with records of the subsequent relief granted, are preserved among the archives of Bordeaux and in the Public Record Office in London. Such is the petition of Libourne to be free of customs, resulting in her admission to equal privileges. Later on, a declaration of Henry IV

[1] *Rotuli Parliamentorum, ut supra*, II, 114; Malvézin, *op. cit.*, I, 262, 280, 323, 332; C. Jullian, *Histoire de Bordeaux* (Bordeaux, 1895), 212–14; cf. *Archives Historiques du Département de la Gironde*, I and II (Société des Archives Historiques du Département de la Gironde, Bordeaux and Paris, 1859–60), 119.

specifically mentioned that the privileges of Bordeaux were
not intended to prejudice Libourne, Bourg or St. Emilion.
Likewise Blaye, a formidable fortress guarding the approach
by wáter to Bordeaux, secured freedom to sell its wines there,
and when English rule in Gascony was ended its privileges
were confirmed by the French king, as were those of
Libourne. Besides these cities on the Dordogne and the
Gironde, some of those on the Garonne, still more at the
mercy of Bordeaux, won treaties assuring them freedom of
trade. Thus La Réole could at one time take a toll on all
wines passing beneath her walls on their way to Bordeaux,
except those of Bordeaux citizens. Resentful of this and of
the restrictions imposed on her own wines in Bordeaux, she
finally gained freedom to sell them there at any time and
also won exemption from local duties there, as did her
neighbour, St. Macaire. These six cities, and perhaps others,
had with some degree of success challenged the supremacy
of Bordeaux in Northern Gascony, securing for themselves
reciprocal treaties, with freedom to sell their wines to the
stranger. Yet Bordeaux still retained her virtual monopoly
of the export trade, and she seems to have been the only
one of the cities to possess sea-going ships.[1]

The pretensions of Bordeaux to control the trade aroused
the hostility not only of her neighbours but also of the
English, who resented both the increased cost of the Haut
Pays wines through the high dues paid at Bordeaux, and the
prohibition from time to time against purchasing them elsewhere. At times they combated the claims of Bordeaux with
success. Thus in 1444 the Commons complained that they
were now forbidden to "bye wynes of the growyng of the
High Countr' in swich tyme as they wer wont to doo",
elsewhere than from Bordeaux or Bayonne. Their petition in
Parliament won them liberty freely to buy and sell anywhere,

<hr>

[1] *Archives historiques, ut supra*, I, 173, 305; II, 139; *Inventaire sommaire
. . . Gironde, ut supra* II, 56, 3, 263, 346; III, 44. *Catalogue des rolles
gascons, normans et françois conservés dans les archives de la Tour de Londres*,
ed. T. Carte (1743), II, 222, 207.

as they had formerly been accustomed to do, while any officials who opposed them were liable to a fine of £20 with treble damages.[1] One privilege at least which the English were allowed throughout the first half of the fifteenth century was that of importing goods into Gascony free of duty.[2] There were thus two classes of privileged merchants in Bordeaux—the English and the merchants of specially favoured towns. Of them all, it was the citizens of Bordeaux whose long-established privileges never fluctuated whilst English rule lasted.

Bayonne, in contrast to Bordeaux, though enjoying some of the same privileges as a centre for export, was not sufficiently influential to insist on controlling the river traffic in her own interests. In 1409, for instance, to her intense but unavailing indignation, the king granted a toll to the redoubtable lord of the stronghold of Mauléon on all wines passing Guiche.[3]

Bordeaux was thus the paramount port for the dispatch of wines to England and elsewhere, with Bayonne as a competitor in the early part of the century. But the citizens of Bordeaux were far behind those of Bayonne in seamanship and relied upon strangers to fetch their wines and even to keep open the gates of their own port in time of danger. Of over 200 ships leaving their harbour in one year, only five were their own, and they were helpless before the threat of a foreign navy. Thus when the French ships lay between them and the open sea, besieging Blaye, the heavily laden merchantmen, ready to depart, dared not venture forth without a convoy. So the town council, meeting day after day to discuss the situation, could only advise immediate dispatch of a vessel to England to crave assistance. It was urged, however, that none of the four craft owned by the town of Bordeaux could with impunity venture across the high seas in November. An English ship had therefore to be persuaded

---

[1] *Rotuli Parliamentorum, ut supra*, V, 113-7.
[2] Malvézin, *op. cit.*, I, 299.
[3] Balasque, *op. cit.*, III, 439.

to take the message, and another hired to go to the relief of Blaye.[1]

The constitutional aversion of the Bordelais to the risks of the open sea stands out in striking contrast to the enterprise of the men of Bayonne. Their vessels not only took wine from their own port, but provided as much freight for that of Bordeaux as she did herself. In 1409–10, for instance, Bordeaux provided five ships, and so did Bayonne. In the winter of 1403–4 no less than nine Bayonne ships brought wine to Bristol, seven of them sailing from Bayonne, and two from Bordeaux, while Bordeaux herself sent not one ship. These figures are typical and not exceptional.[2]

Yet the bulk of the wine exported from Bordeaux was carried not by the ships of Bayonne or of Bordeaux, but by those of England. The elaborate and interesting accounts of the Constable of Bordeaux noting the departure of the wine ships record a few Flemish, Breton, and French vessels, but a multitude of English craft, coming from at least thirty-five English ports from Newcastle in the north to Plymouth, Fowey, and Bristol in the west, and from Welsh ports such as Chepstow, Tenby, and Milford Haven. Among the English ships, those of Dartmouth were the most numerous. During one year (1409–10), between December and March, over 200 ships left Bordeaux, and of these twenty-seven belonged to Dartmouth, thirteen to London, eleven to Hull, nine to Bristol, and nine each to Fowey and Plymouth. Their exact destination is not ascertainable, but amongst those bound for Bristol there must have been ships of Bayonne and Bristol and perhaps of Dartmouth, Plymouth, and Fowey.[3] Certainly more than half Bristol's imports of wine from Gascony came at this time in her own ships, and the rest almost entirely in ships of Bayonne, though occasionally in those of Lynn, St. Jean de Luz, La Rochelle or elsewhere.

[1] P.R.O., K.R. Accounts Various, France, 184/19; Malvézin, *op. cit.*, I, 275.
[2] P.R.O., K.R. Accounts Various, France, 184/19; P.R.O., K.R. Customs Accounts, 17/8 and 10.
[3] P.R.O., K.R. Accounts Various, France, 184/19; cf. P.R.O., K.R. Customs Accounts, 17/37.

These two hundred or more ships, which came each year to Bordeaux for wine, arrived usually in the vintage season or in early spring, returning home in December or March. They set out in large companies for mutual safeguard, fifty of them sometimes leaving Bordeaux within a few days of each other. Royal protection had frequently been granted to such wine fleets in the fourteenth century, and again and again ships were warned not to venture singly. Richard II, for example, once ordered all vessels bound for Bordeaux to assemble at the Isle of Wight, in view of the alarming naval preparations of the French, and to put themselves under the command of the Constable of Bordeaux. Scorning such timorous counsels, Adam of York and his fellows returned alone and fell a prey to the pirates of Talmont and Rochelle. But such royal help was not regular, and became less frequent in the fifteenth century. Now merchants more often combined with each other for mutual protection on outward and homeward voyages, and made their agreements binding by solemn attestation before some public authority such as the Constable of Bordeaux. In 1415, for instance, when a fleet of English ships was laden with wine ready to depart, the chief merchants and masters elected an admiral for the voyage and swore before the Constable that nothing should separate them before their arrival in port. When, therefore, the *Christopher* of Hull was attacked and captured by Spanish pirates, and the others fled away in fear and left her to her fate, the deserters were ordered to make good the damage.[1]

The English ships which left Bordeaux were bound for many different destinations. Some put in at Channel ports such as Southampton, more at Bristol and Hull, and more still at London. The actual journey from London to Bordeaux took about ten days, and the whole expedition there and back usually occupied about two months.[2] At least a month

---

[1] Malvézin, *op. cit.*, I, 278–9; F. Michel, *Histoire du commerce et de la navigation à Bordeaux, principalement sous l'administration anglaise* (Bordeaux, 1867–70), I, 54; *Rotuli Parliamentorum, ut supra*, IV, 85.

[2] P.R.O., K.R. Customs Accounts, 17/8 and 12, 19/14.

must thus have been spent in Bordeaux, repairing the ships, disposing of their cargoes, and bargaining for wine, or purchasing it from the Haut Pays when this was allowed.

In late autumn and in spring these ships often carried no other merchandise but wine, but wine was now by no means the only commodity laden in them. In mid-winter and in summer there came a variety of produce not only from Gascony but from as far away as Brittany to the north and Spain to the south. Chief among these was woad. Casks of this blue dye, made up in the form of dry balls, frequently constituted the whole freight of a ship. Even in the month of March cargoes worth £690 once came to Bristol, and it seems likely that still more was brought in the summer when ships were no longer freighted with wine, and when the woad itself was harvested. How largely Bristol merchants dealt in it may be inferred from the fact that it was a form of property they often bequeathed. Ludovic Mors left a quarter of woad to pay for his burial in St. Mary Redcliffe, and the only other property specified, besides his house in Old Corn Street and his shop on the quay, was twenty pipes of woad to be divided among his three sons; six pipes were in his house, and fourteen in certain ships "returning by the Grace of God from parts beyond the sea". Similarly, Edward Dawes left eight measures of woad towards buying a new pair of organs for St. Werburgh's church. The demand for this woad in the cloth-manufacturing districts of the west, especially in Bristol itself, was very great, for though its cultivation in England had almost ceased, it was one of the commonest dyes, used not only for blue cloth, but as a foundation for other colours. Its importance is evident from the number of regulations made by the town council in Bristol concerning the "assay" of each consignment of woad by sworn members of the dyers' craft, and the appointment of special porters and brokers to assist in this and in the storage and sale of the woad. Other ordinances were passed regulating the actual dyeing processes, and arranging for the proper measurement and marking of each cask before its shipment. Bristol's import of woad was almost entirely in the hands of English merchants, and in the early fifteenth century they shipped it mainly from Bayonne though partly from Bordeaux. The plant from whose leaves it was prepared was grown around Toulouse, Albi, and Montauban, and had long since been used by the cloth manufacturers of Languedoc. They had at times succeeded in prohibiting its export, but this was now permitted subject to a toll. By the fifteenth century Languedoc's own cloth industry had almost vanished, and its harvest of woad was so potent a factor in the growth of England's industries that Bristol merchants might well speak of this trade as the "moost chieff, noblest and ponderoust merchaundys of good & able Wode, thencrece whereof in old tyme causyd, manteynyd and susteynyd the noble and prosperous felicitee of this Worshipfull Town".[1]

Other less important raw materials for fixing the dyes included alum and potash.[2] And from Bordeaux there came also wax and honey from the Landes and Narbonne.[3] Bayonne, however, sent a much more varied assortment of goods than did Bordeaux. For since she was situated close to one of the two land gateways into Spain, many goods came to her thence, and they were sometimes allowed through free of duty to increase her business. Iron was a very usual export, probably from the Cantabrian mountains. Steel came sometimes, but more often manufactured metal goods such as combs—another evidence of the growing importance of the cloth industry in England. Pitch and rosin, bowstaves, beaver, and cordovan (Spanish leather) were often included. For the housewife came many delicacies—honey and sugar, almonds, licorice, and saffron, recommended in all good

[1] P.R.O., K.R. Customs Accounts, 17/10; *Abstracts of Wills, ut supra*, 138–9, 169; *The Little Red Book, ut supra*, II, 16, 39, 81; Great Red Book, *ut supra*, f. 231; Malvézin, *op. cit.*, 310–1; cf. E. M. Carus-Wilson, "La guède française en Angleterre: un grand commerce du Moyen Age", *Revue du Nord*, tome XXXV, No. 138 (1953), 89 *et seq.*

[2] "*Cineres.*"

[3] Cf. Malvézin, *op. cit.*, I, 309.

cookery books of the period to give colour and flavour to such dainties as fritters. If Bayonne sometimes wished that her hostile Spanish neighbours were further off, she must often have been glad to have them so conveniently near as sources of supply for such a variety of produce.

While Gascony throve by exporting her own produce of wine and woad, she became more and more dependent upon foreign lands for such necessaries as cloth, fish, and corn with which she could no longer provide herself. Cloth reached her from Flanders, from Ireland, but above all from England, and the cargoes unloaded by Bristol ships in Bordeaux or Bayonne consisted usually almost entirely of cloth. Gascony was now one of the principal markets for Bristol's cloth, which was sold not only in the wine-growing regions but also as far inland as the woad centres of Languedoc.[1] Hides from Bristol were also an acceptable commodity, though insignificant in comparison with cloth. Some of the coal brought by river craft to Bristol found its way to Gascony, and also small quantities of fish, white and red herring, and hake; but the big demand for fish in Gascony during Lent was met mainly by boats from other ports, especially of Cornwall; the Archbishop of Bordeaux once laid in a stock of 1,000 red herrings from Cornwall in exchange for his wines.[2] Foreign corn was often as much in demand as foreign fish, and for this England was said to be Gascony's chief source of supply. The civic books of Bordeaux record the arrival of corn by land or sea as an event of great moment; its import, unlike that of other goods, was always exempt from duty, and the city as a whole became responsible for ensuring the supply, sometimes borrowing the money with which to pay for it. On some occasions corn was so urgently needed that it was allowed through from the Haut Pays even when that region was in French hands, and thus nominally at war with the English, and sometimes it was stipulated that a certain proportion of

---

[1] Jullian, *op. cit.*, 218; Malvézin, *op. cit.*, II, 199; P.R.O., K.R. Customs Accounts, 17/10 etc.

[2] Jullian, *op. cit.*, 219; P.R.O. K.R. Customs Accounts, *passim*.

corn must be included with every cargo of Haut Pays wine. The overseas supply from England seems, however, to have been intermittent, coming probably in times of famine, siege or other emergency. Thus during the great famine of 1403 permission was given to export grain to Bayonne, and again in 1419 when the Spaniards threatened to besiege Bayonne, and yet again in 1420. Big purchases from England are noted in the civic records of Bordeaux during a time of scarcity and high prices in 1406–7. The amount sent from Bristol it is impossible to ascertain, since corn was sometimes exempt from duty. That Bristol merchants took some share in provisioning Bordeaux and Bayonne is evident, however, not only from the customs accounts, but also from the licences granted when the export of corn was otherwise forbidden. Thus corn to the value of nearly £100 was licensed for shipment from Bristol to Bordeaux in 1442–3; and between 1449 and 1452, when Bordeaux was hemmed in by conquering French armies, Harry May and Patrick Davy of Bristol, with David Selly of Westminster, were commissioned to buy "grain, flesh, and fish" to victual Bordeaux.[1]

This traffic, in which England exchanged her cloth and her foodstuffs for the wealth of the Gascons, was indeed "gret plesur to all estatez and degreez, grete richesse and by the myght of such Nave, gret defence for all this lond". Bordeaux and Bayonne likewise became through it exceedingly opulent. Firmer and firmer economic bonds strengthened their political union under the English crown, and judicious English rulers gave them every opportunity of managing their own affairs as they pleased, unfettered by interfering officials and mulcted of a minimum of taxation by the central authority. Truly had Froissart surmised in 1399 that Bordeaux and Bayonne "wyll never tourne Frenche, for they cannat lyve in their daunger nor they canne

---

[1] Jullian, *op. cit.*, 219; Malvézin, *op. cit.*, I, 297–8, 191, 293; *Rolles gascons, ut supra*, I, 189, 202–3; Balasque, *op. cit.*, 462; P.R.O., L.T.R. Customs Accounts, 19, m. 6d; P.R.O., Early Chancery Proceedings, 19/409.

nat suffre the extorcyon and pollinge of the Frenchemen; for under us they lyve franke and free, and if the Frenchemen shulde be lordes over them they shulde be taxed and tayled and retayled two or thre tymes in a yere the whiche they are nat nowe accustomed unto, which shulde be a harde thyng nowe for them to begynne". The lot of the Gascon cities was indeed a striking contrast to the feudal oppression and the high taxation and official interference under which French towns languished, and eager was their desire to remain under the lenient rule of the English.[1]

The fortunes of the Gascon trade were, however, closely involved in the fortunes of the Hundred Years War and, as the French gradually reconquered Gascony until the link of allegiance to England which had endured for three centuries was snapped, marked changes took place in its volume and character. Trade had already suffered when at the opening of the fifteenth century the English dominion in Southern France had shrunk to little beyond Bordeaux and Bayonne. Goods were more expensive, for higher duties were levied on those from inland enemy districts, and these districts retaliated by extorting duties on merchandise from English possessions. In 1406, for instance, La Réole, which had hitherto been exempt from customs at Bordeaux, became French. Bordeaux forthwith took 10 per cent. on her wines and a tax on other goods; but a petition to the French king's lieutenant in Guienne secured for La Réole permission to exact precisely similar duties on all merchandise taken down the Garonne by the English. When, however, she came again under English rule, La Réole's privileges at Bordeaux were restored. Trade was now not only more costly but also more precarious, both on account of the havoc wrought by war and epidemics on land and because of assaults at sea. In

---

[1] *Rotuli Parliamentorum, ut supra*, V, 113; E. Troplong, "De la fidélité des Gascons aux Anglais pendant le moyen âge (1152–1453)" (*Revue d'Histoire Diplomatique*, Paris, 1902), 52; L. D. Brissaud, *L'administration anglaise et le mouvement communal dans le Bordelais: les Anglais en Guyenne* (Paris, 1875), 234; *The Chronicle of Froissart translated out of French by Sir John Bourchier, Lord Berners, Annis 1523–5*, ed. W. P. Ker (1901–3), II, 164.

spite of the nominal truce, Gascony was attacked in one place
after another in the first decade of the century, and on at
least one occasion all shipping was held up in the Garonne.
Kings gave little help; messages of distress were sent in
desperation to towns such as Bristol; the Archbishop
lamented that he had cried out till he was hoarse, and that
nothing could save the country but the feebleness of the
French.[1] When at last English merchantmen had assisted
in reopening the river and another truce had been signed in
1407, trade revived, and in 1409–10 nine Bristol ships left
Bordeaux heavily laden with wine.

During the next fifteen years local levies raised at Bordeaux
made a determined effort to recapture the wine districts, and
won back strongholds such as St. Macaire and La Réole
which controlled the Garonne route. From that time until
1451 Gascony remained almost entirely outside the theatre
of war, except for a Spanish raid on Bayonne, and for the
sudden alarming incursions of the French in 1438, and again
in 1443, when the great fortress of Dax capitulated.[2] In this
period of virtual immunity from war, Gascony, though often
tormented by *routiers*, enjoyed considerable prosperity. Her
progress was in striking contrast to the fate of the once rich
land between the Loire, the Seine, and the Somme; this lay
overgrown with thorns and brambles, and even the very
sheep and swine fled at the familiar sound of the alarm bell.
But in Gascony trade flourished, and it is remarkable that in
spite of the long and costly wars, of lawlessness on the sea,
and of misgovernment in England, imports of wine to Bristol
increased markedly during this period, reaching their
maximum on the eve of England's final defeat, at a figure
never exceeded throughout the Yorkist and Lancastrian
period. This conclusion is suggested by an investigation of
the enrolled customs accounts. Here it appears that Bristol's

[1] *Archives historiques de la Gironde, ut supra*, I, 310; II, 139, 243;
Troplong, *op. cit.*, 487.
[2] Balasque, *op. cit.*, 462; Jullian, *op. cit.*, 292; L. Puech, *Histoire de la
Gascogne* (La Société Archéologique du Gers, Auch, 1914), 272.

BRISTOL'S IMPORTS OF WINE AND EXPORTS OF CLOTH
1399-1485

WINE IMPORTS

in tuns per annum (Michaelmas to Michaelmas):
the statutory capacity of the tun = 252 gallons

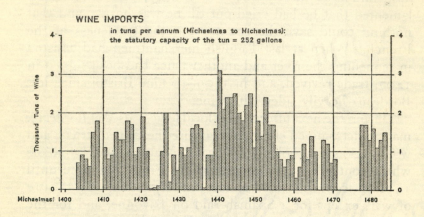

CLOTH EXPORTS

in cloths of assise per annum (Michaelmas to Michaelmas):
the statutory size of the cloth of assise = 26 yards × 6 quarters before fulling
The stippled area represents cloth exported by native merchants.

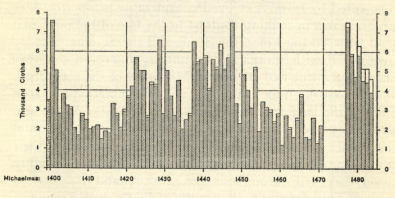

NOTE. Accounts normally cover an Exchequer year from Michaelmas to Michaelmas.
Where this is not so the monthly average over the longer of two adjacent
accounts has been used to adjust both accounts.

wine imports reached their highest figure between 1440 and 1448, and that exports of cloth were largest about the same time. It is impossible precisely to distinguish the origin of these imports, but the Bordeaux accounts confirm the inference that this expansion marks an increase especially in wine from Gascony. These show, for instance, that in the autumn only of 1443, six Bristol ships left Bordeaux with 1,614 tuns of wine [1]; this is almost as much as Bristol's total annual import of wine from all sources early in the century. Again, whereas in 1409–10, of over 200 ships of all nationalities leaving Bordeaux only two had carried as much as 170 tuns, 170 was now the average cargo of Bristol's ships, while the *Marie de Wilshore* carried as much as 249 tuns, 40 per cent. more than any ship in 1407–8. And these were no exceptional cargoes, as later accounts prove.

This remarkable expansion of Bristol's trade with Gascony in the last years of English rule was not, however, due solely to Gascony's immunity from war, nor to the increased size of Bristol's ships and the progressive enterprise of her merchants. It is surely no mere coincidence that the year 1444 saw the successful petition of the Commons that the English might buy wines freely in the Haut Pays, and also the signing of the five years' truce between England and France, a truce that was later on to cost the Duke of Suffolk his head. Ships were then no longer in peril from organized attacks of the enemy; no longer were they liable constantly to be diverted from their peaceful business by being commandeered for the king's service, as were the Bristol ships in the two years preceding the truce. Further, the elaborate scheme of 1443 for the safeguarding of the seas by a permanent naval force, to which Bristol contributed two ships,[2] may not have been without effect, even though these ships were not themselves of blameless reputation. Yet more welcome to the merchants, no doubt, was definite permission to take the law into their own hands. They had in vain

---

[1] P.R.O., K.R. Accounts, Various, France, 194/3.
[2] *Rotuli Parliamentorum, ut supra*, V, 59.

petitioned for the repeal of the stringent statute of 1414 against breakers of truces and safe-conducts, but between 1435 and 1451 this was suspended and they were free to recoup themselves to any extent they thought fit by priva-teering.[1] This new privilege naturally brought about an increase in piracy, but it probably stimulated rather than discouraged enterprise.

This rapid progress of Bristol's merchants was shortly, however, to be checked by circumstances beyond their control. While England's political power in France had been waning gradually, her commercial collapse was to come with startling suddenness. In 1449 England and France went to war once more. On the conclusion of the rapid reconquest of Normandy in that year, the French took up with ardour the reconquest of Gascony, and her strongholds fell one after another before their advance. Finally, when Bourg and Blaye, Libourne and St. Emilion, and almost every Gascon fortress except Bayonne had capitulated, and when the Gironde was swept by French ships, Bordeaux, surrounded by 30,000 French troops, despairing of the help that the English continually promised and never sent, at last sued for peace with her own countrymen (12th June 1451). Even then she did not humble herself. Full of consideration were her conquerors, eager to conciliate these proud and wealthy citizens; all that they required was that they should promise to be good and loyal Frenchmen. Their privileges were all confirmed, merchants were to pay only the accustomed dues, and those who wished to do so were free to depart under safe-conduct within six months.[2] Bayonne, however, suffered a worse fate. Her gates were still closed to the French, and a month later Bristol was ordered to provide ships and mariners for a relieving force. Once more the procrastinating English government was too late, for on 21st August Bayonne was

[1] C. L. Kingsford, *West Country Piracy: the School of English Seamen, in Prejudice and Promise in Fifteenth Century England* (1925), 79–81.
[2] *Ordonnances des Rois de France de la Troisième Race*, XIV, ed. L. G. Oudart Feudrix de Bréquigny (1790), 140.

compelled to surrender, all the goods of the English there were forfeited, and so were the privileges of the town.[1] But so much had the Bordelais come to depend upon England, and so firm was their allegiance to English rule, that they would not become good and loyal Frenchmen. Chafing beneath the yoke of their conquerors, who foolishly provoked them with levies of tribute and of soldiers, they opened their gates to the Earl of Shrewsbury in the following year, and before the year ended had chased the French from the rich valleys of the Garonne and the Dordogne. When their city was at last, after a spirited resistance, recaptured by the French in 1453, they were severely punished for their revolt. Their privileges were suspended, a crushing indemnity was imposed, and twenty of the leaders of the defence had to be surrendered. Six months later the harshness of the terms was in some degree mitigated, but a tax of 25 sous per tun was levied on all wines exported, and further duties on almost all other exports and imports; while instead of being virtually self-governing, Bordeaux became part of an increasingly centralized state with a council nominated largely by the king.[2]

Thus fell Bordeaux from her former greatness; poverty-stricken, oppressed with taxation, and threatened with famine, her vineyards lay desolate, and her houses empty. Trade with the English did not, indeed, wholly cease, but it was much diminished in volume. English merchants were now enemy aliens. Only by special licence from the kings of both France and England could they visit Bordeaux, and risks on the seas were multiplied.[3]

Many of the Gascons came to England, preferring English to French rule, and the number of Bristol's merchants was increased by several of these immigrants. Such were Barnard Bensyn "late of Bordeaux, merchant"; Moses Conterayn, "Gascon and merchant of Bordeaux", who

---

[1] Balasque, *op. cit.*, III, 499–502.
[2] *Ordonnances des Rois de France, ut supra*, 270, 273.
[3] For fuller discussion of the effects of the fall of Bordeaux see chapter VII.

became one of Bristol's most active merchants, and probably also William Lombard, "merchant of Bordeaux", who in 1488 was buried in St. Nicholas' church, Bristol, and whose will is inscribed in the Great Red Book. Many also of those who lost property in Gascony or were captured and had to find ransoms, took to trade to recoup themselves, and the Great Red Book abounds in copies of safe-conducts granted at their request; one is for Petronilla, wife of Bertram de Montferrant, who lost all her goods in Bordeaux and came to England relying on the king; another is for John Ducastet who likewise lost his goods and came to England; another for John Freme, merchant of Bristol, who with others had fallen into the hands of the French and were "ad financiam ducentarum librarum sterling ultra les droitz positi".[1]

Hitherto Bristol's French trade had been almost exclusively with Gascony. Breton boats had sometimes visited her, from Penmarch, Vannes, Conquet, S. Pol de Léon, Quimper, Quimperle, Concarneau, Nantes, Crozon, and Guérande, and some of them brought salt from the Bay of Bourgneuf. But they were usually on their way from ports other than their own, and Bretons were known to Bristol men chiefly as pirates, plundering more ships than they loaded peacefully, and preying on those who passed their rocky coasts bound for the harbours of the south. Neither had Bristol in the past dealt much with Normandy or Flanders, though Bristol merchants were sometimes in Flanders on business, and sometimes shipped goods from Ireland thither. Occasionally a foreign ship called on its way to or from Flanders with hops, wainscot, tar, and madder, but Flanders was more in need of Irish produce such as hides which she could procure direct, and she and Bristol, each with their flourishing cloth industry, had little to give each other. But now, when the direct trade between Gascons and Englishmen was checked,

---

[1] P.R.O., Early Chancery Proceedings, 64/345, 26/474; cf. Commines, Bk. 4, chapters 9 and 10; Great Red Book, *ut supra*, ff. 40, 68; cf. P.R.O., Chancery Enrolments, Treaty Roll, 30 Hen. VI, m. 7; many similar licences are on these Treaty Rolls.

new contacts were developed. Wine came more often in boats of Brittany and via Breton ports, for Brittany, profiting from the embarrassments of England and France, developed her shipping just as she developed her manufactures with the aid of skilled refugees from the English provinces. Even more interesting is the shipment of woad from Caen, the first clear indication of trade between Bristol and Normandy.[1]

In 1461, however, with the accession of Edward IV in England and Louis XI in France, there came an opportunity for Bristol to rebuild its trade with Gascony. Louis' predecessor, Charles VII, had rudely conquered and tried to crush the Gascons. But the astute Louis, "the greatest traveller to win a man that might do him service or harm", realized that in the struggle of the crown to build up a united nation the bourgeois were his strongest support against the nobles. He therefore won their favour by granting privileges to the towns, restoring to many of those in Gascony a large measure of the autonomy which they had enjoyed under English rule. Bordeaux recovered its privileges, foreigners were encouraged to occupy its empty houses, exiles were recalled, and in 1463 a truce was agreed with England. Bristol merchants hastened to take advantage of the renewed opportunity, and went as of old in autumn or spring to seek Gascon wines. The fall in imports of wine was checked and recovery began. Tiresome restrictions, however, still hampered the merchant. Safe-conducts were compulsory; these had to be purchased for a large sum, and lasted only for a year or two. Customs dues were still heavy, and wines could only be purchased inland from Bordeaux citizens and under official supervision. Every ship had to stop on the way to Bordeaux, first at Soulac to fetch her permit, then at Blaye to be certified as a genuine merchantman and to deposit all arms; in each case a fee had to be paid. At Bordeaux

---

[1] P.R.O., Early Chancery Proceedings, 24/211–17; cf. *Abstracts of Wills, ut supra*, 162, and P.R.O., K.R. Memoranda Rolls, Mich. 12 Hen. VI, m. 34; Troplong, *op. cit.* 521; P.R.O., K.R. Customs Accounts, 19/14; cf. licences to ships of Caen in the Treaty Rolls, e.g. 31 Hen. VI, mm. 6, 7.

merchants had to obtain a special licence, lasting only a month, to dwell in the city; they might lodge only in specified houses, and might not emerge thence before 7 a.m. or after 5 p.m. These petty annoyances in Bordeaux itself had their counterpart in similar restrictions on foreigners in Bristol. No ship was allowed into port until it had forwarded its safe-conduct from Kingrode, had been inspected by officials in the city, and had deposited all its arms. Every Frenchman, merchant or mariner, must purchase a licence to be kept ever on his person; he must dwell in the lodgings assigned to him, and must always wear a white cross upon his shoulder. Intercourse therefore was still difficult and precarious. Moreover, England and France were not yet formally at peace. Each sought opportunity to strike a blow at his adversary, and, in spite of safe-conducts, many boats fell a victim to pirates or privateers.[1]

It was with the Treaty of Picquigny in 1475 that trade with Gascony made a further marked recovery. Then at last the long rivalry between the two nations was brought to a formal close, and the merchant was encouraged not only by the greater security thus given, but by the removal of many hindrances. Now, as of old, he might sail freely to Bordeaux, and there dwell where he pleased for as long as he pleased as freely as any of its citizens. Customs and dues were modified, and the only restrictions remaining were those on the purchase of wine.

Commines, true type of the diligent chronicler of the time, in describing this treaty details elaborately those articles touching the wars of kings and their unruly barons, adding but briefly—"Divers other trifling articles there were touching matters of entercourse, which I overpasse." The people of Bordeaux, however, rightly estimated the worth of this treaty's "trifling" commercial provisions, gratefully naming it

---

[1] Jullian, *op. cit.*, 306; Troplong, *op. cit.*, 519, 521; Malvézin, *op. cit.*, II, 21, 23, 26; P.R.O., K.R. Customs Accounts, 19/1, 3 and 4; P.R.O., Early Chancery Proceedings, 27/383; Great Red Book, *ut supra*, f. 97; *Calendar of Patent Rolls*, 1452–61, 347, 608, 612, 614, 649.

the "paix marchande". For Louis XI saw further ahead than most of his contemporaries in insisting that political separation should not imply economic estrangement, and Edward IV had the shrewd sense to win the advantages of peace by the display of war, and thus to revive England's languishing commerce. Before long Bristol's imports of wine had risen to a level at least as high as at the beginning of the century, while her exports of cloth reached an average equal to that during their zenith before the loss of Gascony. So much did the English profit from the removal of hindrances that, thirty years after their expulsion, it was said that during the vintage season there were no less than 6,000 of them in the city of Bordeaux,[1] though never again were their imports of Gascon wine to reach the levels attained before the disturbances of the Hundred Years War.

§ 4

THE IBERIAN PENINSULA

The author of the *Libelle of Englyshe Polycye*, writing probably in 1436, calls the Englishman a donkey for not seizing his opportunities of trade with Spain. Why does he allow Spanish ships, laden with wine and other precious wares, to sail up the English Channel direct to Flanders, there to traffic with the Low Countries for cloth made of English wool? Why does he not detain them in English ports, and himself sell them cloth made in his own country:

> "Thanne may hit not synke in mannes brayne,
> But that hit most, this marchaundy of Spayne,
> Bothe oute and inne by oure coostes passe?
> He that seyth nay in wytte is lyche an asse." [2]

Bristol, however, hardly deserved the taunt. Her busy looms and those of her hinterland were each year contributing about 6,000 pieces to that steadily increasing output of

---

[1] Troplong, *op. cit.*, 251.
[2] *Libelle of Englyshe Polycye*, ed. Sir G. Warner (1926), 5.

English cloth which was now rapidly replacing England's export of wool. Already a few Spanish ships were visiting Bristol and taking thence large quantities of cloth, while many Bristol ships were sailing each year to Spain, heavily laden, to exchange their cargoes of cloth for the luxuries of the south.

Spanish produce was particularly welcome in England as England's hold on Gascony weakened. Already at the opening of the century Spanish wines were supplementing those of France, though even at its close the amount imported to Bristol from Spain did not exceed a quarter of that which came from Gascony. The wine ships from Spain, like those from France, protected themselves by sailing together in a fleet during the vintage season and in spring, and on one occasion nine of them arrived together in Bristol.[1] But wine, though one of the chief, was by no means the only import from Spain, and the increasing variety of luxuries brought to Bristol points certainly to a rising standard of comfort in England. Foreign fruits, like figs, raisins, and dates, were especially welcome during the winter months, but in summer the expense of transport was not worth while. Thus when Moses Conterayn was shipping wheat at Bristol in the *John de la Passage*, he asked the master, Nicholas Palmer, to sail to Southern Spain, there to sell the wheat on his behalf and to reload with "certeyn tonnes of frute called fyges and resans".[2] Palmer did this, but because of great tempests and "lake of Wynde and Weders" he had to put into so many ports on the way that he only reached England at Easter. The season was then too far advanced for the fruit to be profitably sold, and Conterayn sued Palmer for damages in the Tolsey Court at Bristol.

Other southern delicacies came also for the housewife in increasing quantities during the century—honey, almonds, licorice, and saffron, with vinegar, lard, and occasionally tunny-fish and rice. But the Spanish trade was not merely one

[1] P.R.O., K.R. Customs Accounts, 17/8 and 10.
[2] P.R.O., Early Chancery Proceedings, 48/114.

in luxuries. Valuable raw materials came also for England's industries. Iron (probably from the Cantabrian mountains) is scarcely mentioned in early Bristol accounts of the century, but it soon became one of Spain's chief exports to Bristol, and was usually shipped in the summer, when the wine and fruit seasons were over, together with manufactured iron goods, from brigandines, crossbows, and anchors down to nails and combs, probably for the wool-combers. Southern Spain was one of the chief sources of supply for oil, so that "laden with wine and oil" was a common description of ships which had suffered shipwreck or piracy. Oil also came in the form of ready-made soap from Castile, and as "smigmates", a species of soap, as may be inferred from the fact that some was purchased at Durham for washing the linen of the lord prior. Other raw materials included wax, tallow, rosin, tar, white cork, beaver, boards, bowstaves, and grindstones, while the dyers obtained alum used in fixing the dyes, and sometimes the scarlet dye which came more often from Portugal. Woad came also now and again from the ports of North-East Spain, but this had probably found its way thither from Southern France, just as Spanish iron was sometimes shipped from Bayonne. Leather of Cordova had already given more than one word to the English language, for merchants dealt often in Cordovan, while kid skins, goat skins, and other "wild ware" were especially useful for laces and such articles as demanded strong leather, so that cheap imitations were sometimes made in England to resemble the "Civill (i.e. Seville) and Spannish skynnes".[1]

The entry most commonly met with after wine, oil, and fruit, is that of salt. The low sand-dunes in the south-west of Spain, broken by lagoons, lent themselves to its production, and Spanish salt was supplementing that from the Bay of Bourgneuf.

[1] P.R.O., K.R. Customs Accounts, *passim*; *Calendar of Patent Rolls*, 1401–5, 437, 507; *ibid.*, 1446–52, 238; *Extracts from the Accounts Rolls of the Abbey of Durham*, ed. J. T. Fowler (Surtees Society, 1898–1901), III, 616; cf. 391, 697; Salzman, *op. cit.*, 251–2.

Variety was thus the conspicuous feature of imports from Spain:—

"fygues, raysyns, wyne, bastarde and dates,
And lycorys, Syvyle oyle and also grayne,
Whyte Castell sope and wax is not in vayne,
Iren, wolle, wadmole, gotefel, kydefel also,
(For poyntmakers full nedeful be the ij.)
Saffron, quicksilver." [1]

In comparison with these varied luxuries and raw materials the goods shipped from Bristol to Spain seem uninteresting, though significant, since vessels were usually laden almost entirely with cloth. Most of this was ungrained broadcloth, of which a ship on one occasion took over 200 pieces,[2] though sometimes cheaper qualities were sent. Thus Henry Vaughan alleged that he shipped 136 broad cloths, 32 narrow cloths, and 20 cloths of Welsh frieze in the *Mary* of Ipusco[3] "whereof Ochoa Daramayo after God was master". In this same ship a Spanish merchant once took 18 broad cloths and 124 kerseys. Frieze of Kendal and Irish mantles went also occasionally. Thus it would appear that Spain was becoming more and more directly indebted to England for her cloth, and found less need to ship "full craftily" to Flanders figs, raisins, and the like, there to reload with Flemish cloth made of English wool. While cloth was the regular export from Bristol to Spain, fish such as herring and hake was sometimes included in the cargo, with tanned hides, lead, tin, and now and then carved alabaster. But the only considerable export after cloth was corn and beans, sent probably at times of superfluity in England and dearth in Spain. The *Mary* of Guetaria was once, except for five broad cloths, entirely charged with corn, and during three months in 1475 there were twelve shipments of corn from Bristol, valued in the customs at nearly £400. The arrival of these ships, perhaps as many as twenty in one summer, laden with cloth and corn,

---

[1] *Libelle of Englyshe Polycye, ut supra,* 4.
[2] P.R.O., K.R. Customs Accounts, 19/14.
[3] i.e. Guipuscoa, P.R.O., Early Chancery Proceedings, 30/40.

must have been of no little importance to the Spaniards, and to Bristol the trade was equally advantageous since Spain with its neighbour Portugal were the nearest lands whence such products as oil, figs, and raisins could be procured.

To the Bristol merchant Spain implied Castile; with Aragon he had no dealings. Southwards his ships sailed to far-famed Seville, seeking wine, oil, or fruit, sometimes calling on the way at Saltes, Huelva, or S. Lucar Barrameda. Spanish ships and seamen ventured with them in the trade, but these came not from the south, but from those rocky northern shores which, like the coasts of Cornwall, bred a race of seamen as bold as they were unscrupulous. In Guipuscoa and its neighbouring provinces of Biscay and Santander there were at least twelve havens whose ships visited Bristol in the fifteenth century—Fuenterrabia, Passage, Renteria, San Sebastian, Guetaria, Deva, Motrico, Bilbao, Portugalete, Castro, La Redo, and Santander. Ambassadors of Guipuscoa came often to negotiate with Edward IV, and its merchants did much business with Bristol, where some, like Domingo de Fuenterrabia, were admitted to the liberties of the Staple. Their ships and their seamen were frequently used by Bristol merchants. Henry Vaughan, amongst others, shipped cloth in vessels of Guetaria, and the *S. Sebastien* of Guetaria, when in Flanders, was once freighted by Bristol merchants with madder, tar, wainscots, and hops, and brought to Bristol, where her Spanish captain took on board in his own name a cargo of English and Welsh cloth for the return voyage to Spain. This district especially was haunted by pirates, as may be gathered from Bristol's complaints, such as this typical one of about 1400: four Biscay ships had captured the *Trinity* on her way from Seville, and another Biscay ship had captured the *Mary*; the *Katherine* had been seized by a ship of Motrico, and the *Alison* by four ships of Santander. Westwards, beyond Santander, the coast was a forbidding one, with only "verie naughty havens for great shippes" until Galicia was reached. There where the mountains, hitherto parallel to the shore, run out into the sea, deep sheltered gulfs are hidden between their ridges. Yet these really good ports in Galicia seem scarcely to have been used by Bristol, doubtless because of their distance from the chief wine and iron districts. Only one kind of traffic was carried on there, that in pilgrims for the shrine of St. James at Compostella. Bristol ships could convey a hundred or more of these wayfarers, and were often licensed to do so. It seems likely that they took some of their passengers on board at Plymouth, where they sometimes called on the way, and those unaccustomed to the sea would surely prefer the four days' voyage thence to the prolonged woes, so vividly pictured in a late medieval poem, of those who took to sea—

> "At Sandwyche, or at Wynchylsee,
> At Brystow, or where that hit bee." [1]

Some pilgrims certainly ventured the whole way from Bristol. Such were those who on their way stole some of the books for which the library of All Saints Church was renowned; so highly prized were these volumes that two priests were sent after them, and a special iron cage was meanwhile made for their custody. The accounts of All Saints also contain entries of gifts from those on their way to St. James.

There is no record of pilgrims entrusting themselves to Spaniards, but in other branches of traffic Spaniards, little in evidence early in the century, took an increasingly active part. Sometimes they shipped in their own and sometimes in English vessels. Frequently, even when a Spanish ship carried mainly goods of English merchants, the Spanish captain himself took a share in the venture, as did John Renamond of the *James* of Guipuscoa, and at least one Spanish captain was admitted to the liberties of the Staple

[1] P.R.O., K.R. Customs Accounts, *passim*; Tolsey Court Book, *ut supra*, 1487–97, ff. 157, 172; P.R.O., K.R. Parliamentary and Council Proceedings, roll 28; A. Ashley, *The Mariners Mirrour . . . Luke Wagenar* (H. Hasselup, ?London), 12; P.R.O., Chancery Enrolments, Treaty Rolls, 6 Hen. VI, m. 8; B.M. Harleian MS. 433, ff. 171–2; *The Itineraries of William Wey*, ed. B. Bandinel (1857), 153–5; *The Pilgrim's Sea Voyage*, quoted in Coulton, *op. cit.*, 427.

in Bristol. Prominent English merchants sometimes acted as factors for the foreigner, as did Jordan Spryng, "factor for John de Varrole merchant and owner of the *Marie* of Navarre", and throughout the century Englishmen and Spaniards, jointly or severally, seem entirely to have controlled the Spanish trade with Bristol in contrast to that with other ports. Italians, as the *Libelle* complains, had got into their hands much of the Spanish trade with London and Southampton, but Bristol, with its flourishing native trade, was singularly free from their influence. Its independence and its close co-operation with Spanish merchants is illustrated by a petition from certain aggrieved Genoese, who had freighted the *Julian* in Spain with wine, oil, and other goods for London or Southampton. Since her master, Godfred de Sasiola, had taken her to Bristol instead, he had there been arrested at the suit of the Italian merchants. These complained, however, that the mayor and other great officers and merchants of Bristol owe the nation of Spain "so great love and affiance" that they propose to let the merchandise remain in Bristol, and to make the Genoese pay for its freight.[1]

Spanish ships, like Spanish merchants, increased noticeably in numbers during the century, and merchants of either country employed each other's ships and seamen as occasion served. Sometimes a partnership of Bristol merchants used almost the whole tunnage of a Spanish vessel, as when the *James* of Guipuscoa arrived at Bristol with goods of John Shipward and his associates, and left with cloth of William Canynges and his associates, in both cases in the charge of English factors. While early in the century a Spanish ship was seldom seen in Bristol, towards its close about the same number of Spanish as of Bristol ships seem to have been engaged in the trade. It is clear, therefore, that Spaniards were becoming more actively concerned in intercourse with

---

[1] P.R.O., K.R. Customs Accounts, 19/14; Tolsey Court Book, *ut supra*, 1487–97, cf. *Calendar of State Papers, Spanish*, I, 4; *Calendar of Patent Rolls*, 1452–61, 440; P.R.O., Early Chancery Proceedings, 64/459.

Bristol during the century. No precise estimate, however, is possible of the general growth of the trade. For the detailed customs accounts survive only in fragments, and even conclusions drawn from these may be very misleading, when in any one year as many as seven Spanish ships might fall a prey to pirates.[1]

This constant peril from pirates made the Spanish trade, profitable though it was, the most precarious of all Bristol's regular enterprises. Piracy was endemic owing to the doubtful relations between the rulers of England and of Castile. For during the Hundred Years War Castile had allowed herself, in spite of her goodwill towards England itself, to be drawn into an unusually prolonged alliance with France against the neighbouring English provinces. This alliance lasted almost without interruption for 130 years, and was renewed by each successive sovereign. Yet so anxious was Castile to live at peace with all men except the Moors, that France could scarcely persuade her to translate words into action, and even when she did make war upon the English she hastened to conclude peace at the earliest possible moment.[2] The English, not unnaturally, regarded this long-standing, though passive, ally of France as their "notorious enemy". Hence sea-rovers on either side plundered with impunity, knowing that merchants had slight chance of restitution. If indeed an interval of peace came, the successful pirate might be required to disgorge his gains. When, for instance, the truce of 1403 included England as an ally of both Portugal and Castile, there was a sudden increase not, as might appear, in piracy but in the number of commissions appointed to deal with it, and inquiries were set on foot concerning no less than seven Spanish ships, captured in October 1403 by a gang under Thomas Norton of Bristol and the notorious John Hawley. These efforts were of little avail, for

---

[1] *Calendar of Patent Rolls*, 1401–5, 360, 363, 426–8.
[2] G. Daumet, *Étude sur l'alliance de la France et de la Castile au XIVe et XVe siècles* (Paris, 1898), viii; R. B. Merriman, *The Rise of the Spanish Empire in the Old World and in the New* (New York, 1918–25), I, 132.

Hawley at least was a man of considerable influence who would not lightly yield what he had won at the risk of his life. In fact, such prominent pirates as he were often themselves on the commissions, and even less redoubtable rovers, when alliances were being constantly made and unmade, could easily plead that they had not been present when the sheriff proclaimed the truce. Thus seldom and only with difficulty could Spanish or English merchants secure legal redress. Despairing of it, both were driven to reprisals, with or without the sanction of their governments. When William Skyrmot's ship the *Petre* of Bristol, bound with cloth for Bayonne in 1449, was captured by a ship of Motrico and taken to Spain, Skyrmot sued vainly before the king of Castile, and was finally permitted by the king of England to retain the *Marie* of Motrico, then lying at Bristol under arrest. The king of Castile once issued letters of marque against all English subjects, but the more cautious Edward IV, anxious to avoid any vigorous action and to stand well with both parties, indemnified at the same time both Spanish and English merchants. Thus in 1476 he granted 3,000 crowns from the customs revenue as an indemnity to the men of Guipuscoa, and five years later 3,600 crowns to one of his own merchants, John Payn, who had fallen a victim to them. Payn, a merchant of Bristol, in spite of letters of safe-conduct bearing the seal of the province of Guipuscoa, had under letters of marque been seized at Deva with his partner John George and his ship and goods. Four times he secured letters from the king of England "for the reformation of his injuries", once to the king of Castile and thrice to the governors of Guipuscoa. These he delivered himself, crossing three times to Spain for the purpose, but no reply was vouchsafed. Then "by the advice of learned council in those parts following the law there" he protested to the king of Castile by writing placed on the doors of his chamber and those of his council. For this John George was killed and John Payn for fear of death "retreated to England". Remonstrances now and again passed to and fro between the governments, but they were often answered merely by counter remonstrances; when the king of England wrote in 1411, asking for the restitution of the *Marie* of Bristol, the queen of Castile wrote back that she could not reply to the request since she had not yet received an answer to her last letter.[1]

Gradually, however, after the Hundred Years War was over, and the English were no longer near neighbours of the Spaniards in Southern France, the two peoples came together and the bonds between Castile and France were loosed. In 1466 a formal treaty of peace was concluded. This new alliance was from time to time almost nullified, as when France renewed her alliance in 1470 and again in 1478; merchants still made frequent complaint of ill-treatment; and it was not until the advent of the Tudors that the new friendship was finally sealed by the marriage of Prince Arthur with Katherine of Aragon. By this time, however, the route from Bristol to Spain was considered so safe that letters of state were not even written in cipher. Bristol was now evidently one of the principal ports for Spain. The ambassador De Puebla, very likely on his way from Spain, wrote home in 1495 from Bristol. Two years later, Ferdinand and Isabella directed him to select a trustworthy person in Bristol to receive and forward their letters. It was through Bristol that the negotiations for the marriage of Katherine of Aragon were carried on, and Bristol was named as one of the fittest ports for her arrival.[2]

There is a marked contrast between the dealings of Bristol with Castile and with Portugal, since Portugal's relations with England were consistently friendly. These two states were naturally disposed to be allies, since neither of them was on good terms with Castile. There was also kinship between their dynasties, and the men of both countries were

[1] *Calendar of Patent Rolls*, 1401–5, 360, 426–8; *ibid.*, 1446–52, 215; *ibid.*, 1467–76, 599; *ibid.*, 1476–85, 271; see Kingsford, *op. cit.*, 83 *et seq.*, for a full account of Hawley's career.

[2] Merriman, *op. cit.*, 138; Daumet, *op. cit.*, 115–22; *Calendar of State Papers, Spanish*, I, 57, 112, 136, 250, 255.

born seamen and adventurers. Prince Henry the Navigator was great-nephew to the Black Prince, and he and his successors made their little country the foremost maritime power in Europe. The friendship sealed in 1386 by the Treaty of Windsor between Richard II and John I of Portugal lasted on in spite of temporary ruptures through acts of violence and changes of dynasty in England; throughout the fifteenth century the provisions made in this charter of commerce were confirmed, and the kings of both countries were pledged to punish infractions of it. Privileges hitherto enjoyed by the merchants of Genoa and Pisa only were now extended to merchants of England, who were as secure in Lisbon or Oporto as were natives of Portugal. Portugal's desire to favour them showed itself also in the choice of a special proctor at Lisbon to ensure prompt payment for cloth sold; in the appointment of a single judge in place of a jury of foreigners to settle disputes between English and Portuguese; and in the greater security from the malpractices of customs officials afforded them in response to their petitions of 1454 and 1458.[1]

The Bristol merchant had thus exceptional opportunities of doing business unmolested in Lisbon and Oporto. Moreover, he found there goods specially acceptable in England. Although Portugal is in many places infertile, the vines grown in its sheltered valleys rivalled those of Gascony and competed favourably with those of Castile. When the Hundred Years War ended, it was only at exorbitant prices, by French favour and under French supervision, that English merchants could buy wine in Gascony, and trade with Castile, their other chief source of supply, was still precarious. Hence the demand grew for wine from Portugal. Whereas two Bristol customs accounts early in the century mention wines only from Gascony and Spain, in the winter and spring of 1465–6 six ships came from Portugal bringing nearly 500 tuns of wine, and from this

[1] V. M. Shillington and A. B. W. Chapman, *The Commercial Relations of England and Portugal* (1907), 13, 14, 18, 49, 56, 68, 110 *et seq.*

time such entries recur in each account. Nor was wine the only import. For many years cork was obtainable only from Portugal and sugar from Portugal's first colony, Madeira. Sugar was a luxury unknown to the author of the *Libelle*, and occurs for the first time as an import to Bristol in a customs account of the time of Edward IV. "Ther is also grete salt", as the merchants' handbook noted, and one summer a whole shipload of this came into Bristol, though there was never any very considerable import. Wax came also, and olive oil "wiche is most holswmyst for mannys mette and medicins", and which when old was used for wool oil. The sunny southern provinces yielded quantities of fruit, and Sir John Vasquez, who exported from England lances for the king of Portugal, once imported steel. Most valuable of all Portugal's products in England was perhaps the "grain" used in the dyeing of the precious scarlet cloth. The tiny insect—*kermes*—from which this dye was derived was found in great plenty on the oak trees of Portugal, which became England's chief source of supply.[1]

Thus Portugal, as the *Libelle* observes, had many useful commodities to offer the English, in contrast to the "nifles, trifles" palmed off on them by some. Nor was Bristol at a loss for return cargoes. English cloth was in great demand in Portugal, and in 1482 the Portuguese even demanded that the wearing of garments of any other cloth should be forbidden. Ships often took nothing but cloth, though occasionally the monotony was varied by iron, lead, halyards, hats, barrel staves, or an alabaster reredos. Corn was sometimes sent, and ships occasionally took fish, calling perhaps in Brittany on the way home for salt for their next cargo from the bay of Bourgneuf.[2]

[1] P.R.O., K.R. Customs Accounts, *passim*; *The Noumbre of Weyghtes, ut supra*, f. 100d; *Calendar of French Rolls, Henry V and Henry VI*. Reports of the Deputy Keeper of the Public Records, XLIV, XLVIII (1883, 87), XLIV, 555.

[2] Shillington and Chapman, *op. cit.*, 59, 70; *Calendar of French Rolls, ut supra*, XLIV, 549 *et. seq*; P.R.O., K.R. Memoranda Rolls, Mich. 12 Hen. VI, m. 34, cf. *The Noumbre of Weyghtes, ut supra*, f. 100d.

At first it had been the Portuguese who brought their own goods to England.[1] In the fifteenth century, however, England's seamen were overtaking those of Portugal, and the largest consignments of goods landed in Bristol were those of Bristol merchants in Bristol ships. Thus in 1479–80 only two Portuguese, but ten or eleven Bristol ships, were engaged in the trade, together with two or three ships of Brittany. The Portuguese were no doubt taken up more and more with their colonial ventures, but though they jealously tried to keep their colonial trade to themselves [2] at least one Breton ship, from Quimperle, took cloth of Bristol merchants to Madeira. Bristol seamen, even if they did not visit Madeira themselves, must have learnt much, through their constant contact with the Portuguese, of these isles in the Atlantic.

English ships seem to have carried only English goods, but Portuguese ships were often used by English merchants. Most of the well-known Bristol merchants took part in the Portuguese trade, and sixty-seven of them once contributed to the cargo of the *Mary Redcliffe* when she was bound for Portugal. Nor did the trade attract only English and Portuguese. Ever since King Diniz in 1317 had appointed a Genoese to be an Admiral in his navy, the Portuguese, with ambitions on the high seas, had availed themselves of the skill and initiative of foreigners, thus training themselves in the science of navigation. And even in the fifteenth century Italians were still in evidence in the Portuguese trade, and occasionally came to Bristol. Thus Jerome de Ozerio, merchant of Genoa, asked for a safe-conduct for himself, his factors, attorneys, and servants, and for diverse goods in the *James* of Bristol, of which an Englishman, Richard William, was master.

The most frequented of all Portuguese harbours was Lisbon, whose spacious port at the outlet of the Tagus was safe from all gales except those of the west. Favoured at the expense of all other cities by royal decrees, the one place in

[1] Shillington and Chapman, *op. cit.*, 46–49.
[2] *Ibid.*, 71; Customs Accounts, *ut supra*, 19/14.

which foreigners, by an ordinance of 1423, were permitted to buy merchandise, it had become (said one observer) as large as London. Its fine English church of San Domingo marked it out as the centre of our whole trade with Portugal —at any rate until the decree of 1451 permitted the purchase of fruit and wine in Algarve. Portuguese ships, however, sailed sometimes from Oporto, and this had one advantage over Lisbon in that within easy reach of it grew some of the finest vines on the sunny northern slopes of the Douro valley, sheltered by the lofty Sierra de Marao. From Viana, further to the north, a cargo of steel came once in a Portuguese boat.

Though the progress of this peaceful trade between England and Portugal is in striking contrast to the story of our relations with Castile, it had perils of its own in the many pirates, Cornish, Breton, Gascon, or Castilian, who were often encountered during the long voyage involved. Especially was this the case during the disorders of the middle of the century, when Portuguese and English preyed equally upon each other's shipping in spite of royal injunctions that treaties should be kept; reprisals and counter-reprisals were resorted to, and special protections applied for, as by William Canynges and John Alberton of Bristol.[1] One typical illustration may be found in documents preserved among the Early Chancery Proceedings.[2] In 1443 the *Anthony* of Faro was laden in Algarve with fruit and wine belonging to four merchants who sailed with her—John Veilho, Gunsallo Gile, Vasqueannus, and Alfonso Gile. On her voyage she was taken captive by Hankyn Selander, one of the most notorious of west country pirates. Thereupon a ship of Henry May, the *Trinity* of Bristol, came to the rescue, and with the help of the Portuguese themselves restored them to their ship, gave them armour for six men, and (so said the English) meat and

[1] *Calendar of Patent Rolls*, 1452–61, 225; *Foedera, Conventiones, etc.*, ed. T. Rymer (3rd edition, The Hague, 1739–42), V, i, 37; Shillington and Chapman, *op. cit.*, 62, 99, 307: "William Canis . . . his ship La Mary Redclyff". This must refer to William Canynges.

[2] P.R.O., Early Chancery Proceedings, 9/488.

drink for a day and a night for sixty men. In spite of his repulse, however, Hankyn again attacked the *Anthony*, captured her, put her master, merchants, and mariners on shore in Brittany, took the ship to Fowey, and there sold both her and her goods. Veilho in course of time made his way to Bristol and begged help from the mayor through Henry May. When no help was forthcoming, May wrote several letters for him "in frendly wise" to John Chirche, Stephen Stychemersh, and Piers Alford of London, and through their good offices the case was finally brought into Chancery. Meanwhile Henry's brother, Richard May, merchant of London, was in Lisbon with goods of his own in the *George Heron*. The other merchants concerned in the *Anthony*, therefore, declaring that Henry was responsible for her fate and had acted in collusion with Hankyn, took action against Richard. All his property and his goods in the *George Heron* were seized, the ship was delayed five weeks in Lisbon so that her owners demanded heavy compensation, and finally Richard himself was cast into prison. Richard and Henry then appealed together to the Chancellor, begging him to consider the great "trouth, gode wille and favour" done by them to John Veilho and his fellow merchants of Portugal, and the "grete untrouth wrong and iniurie" done to them by John Veilho.

Veilho in his reply did not deny that Henry May brought him good cheer, though as to keeping sixty Portuguese in food and drink for a night and a day, that was impossible, since there were not more than twenty men on board, and they had "sufficence of vitailles" though "som of theym drank with them oo nyght". He declared, however, that the English had soon wearied of well-doing, for that John Fleming, on learning that the pirate ship was English, said he would not for a great sum have done as he did, and that he would no more meddle in the matter because he had been given nothing for his pains. So the Portuguese had offered half of all the merchandise in their ship as the price of an escort to Bristol, and in spite of this the *Trinity* had left them to the mercy of Hankyn. Yet Veilho protested vigorously that had he been in Lisbon and not stranded in Brittany, Richard May should never have been molested. On the strength of this, though the *Trinity*'s men were entirely exonerated, each side had apparently to bear its own loss.

Such an incident illustrates not only the perils of the Portuguese trade, but the frequent collaboration between merchants of the two lands. One further instance may be added showing the close and friendly relations between the two in peace as well as in war. When English and Portuguese ships had together blockaded Rochelle in 1403, the men of Rochelle had retaliated by preying upon Portuguese as well as English vessels. They had captured a ship of Bristol laden with cloth and two other ships with produce of Portugal. So close was the alliance between Portugal and England that, it was said, the Portuguese were taken flying English colours, bearing the red cross on their banners in the English manner.[1]

§ 5

THE MEDITERRANEAN

The stately vessels of Venice and Genoa, bringing the luxuries of the Mediterranean and of the Far East to the shores of England, there to exchange them for her more homely wares—wool and tin and cloth—deigned not to visit Bristol. In London, in Southampton, and in Sandwich they unloaded silks and damasks, fruits and spices, finely wrought armour, delicate goldsmiths' work, and many another precious ware down to "apes and japes and marmasettes tailed", and there they were privileged to ship staple English goods direct to southern Europe and the Levant.[2]

Yet Bristol was not quite unrepresented in this trade. Its

<hr/>

[1] H. G. Richardson, " Illustrations of English History in the Mediaeval Registers of the Parlement of Paris ", in *Transactions of the Royal Historical Society*, Fourth Series, X (1927), 74.

[2] *Rotuli Parliamentorum, ut supra*, III, 429, 662.

riches were needed to minister to the growing luxury of her burghers, and therefore, when the Italian fleet lay at anchor off Southampton, Bristol cloth and other goods were dispatched thither overland, and there, no doubt, silks and spices were purchased. Thus in 1478, when the *Andrew* and the *Salva Deo* were in Southampton harbour, Petrus de Antina and Nicholas Nadale sent overland from Bristol for shipment in them a cargo of cloth and hides.[1]

But though the great fleets of the Mediterranean kept to the Channel, diverging thence for the Flemish or English ports, a stray vessel of Venice or Genoa, bound possibly for Ireland, found its way now and again into the Severn laden with goods of Spain and Portugal. Such wayfarers were more than once set upon, doubtless with joy, by Bristol mariners. A carrack of Venice in 1421 put in at Goldhap in Wales, and was there seized, with its raisins, figs, and almonds, by three ships of Bristol and a barge of Plymouth. Again a rich cargo of Balthasar Gentilis was, in 1458, brought into Bristol from a carrack wrecked near by.[2]

Great must have been the awe roused in the English mariners when their sturdy little boats met these portly Italian vessels; keen must have been their jealousy of the opulent foreigners who bore the merchandise not merely of their own states and of the East, but also of Spain, Portugal, and France; eager their desire to snatch from them the carrying trade to their own ports, and to challenge their virtual monopoly of the Mediterranean. But whereas in the vast spaces of the North Sea the claims of the Hanse might be flouted at times with impunity, the Mediterranean was an enclosed lake where traps for the intruder could easily be set at Gibraltar, Malta or elsewhere, and from the Pillars of Hercules to the gateways of the East, where caravans discharged their precious burdens, the merchants of Venice and Genoa still reigned supreme in the early fifteenth century. In vain the English petitioned against the lavish privileges

---

[1] P.R.O., K.R. Customs Accounts, 19/13.
[2] *Calendar of Patent Rolls*, 1416–22, 418; *ibid.*, 1452–61, 438, 443.

obtained with a great sum by these merchants from needy
kings whose financiers they had become, begging that they
might be restricted to bringing goods of their own manufacture; unable to vie with the mighty Italian cities in wealth,
the little English towns received scant attention.

Nevertheless the men of Bristol, Hull, and other rising
ports were not content to ply their trade only with lands
where no powerful interests contested their authority. Away
in the far north, as is elsewhere related, they had already
recklessly ignored the monopoly of Bergen and the privileges
of the Hanse, opening across uncharted seas a new route to
the shadowy realm of Iceland. Now the same intrepid spirit
of daring impelled them also to seek new highways for their
ships in waters frequented from the dawn of history. Boldly
they pushed through the Straits of Marrok to fetch for
themselves the spices which they had hitherto meekly
received from foreigners. The history of Bristol's earliest
attempt to penetrate the Mediterranean is inseparably bound
up with the name of the great pioneer Robert Sturmy, one
of the most notable but least known of Bristol's citizens.
His last ill-fated expedition arrested the attention of more
than one fifteenth century chronicler, but the allusions to him
in modern histories (like those to John Taverner of Hull,
and other pioneers beyond the straits) are slight and misleading.[1] It may therefore be of interest here to set down
what evidence has come to light of one commemorated in
Bristol as a "ful notable worshipful marchaunt".[2]

Little is known of his early career. In contrast to William
Canynges and his distinguished family he stands out as a
solitary figure of obscure origin. Unluckily no detailed
customs accounts survive for the two decades during which
he must have traded most actively. Hence there is no means
of knowing in what goods he trafficked or with what lands he

[1] E.g., A. Abram, *Social England in the Fifteenth Century* (1909), where it
is stated that Sturmy "carried on a considerable trade in the Levant".
[2] J. Latimer, *The History of the Society of Merchant Venturers of the City
of Bristol, with some account of the anterior merchants' guilds* (1903), 16.

had dealings in an ordinary way. Almost his only recorded transactions are those exceptional enough to need licences; his only known ventures those which came to a tragic end. His experience as a merchant was gained in part through provisioning the king's forces in France, whither he sent corn in 1441–2, and by this time he possessed at any rate a share in a ship.[1]

By 1444 he was sufficiently well known in Bristol to be chosen bailiff. In the following year the Venetians were driven out of Egypt, and the monopoly of the Italians in the Levant was threatened. Not long after, with shrewd insight, Sturmy was planning his first recorded expedition to the Mediterranean, and procuring for it the *Cog Anne* and a special licence enabling him to share the privilege of shipping staple goods elsewhere than to Calais. Three English commodities were certain of a Mediterranean sale—wool, tin, and cloth. For cloth he needed no permit, so the licence was made out on 3rd November 1446 for him to ship forty sacks of wool and 100 pieces of tin (26,000 lb. in weight) by his attorneys or deputies, "by way of the Straits of Morocco" to Pisa.[2] By sending to Pisa he designed to avoid Venice and Genoa, and to deal with a now humbler rival in commerce, namely Florence. But the *Cog Anne*'s journey was not to end at Pisa. For she was on her way to fetch from the gateways of the East the spices—pepper, ginger, and the like—which were the most coveted of the infidels' goods. For this, what outward freight could be better than pilgrims for the Holy Sepulchre?

In 1446, then, the *Cog Anne*, with 160 pilgrims and a crew of thirty-seven, charged with 20½ sacks and 12 cloves of wool, and probably other goods too, set sail from Kingrode for Pisa. Tin may have been taken on board at some Cornish or Devon port. Who was the luckless captain, and who went as Sturmy's representative to parley with the Turks, is

[1] P.R.O., L.T.R. Customs Accounts, 19, m. 6d; P.R.O., K.R. Memoranda Roll, Trin. 20 Hen. VI, m. 2.
[2] P.R.O., Chancery Enrolments, Treaty Rolls, 25 Hen. VI, m. 20.

unknown. Calling at Seville, she passed the ill-omened straits, defiantly entered the Mediterranean, and, perhaps because she was quite an unexpected apparition, arrived safely at Joppa, her goal, and landed her pilgrims. These travellers very likely returned by the overland route, then often preferred to the long journey by sea. At any rate the *Cog Anne* did her business and set out for home without them. It is not known whether she had secured her spices, for on a dark and gloomy night in mid-winter (23rd December), as she sailed along the rugged coast of southern Greece, there arose a sudden tempest and a mighty wind; the *Cog Anne* was driven on to the rocks off the island of Modon and dashed to pieces, and there her whole crew perished "to the extreme grief of their wives and their friends at Bristol". Then came a certain faithful bishop of Modon, who gave honourable burial to the thirty-seven bodies, and built and consecrated a chapel from which prayers might arise for the souls of these ill-fated adventurers. Such is the story, as given in two places by William of Worcester. How great a sensation the calamity made is apparent from the stress laid on it in his usually terse and unemotional pages.[1]

Sturmy seems to have been neither ruined nor daunted by so melancholy a shattering of his hopes—he had at least not fallen into the clutches of the grasping Italians, whom his petty traffickers must have dreaded more than the elements. During the next ten years he figures as a prosperous and respected (*venerabilis*) citizen, doing his duty in such civic offices as only a man of wealth could afford to fill. We find him attending a meeting of the town council (in 1450) to arrange for the spending of money bequeathed by a fellow merchant for the repair of the town walls; being chosen (in 1451) as sheriff; assisting (in 1452) to pass a decree degrading from office an unworthy steward; and finally elected by his fellow-councillors as their mayor for 1453–4. More councils had now to be attended, ordinances for the welfare

[1] P.R.O., L.T.R. Customs Accounts, 19, m. 7d; *Antiquities of Bristow, ut supra*, 78, 109.

THE OVERSEAS TRADE OF BRISTOL

of the town passed, elections presided over, industrial disputes between masters and men settled; courts held constantly—the Tolsey court sat at least three times a week; quarrels heard between natives and aliens, customs officer and refractory shipowner, and judgment given sometimes under threat of vengeance from the loser. Royal mandates, too, had to be carried out, such as that to Sturmy and three others to levy £150 in Bristol for the wages of certain lords and others associated with them for the keeping of the sea. A special effort had been made this year under the new Protectorate to remedy the chronic state of piracy on the seas, and it had been ordained in Parliament that money should be collected promptly from the chief ports. Bristol's allotted share was more than that of any city except London, yet so public-spirited was Sturmy, or so thoughtful for royal favours to come, that he further assisted matters himself by making "new at Brystow . . . a stately vessell, only for the warre". Prominent in private as in public life, he was long remembered for his liberal hospitalty and his generosity to fellow-merchants whether foreign or otherwise. We can well imagine him in his fur-trimmed gown of rich scarlet and his golden girdle, with the help of Mistress Ellen his wife sumptuously entertaining in his hall some distinguished visitors from foreign parts, and keenly questioning them on the distant lands which he purposed to visit.[1]

In these years of strenuous public duty, Sturmy can have had little time for business enterprises out of the usual, but as soon as his mayoralty was over, new ventures claimed him. Again in 1456 he procured a licence to take pilgrims, this time to Compostella, to the number of sixty in his own ship the *Katharine Sturmy*. Very likely this was the one from Bristol which joined company with five others at Plymouth.[2]

---

[1] Great Red Book, *ut supra*, ff. 17, 18, 186, 78, 93; *The Little Red Book*, *ut supra*, II, 151; P.R.O., Early Chancery Proceedings, 19/122, 24/221; *Calendar of Patent Rolls*, 1452–61, 156; *Rotuli Parliamentorum*, *ut supra*, V, 245; *Paston Letters*, *ut supra*, No. 208; *Antiquities of Bristow, ut supra*, 112; Register of Wills proved in the Prerogative Court of Canterbury, Stokton, 14.
[2] *Foedera, ut supra*, V, ii, 67; *Itineraries of William Wey, ut supra*, 153.

This voyage was for the *Katharine* but a prelude to a far more daring one the following year. By 1457, when English merchants, driven from Gascony, must have had much cloth on their hands, the Italian merchants were losing their grip on the Levant as the tide of Ottoman invasion steadily advanced. When Constantinople at last fell in 1453, Genoa lost her rich colony at Pera, and her merchants were becoming more and more exhausted by the struggle to protect their Black Sea colonies from the Turks as well as their western possessions from the growing menace of the Catalan fleet. Venice, with greater influence in the Near East by reason of her situation and her superior naval strength, was still able to conclude a treaty with the Sultan preserving her rights of free trade and of self-government in Constantinople. Such a time of upheaval must have seemed opportune to Sturmy, who had the vigour and initiative to adapt old resources to changing needs. Once again he resolved that an English ship should fetch spices from the Levant, venturing not alone, but with two attendant caravels, and that he himself would go with them. Once again, on 8th February 1457, a licence was procured. Its figures give some idea of the magnitude of the venture conceived by Sturmy. For even if he sold a part of the licence to other merchants, it indicates an English Mediterranean enterprise of an altogether exceptional character. He had permission to ship 100 fothers of lead, 10,000 pieces of tin, 600 sarplers of wool, and 6,000 pieces of cloth—that is cloth then worth at least £20,000. Security to the extent of 500 marks was to be left with the customers that the goods were to be sent "beyond the mountains by the straits of Marrok" and nowhere else, and a certificate of their unloading was to be delivered within one year. A month later Sturmy procured a further licence for 40 quarters of wheat to be carried to Italy with other goods. Three months more must have been spent with John Eyton, who provided one of the ships, in repairing and victualling them, and in collecting cargo. At last on 27th June Sturmy made his will, beginning as follows:—"In the name of God, Amen. The 27 day of June in the yere of our Lord m¹cccc^mo lvii, I, Robert Sturmy, Burgeys and marchant of Bristowe, make my Testament in this wise. First I bequethe my soule to God and to our Lady Seint Mary, and to alle þe seintes of hevyn, and for as much as I am now passinge over the see under the mercy of god I bequethe my body to be buryed ther as is moost plesing to God." He must have been hoping for considerable profits from this voyage, for the legacies to his family and to his servants were to be doubled if his ship returned in safety, many more masses were to be sung for his soul, and further sums of money were to be given to the overseers of his will, the Vicar of St. Nicholas and a Ludlow draper.[1]

There is no clue as to the date of embarkation or as to the precise cargo, though it seems most probable that the *Katharine* set out in 1457. Safely she sailed into the Mediterranean and on into "divers parts of the Levant" ("hetheness", as the London chronicler expresses it), "and other parts of the East". Of this stage of the trip only hearsay reached the chronicler, though official documents amply corroborate the main facts. Then, continues Fabyan, "for so much as the fame ran upon him, that he had gotten some green pepper and other spices to have set and sown in England (as the fame went)", the Genoese determined that the *Katharine* should never reach home. So they lay in wait for Sturmy near Malta, and there they spoiled his ship and another.[2]

Thus provokingly brief are State records and chronicles alike, but, whatever the damage done, the outrage roused the wrath of the English. All the Genoese in London (their chief English depot) were arrested and incarcerated in the Fleet, and their goods were confiscated. Relations between England

[1] P.R.O., K.R. Memoranda Roll, Easter, 36 Hen. VI, m. 37; P.R.O., Chancery Enrolments, Treaty Rolls, 35 Hen. VI, mm. 20, 6; Register of Wills proved in the Prerogative Court of Canterbury, Stokton, 14.

[2] *Chronicles of London*, ed. C. L. Kingsford (1905), 169; *Ricart's Kalendar, ut supra*, 41; *Six Town Chronicles of England*, ed. R. Flenley (1911), 112, 161; *Calendar of Patent Rolls*, 1452–61, 517.

and Genoa were further complicated at this time since in 1458 Genoa, desperately seeking aid against the Turks and against Alfonso of Naples with his troublesome Catalan fleet, had persuaded Charles VII of France to become her overlord. In that year, therefore, French soldiers were assisting to defend the harbour of Genoa against the Catalans. Moreover, French ships had in the previous year been responsible for the sacking of Sandwich and the burning of Fowey, and were now being vigorously chastised with those of their allies the Castilians by the Earl of Warwick. It is therefore highly probable that the French instigated the seizure of Sturmy's ships by the Genoese. Indeed, it has even been suggested that the arrest of their ships and goods in England in that year was merely the natural sequel to their accepting the French as overlords; [1] it seems, however, more likely that, as the chronicles relate, the attack on Sturmy immediately prompted such drastic action, especially in view of the magnitude of the damages extorted for it before the Genoese could be delivered. For there now began a great lawsuit when Philip Mede, Mayor of Bristol, "sewid byfore the kyng and his counseile al the Lumbards Janueys at that time in Englande, bicause of the takyng of Robert Sturmy and of his shippes. Which Janueys, after long sewte of the same, were judged and condempned to pay the saide maire and his brothern the some of 9,000 marcs, to be paide at certein termes." In due time, on 25th July 1459, Sir John Stourton, Philip Mede, John Eyton, William Canynges, Richard Chok, and William Coder were commissioned to receive from the Treasurer £6,000 to be distributed among those involved in the venture, and the Genoese were delivered from prison. The fate of Sturmy himself is an unsolved mystery. But at least it is clear that he perished in the very year of the disaster, for his will was proved on 12th December 1458. Its administration was entrusted to his wife, who lived

---

[1] *Letters of the Fifteenth and Sixteenth Centuries from the Archives of Southampton*, ed. R. C. Anderson (Southampton Record Society Publications, 22, 1921–2), 14–6.

on in Bristol, renting a house in Baldwin Street, and leaving the princely mansion on the Back to become the meeting-place of the first society of Merchant Venturers in Bristol.[1]

The tragedy of Sturmy is but an episode in the story of Bristol's trade at the close of the Middle Ages. No other record has come to light of similar Mediterranean ventures thence before the time of the Tudors. In the south, even more than in Iceland, the English were sharply rebuffed in their attempt to penetrate the spheres of their formidable rivals. It was not until the middle of the sixteenth century that the monopoly of the Mediterranean was wrested from the Italians, and even then the tradition of their ascendancy over the "petty traffickers" died hard. Yet already by the time of Henry VII England had a consul at Pisa, whither Sturmy had taken wool, and by 1511 "divers tall ships of London" with ships of Southampton and Bristol were voyaging still further to Candia, Cyprus, and even to Bey-rout. Thus Sturmy was but a little before his time in sailing with his three English ships past the Straits of Marrok into "so jeopardous and far parts".

§ 6

THE MERCHANT OF BRISTOL

Merchandise rather than merchants has hitherto been the subject of this essay. The routes have been traced by which the wares of Bristol were carried over almost the whole of Europe; reckoning has been made of the rich and varied imports unloaded at her quays. What of the persons who trafficked in these things? Were they Englishmen or strangers? What was their status in society and what their influence over the city's government? Did they build and own the ships to which they committed their precious

---

[1] *Ricart's Kalendar, ut supra,* 41–2; in *Chronicles of London* and *Six Town Chronicles, ut supra,* the sum is 6000 marcs; *Calendar of Patent Rolls,* 1452–61, 517; *Abstracts of Wills, ut supra,* 137; Latimer, *op. cit.,* 16, 17; *supra,* p. xxviii.

freights? Who helped them at home and transacted their
business abroad? How large were the fortunes they amassed,
and how did they spend their wealth when they had won it?
Such are a few of the innumerable questions whose answers
might well fill a bulky book, had letters or private papers of
the merchants survived. But the absence of these is so complete that it is now only possible to catch an occasional
glimpse into their manner of life through their legal transactions, their civic activities, their contact with the customs
officers and other officials, and their dealings with the church.
Through these they may be pictured resplendent in robes of
scarlet, violet, blue, green, and murrey, edged with the finest
of costly furs, girdled with gold and silver, and adorned with
chains of gold and rings of great price; proud mayors past
and present, in black velvet hoods with scarlet trains borne
behind them, entertaining the highest in the land in their
lofty timbered and tapestried halls.[1] Right royal was the
reception given by these opulent burghers to the ill-fated
Margaret of Anjou, to Henry VI, and, in happier circumstances, to Edward IV. Brilliant was the pageant prepared
for the new sovereign in 1461. "First atte the comyng ynne
atte Temple Gate there stode Wylliam Conquerour with
iij lordis, and these were his wordis:—

'Well come Edwarde, oure son of high degre,
Many yeeris hast þou lakkyd owte of this londe,
I am thy fore fader, Wylliam of Normandye,
To see thy welefare here thrugh goddys sond.'

Over the same gate stondyng a great Gyaunt delyveryng
the keyes. The Receyvyng atte Temple Crosse next
folowyng. There was seynt George on horsbakke uppon a
tent fyghtyng with a dragon, and þe kyng and þe quene
on hygh in a castell, and his doughter benethe with a
lambe. And atte the sleying of the dragon ther was a great
melody of aungellys."[2]

[1] *Abstracts of Wills, ut supra, passim.*
[2] Lambeth Palace MSS., CCCVI, f. 132, quoted in the Introduction to
Ricart's Kalendar, p. xviii.

The merchants' houses were indeed not unworthy to shelter kings, built as they were with great attention to comfort and, with the increasing use of glass, to a novel craving for light and air. Of no mean proportions were those in the fashionable and less congested quarter of Redcliffe, set among gardens and meadows stretching down to the brink of the river. Pre-eminent among them was the mansion of William Canynges the younger, five times mayor of Bristol. Its central feature was the great hall, probably older than the fifteenth century, with its steep-pitched timbered roof, whose mutilated and much obscured remains may still be seen. Such an apartment had probably originally been at once hall, dining-room, and parlour. But later on more rooms had been added, and down by the river had been built a "tower" of great beauty, with many chambers and four of the new-fashioned "Bay-wyndowes", the whole nearly fifty feet long.[1] No doubt there was also a solar besides the bed-chambers and kitchens and other offices quite adequate to produce a feast for the king himself. William of Worcester does not make clear whether these were grouped round a courtyard, as in a country house of the period, with the hall under its own roof on one side, and the tower on the other, nor whether this tower was built (as seems probable) of stone, with delicately mullioned stone bays like those of the George Inn at Glastonbury. "A mansion of great stones" is Worcester's description of another luxurious house nearby, called Vyell Place after its owner, and many a merchant lodged in a stone tower upon the city wall on to which chambers had been built out. But a stone house remained a landmark, though many another possessed ample accommodation with hall, parlour, kitchen, and chambers. In the more constricted central thoroughfares of Old Bristol the wealthy burgher's house could not stand in grounds of its own, and was chiefly distinguished by its superior height or adornment. The High Street, with its buzzing market,

---

[1] *Antiquities of Bristow, ut supra*, 145. Since this was written the hall of Canynges' house has been demolished.

boasted the house of more than one important merchant, jostled by the shops of tailors, goldsmiths, drapers, and saddlers. Here dwelt Clement Wiltshire at "le Cok in the Hope"; near by John Compton might be found at "le Grene Latyce"; and here the widow Alice Chester, who traded in cloth with Spain and Flanders, rebuilt her house between "the Bull" and the dwelling of John de Cork, corvesor. Her agreement with the Welsh carpenter, Stephen Morgan, is preserved among the archives of All Saints, and is of some interest, since the planning of medieval town houses is very much a matter of conjecture. Stephen was to build it of good timber and boards; it was to be only 10 ft. 5 in. wide, but nearly 20 feet in length; on the ground floor was to be a shop, over it a hall with an oriel window, above this a chamber, also with an oriel, and on the fourth floor yet another chamber. Such oriel windows are rarely depicted in manuscripts of the period, so that Alice Chester's house must have been a distinctive one. The windows were probably leaded, for the lattices were to be completed by another hand; the timber walls were later to be covered with lath and plaster; but the whole framework of this compact but lofty house, with floors, doors, and partitions, was to be Morgan's work, and he was to receive for it £6, 13s. 4d. (paid in instalments) with all the timber of the old building.

Thus some of these narrow houses in the busy highways of Bristol were four storeys high, with shops below open to the street and projecting upper storeys nodding to their neighbours on the other side. Equally important, however, were the one or more storeys below the ground, dark vaults burrowed out even under the street for the storage of casks of wine, woad, salt, and other bulky merchandise. The letting of these underground cellars apart from the house above must surely have given cause for strife unless they were all very soundly made, like those which were finely vaulted in stone. Behind the house were stables, for many a merchant possessed his own horse, while others hired them— once at a cost of 4d. a day—when going on a journey. To ride to Salisbury and back, one merchant paid 3s. 4d. for his mount.[1]

In such wise were the houses of the merchants designed on the outside. Within they were partitioned into sundry rooms, each often hung with its distinctive tapestry or brightly coloured cloth, or perhaps lined with English oak or with wainscotting imported from eastern lands. Their furniture was scanty. A "joined" table had seldom superseded the customary trestles; John Gaywode mentions one in his will, of wainscot with four feet and "a beast carved therein", but then Gaywode was a prince among merchants, a partner with Canynges, owning a mansion not far from him in Redcliffe Street, in the height of luxury as then understood. Tapestries enriched his hall and parlour, and to match each set were "bankers"—covers for the wainscotted benches, and cushions to make snug seats in them and in the embrasures of the windows. In his hall hung a candelabra of laten; since candles were still a costly indulgence, to judge by the price paid by Elizabeth Stonor, this may have been reserved for special occasions, as were the two great andirons for the yule-log. The rapidly rising standard of comfort can be even more clearly perceived in the bed-chamber fittings of the merchant's house. Richly garnished with coverlets of tapestry or brightly patterned cloth, in blue and white, or green and yellow, the beds were canopied by testers to match, and screened with curtains. So elaborate were these fittings that the bequest of a "bed" often meant that of a coverlet and tester. Even at the close of the fourteenth century a house in Redcliffe Street had three such beds, one white embroidered, one blue embroidered with an eagle, and one red embroidered with a hawk. The ten beds bequeathed by John Hunt, including the one "wherein I have lain for the last two weeks", can scarcely all of them have been so complex. Feather beds and pillows were highly prized at a time when many a man thought himself fortunate to be able

[1] *Abstracts of Wills, ut supra, passim; Ricart's Kalendar, ut supra,* 46; Tolsey Court Book 1480–1, ff. 26, 113.

to purchase a flock bed and "thereto a sack of chaff to rest his head upon". Already known at the end of the fourteenth century, they were more usual, though not common, a century later, when Edward Kyte left his "optimum ffethirbedde" to his daughter Joan, and John Esterfeld a featherbed and bolster and "ij pylowes garnesshed", such as were then, if we are to believe Harrison, thought "meet only for sick women". Sheets were also sufficiently valuable to be sometimes specified in wills, and of these one merchant's widow left four pairs with a towel. Blankets, as was natural in Bristol, were well known. Little else besides the bed can there have been in the chambers except shining basins, ewers, and the ubiquitous wooden chest, serving, amongst other functions, that of a "press for my clothes". In chambers, hall, and parlour the sparseness of the furniture must have given full value to the rich glow from the brightly coloured hangings and cushions, and, on state occasions, the gleam of plate. John Gaywode possessed a Parisian cup with a coloured design in enamels; James Cokkes' great silver cup weighed over two pounds; and William Bird had to adorn his table five cups with covers, two flat cups, two gilt bell cups, and two gilt standing cups, also two dishes, one of them covered, for the precious spices that flavoured the food, and two and a half dozen spoons, and, as principal ornament, one silver salt cellar and two of the best gilt salt cellars.[1] Clearly there was a "great amendment of lodging" during this century among the wealthier burghers, as during the succeeding one when bequests become still more rich and varied. The average standard of comfort of the merchant of the fifteenth century must have been very much that of the farmers and lesser artificers of a century later, who, according to Harrison, had learned "to garnish their cupboards with plate, their joined beds with tapestry and silk hangings, and their tables with carpets and fine nappery, whereby the wealth of our country (God be praised therefore, and give us grace to employ it well) doth infinitely appear".

---

[1] *Wills, ut supra*, 42, 60, 87, 164, etc.; *Great Red Book, ut supra*, f. 248.

Moreover few ambitious merchants were content if they had not laid up enough by their trafficking to purchase land, then almost the only practicable form of investment, procuring on a long lease at any rate a tenement here and there in the city or the suburbs or perchance beyond. Clement Wiltshire, mayor of Bristol, purchased his own house "le Cok in the Hope" and two other tenements in High Street, two tenements in Temple Street and Winch Street, and two cellars near the Welsh Back. John Shipward, another famous mayor, possessed at his death four tenements and a stable in High Street, with cellars and a tenement in St. Nicholas' Street, seven acres of meadow in Redcliffe Mead, five gardens and a tower with a large garden at Llafford's Gate. William Canynges the younger held, besides fourteen shops, at least seventeen tenements, a close and two gardens in Bristol, and lands in Wells, the hundred of Wells and Westbury on Trym. Similarly Philip Mede, mayor, owned lands in the counties of Somerset and Bristol; Hugh Withiford, mayor, left lands in Shropshire in Oswestry and round about; and another mayor, Robert Jakes, had extensive property in various parts of Leicestershire. Which of these worthies were squires' sons who had taken to trade, and which were traders destined to become landed gentry it is difficult to determine. Clearly, however, the aristocrats among the merchants were accepted then as readily as now in county society. Philip Mede married his daughter to Sir Maurice Berkeley, lord of Beverston; and the famous Canynges' son and heir, John, was considered an eligible match for Elizabeth, daughter of Thomas Middleton, Esq., of Stanton Drewe. When Canynges drew up the marriage agreement he promised that he would "competently find" John and Elizabeth in meat, drink and clothing, and all things necessary to their degrees during his life, and would leave his son as well off as any man left his son in Bristol within a hundred years, "saving only Robert Cheddar".[1]

[1] *Abstracts of Wills, ut supra, passim*; *A Catalogue of Deeds* (*chiefly relating to Bristol*) *collected by G. W. Braikenridge*, ed. F. B. Bickley (Edinburgh,

At any rate traders in Bristol wares were recruited from many quarters, and its population became more and more cosmopolitan. Englishmen from neighbouring counties—Malmesburys, Ludlowes, and Devonshires—sometimes, like Philip Excestre, founded a family of merchants. Irishmen such as "Harry May" and "Patrick Irishman" were too numerous to be welcome; and Welshmen, more readily absorbed than the Irish, were almost as common as Englishmen, as is shown by the notable array of Vaughans, Goughs, Lloyds, ap Ryses, ap Meryks, and so forth. Frenchmen such as Barnard Bensyn [1]; Spaniards like Simon Aragon; Genoese, and perhaps Venetians, such as John Lombard and the more renowned Cabots, made Bristol their headquarters, and the Gascon Moses Conterayn, who became a Bristol merchant, must have been of Jewish origin. While, however, some foreigners sought admission to the liberties of the Staple at Bristol, the evidence of many living there is slight. In Bristol there was no parallel to the foreign colony of Englishmen in Lisbon, nor to the Hanseatic colony in London. Detailed records of Bristol's dealings with her various customers prove that her trade was mainly in English hands, and reveal a rich and powerful group of native merchants, controlling all the affairs of her city.

Sometimes a commercial enterprise was carried on from generation to generation, as was the case in the Canynges family. William Canynges, burgess and merchant, who died in 1396, left his share in the ship *Rodecog* to his son Simon, and the rest of his property (after his wife's death) to his son John. This John traded with the talents committed to him, continued like his father to deal in cloth, shipped it to Spain and Bayonne, imported thence woad and iron, and in 1399 was elected mayor. He survived his father barely nine years, and died in 1405, possessed of three halls and five gardens, six tenements, twenty-two shops, and other lands and " void

privately printed, 1899), 9; B.M. Additional MS. 29866; P.R.O., Early Chancery Proceedings, 44/163.

[1] See above, p. 45.

places" in Bristol, leaving six young children under age. His wife thereupon was married again to a prosperous merchant, Thomas Yonge, and three of her children distinguished themselves. One, Thomas Yonge, deserted trade for the law and became the well-known judge and member of Parliament who in 1451, for petitioning that the Duke of York should be declared heir to the throne, was cast into the Tower. Another, Thomas Canynges, made his way in London as a grocer, until in 1456 he was elected mayor there; and a third, William Canynges, followed his father's profession in Bristol, sent his ships to Iceland, the Baltic, Spain and Portugal, France, and the Netherlands, increased the family property, and was mayor five times. He outlived both his childless sons; at his death the family vanished from Bristol, though his great-nephew and heir occasionally imported goods thither, and it was from the mayor of London that the nineteenth century statesman, George Canning, was descended.[1]

Many another merchant's son or grandson chose thus to follow him, acted as his father's representative, and then launched out on his own. For the outsider, apprenticeship for seven or eight years was normally the first rung on the ladder. Thus the "Childe of Bristow", somewhat priggishly declining to perjure his soul by amassing wealth through the law, resolved to take himself to Bristol and bind himself to a respected merchant there.

> "Hit hath ever be myn avise
> to lede my lyf by marchandise,
> to lerne to bye and selle;
> that good getyn by marchantye,
> it is truthe, as thynketh me,
> there with will I melle.

> "Here at Bristow dwelleth on
> is held right a juste trew man,
> as y here now telle;
> his prentice will y be vii yer,
> his science truly for to lere,
> and with hym will y dwelle."

---

[1] *Abstracts of Wills, ut supra*, 48, 77; P.R.O., K.R. Accounts, Various, Ulnage, 339/2; P.R.O., K.R. Customs Accounts, 17/1, 17/8, 19/14.

In like manner a Worcestershire lad, Richard Denton, was apprenticed by his father to Robert Gaynard and his wife for seven years. On Gaynard's death his wife married a second husband, John Gawge, who did business with Bordeaux and Bayonne. Then the young Richard, giving as his excuse an outbreak of plague in the city and a slump in business, "when Gawge kepith noon occupation and they die dayly in Bristowe", ran away to his father in Worcestershire. Evidently heavy penalties could be imposed on refractory apprentices, for when the father sent him back, as he alleged, Gawge refused to receive him and won £100 damages. Part of their training was to do business for the merchant abroad, until they had sufficiently learned the science of commerce to become, like the exemplary "Childe", the more responsible factor, trusted agent, and finally perhaps heir to the merchant.[1]

The position of factor was normally the next step taken by the ambitious apprentice when he was no longer a "Childe", though still young and ready to see the world before marrying and settling down in Bristol. This would probably mean living abroad, for the merchant usually kept a resident factor in towns with which he dealt constantly, with fuller powers of transacting business than his apprentices. Often the factor was a younger member of his family like John Canynges who seems to have been factor for his father, William Canynges. Much loss must have been suffered through the dishonesty of some of these agents, who had to be trusted to carry on business abroad with little supervision from home. Robert Russell once had occasion to complain of his factor, Thomas Hoper, in Bayonne. Cloth and other goods had been sent to him, but Hoper had converted these to his own use, married a woman of Bayonne, and was so "meintenuz et sustenuz par les Cosyns et alliez de sa dite femme" that Russell could not secure legal redress. The best that he could apparently do was to appoint one William

[1] *The Charm of the West Country*, ed. T. Burke (1913), 223; P.R.O., Early Chancery Proceedings, 79/43, and cf. *ibid.*, 19/263 and 64/42.

Roger, a merchant, as his attorney beneath the great seal of Bristol, to sue Hoper on his behalf, a journey abroad being then a tedious and difficult enterprise for a busy man.[1]

The attorney was usually, as in the case of William Roger, an agent appointed to transact a particular piece of business, though the words "factor" and "attorney" were sometimes used indiscriminately, and not in the strict legal sense in which the attorney, with more complete powers than the factor, would have fuller authority to act for another. Thus the master of a ship or a merchant trading abroad on his own account would take charge of a consignment of goods for another merchant or group of merchants. When the word is used, however, in connection with customs payments, it has sometimes a peculiar significance. For if a merchant shipped goods in virtue of a special licence granted to another, having perhaps purchased a share in the licence, he would enter the goods in the name of the licencee, naming himself as the attorney. From the customs, for instance, it would appear as though Canynges, Shipward, Gaywode, and Baron, in partnership, once during four months (1465–6) shipped goods through no less than seventy-one attorneys, monopolizing almost the whole of the native trade of Bristol. But the fact that Canynges and his associates then had a licence to ship customs free[2] makes it plain that the attorneys were the real owners of the goods, and succeeded in shipping them under the name of this influential partnership in order to benefit by their privileges. Indeed, the customs accounts themselves disprove the inference that such a partnership ever dominated the trade of Bristol. For the group makes its first appearance simultaneously with the granting of the licence and vanishes again later.

It is further remarkable that the other extant customs accounts at this time not only yield no evidence of such a

[1] *Ibid.*, 64/345, 59/22, 32/31; P.R.O., Exchequer, Treasury of Receipt, Council and Privy Seal Records, File 46, 3 Hen. VI.

[2] P.R.O., K.R. Customs Accounts, 19/14; Canynges had recently lent £333, 6s. 8d. to the King: P.R.O., K.R. Memoranda Roll, Easter, 3 Edw. IV, m. 6d.

partnership, but scarcely even mention the name of Canynges. Now this period was the very climax of Canynges' career, and it seems at first strange that he, traditionally the greatest Bristol merchant of the century, should appear to be taking so little active part in foreign trade. The story of Canynges, however, marks a new stage in the evolution of Bristol's trade. For one of the most notable features of the time is the emergence of the shipowner as a still more wealthy and influential citizen of Bristol than the merchant.

The shipowner on a large scale, as distinct from the merchant, was a new phenomenon in Bristol's history, and had developed probably from that newly emerged class of merchants making their fortunes entirely by foreign trade. It was in fact the latest of a series of changes in mercantile organization which accompanied the rapid expansion of England's foreign trade, each change tending towards greater specialization.

Early in the century there were few "merchants" concerning themselves primarily with foreign trade in a variety of commodities. Ship-masters took goods abroad on their own account; others concerned in the production of cloth were themselves responsible for its shipment abroad.[1] Thus William Symondes of Bristol, shearman, commissioned Richard Davy, who was setting out for Bordeaux, to take thither for him twelve broad murrey cloths to deliver to John Essey of Bordeaux.[2] Out of fifty-nine burgesses making their wills between 1380 and 1400, only five, including William Canynges the elder, were designated "merchant", though the epithet is a common one later. Rapid changes were, however, taking place in both industry and transport, and the significance of many terms connected with them changed also. As the towns abandoned their original attempt to confine the cloth industry within their walls, and it grew with ever-increasing speed beyond them in the country districts,

---

[1] As shown by a comparison of the more reliable Ulnage Accounts with the K.R. Customs Accounts.
[2] P.R.O., Early Chancery Proceedings, 16/473.

a new class of "clothiers" emerged who arranged for every stage in the making of the cloth and sold the finished product to the drapers. So William Lewys bought of Philip Coke, clothier, three broad woollen cloths.[1] Not only in its manufacture, but also in its export, there were marked changes, as the English cloth trade expanded and the drapers, who purchased the cloth in England from the clothiers, ceased gradually to concern themselves with its sale abroad. In the second half of the century, while those concerned in its production still occasionally shipped it overseas themselves, most of those who exported cloth were not merely drapers but merchants, for they dealt in many other things. Thus developed a distinctive merchant class, specializing in foreign trade, no matter in what commodity, not always ceasing to be concerned in production, but more and more exclusively mercantile. Since these middlemen, doing business in many commodities, seem often to have been connected with the production of cloth,[2] it may possibly have been from among the drapers that this distinctive mercantile class arose. The fortunes of the Canynges family were very likely typical. In Richard II's reign John Canynges and William the elder were concerned both in the production and in the export of cloth.[3] But in a list of over 240 people accounting to the ulnager for over a thousand cloths early in the reign of Henry VI, and in all later accounts, the name of Canynges never appears. William Canynges the younger was therefore probably in the first instance purely a foreign merchant, procuring the cloth which he exported from drapers or clothiers. Just as the cloth producers and cloth dealers in England were thus ceasing to trade abroad on their own account, giving place to the foreign merchant, so the ship-

[1] W. J. Ashley, *The Early History of the English Woollen Industry* (Baltimore, 1887), 62, 75, 80 *et seq.*; P.R.O., Early Chancery Proceedings, 48/85, cf. *Calendar of Patent Rolls*, 1485–94, 447, for "merchant's" debts to "clothier".

[2] Cf. P.R.O., K.R. Accounts, Various, Ulnage, 346/23, one of the more reliable accounts, with K.R. Customs Accounts, 19/14.

[3] P.R.O., K.R. Accounts, Various, Ulnage, 339/2; Customs Accounts, 17/1.

master now seldom entered goods in his own name, but, leaving them in the charge of the foreign merchant, became more exclusively concerned with navigation.

But now in this new group of foreign merchants itself yet further specialization took place. Early in the century many merchants were themselves shipowners, having perhaps a share in a ship with five or six others. Such shares were a form of property often bequeathed. Walter Derby left to his servant Nicholas half of the *Nicholas* and half of the balinger called the *Trinity*, and to his servants William and John half of the *Marie* and *Nicholas* respectively. Ships sometimes came into the hands of women. Thomas Sampson left the whole of the *Cog Joan* to his wife Joan, and William Spaynell left three-quarters of his "barge" to his wife Soneta and his two sons, bequeathing also money to "old John Wynne of the balinger" of whom we should like to know more.[1] Later in the century, however, while some merchants still had shares in ships, many more owned the whole of a ship, and gradually a wealthy class of shipowners appeared possessing small private fleets of ten or more vessels. These great shipowners, employers of several hundreds of men, fully occupied with the building, equipment, and management of their craft, concerned themselves little, if at all, with the buying and selling of goods, but made their profits on the freights paid by merchants whose goods they carried.

Pre-eminent among such shipowners was William Canynges the younger, himself once a foreign merchant. According to his contemporary and fellow-citizen, William of Worcester, he kept 800 men for eight years employed in his ships, and had workmen, carpenters, masons etc. to the number of a hundred men. Worcester enumerates ten ships as his, including one lost in Iceland, and says that six years after his death, in 1480, Thomas Strange possessed about twelve ships and John Godeman several more, while there were ten other ships belonging to Bristol in that year (*naves Bristolliae pertinentes*). This figure is corroborated by the

[1] *Abstracts of Wills, ut supra*, 16, 17, 30.

customs records, which mention at least twenty Bristol ships, many of which can be identified in Worcester's list. These Bristol ships account for rather more than half the total trade of Bristol, leaving out of account the Irish trade, where Irish ships were in the majority. Canynges, therefore, controlled perhaps a quarter of all the shipping at the port of Bristol, owning nearly half of Bristol's ships, and amassed his wealth not by dealing in cloth or in other wares, but by carrying the merchandise of others who paid freight on the goods they entrusted to his ships. These freights were usually paid on the safe delivery of the cargo, a very small sum being sometimes paid in advance. Thus when the *Marie* came into port from Bayonne, her master received from Bristol merchants with goods in the ship over £100 *in plenam solucionem tocius affretamenti predicte navis* for the owners of the ship or for whoever else might claim it. Similarly John Heyton, merchant of Bristol, made an agreement with Clement Bagot, owner of the *Julian*. Bagot was to freight his ship for Lisbon at the pleasure of Heyton, reserving to himself only ten "tontight". The rate of payment was high, since risks were considerable; for wine it was usually at least a sixth of its price in England. Heyton was to pay £1 for every tun of wine brought from Lisbon to Ireland, and out of the total, twenty marks were to be paid to the mariners within six weeks of their arrival. Another merchant, shipping wine from Bordeaux to England, agreed to pay 21*s.* a tun within three weeks of its discharge, and handed over in advance in the church of St. Peter at Bordeaux the small sum of 3*s.* 4*d.*[1]

The appearance of the specialized shipowner was accompanied by a marked development in Bristol's ships. These differed widely in size and character. Some were little "crayers", a term often applied to river boats. Others, used commonly as fishing boats and in trade with Ireland, were "picards", named often in the Tolsey Court books as

[1] *Antiquities of Bristow, ut supra*, 114–5; Great Red Book, *ut supra*, f. 78; P.R.O., Early Chancery Proceedings, 24/211 and 217, 26/474.

pledges for debts, and worth about £8. For larger vessels
the terms ship, barge, balinger, cog, and caravel, are often
used indiscriminately, nor is there any clear distinction
between the two most usual expressions "navis" and
"batella". The "ship" usually designates one of the larger
trading vessels, the cog or the caravel. The broadly built cog,
evolved during the thirteenth century, was pre-eminently a
cargo ship. At the opening of the fifteenth century it
could carry about 200 tuns, and was the commonest type
of merchant ship, though before long England began to
imitate the Portuguese caravel, built with planks edge to
edge instead of clinker fashion with overlapping edges.
Sturmy, for instance, sent the *Cog Anne* on his first expedition
to the Mediterranean, and the second time had two attendant
caravels. The barge was, strictly speaking, smaller than
the "ship", and the balinger smaller than the barge. Both
had originally oars, but the barge had by the fifteenth
century been built up into a high vessel of the sailing type,
while the balinger was then the typical pirate ship.[1]

Early in the century few of Bristol's ocean vessels can have
carried more than 100 tuns, and the average cargo of the
Bordeaux wine ships was 88 tuns, though one ship loaded
179 tuns. By the middle of the century, however, ships from
Bordeaux were bringing on an average 150 tuns and some
carried as many as 250 tuns. This may be compared with the
figures for French and Spanish ships visiting Bristol, given
in the lists of safe-conducts for this period in the Great Red
Book. These vary from 80 to 250 tuns, occasionally reaching
300 tuns. Such figures are more likely to be purely formal
than those given in the customs account of amounts actually
carried; but it is clear that by the middle of the century
Bristol boats had considerably increased in size, that 200 tuns
of wine was no unusual cargo, and that they compared

[1] Great Red Book, *ut supra*, f. 331; P.R.O., Early Chancery Proceedings,
64/533; B.M. Additional MS. 29866; P.R.O., K.R. Accounts, Various,
France, 185/7; cf. W. Vogel, *Geschichte der deutschen Seeschiffahrt, I: von
der Unzeit bis zum Ende des XV Jahrhunderts* (Berlin, 1915), 491-2, 498-9;
see above, p. 228; *Rotuli Parliamentorum, ut supra*, V, 59.

favourably in size with those of France and Spain. This marked increase tends also to confirm William of Worcester's oft-criticized figures for the last quarter of the century, the time of the great shipbuilders, Canynges and Strange. Worcester puts four of Canynges' ships at under 200 tuns, three more between 200 and 250 tuns, the *Mary Canynges* at 400 tuns, and the *Mary Redcliffe* at 500 tuns, the size of the largest of Warwick's ships in 1464. The most difficult figure to believe is that of 900 tuns for the *Mary and John*. Worcester, however, was scrupulous in those measurements of his which we can check to-day in Bristol; he was cautious, for he admits that he does not know the exact tunnage of the ship lost in Iceland, stating it to be "about 160 tuns"; and it is evident that the *Mary and John* was quite exceptional, for he states that she cost Canynges the great sum of 4,000 marks to build. Why should not Canynges, like John Taverner of Hull, have built a ship "as large as a carrack or larger"? [1]

The total tunnage of Canynges' ships must thus have amounted to close on 3,000. Each ship usually made one of the longer voyages twice a year, and thus if we estimate on the basis of the freights paid on wine, Canynges might have received in freights during one year over £10,000, though it is impossible to judge how much of this would be profit. With such a large scale shipping enterprise Canynges must have been remarkable as an employer of labour alone. Crews then were much larger than in sailing ships of the nineteenth century. In the safe-conducts in the Great Red Book ships of about 300 tuns are described as having crews of from sixty to eighty, and ships of about 80 tuns from twenty to thirty men, though these figures no doubt include convoys as well as actual crews. According to this, Canynges' ships would

[1] P.R.O., K.R. Accounts, Various, France, 184/19, 193/4, 195/19; Great Red Book, *ut supra*, ff. 38–161; C. L. Scofield, *The Life and Reign of Edward the Fourth* (1923), II, 417; cf. prices paid by Edward IV for ships, from £80 to £600 (Scofield, *op. cit.*, II, 410–4), and the cost of the *Margaret Cely* (?200 tuns), £28 (Cely Papers, ed. H. E. Malden (Camden Society Publications, 3rd series, I, 1900), 176–7).

have employed 600–800 men, and since this last figure exactly coincides with that given by Worcester, apart from those engaged in building the ships, such an estimate of Canynges' employees may be roughly correct.[1]

Canynges was not the only Bristol owner who built his ships at home, though some purchased them abroad, for example in Prussia. The tower beside which was built the famous *Nicholas de la Tour*, in whose boat Suffolk's head was smitten off with a rusty sword by "oon of the lewdeste of the shippe", was for long pointed out in Bristol; and when Edward IV visited the town in October 1474 he promised a reward to any who would build a ship of considerable value. Perhaps as a result of this, ten Bristol merchants in the following November were licensed, "for the continuance and increase of shipping in the port of Bristol", to take their four ships to Spain or Portugal and back, customs free; while the following May similar permission was given to William de la Founte, because he had "fully made and apparelled a ship of the portage of 200 tuns or under".[2]

Large and valuable cargoes went in these new ships in the latter part of the century. The *George*, for instance, probably the one enumerated by Worcester as of 511 tuns, was freighted, in the very year in which he wrote, with the goods of sixty-three merchants worth altogether over £1,000. Such a multifarious division of the cargo was very common when merchants preferred not to risk too large a consignment in one vessel. Each merchant distinguished his particular goods by a "mark" of his own, and this was legally recognized as establishing at least *prima facie* evidence of ownership in case of shipwreck, piracy, or other mishap.[3]

---

[1] P.R.O., K.R. Customs Accounts, *passim*; Vogel (*op. cit.*, 452) estimates only one man to 5 lasts (i.e. 10 tons). Worcester's tunnage figures are confirmed by the K.R. Customs Accounts, e.g. the *Mary Bird* "of 100 tuns" carried 101 tuns in 1479; P.R.O., K.R. Customs Accounts, 19/15.

[2] P.R.O., Early Chancery Proceedings, 9/223; *Antiquities of Bristow, ut supra*, 140; *Paston Letters, ut supra*, No. 93; Scofield, *op. cit.*, II, 416.

[3] P.R.O., K.R. Customs Accounts, 19/14; F. I. Schechter, *The Historical Foundations of the Law relating to Trade Marks* (New York, 1925), 26–34.

Risks indeed were great. Although laws of the sea existed, lawlessness had become a habit. Losses from piracy, from wrecks and the plundering of wrecks, legalized or arbitrary, were constantly recorded, and ships were in peril even at Kingrode; there in 1488 "a grete ship", the *Antony*, was lost; there, four years earlier, she and a ship of Bilbao had run aground, and other boats and cogs had been sunk in a fierce storm, whose effects had been felt even in Bristol, where the cellars had been flooded and much merchandise spoilt. Many a ship, like Canynges', must have perished in the fogs off Iceland, and others by fire through carelessness.[1] Little wonder was it that merchants sought heaven's protection against the elements, and that parish accounts contain such entries as "Item of John Foster, merchant, at his going to sea, 4*d*". Against piracy and the risks of war the only and very ineffectual protection, beyond their own armed resistance, was a safe-conduct. This lasted usually only for a year or two, and was purchased for a great price from their own or a foreign monarch. Some foreigners who once procured a safe-conduct through Bristol merchants offered in payment £12 for every voyage made. John Wylly, a Bristol brewer, and his son-in-law promised to pay forty marks for a safe-conduct from the French king. Their petition to Chancery illustrates yet another menace at a time when there was scarcely any royal navy—that of the commandeering of their vessels in time of war. Their ship, the *Julian* of Fowey, fell in with the Earl of Warwick on his way to Ireland "in his grete wrongfull trouble" to bring the Duke of York to England. It was seized by the Earl and detained for six months, and by this time the safe-conduct had expired and was worthless. Meanwhile the merchants shipping in the *Julian* had taken action against Wylly at Bristol for not delivering their goods. On occasions such as these the goods seem often to have been landed at the nearest port, and the merchant had to profit by them or not as he

---

[1] E.g. P.R.O., Early Chancery Proceedings, 47/62, 68/200; cf. Michel, *op. cit.*, I, 72; *Ricart's Kalendar, ut supra*, 46, 47.

could. The shipowner's compensation for the use of his ship was, when obtainable, 3*s*. 4*d*. per tun per quarter from the crown. There were usually three or four merchants travelling in each ship, and when one of these was captured the pirates made a goodly profit. For Thomas Canynges, sent overseas on business by his father (nephew of the great William), the Bretons asked £100, and to pay this land had to be mortgaged in Bristol. John Wode, factor of Thomas Wode, was of a less distinguished family, and for him and his ship and goods in Zealand the Scots asked only £28. John Wode was unable to pay, and so the factor of one John Seglysthorn lent him the money.[1]

Merchants must often have helped each other thus abroad, in days before consuls and permanent ambassadors existed. One John Pavy with goods worth £500 or more in France charged two fellow citizens, as he lay dying at Bayonne, to restore his property to his wife and children in Bristol. William Rowley, junior, who died in Bordeaux in 1478, entrusted to John Chester the return of the ship and goods for which he was responsible. The following year his uncle, William Rowley, senior, died in the Netherlands at Damme, in the house of "the honourable Roger of Dam", and was buried in the ambulatory of St. Mary's there, only a few months after his elder brother, Thomas, had died in Bristol.[2]

When a merchant's business was thus suddenly cut short, his wife frequently wound it up for him. Thus Joanna, widow of William Rowley, senior, received sugar from Lisbon in 1479, and in the following year oil and wax from Lisbon and woad and wine from Spain. Similarly in the name of Margaret, widow of Thomas Rowley, came three shipments of wine from Bordeaux and one of oil from Seville. Often when the husband was away the wife had to receive the goods

[1] Churchwardens' Account Book, Church of St. Ewen, Bristol, f. 61; P.R.O., Early Chancery Proceedings, 29/390, 27/383 and 471, 64/131, 59/92; *Rotuli Parliamentorum, ut supra*, III, 554.

[2] P.R.O., Early Chancery Proceedings, 10/136; *Abstracts of Wills, ut supra*, 161–2; Inscription on brass in church of St. John, Bristol, and cf. Great Red Book, *ut supra*, 197–8.

or money due to him, though sometimes she refused to take the responsibility of handing over the bond.[1]

Some able and energetic women ventured into foreign trade on their own account, though not often to such an extent as Margery Russell of Coventry, who was robbed of goods worth £800 by the men of Santander.[2] The customs accounts of the reign of Edward IV name seven women merchants who were probably widows, and eight others who made a few small shipments, all of them imports. Elizabeth Jakes, wife of a merchant and mayor, three years after her husband's death exported cloth and an alabaster reredos to Lisbon. Still more enterprising was the wealthy widow of Henry Chester who died in 1470. Alice lived on in High Street, and two years later arranged for the building of her new and elegant house there. Both she and her son carried on a varied business, importing iron from Spain, sending cloth to Lisbon, to Flanders, and so forth. Meanwhile she earned the gratitude of both citizens and strangers by making a crane on the Back by Marsh Gate, where there had been none before, at a cost of £41, "for the saving of merchants' goods of the town and of strangers". The accounts of All Saints record also a number of munificent benefactions made by her and her husband and their son John, "also a well-wisher in all this business". These show that she must have amassed a considerable fortune, as does the mention of her loan of £20 to the Prior of Taunton, when he was in great poverty and could neither repair his house nor pay his debts. Seven years after the building of the crane, "being in good prosperity and health of body, considering that the rood loft of the church was but single and nothing of beauty", Alice took counsel with the "worshipful of the parish and with others having the best understanding and sights in carving". Then she had made a new rood loft resting on two pillars, each with four saints in carved niches, with three principal images of the

---

[1] P.R.O., K.R. Customs Accounts, 19/14, 19/15; Early Chancery Proceedings, 63/143.
[2] A. Abram, *English Life and Manners in the Later Middle Ages* (1913), 36.

Trinity, St. Christopher and St. Michael, twenty-two images in all. Alice also had a new front carved for the altar in the south aisle, gilded the altar of Our Lady, and made an elaborate tabernacle there; and besides many vestments, altar cloths and ornaments, she gave "a cross of silver gilt enamelled with Mary and John", costing £20 and weighing sixty ounces, for hitherto the best cross had always to be used. On 16th December 1485, concludes the All Saints record, "the soul of this blessed woman departed out of this world".[1]

Alice Chester's work is to-day but a tradition hidden among the archives of All Saints, for the excellent carved work of the fifteenth century has long been broken down. Others have left more enduring memorials. The stately tower of St. Stephen's, whose pinnacles rise high above all others in the old city, was erected at the sole expense of the merchant and mayor, John Shipward, whose house stood near by. William Canynges, his yet more renowned partner in trade, shipowner, shipbuilder, and five times mayor of Bristol, splendidly completed the work of his father and grandfather beyond the city walls, earning the title of "renovator et quasi alter fundator ac inter ceteros specialissimus benefactor ecclesie de Redeclif",[2] and leaving behind him one of the last and greatest achievements of English Gothic. With no son to succeed him, since both had died young, he roused the wrath of his daughter-in-law's family by bestowing more and more of his great wealth upon the church.[3] Like the merchant saint, Godric, he "began to yearn for solitude and to hold his merchandise in less esteem than heretofore", until finally he purposed to give himself also to the church, and retired at the close of his fifth mayoral year, to become first presbyter and then dean of Westbury-on-Trym. There, in 1474, he died—"ditissimus et sapientissimus mercator villae Bristolliae".

---

[1] Cf. *supra*, 76; *The Little Red Book, ut supra*, II, 133; MSS. notes of Churchwardens' Accounts, Church of All Saints, Bristol; P.R.O., Early Chancery Proceedings, 60/62; Customs Accounts, *ut supra*, 19/1, 10a, 13, 14, 15.

[2] Great Red Book, *ut supra*, f. 247.

[3] P.R.O., Chancery Proceedings, 44/163.

The Bristol merchant was no doubt a hard-headed business man, yet the grace and perfect proportions of his buildings show that he was not lacking in appreciation of other than mere monetary values. He cared for learning and collected books, as the Book of Wills testifies. John Esterfield, merchant and mayor, left two matins books, a mass book, and a psalter; William Pavy possessed more than one missal besides a "good psalter" and legends of the saints; William Coder had many Latin books in a chest in his house, and others which he had lent to a kinsman; several merchants presented missals and psalters to their parish churches. Probably their brothers who became men of law acquired more secular books and read more widely, as did Thomas Yonge who borrowed from William of Worcester a book on ethics and "le Myrrour de dames" covered in red leather. And some of the merchants must have sent their sons to college as the Bristol glover sent his son, William of Worcester.

The merchants' local patriotism prompted them not only to endow noble churches but to appropriate a large share of the burdens of office. The government of the town was almost entirely in their hands, and all except five of the mayors between 1450 and 1490 were well-known merchants. That their duties were arduous is evident from the list of functions that had to be attended,[1] from the almost daily session of the Tolsey Court to such celebrations as those of St. Katherine's eve, when there were "drynkyngs with Spysid Cake brede" in the Weavers' Hall, and performances by the St. Katherine's players at the doors of the civic dignitaries.

Now and then they took part in the public affairs of the nation, serving in Parliament, lending ships, money or men. But only grudgingly did they contribute to the Exchequer, and in dynastic struggles they interfered little. Their loans were usually in direct relation to favours expected,[2] and on the whole they were more concerned with the ordinances of their city than with the laws of their country, which gave them little protection at home or abroad. Scant support could

---

[1] *Ricart's Kalendar, ut supra*, 80 *et seq.*   [2] See above, p. 83, n. 2.

they look for from sovereigns who, unlike their cousins of Portugal, preferred adventures in France to adventures on the sea, or who, in contrast to the rulers of Spain, encouraged pioneers only after they had proved successful.

The peace and prosperity of the city which they governed stands out in striking contrast to the disorder and misery occasioned by partisan strife elsewhere. For while the barons were wearing themselves out in the elaborately recorded Wars of the Roses, such vigorous and self-reliant men as these merchants were quietly amassing wealth and worldly wisdom. Despite England's lack of governance at home, her defeats abroad and her failure to keep the sea, these citizens, refusing to be intimidated by marauding foreigner, "overmighty subject", or Yorkist or Lancastrian army, were steadily extending their trade and commerce.

Though the volume of their trade was as yet comparatively small, their knowledge of the seas was now wider than that of either of the traditional sea-powers of Europe, who so stubbornly resisted their intrusion. For while the trade of the Italians extended from the Levant to the English Channel, and that of the Hanseatics from thence to the Baltic, and so to Norway and Iceland, the men of Bristol were acquainted with all these routes, from southern Joppa to the frozen north. Nor had they merely groped darkly round the coasts of Europe, for in sailing to Iceland they had launched out boldly across the ocean, thereby spanning a distance nearly half as great as that to the still undiscovered New World.

Their main business throughout was on the Atlantic. For Bristol's reputation as the second port in the kingdom was built up, not in a perilous and uncertain competition with Italians or Hanseatics in the Baltic or the Mediterranean, not in the traditional marts of the Netherlands, nor in the ancient wool trade with Flanders, soon doomed to extinction, but in a steady and mainly uneventful traffic on the western shores of Europe, less chronicled since less disputed. Rebuffed in the north by the arrogance of the Hanse, in the south by the exclusiveness of the long-established

Italians, inevitably they concentrated more and more on this Atlantic trade and pushed out towards the west. Not only did they rebuild successfully their ancient trade with Gascony, but, turning their backs upon Europe, they sought new outlets for their enterprise in those fabled isles lying beyond Ireland, far out in the unknown Western Ocean. In the summer of 1480 two ships, the *George* and the *Trinity*, were laden in the port of Bristol "not for the purpose of trading, but to seek and discover a certain island called the *Ile of Brasile*". The venture was a joint one, in which several Bristol merchants co-operated, amongst them being John Jay, who apparently provided one of the ships, and Thomas Croft, whose share was one-eighth in each ship. The navigation was entrusted to a Welshman, one Lloyd, "the most scientific mariner of all England". On 15th July the ships set sail, under the protection of the Virgin (*fulcando Maria*), towards the "Island of Brasylle in the western part of Ireland". For two months they sought it, till, tossed by the sea, they were driven into port in Ireland, and the news of their failure reached Bristol on the 18th September.[1]

Baffled though the Bristol merchants seemed at this moment, their failure was but the prelude to adventures of undreamed-of magnitude. For the foundations they had well and truly laid of a purely English trade upon the Atlantic, based on a flourishing industrial hinterland, and their proved readiness to venture their wealth in search of new lands, had prepared the way for achievements more notable than those of their rivals the Italians or the Hanseatics. They had already staked out a claim on the highway of the future, and it was with a true instinct that the Venetian citizen Cabot now departed from Italy and made his home in Bristol, there to find among its merchants support for his ventures across uncharted seas to the wide lands of the New World.

[1] P.R.O., K.R. Memoranda Rolls, Hil. I Hen. VII, m. 30; see W. E. C. Harrison, "An Early Voyage of Discovery", in *The Mariner's Mirror*, XVI (April 1930), 198–9; *Itineraria Symonis Simeonis, ut supra*, 153. Lloyd was then usually spelt phonetically as "Thlyde".

II

THE ICELAND VENTURE

"Of Yseland to wryte is lytill nede
Save of stokfische; yit for sothe in dede
Out of Bristow and costis many one
Men have practised by nedle and by stone
Thiderwardes wythine a lytel whylle,
Wythine xij yeres, and wythoute parille,
Gone and comen, as men were wonte of olde
Of Scarborowgh, unto the costes colde."[1]

§ I

THE ESTABLISHMENT OF THE TRADE

To the Englishman at the close of the fourteenth century Iceland was a land of myth and fable, perilously poised on the outer edge of that "sea of darkness" which encircled the whole known world. He might perhaps read in monkish books, mere echoes of ancient geographers, of how "Iceland is an isle, having on the south Norway, on the north the sea congealed"; of "white bears breaking the frozen water to draw out fishes"; and of its people "short of language, covered with the skins of wild beasts, giving their labour to fishing". He might learn also that it was reputed distant from Britain "by the sailing of three days".[2] But such reports were scarcely to be relied upon; of first-hand information he had none; for certain knowledge he must go to Norway. There in the harbour of Bergen he might see Norwegian or German traders unloading cargoes of stockfish from Iceland's newly-exploited fisheries. There he might even see that excellent ship the "Bishop's Buss", bearing Bishop William, its builder, "of venerable memory", to his

---

[1] *Libelle of Englyshe Polycye*, ed. Sir G. Warner (1926), 41.
[2] *Polychronicon Ranulphi Higden Monachi Cestrensis*, ed. C. Babington (Rolls Series, 1856–86), I, 322; cf. *Giraldus Cambrensis, Opera* (Rolls Series, 1861–68), V, 22, 25, 95.

remote see of Skálholt.[1] Then he might realize that Skálholt was a yet longer journey from Norway than it was reputed to be from Britain, though no English sailors now put this matter to the proof.

Yet there had once been a time when Iceland, geographically nearer to Ireland than to Norway, was closely linked with our own islands. It was from Ireland in very early Christian days that saints and scholars had sailed to that larger but more remote Atlantic isle, seeking sanctuary from the tumults of a changing world. Rudely they had been driven forth when the fierce Norse rovers first appeared, and in their flight they had left behind them "books, bells, and croziers". The Norsemen themselves, it is said, were in some degree indebted to the Irish for their safe arrival in Iceland, for they traversed the ocean successfully with the aid of Irish captives who, by their long sea experience, saved the lives of their captors. Ere long evangelizing zeal prompted further voyages to the Norse colonists in Iceland. Missionaries from the British Isles, such as Bishop John the Irishman, were among those who won the north once again for Christendom, and Örlyg, trained by Bishop Patrick of the Hebrides, brought to Iceland timber for a church, a church bell, and some consecrated soil. Along with the missionaries went traders, and merchant ships plied to and fro, such as one from Dublin which anchored off Snaefellness in the year 1000. In this came an enterprising lady Thorgunna, proud possessor of a large chest with "bed clothes beautifully embroidered, English sheets, a silken quilt, and other valuable wares, the like of which were rare in Iceland". The Irish were indeed pioneers in voyaging across the ocean to Iceland, though before long contacts with England became not less close. Ships from Iceland put into East Coast ports, and it was from England that the light of the twelfth century Renaissance reached Iceland. St. Thorlak, from Iceland, then studied at Lincoln, and in England his compatriot

[1] *Annales Islandici posteriorum saeculorum: Annálar 1400–1800* (Reykjavik, 1922–48), I, i.

Bishop Paul got great wisdom, and so "surpassed all other men in Iceland in courtliness and in his learning and in making of verse and in book lore". By this time Britain's horizon had widened even beyond Iceland to the far western shores of the Atlantic. Explorers of the lands of "forest and self-sown wheat" in North America had put in to Irish harbours; settlers in Greenland had traded with England. The detailed knowledge of Greenland in the thirteenth century is remarkable, and is a striking contrast to the darkness which shrouded it at the opening of the fifteenth century.[1]

For the promise of earlier days was not to be fulfilled. The bounds of the known world expanded no further but shrank. The "rich lands" beyond Greenland's barren wastes faded away into a myth. Soon the Greenland settlements also receded into outer darkness. Their settlers, isolated, struggling against the encroaching Eskimo, degenerated, lapsed into heathenism, and perhaps perished utterly. At any rate voyages thither ceased almost completely during the latter half of the fourteenth century. Iceland herself was now losing touch with the outer world, and from Britain she seems to have become completely estranged. The Icelandic annals, which carefully enumerate ships arriving from Norway, and in the next century record the visits of ships from England, are as silent as the English records of this period about any communication with our islands, save when a shipload of Scotsmen was driven inadvertently on to the coast of Iceland

[1] Dicuil, *De Mensura Orbis Terrae*, VII (see C. R. Beazley, *The Dawn of Modern Geography*, 1897–1906, I, 227); A. S. Green, *Irish History Studies*, first series (1927), 10; *Origines Islandicae*, ed. and trans. G. Vigfusson and F. Y. Powell (1905), I, 431; K. Gjerset, *History of Iceland* (1924), 26; A. Walsh, *Scandinavian Relations with Ireland during the Viking Period* (Dublin, 1922), 31; *Diplomatarium Islandicum* (Hinu Islenzka Bókmenta-félagi, Copenhagen, Reykjavik, 1857, etc.), I, 481 n.; cf. *ibid.*, II, 439, 435, 453; *Rotuli Litterarum Clausarum*, ed. T. D. Hardy (Record Commission, 1833), I, 617b, 642b; *Origines Islandicae, ut supra*, I, 463, 503; Gjerset, *op. cit.*, 100, 108; A. E. Nordenskiöld, *Facsimile Atlas till Kartografiens Åddsta Historia* (Stockholm, 1889), 52–4; Nordenskiöld, *Periplus* (Stockholm, 1897), 92; cf. sailing directions from Iceland to Greenland and to Ireland in Olaf Tryggvason's Saga (thirteenth century), *ibid.*, 101.

and "none understood their language". These annals show, also, that even between Norway and Iceland intercourse was very spasmodic during the fourteenth century, so that on more than one occasion the annalist had sorrowfully to record at the end of the year "No news from Norway to Iceland", and the Icelanders made bitter complaints of this neglect.[1]

The isolation of Iceland at the close of the fourteenth century is very evident, and her decline is as marked in the economic as in the intellectual sphere. The reasons for such isolation are less obvious, and it has given rise to many conjectures. It is certainly clear that the great days of Viking venture were ended and that Scandinavian sea-power was waning. The Icelanders especially, ever ready to bewail their desertion by others, now showed little enterprise upon the sea. Had they indeed kept up the character of sea rovers in a land almost destitute of the raw materials for ships, theirs would have been a remarkable achievement. When, therefore, they agreed to the union with Norway in 1262 they stipulated that she should send them six ships annually. Their reiterated complaints that this promise was not kept indicate clearly that, left to themselves, they were helpless, even though a bishop or a "lawman" might occasionally fare forth across the sea in his own ship.[2]

The complaints that the Icelanders sent to Norway must, however, lead us there to seek further, in the policy of their rulers and in the eclipse of Norwegian shipping also, the cause of Iceland's isolation and detachment from the rest of Europe, and in particular of the severance of the link with England. Norway, regarding Iceland merely as a potential

---

[1] Beazley, *op. cit.*, III, 455–6, 495; Gjerset, *op. cit.*, 115; H. J. Shepstone, "Solving Greenland's Historic Mystery", *Discovery*, VI, No. 71 (November 1925), 415; *Annales Islandici, ut supra*, I, i, 18. No evidence seems available today to corroborate the assertion in R. Hakluyt, *The Principal Navigations* (Everyman edition, 1907), I, 303, that Blakeney men fished off Iceland temp. Edw. III, though they certainly fished off Norway.

[2] *Diplomatarium Islandicum, ut supra*, I, No. 152; Gjerset, *op. cit.*, 230, 235; T. Thoroddsen, *Landfraeðissaga Islands* (Hinu Islenzka Bókmenta-félagi, Reykjavik, 1892–6), I, 101 *et seq.*

source of revenue, was quick to turn the union of 1262 to her own advantage. Before long, Iceland was transformed into a complete dependency, whose commerce, existing solely for the benefit of the mother country, was strictly controlled by the Norwegian kings. To facilitate such control, trade was concentrated at Bergen, which became the staple town for all dependencies and was forbidden to all but Norwegians. It finally became virtually a royal monopoly, hampered by excessive tolls, and permitted only through licence from the king, who himself owned a quarter of every ship concerned. Even the notable son of an Icelandic chieftain, named Jorsalafari on account of his adventurous travels to Jerusalem, was once arrested for voyaging to Greenland without the royal sanction.[1] Thus Iceland, destitute herself of ships, might look for assistance only from Norwegian merchants in Bergen. Had the Norwegians been still a great seafaring nation, the Icelandic trade now left in their hands might yet have prospered. But their shipping, too, was decaying, and its decline was hastened by the rise of a rival commercial power on the north coast of Germany, destined ere long to dominate the commerce of Scandinavia. Already by the fourteenth century the Hanseatic League had driven the Norwegians from the southern coasts of the North Sea and the Baltic, thrusting them back upon their own dependencies. Hence, momentarily, trade with Iceland was stimulated, and so vigorously did the Norwegians develop it, that Iceland, alarmed at the vast cargoes of fish shipped from her harbours, was moved to remonstrate that she was left without sufficient for her own consumption.[2]

---

[1] A. Bugge, *Studier over de norske byers selvstyre og handel før Hanseaternes tid*, 115 (Supplement to Historisk Tidsskrift, No. 16, Norsk Historisk Forening, Oslo, 1899); *Diplomatarium Islandicum, ut supra*, II, No. 176; *Norges Gamle Love indtil 1387*, I–III, ed. R. Keyser and P. A. Munch (Den Kongelige Norske Videnskabers Selskab, Christiania, 1846–9), III, 134, 118, 119; *Diplomatarium Islandicum, ut supra*, IV, No. 381; Gjerset, *op. cit.*, 257.

[2] A. Bugge, *Den Norske Traelasthandels Historie*, pt. 1: *Fra de aeldste Tider indtil Freden i Speier 1544* (Skien, 1928), 186 *et seq.*; Gjerset, *op. cit.*, 236; cf. *Diplomatarium Norvegicum*, ed. A. Bugge and others (1894, etc.), II, i, 235.

But the ever-encroaching Hanseatics, not content with expelling the Norwegians from the south, went on to challenge their monopoly even in Bergen, so that the restrictions on trade with the dependencies were from time to time relaxed in their favour. Slowly and steadily they undermined the naval power of Norway until her trade, even with her own colonies, languished and died. Iceland, already cut off from her former friends in Western Europe, could now look for scant succour even from Bergen, whence came no regular traffic, but only occasionally a German or Norwegian ship.[1] Thus we may seek a reason for Iceland's isolation and for her estrangement from Britain not only in the decay of the Icelanders' original spirit of enterprise, but in their political union with Norway, and in the restrictive policy which limited their trade, drew it all towards Bergen, and heavily taxed it, leaving them thus altogether stranded as Scandinavian shipping declined and was destroyed by the Hanse.

Iceland's plight was indeed pitiable when she was thus left to her own slight resources. "The desert in the ocean" is the apt description of the island by one monkish chronicler.[2] Far out to the north-west she lay, in the midst of the ocean, a solitary outpost of civilization. There, amidst a dreary waste of icy waters, rose this snow-capped volcanic tableland, girt on the north by ice-floes, and shrouded by fog till far on into the summer. Even its valleys and its meagre fringe of habitable coast, rich in green pastures when the snow had vanished, yielded little corn. The Icelanders, therefore, clung to the shore. Fish was their staple food, and with this they were bountifully provided; some cattle were kept; their clothing was made from the rough *vaðmál* woven from their own sheep's wool; but for the supply of their other needs they looked out anxiously across the ocean. From earliest times corn came to them from other lands, drift wood was

[1] Gjerset, *op. cit.*, 243 (i.e., 1343–8, 1361, 1376–80); Bugge, *Den Norske Traelasthandels Historie, ut supra*, 194 *et seq.* There is no evidence that the Hanseatics actively developed the Icelandic trade at that time.
[2] *Adamnani, Vita S. Columbae*, ed. J. T. Fowler (1920), 156.

eagerly collected by the shore, and big timber for the building of churches was laboriously brought in long ships across the ocean.[1] Thus it was, when the days of their own sea-roving were over, that they depended so much upon the visits of foreigners, and lamented so loudly when the Norwegian ships failed to arrive and the sorely needed provisions could not be obtained through Bergen. Their difficulties were aggravated in the later fourteenth century by a concurrence of natural calamities: violent volcanic eruptions, winters of exceptional severity, the Black Death and other widespread epidemics bringing famine and want in their train.

Still worse became Iceland's condition at this time, since both she and Norway came under the rule of far distant Danish sovereigns until finally these three countries, with Sweden, were formally united by the Union of Kalmar in 1397. Before long her claims, like those of Norway and Sweden, were entirely subordinated to those of Denmark, the strongest and most populous partner in the union. Brought beneath the sway of self-centred, narrow-minded strangers with no interest in her welfare, anxious only to fill their own coffers and absorbed in their own concerns, she became a prey—albeit a restless one—to the extortion of governors (hirðstjórar) appointed by aliens, and to the selfish greed of foreign bishops who "travelled through the land collecting taxes from learned as well as from laymen, whatever they could get; and under the oppression of such burdens the people had to remain". With complete indifference to her troubles, and contrary to the agreement of union, new and burdensome taxes were laid on the country and on any exports thence,[2] though no provision was made to ensure the stipulated visit of six ships annually. It was little wonder that when Bergen seemed unable to help, and the distant Danish government seemed deaf to their entreaties, the angry Icelanders were ready to ignore Bergen's monopoly, and to welcome eagerly the first foreign ships which came their way.

[1] Beazley, op. cit., II, 109; Gjerset, op. cit., 26.
[2] Norges Gamle Love, ut supra, III, 118, 119.

Not long were they to remain virtually deserted, dependent upon spasmodic visits from Bergen, and cut off from their old connections with the British Isles. For while famished Iceland was looking out anxiously for assistance, many circumstances were combining to bring about a renewal of English ventures thither, and to draw her once again within the orbit of England's trade. England, now rapidly developing as an industrial country, was seeking far and wide new markets not already captured by the cloth-makers of the Low Countries, while to feed her own people there was an increasing demand for fish, and English fishers, growing ever more venturesome, were exploring every region profitable to them, no matter what the hindrance might be. Already during the fourteenth century, while the amount of cloth sent out of England grew steadily greater, more and more codfish came into England from Norway and more and more English merchantmen went to fetch it themselves. English fishers as well as English merchants sought the coasts of Norway for fish, like certain "fishers of salt fish of Cromer and Blakeney", who carried on fishing "on the coasts of Norway and Denmark".[1]

At the same time a striking advance was being made in English shipbuilding, rendering ocean trade practicable to an unprecedented degree. The single masted vessel with its one square sail, familiar from the days of the Vikings to the fourteenth century, had by the fifteenth century developed into a two or three masted vessel more adaptable to ocean gales, with high pointed bows to resist the buffetings of a strong head sea. Such an English ship was then carved on a pew end in the new church at Lynn, a church described in 1419 as "that most beautiful chapel of St. Nicholas newly built and constructed by the alms of the benevolent". The ship has two masts; the mainmast is square rigged as of

---

[1] P.R.O., Ancient Petition, 5100 (?1383); A. Bugge, *Handelen mellem England og Norge indtil Begyndelsen af det 15de Aarhundrede* (Historisk Tidsskrift, Raekke III, Bind 4, Den Norske Historiske Forening, Christiania, 1898), 56, 83, 88.

old, but the mizzen has the new three-cornered lateen sail, recently borrowed from the Mediterranean; this greatly facilitated the working of the ship by making it possible to sail nearer to the wind. The castles built up at stem and stern are now an integral part of the ship itself, the "forecastle" being noticeably the higher of the two. The mainmast has a stalwart fighting top, and is supported by elaborate rigging coming down abaft amidships; while there are many more forestays and backstays, for greater strength, than in earlier ships.[1]

This marked development in shipbuilding, which enabled the seaman to master his vessel as never before, was perhaps even more important than the contemporary improvement of the compass. For though at first men had fared perilously across the ocean to Iceland with the aid of birds, already by the twelfth century the principle of the compass was understood in Northern Europe, and when clouds obscured the Pole Star the pilot discovered the north by rubbing a needle with a lodestone, mounting it upon a piece of wood, and floating it on the water. Alexander Neckam, writing probably before 1200, described fully the sailor's use of this magnetized needle. A century later, Hauk Erlandsson, editing the ancient *Landnámabók*, commented on the striking contrast between the improved method of steering in his own day and that of the earliest Icelandic voyages when "the sailors of the north countries had not yet any lodestone". Such a primitive device, however, though it could be used occasionally to find the direction of the Pole Star, could not be used continuously for steering, since the rubbing had to be repeated every time the needle was consulted. The really practical mariner's compass with a pivoted needle and compass card, or "Rose of the Winds", was only commonly adopted by the Italians in the fourteenth century, and was not in general use in the north until the fifteenth century.

[1] The carving, once sold by the churchwardens, is now to be seen in the Victoria and Albert Museum; cf. E. M. Beloe, *Our Borough: Our Churches: King's Lynn, Norfolk* (1899), 82–3.

Northern Europe, foremost in the use of the lodestone, lagged behind the south in superseding the lodestone and needle by the completed "compass". While the Mediterranean had with its aid been accurately mapped before the end of the fourteenth century, no comparable charts have been found for the northern seas dating before the sixteenth century. English ships were still purchasing "lodestones" in 1345, and the term was still as usual as that of "compass" was uncommon; no compass has been traced in a German ship's inventory until 1460. Fra Mauro, on his map made in 1458, wrote that the seamen of the Baltic sail "neither with chart nor with compass". The familiar reference in the *Libelle of Englyshe Polycye* (?1436) to the needle and the stone by which men found their way to Iceland can indicate only the primitive instrument, and shows that even this was resorted to only for voyages across the deeps of the open ocean. Hence the latest improvements cannot have been generally adopted in England by the opening of the fifteenth century. The mariner's compass was not, therefore, an important factor in the reopening of communication with Iceland, though its increasing use during the century must greatly have facilitated and stimulated the trade.[1]

England's progress in the art of navigation, and the enterprise of her merchants and fishers in pushing her wares into new markets and striving to open new sources of supply, might alone have taken her ships to Iceland. A more direct

[1] P. Benjamin, *The Intellectual Rise in Electricity* (1895), 113, 129; Nordenskiöld, *Periplus*, 50; W. Vogel, *Geschichte der deutschen Seeschiffahrt, I: Von der Unzeit bis zum Ende des XV Jahrhunderts* (Berlin, 1915), 520–1; *Libelle of Englyshe Polycye, ut supra*, 41. The fifteenth-century "Sea-books" of northern Europe [see e.g. *Sailing Directions for the Circumnavigation of England, and for a voyage to the Straits of Gibraltar*, ed. J. Gairdner, appended to *Tractatus de Globis, et eorum usu. Robert Hues*, ed. C. R. Markham (Hakluyt Society, No. 79, 1889); and *Das Seebuch*, ed. K. Koppmann (Niederdeutsche Denkmäler, I, Bremen, 1876)] show that in the shallow North and Baltic Seas sailors made extensive use of soundings, as Fra Mauro says; cf. Vogel, *op. cit.*, and Nordenskiöld, *Periplus, ut supra*. Some compasses were supplied to Henry V's warships, but their use seems exceptional, see L. F. Salzman, *English Trade in the Middle Ages* (1931), 242.

impetus, however, came from Norway herself, in the many hindrances to the English traffic there at the opening of the fifteenth century. All fish caught off the coasts of Norway or any of its dependencies had to be brought before export to the Staple at Bergen, where heavy dues were exacted. This restriction, tiresome though it was, was nothing new, but it now became peculiarly obnoxious owing to the rapid advance of the Hanse in Bergen. Though their privileges there had for a time been cancelled on the death of King Haakon in 1380, and the English were then able to make much progress, by 1410 the Wendish group among the Hanseatics dominated the city; pursuing a policy of arrogant exclusiveness, they now did their utmost to oust all other foreigners, whether English or Hanseatic.[1] Thus while Bergen remained the Staple and the Hanse controlled Bergen, the English could have little recognized part in the trade and fisheries of Norway or her dependencies. They therefore boldly defied the law, opened up a direct trade with Iceland, and before long became so firmly established that they could not be dislodged and the Bergen rules were perforce relaxed.

Where saints and scholars had once led the way across the ocean, braving monsters "passing dreadful", fishermen now opened anew the traffic between Iceland and the British Isles, thus re-establishing a connection older than that between Iceland and Norway. In the very year (1412) when the annalist had sorrowfully to record "No news from Norway to Iceland", a strange ship appeared off Dyrholm isle. Men rowed towards it, and there discovered "fishermen out from England". Henceforth more and more fishermen arrived. The next year "thirty or more" fishing doggers came from England to the Vestmann Isles off the south coast, and some of the crew rowed over to the mainland, twelve of them in a boat. There they sought to replenish

---

[1] Bugge, *Handelen mellen England og Norge, ut supra*, 89–90; E. R. Daenell, *Die Blütezeit der deutschen Hanse. Hansische Geschichte von der zweiten Hälfte des XIV bis zum lezten Viertel des XV Jahrhunderts* (Berlin, 1905–6), I, 151 *et seq.*

their provisions, and because they were trafficking with a people whose language they knew not, they "put down money" and took from a farmer cattle in exchange. Some wandered far, to the north and to the east, and five lost sight of their ship and were stranded for the winter.[1]

Fishers were the forerunners of merchants. These at first succeeded in obtaining the necessary licence from the new king Eric, who, with his English wife, showed himself to be favourably disposed to the English.[2] For in this same year, besides thirty or more fishing doggers, there arrived in Iceland an English merchantman, whose captain carried letters from King Eric "to the effect that he might sail with his wares into the realm without toll". Taking oath to be faithful and loyal to the land, he called at many ports including Hafnarfjördur and Horn, and rode inland to Skálholt, doing meanwhile a good trade. Thus both fishers and merchants began to desert the coasts of Norway, where so many hindrances beset them, and England and Iceland supplied each other's needs direct, ignoring the Staple at Bergen. But the next year King Eric, apprehensive perhaps of the proportions the trade was assuming, sent letters to Iceland forbidding all trade with the "outlandish men". The English, however, had already set out, armed with letters from their own king, who was himself tempted to risk a ship in the venture. This vessel, with four other merchantmen, arrrived in the Vestmann Isles in the summer of 1414, bringing letters addressed by Henry V "to the people and chief men of Iceland, to the effect that licence should be given to transact business especially that relating to the king's own ship". The Icelanders, mindful of King Eric's letter, demurred at first and spoke, like dutiful subjects, of the Staple at Bergen. But, seeing that the English would have nothing to do with that, they swallowed their scruples and did business. The next summer six English ships rode at anchor in Hafnarfjördur. On their return voyage the

---

[1] *Annales Islandici, ut supra*, I, i, 18–19.
[2] See Daenell, *op. cit.*, I, 228.

hirðstjóri himself, Vigfus Ivarsson, embarked for England, taking with him fifty lasts of dried fish and silver of great price, that he might pay his vows at the shrine of St. Thomas of Canterbury. Fogs and snowstorms took their toll, once of no less than twenty-five English ships in a single day, but traders and fisherfolk, long bred to hardship on rough northern seas, persisted in the venture, flouting openly the monopoly of Bergen.[1]

So great was the sudden influx of fishermen, and so ungoverned were they, that in 1415 King Eric was moved to write to King Henry, complaining of the damage done by them in Iceland and the adjoining islands. His letter was answered during Henry's absence in France by the Duke of Bedford, who declared that for the next year none should sail to Iceland "except in accordance with ancient custom", thus prohibiting intercourse except through Bergen. Such a prohibition provoked an immediate petition to the English Parliament, expressing indignation that "certain of Norway and Denmark" should have been endeavouring to exclude the English fishermen. The Commons declared that since the fish had forsaken their former haunts, "as is well known", the fishers had searched elsewhere and found great plenty in Iceland, where they had fished six or seven years past. It is impossible now to judge whether the difficulty in procuring fish off Norway was due, as the petition alleged, to the migration or to the extermination of the fish, or merely to the Staple restrictions of the Norwegian kings, which made it a troublesome business. At any rate the protest proved ineffectual and the prohibition was proclaimed in sixteen ports throughout the East Coast of England.[2]

[1] *Annales Islandici, ut supra*, I, i, 19–21; *Literae Cantuarienses*, ed. J. B. Sheppard (Rolls Series, 1887–9), III, 137; *Inventaire-sommaire des archives départementales antérieures à 1790. Nord: Archives Civiles, Série B, Chambre des Comptes de Lille, Nos.* 1 à 1241, ed. A. Le Glay (Lille, 1863), I, 329.

[2] *Diplomatarium Norvegicum, ut supra*, XX, pt. 1, Nos. 733, 755; *Rotuli Parliamentorum, ut et Petitiones et Placita in Parliamento*, etc. (Record Commission, 1767–77), IV, 796; *Foedera, Conventiones etc.*, ed. T. Rymer (3rd edition, The Hague, 1739–42), IV, ii, 150.

But the arbitrary decrees of distant kings, whether in London or in Copenhagen, could not actually put a stop to a business which in Iceland was equally opportune to both parties. Unable now to obtain letters from the King of Norway or from their own king, the English contented themselves with a licence procured in Iceland from the governor, and with his permission they engaged in the fisheries and bought and sold freely throughout the island. The Icelanders were not indeed particularly glad to see the English fishermen, for none of them had much to offer and some were hardy ruffians, quick to take advantage of Iceland's lack of governance. But for the English merchants they had a ready welcome. Sorely stricken by famine and want, despairing of succour from Bergen, they cared little for the decrees of an alien king. "Our laws provide," they wrote to King Eric in 1419, "that six ships should come hither from Norway every year, which has not happened for a long time, a cause from which your Grace and our poor country has suffered most grievous harm. Therefore, trusting in God's grace and your help, we have traded with foreigners who have come hither peacefully on legitimate business, but we have punished those fishermen and owners of fishing smacks who have robbed and caused disturbance on the sea." Armed with this explanation of the licences he had granted, the *hirðstjóri* now set sail for Norway, and it is perhaps significant that he did not again appear as governor. Thus the Icelanders took matters into their own hands, recognizing gladly that trade with the English was an established fact. Instead of opposing it, they strove to control and to regulate it, checking the lawlessness of the more unprincipled fishermen, and calling to account those who exceeded their privileges.[1]

Encouraged by their readiness to trade, more and more English merchants forsook Bergen for Iceland. Before long Lynn had its recognized body of "merchants of Iceland",

[1] *Diplomatarium Norvegicum, ut supra*, XX, pt. 1, No. 749; *Diplomatarium Islandicum, ut supra*, IV, No. 330.

who in 1424 elected two of their number for taxing the merchants, as did "merchants of Norway", "merchants of Prussia", and "other merchants". The owner of the "navis Roberti Holm", which was in Iceland in 1420, was probably the notable citizen of Hull, Robert Holm, merchant and thrice mayor. Bristol men were not far behind those of Lynn and Hull, though they had no previous connection with Bergen. The earliest trace of them is in the *Libelle of Englyshe Polycye*, and if we put the date of this at 1436 we may infer that they too found their way to Iceland "by nedle and by stone" about 1424.[1]

This rapid development of the Icelandic trade and fisheries naturally roused the bitter resentment of those who controlled the staple market. The English had now to reckon not merely with the disapproval of the Danish king, who, after all, could collect his dues as well in Iceland as in Norway, but with the active hostility of the Hanse merchants in Bergen. These, despite their firm hold upon the city, now saw much of its business slipping from their grasp, as the direct Icelandic trade was vigorously exploited and England ceased to demand fish from Norway. They therefore strenuously opposed all interlopers, whether English or German, and used all their influence to prevent any relaxation of the staple restrictions.

In 1420 there arrived from Denmark a new *hirðstjóri*, Hannes Pálsson, bringing with him many alien Danes. These were as unpopular as their grasping master who, with his companion Balthasar van Dammin, "made the most of the king's gift to them of that land in fief". "That", continues the annalist, "became a cause of little concord to themselves afterwards." Pálsson began not by stopping the trade, but by endeavouring to control it. He established a market in the Vestmann Islands, fixed prices, and brought to judgment those who exceeded their licences by wintering and building

---

[1] Congregation Book, I, f. 84 (Archives of the Corporation of King's Lynn); Bench Book, III, f. 95 (Archives of the Corporation of Kingston-upon-Hull); *Diplomatarium Islandicum, ut supra*, IV, No. 381; see above, 98.

houses in the islands. But Danes and English were not the only strangers in Iceland. In this same year a German, one Stephen Schellendorp, was there spying out the land. Whether he was actually an agent of the Hanse is not clear, but he certainly served their interests well. Towards the end of the trading season he wrote to King Eric of Denmark an obsequious letter, fulsome in its protestations of disinterested service. Here he declared that English merchants and fishermen had acquired so firm a footing in Iceland that, unless their voyages were stopped, the land would certainly be lost to the Danish crown. Schellendorp's specious insinuations, however, perhaps assisted the cause of the Bergen merchants less than the high-handed behaviour of some of the English. Neglected Iceland offered a fair field to adventurers of every description, and among the fishermen especially were many rascals who, emboldened by the feebleness of the administration, defied all law and order, pillaging churches and carrying off flocks and herds. Both merchants and fishers, well aware that they were interlopers, came fully armed and, when hindered in their business, showed scant respect for royal decrees or for royal officials enforcing them. Crews landed in full battle array with trumpets and flying ensigns, governors were seized and obstructing officials slain, and when Pálsson and van Dammin, after five years of office, attempted to arrest the English ships in the Vestmann Islands, they were repelled with bows and arrows, captured, and carried off to England. There in the heat of his indignation Pálsson composed a shattering indictment of the English, point by point at tedious length enumerating their crimes during his five years of office, to the number of thirty-seven.[1] It is to this almost interminable complaint of the deeply injured governor that we owe the whole of our evidence of the misdeeds of the English in Iceland during the first quarter of the century, misdeeds which have caused them without discrimination to

[1] *Annales Islandici, ut supra*, I, i, 22–4; *Diplomatarium Norvegicum, ut supra*, XX, pt. 1, Nos. 753, 749; *Diplomatarium Islandicum, ut supra*, IV, Nos. 343, 381.

be branded as the most unscrupulous of pirates.[1] Every recorded misdemeanour can be traced to this same source. It is therefore of interest to examine its allegations, with the help of the records of those English towns trading to Iceland, where the names of many of the delinquents may be found. At least half the complaints concern the same gang, many of whom prove to be mariners of Hull, where their leader, John Percy, figures not creditably in one of the unpublished Bench Books. Hull, carrying much of the merchandise of York, was itself predominantly a city of seamen rather than of merchants, as the lists of burgesses show; hence it was always more of a centre for piracy than cities such as Bristol and Lynn, with their influential bodies of responsible merchants.[2] No name which can be traced to either Bristol or Lynn figures once in the report. Most of the merchants therefore probably carried on a peaceful trade to the advantage of all concerned.

A further scrutiny of the complaints reveals the fact that out of twenty-nine specific accusations at least eighteen concern disputes with Danish officials and alleged "thefts" of fish from them. Thus it is clear that on the whole it was not the Icelanders whom the English attacked, but rather the Danish officials who endeavoured, if not to abolish the trade, to extort the exorbitant dues claimed in the name of their king. The English resistance to such alien officials, and even the kidnapping of one of them, would seem from the Icelandic annals to have been actually applauded by the Icelanders. For Hannes' voluble report may well be put side by side with the one act of violence recorded in the annals during these years. "The cloister of Helgafell despoiled and the church; the servants of Lord Hans did that." And when

---

[1] See e.g. F. Magnusen, *Om de Engelskes Handel og Foerd paa Island i det 15de Aarhundrede* (Nordisk Tidsskrift for Oldkyndighed, II. Kongelige Nordiske Oldskrift-Selskab, Copenhagen, 1833), 119; J. Espolin, *Islands Arbaekur i sögu-formi* (Islendska Bókmentafélag, Copenhagen, 1823), II, chs. 13, 14.

[2] Bench Book, *ut supra*, II, f. 246 *et seq.*; Raulyn de Bek, Robert Thorkill, J. Pasdale, etc. admitted burgesses.

Hannes was carried away in an English ship the annalist laconically concludes: "Few were sorry at that." [1]

Icelanders evidently welcomed the English traders, if not the English fishermen, and bade joyful farewells to Pálsson, yet it was the Danish Pálsson and the German Schellendorp whom the king of Denmark heeded, rather than his neglected subjects. In the same year he issued orders that all sailing to Iceland without his permission were to be called to account. Meanwhile the "Consules Bergenses" had been diligently examining Pálsson's evidence with the aid of witnesses, and they now declared that the half had not been told, but that at present they would spare their readers and forbear to relate the many other wrongs perpetrated. King Eric's warnings reached the English ports, where, early next spring when the time came for the usual voyages, merchants and mayors took counsel together. At Lynn, in a Congregation of February 1426, the decrees were read in an English translation, and the following week all the merchants frequenting Iceland were summoned to the Guildhall and there forbidden to set sail under pain of forfeiture of their goods. Ten days later an ordinance forbidding the voyage was drawn up, sealed with the consent of the majority of the Congregation, and subsequently read out by the common clerk with the letters from the Danish king.[2]

Meanwhile the captive Pálsson had lodged his voluminous indictment with the Council of England, and the Admiral, the Duke of Exeter, duly impressed, forbade the voyage to Iceland. This prohibition also was read out in a Congregation at Lynn, and the Mayor, acting upon it, a few days later arrested a boat which was about to sail for Iceland. Tense was the situation when, that autumn, a London boat put in at Lynn on its return from Iceland. John Vache, its captain, must have taunted the Lynn men for deserting Iceland so readily, for in solemn council privily held, the Mayor himself

---

[1] *Annales Islandici, ut supra*, I, i, 24.
[2] *Diplomatarium Islandicum, ut supra*, IV, Nos. 380, 386; Congregation Book, *ut supra*, I, ff. 111, 114, 115.

declared that Vache had called the Lynn merchants traitors, and Vache, before he was set free, was made to swear upon the gospels "that he never used those words".[1]

The Congregation of merchants at Lynn, who thus by a majority banned the Iceland voyage, were no doubt actuated by a desire not to provoke the Danish king, because of the old-established connection with Bergen on which the prosperity of their city largely depended. And since King Eric was now on the point of war with the Hanse, they may have hoped, by falling in with his wishes, to secure from him greater favours for themselves.[2] At Bristol, on the contrary, which had no interest to maintain in other dominions of the Danish king, there is no trace of any action taken by the city itself to enforce the prohibition, nor is there at Hull, which, as we have seen, was a city of sailors rather than of merchants. At Bristol and Hull, however, no such complete minutes of the council meetings exist, though both have records of ordinances passed.

But if some of the English thought by abandoning Iceland to strengthen their position in Bergen, they were doomed to disappointment. For in 1428 and 1429 Bartholomew Voet and his fellow pirates, aided by the Hamburg *Bergenfahrer*, plundered the city of Bergen, so that the English fled in terror. Many therefore persisted in journeying to Iceland, so that in the spring of 1429 the sheriffs were again ordered to proclaim that the Staple was at Bergen. Then the Lynn council held further debates on the matter. Those who for some years had visited Iceland begged that they might sail just once again; those who frequented Bergen and Prussia, fearing that Danish reprisals might fall upon their heads, protested, reminding the council of the ordinance of 1426. The discussion continued while those principally concerned were sent out of the room, and finally the Icelandic merchants were compelled to abandon the venture on condition that they too might traffic in Bergen. The Lynn council not only

[1] *Diplomatarium Islandicum, ut supra*, IV, No. 386; Congregation Book, *ut supra*, I, ff. 99, 103.   [2] Daenell, *op. cit.*, I, 231.

did its best to stop the voyage to Iceland, but also tried to call to account those who had misbehaved there, particularly by carrying off young Icelanders. The fate of these children has given rise to much speculation. Behaim, writing of Iceland on his globe of 1492, declared that the famished Icelanders sold their children into servitude to secure bread for those that remained. At Lynn five boys and three girls were found in 1429, and, whether they had been bought or stolen or lured away, their captors were ordered to restore them the following year. Many must nevertheless have remained to swell the number of England's foreign immigrants, such as those Icelandmen and Icelandwomen who now and again occur in the Subsidy Rolls, or those "born in Iceland" who take the oath of fealty.[1]

Next year the King of England, in conformity with the Danish ordinances, reinforced his proclamations by an Act of Parliament to regulate the Icelandic trade. The statute of 1430, after reciting the Danish king's ordinance that "all strangers coming by ship to his dominions for fish or other goods shall come to Northbern", forbade any "by the audacitie of their follie" to go elsewhere in the Danish king's dominions. A petition was immediately presented in Parliament against this "too grievous ordinance", but the petitioners had to content themselves with the assurance that the King was sending ambassadors to Denmark to treat of the welfare of the merchants. The citizens of Lynn sent further ambassadors at their own expense to discuss their difficulties at Bergen, where they still hoped to retain their trade instead of resorting to Iceland. Many were the grievances to which the English ambassadors had to listen in Denmark; vast was the compensation demanded for "twenty years'" ravages in Iceland and other colonies, such as Finmark, which the English had frequented for fish.

[1] *Ibid.*, I, 234, but the English did not entirely abandon the trade to Bergen as suggested here; Congregation Book, *ut supra*, I, ff. 200–1, 247 (incorrectly quoted in *Diplomatarium Norvegicum*); *ibid.*, ff. 147, 262; Nordenskiöld, *Periplus, ut supra*, 92; *Calendar of Patent Rolls*, 1476–85, 242, cf. 178; P.R.O., Subsidy Rolls, Lay Series, 192/99, 217/67.

These tales had the desired effect on the English envoys, who meekly did as they were bid and promised that captives should be liberated, the plundered satisfied, the relatives of the slain compensated, and also that the merchants should peacefully visit one another's lands in places not prohibited. To give the treaty a simulated appearance of reciprocity, it was solemnly added that while the English might not go to Iceland or Finmark on pain of loss of life and goods, so Danish subjects on pain of similar penalties might not visit prohibited places in England. Accordingly once again proclamation was made of the Bergen Staple throughout the ports of England, and once again the English merchants replied by complaining of their maltreatment in Bergen. Lynn sent envoys to London, and Hull sent its Mayor and another, and a complaint was laid before Parliament asserting that the king's people "be greatly impoverished and undone and in part destroyed by the king of Denmark and his lieges, because they do daily take of the subjects their goods; of the merchants of York and Hull goods to the value of £5,000 within a year, and of other lieges and merchants of England to the value of £20,000, whereof they have no remedy because none of the subjects of the king of Denmark come to England or have anything in England". The king promised to provide "convenable remedy", but the way to Bergen, the one place they might go to in the parts of the north, was evidently still fraught with difficulty.[1]

Thus the direct road to Iceland was definitely closed to all legitimate English traffic. But the English venturers who had beaten a path across the trackless ocean were not to be daunted by the decrees of a distant Danish king. Scant respect had they also for the discredited English Council,

[1] Hakluyt, *op. cit.*, I, 111; *Rotuli Parliamentorum, ut supra*, IV, 378; P.R.O., Treaty Roll, 9 Hen. VI, m. 11; Congregation Book, *ut supra*, II, ff. 1, 2, 5, 6, 7, 9, 20; Gjerset, *op. cit.*, 263; *Diplomatarium Norvegicum, ut supra*, XX, pt. 1, No. 800; *Foedera, ut supra*, IV, iv, 177; Chamberlain's Account Roll, 11 Hen. VI (Archives of the Corporation of Kingston-upon-Hull); *The Statutes of the Realm*, ed. J. E. Tomlins, J. Raithby, J. Caley, W. Elliott (1810–22), 10 Hen. VI, c. 3.

and the liberty which they could not secure by diplomacy they were prepared to win by force if necessary. Scorning the royal prohibitions, they continued to voyage to Iceland, there loading their vessels "according to their own pleasure", skilfully outwitting the royal officials whether Danish or English. Some flouted openly the monopoly of Bergen, trusting to their own wits to save them. Of such we hear only when disaster befell them. The official records of the years following 1430 are strewn with the relics of ships and their cargoes forfeited to the king, of warnings proclaimed, of commissions appointed, and of instructions to officials to imprison and forfeit. Cloth in the ship of a Coventry merchant was seized at Boston. Stockfish from Iceland was discovered at Bristol and Hull, at Cromer and Scarborough; more was probably smuggled into less obvious harbours, for commissions and proclamations concerned not only all East Coast ports from London to Newcastle, but also Devon and Cornwall, Somerset and Wales. Frequently offenders put in at Chepstow, while mariners of Fowey and of Saltash were fined for breach of the statute. Ships as well as fish were arrested, from doggers of Cromer worth £40 with fish worth nearly £100, to merchant ships of Hull or Bristol with cargoes worth from £200 to £300. Large rewards tempted stay-at-home seamen to prey upon the more adventurous. A Bristol ship home from Iceland fell a victim to two piratical ships of Newcastle, and while her cargo was handed over to the Danes, her sailors were thrown into Newgate prison, and the vessel herself was sold to the profit of the king and the men of Newcastle.[1]

[1] *Foedera, ut supra*, V, i, 132; *Calendar of Patent Rolls*, 1436–41, 232, 233, 235, 315; 1446–52, 137, 156, 175, 474; *Proceedings and Ordinances of the Privy Council of England*, ed. H. Nicolas (1834–7), IV, 208; P.R.O., K.R. Memoranda Roll, Mich. 9 Hen. VI, m. 19; Mich. 13 Hen. VI, m. 5; Mich. 15 Hen. VI, m. 20; Mich. 12 Hen. VI, m. 14; Mich. 18 Hen. VI, m. 19; Trin. 18 Hen. VI, m. 9; Mich. 19 Hen. VI, m. 27; Hil. 19 Hen. VI, m. 82; Mich. 13 Hen. VI, m. 5; Hil. 13 Hen. VI, m. 17 *et seq.*; Easter, 26 Hen. VI, m. 6; Easter, 28 Hen. VI, m. 4; Hil. 14 Hen. VI, m. 12; Hil. 18 Hen. VI, m. 82; Hil. 28 Hen. VI, m. 18; Hil. 17 Hen. VI, m. 20; P.R.O., Exchequer, K.R., Extents and Inquisitions, General Series, 143/22.

A declaration of forfeiture, however, was not always effective, and a shrewd shipowner must often have outwitted a royal official. Such a one was the cunning and audacious John Wyche of Bristol who, when himself a surveyor of customs, was evidently suspected of illegal practices, since a commission was appointed to inquire into his behaviour. His ship the *Mary* was arrested by his successor in office, John Maryot, on her return from Iceland laden with fish. The ingenious Wyche, however, forestalled the surveyor, promptly handed over all the fish to the Mayor in payment of certain debts to him, and sold the ship. The surveyor, nonplussed, appealed to Chancery.[1]

The immunity that craft and daring achieved for Wyche was won by others through wealth or influence. William Canynges, five times Mayor of Bristol, who lent large sums to the king, traded to Iceland in the *Katherine* of Bristol, owned jointly with Stephen Forster. Not only were he and Forster pardoned for this, but they were given permission to take the *Katherine* and the *Mary Redcliffe* to Iceland for four years, despite the statute.[2] Smuggling, after all, was risky. Kings, such as those of England and Denmark, were sorely in need of money. Privileges and immunities were therefore not difficult to procure, and were amply worth paying for when the return cargo from a single ship might be sold for £700 or more.[3] Thus, paradoxically, the English trade to Iceland increased rather than diminished in the years following its unsparing official condemnation by both parties. A flourishing licensed trade grew up, licensed by the King of England, the King of Denmark, or both. Fishing boats cannot be enumerated, but of actual merchant vessels there were for instance nineteen licensed in 1443, and fourteen in 1442 and 1444–5. It is improbable that so many actually sailed, but the particular customs accounts are too

---

[1] *Calendar of Patent Rolls*, 1436–41, 572; 1441–46, 274; P.R.O., Early Chancery Proceedings, 19/316.
[2] *Calendar of Patent Rolls*, 1441–6, 81.
[3] See below, 132.

fragmentary to determine this. At any rate the great bulk of the trade must have been in English hands, and Iceland, which had once begged for six ships annually, was now visited by from ten to twenty merchant ships, apart from the fishing boats. These licences, found scattered throughout the Treaty Rolls, were granted mainly to merchants of Bristol, often to merchants of Hull or of London, occasionally to shipowners of Newcastle, Dartmouth, Swansea, and Cromer, while one was for a Sandwich boat equipped by London merchants. Some are specifically to fishmongers such as Napton of Coventry, and some to stockfishmongers such as Robert Weston of London and Curteys of London.[1]

The most singular, and the earliest, licences granted by the English king were those to certain of his own subjects doomed to live in Iceland with neither bread, wine, beer, nor cloth fit to dress themselves and their servants.[2] For the Danish synod appointed at least two Englishmen as bishops, perhaps because they hoped they might keep their obstreperous countrymen in order, or because no Dane or Norwegian was eager to be thus ostracized; or was it that the Englishmen in question had sufficient influence to obtain a post with lucrative possibilities? Icelandic priests at this time were men of little education, and, with a few striking exceptions, the bishops, most of them foreigners, seem to have been more careful to supply themselves with beer than their flocks with instruction. English merchants were quick to take advantage of their need, and it was on the pretext of supplying the bishops that the first licensed trade, dating from 1427, was inaugurated. Between 1427 and 1440 four licences were given to Bishops of Hólar and three to Bishops of Skálholt. John Johnson, for instance, an Englishman by birth, was appointed bishop of the northern diocese of Hólar in 1427.[3]

[1] P.R.O., Treaty Rolls, *passim*; for Sandwich see *ibid.*, 36 Hen. VI, m. 6; for Coventry, *ibid.*, 38 Hen. VI, m. 12; 1 Edw. IV, m. 10; *Calendar of Patent Rolls*, 1436–41, 58.
[2] *Foedera, ut supra*, V, i, 75.
[3] C. Eubel, *Hierarchia Catholica medii aevi* (Librariae Regensbergianiae Monasterii, 1901), II, 183.

Before his departure for his see he secured permission to buy
in England 1,000 qrs. of wheat and 500 qrs. of malt or
barley for his beer, and to transport them to Iceland from
Lynn, Hull, or Newcastle. Accompanied by two priests he
then set sail in an English ship and duly arrived at Hafnarfjördur on the west coast. There the documents brought with
him were read in a general council, but when he pursued
his way northwards the inhabitants looked askance upon him,
he quickly lost heart, and without even seeing his cathedral
see set sail again the same summer, after ordaining four
priests and some deacons. The following year he paid one
more flying visit, which seems to have been his last, and
commended the bishopric to John Williamson, also probably
an Englishman.[1] English venturers of the baser sort must
have hailed with delight the arrival of such compatriots.
Once when in difficulties they fled into the cathedral of Hólar.
Bishop Williamson kept at bay their pursuers, declared them
to be in sanctuary, and drew up a document to the effect that
he had purchased half their ship the *Bartholomew*, then
lying off Skagafjörd, for twelve lasts of fish, so that she
might now proceed to England under the solemn protection
of the holy see. Bishop Williamson, when translated to
Skálholt in 1435, continued his trading enterprises as a
means of satisfying his creditors, and secured licences for
this purpose both in 1436 and 1438. When his ventures
failed, ruin faced him, if we are to believe the story told in
Chancery by John Richeman, citizen and stockfishmonger
of London. The bishop, being in debt to the merchant,
"gatte a licence" to send to Iceland wheat, wine, and other
victuals and merchandise, and ordained Richeman his
deputy so that the debts might be satisfied. But the ship, duly
freighted, was taken treacherously by the pilot to Ireland
instead. Richeman, in fear of his life, escaped thence to
England, and the bishop "hearing of the disposition above-
said sorrowed greatly, because he knew and well understood

---

[1] *Calendar of Patent Rolls*, 1422–9, 394; *Annales Islandici, ut supra*, I, i,
24–5; Magnusen, *op. cit.*, 119.

that he had not the wherewithal to live here. And he was taken in of alms into 'St. Thomas Spitell' in Southwark, and there died." [1]

Other bishops were entirely non-resident and lived on the profits of the see, paying their creditors with licences to trade to Iceland. Such was John Bloxwich, Williamson's English successor at Hólar. Declaring that he feared exceedingly to visit his diocese on account of the great perils by sea and by land, in 1436 he appointed a Hull merchant to bring him thence news—and no doubt wealth. In the following year he commissioned Robert Weston, stockfishmonger of London, for the same purpose, and in 1438 he procured another licence to send two ships to Iceland with foodstuffs and to bring back the first-fruits, lest the papal bulls, held in pledge by certain London merchants, should be returned to Rome.[2]

Nor was it only bishops of English birth who were in close touch with England. John Geriksen, a former archbishop of Upsala, had been dispatched for his unlawful deeds to Skálholt, there to dwell in "a remote land among people well nigh barbarian". He wintered in England and started thence for his diocese in 1430. Two priests went with him, one of whom soon took to trading and returned to England in the same year with stockfish of the bishop's, "for he was a great gatherer of stockfish and other things". With the bishop was also a retinue of thirty serving men; these pretended to be Danes but were in reality Irishmen, so turbulent that the bishop "ruled them little or not at all". These strange followers brought small credit to the Church. They seized the chief men of Iceland and put them in irons, and the bishop was further discredited by one Magnus who, as some said, was his son. Magnus wooed Margaret,

---

[1] *Diplomatarium Norvegicum, ut supra*, XX, pt. 1, No. 790; Eubel, *op. cit.*, II, 255; *Calendar of Patent Rolls*, 1436–41, 32; P.R.O., Early Chancery Proceedings, 43/278.

[2] *Calendar of the Entries in the Papal Registers relating to Great Britain and Ireland: Papal Letters*, VIII, A.D. 1427–47, ed. J. A. Twemlow (1909), 499; P.R.O., Treaty Roll, 14 Hen. VI, m. 9; *Calendar of Patent Rolls*, 1436–41, 58, 140, 224.

sister of Ivar Vigfusson, and, receiving little encouragement, led a raid on Kirkjubaer and set fire to the town. In the skirmish Ivar was killed. Margaret declared that she would wed none but the man who avenged her brother, and the challenge was taken up by Thorvard Lopt. Riding with an army upon Skálholt, he followed the bishop into his cathedral, seized him as he stood clad in his vestments before the altar, dragged him to the river, and there drowned him with coils of ropes weighted with stones. Yet so accustomed were the Danes to attributing all harm to the English, that in the treaty signed a year earlier the English had actually been made to promise amends for damages to this very bishop and his followers.[1]

§ 2

THE TRADE AT ITS HEIGHT

So the trade went on into the middle years of the fifteenth century, actively and profitably. Even the Danish king was compelled by its very magnitude to recognize it. And though he still strove to insist that each ship must have his licence, the matter of the Bergen Staple was tacitly ignored. Rivals as yet were few. The traces of other foreign competitors during the first half of the century are slight. The *Holy Ghost* of Schiedam sailed for Iceland in 1431, but she carried an English cargo from Hull; eight years later the *Marie Knight* of Amsterdam took fish from Iceland to Ireland. German merchants are first heard of in 1431, when the Althing forbade both English and Germans to winter in Iceland. But their advance was delayed by the exclusiveness of the Bergen merchants, who insisted in their own interests that the Hanse should forbid the direct voyage to Iceland from any of the German cities; not till the second half of the century is there evidence of great Hanseatic acitivity in the

---

[1] Eubel, *op. cit.*, I, 479; *Annales Islandici, ut supra*, I, i, 56-7. F. Jónsson, *Historia Ecclesiastica Islandiae* (Havniae, 1772-4), II, 471 *et seq.; Diplomatarium Norvegicum, ut supra*, XX, pt. 1, 800.

trade. Thus the commerce of Iceland came completely under English control, though there was no sign that the English proposed, as Schellendorp insinuated, to follow this up by annexing the island. Indeed the enfeebled English government was then more disposed to relinquish than to acquire overseas possessions, and merchants had to expect from the State not encouragement but obstruction.[1]

Great was the congregation of English off the coasts of Iceland every summer—big trading vessels bound perhaps for France during the following winter,[2] with merchants or their factors on board; little doggers with adventurous fishermen whose furthest goal had hitherto been Norway. Round the Vestmann Isles in particular they clustered, "where is the best fishing of all Iceland". There, it was reported to the Danish king, "they build houses, erect tents, dig up the ground, and carry on fishery as if it were their own property".[3]

The fishing doggers, small though they were, were greatly superior to those of the Icelanders, who had but "the smallest skiffs (*scaphas*) because there is scarcely any wood suitable for ships". Hence before long the English had almost entirely wrested the fishing industry from the Icelanders. Early in the sixteenth century the Althing was moved to complain of this, explaining that with their larger boats the English could fish at a greater distance from the shore, with long lines and many hooks fastened upon them, and thus prevented the approach of the fish nearer inshore, so that the Icelanders waited in vain in their little boats. As to the exact size of the doggers, and the amount which they caught, we

---

[1] P.R.O., Exchequer, K.R. Customs Accounts, 61/32; *Calendar of Patent Rolls*, 1436–41, 270; *Diplomatarium Norvegicum, ut supra*, XX, pt. 1, No. 789; *Hanserecesse*, 1431–76. Zweite Abtheilung, I–VII, ed. G. von der Ropp (Verein für Hansische Geschichte, Leipzig, 1876–92), II, i, 318; E. Baasch, *Die Islandfahrt der Deutschen, namentlich der Hamburger, vom* 15 *bis* 17 *Jahrhundert* (Forschungen zur hamburgischen Handelsgeschichte, No. 1, Hamburg, 1889), 6–8.

[2] P.R.O., K.R. Customs Accounts, 19/10.

[3] *Diplomatarium Islandicum, ut supra*, IV, No. 381.

have little information. The men of Cromer and Blakeney, it is true, had pleaded that their vessels were so small—"about 10 or 12 or at most 18 tuns"—that they could not carry horses across the channel for the king, but less biased corroboration of this small figure is not forthcoming. At any rate one dogger could carry 15 lasts of stockfish valued at nearly £100. Whatever its size, every dogger had to take, besides from five to ten fishermen, a good store of provisions for the whole summer, since Iceland could scarcely be depended upon for these. Many a fifteenth century ship must have been equipped like that of Henry Tooley, which early in the sixteenth century was stocked with barrels of beer and meal, flitches of bacon, salt fish, a barrel of beef, a firkin of butter, and some herrings. The 18 weys of salt and the 3200 hooks which, besides warlike weapons, completed his equipment, tell much of the methods of the business. For the English were pre-eminently "fishers of salt fish", and as the fishing continued salting proceeded busily also, so that at the end of the season the mariners might hope to return with all their original cargo of salt absorbed into merchandise—salted codfish, ling, or keling, which found a ready sale at home in October and November.[1]

A case recorded in the Memoranda Rolls pictures vividly what must have been a possible if not an actual happening.[2] Thomas Erlyngham, accused of trading illegally with Iceland, tried to account for the quantity of salt fish in his ship by relating that he sent her under John Dickinson with eight other mariners, fishers, and servants, "on to the high seas towards the north for fishing and taking fish to salt". From 20th May till 4th September they were out on the sea fishing, and diverse fish "called lyng and kelyng" were

[1] *Ibid.*; Baasch, *op. cit.*, 58; Ancient Petition, 5100; P.R.O., K.R. Memoranda Roll, Mich. 19 Hen. VI, m. 27; Henry Tooley's Account Book, f. 99 (Archives of the Corporation of Ipswich; transcript lent by V. B. Redstone, Esq.); *Rotuli Parliamentorum, ut supra*, IV, 79. For the number of men carried see below, and cf. many refs. in *Annales Islandici*, K.R. Memoranda Rolls, etc.

[2] P.R.O., K.R. Memoranda Roll, Easter, 9 Hen. VI, m. 13.

taken "to the use of Thomas" and salted. Such, if not actual
fact, was very likely the common custom of fishers of salt
fish, very similar to that of the more recent Bretons as
vividly described in Pierre Loti's *Pêcheurs d'Island*. Erlyngham scarcely explains satisfactorily the presence of a large
quantity of stockfish by an alleged transaction upon the high
seas with certain famished foreigners, who bartered their
stockfish for the Englishman's victuals. Evidently he had
landed in Iceland and done business there. In fact the
distinction between fishermen and merchants was often an
impossible one. If the fishermen took more food than they
actually needed, they could be sure of a ready sale for it in
Iceland, in return for an addition to their own cargo of
fish. Such a practice became so widespread that it had
to be specifically prohibited by Henry VII. In attempting to
regulate the fishing he insisted that the doggers should find
surety "that they will only have grain for their victualling".[1]

The fishing doggers which congregated off Iceland each
summer were drawn from a wide area, but predominantly
from the East Coast of England. A Cromer fisherman,
Robert Bacon, is said to have "discovered Iceland" early in
the fifteenth century,[2] and the assertion is not improbable.
For fishers of Cromer and Blakeney were, as is shown above,
among those who frequented the coasts of Norway, and a
Cromer dogger certainly visited Iceland in 1439, though
possibly not for fishing. Cromer mariners were also in
Iceland in 1433, and in 1438 Roger Fouler of Cromer
freighted for Iceland a ship of which he was the master,
owned by Adam Horn of Cley. Cromer was closely linked
with Cley and Blakeney, into whose harbours its boats
frequently came, and shipmen of both these ports were
acquainted with Iceland. Norfolk fishing doggers may also
have gone thither from Burnham and Dersingham, for these
then flourishing havens were included in a proclamation of

---

[1] *Paston Letters*, ed. J. Gairdner (1900–8), No. 367.
[2] F. Blomefield, *An Essay towards a Topographical History of the County of
Norfolk* (contd. by C. Parkin, 1805–10), VIII, 104.   No authority is given.

1415 against visiting Iceland for fishing. The same proclamation was made in sixteen East Coast ports from
Newcastle to Orwell, including the fishing centres of Whitby,
Grimsby, and Scarborough. At least one Scarborough boat,
owned jointly by a Londoner and a Scarborough man, "went
out of the Humber to Iceland" in 1437, and the *Libelle*
implies that this was not the first time that Scarborough
fishermen had visited Iceland. Suffolk also probably sent
its doggers to Iceland. Such of its local records—account
books of Dunwich, Southwold, and Walberswick—as
Thomas Gardner discovered in private hands when he wrote
his *Historical Account of Dunwich* in 1754 seem now to have
vanished. But if we may trust Gardner's quotation, Walberswick at any rate had "13 barks trading to Iceland, Farra, and
the North Seas" in 1451, and by 1509 William Godell of
Southwold left in his will all his ships "that be in Iceland".[1]
Some of these fishermen visited other far northern dependencies of Denmark, such as the Faroë Islands and that most
northerly of all Norway's domains, Finmark, where still
to-day fishermen gather round the Lofoten Isles. Finmark
is almost always mentioned with Iceland in decrees and
prohibitions, and in 1439 four mariners were pardoned for
sailing there in the *Nicholas* of Saltash.[2] Clearly the Cornish
fishermen did not leave the exploitation of the Norwegian
fisheries entirely to their more conveniently situated brethren
on the East Coast of England.

The greater merchant vessels, taking English goods to
barter in Iceland for stockfish, sailed usually from Bristol,
Hull, or Lynn. East Coast ports, with old-established stock-

[1] For Cromer, see P.R.O., K.R. Memoranda Rolls, Mich. 19 Hen. VI,
m. 27; Mich. 12 Hen. VI, m. 14; Hil. 18 Hen. VI, m. 82; for Cley and
Blakeney, see e.g. *ibid.*, Mich. 19 Hen. VI, m. 27, and Exchequer, K.R.,
Extents and Inquisitions, General Series, 143/22; for Burnham and Dersing-
ham, see *Foedera, ut supra,* IV, ii, 150; for Scarborough, see K.R. Memoranda
Roll, 25 Hen. VI, m. 38; for Suffolk, see T. Gardner, *An Historical Account of
Dunwich, Anciently a City* (1754), 145, 248; cf. E. R. Cooper, *A Brief
History of Southwold Haven* (1907), 4.
[2] Gardner, *op. cit.*, 145, "Farra"; *Diplomatarium Islandicum, ut supra,* IV,
No. 381; *Calendar of Patent Rolls,* 1436–41, 232, 234, 235.

fishmongers and "stockfish rows",[1] hard hit by the collapse of business with Bergen, were naturally foremost in developing the possibilities of Iceland. Lynn, with its group of "merchants of Iceland", was already deeply involved in the first quarter of the century. And though later on its merchants were forbidden to traffic there and never sought licences from the English king, it would seem from Danish accusations that they cannot have entirely abandoned the enterprise. Hull was a more active centre. Here the Iceland trade became a civic venture, and in the time of Edward IV the city regularly freighted three or four ships for Iceland in the name of "the mayor and burgesses". London merchants and stockfishmongers seem also to have preferred the shipping of Hull to their own, and it was seldom that a merchantman of London or of other eastern ports such as Newcastle sailed for Iceland. Merchants of inland cities, such as Thomas Napton, fishmonger of Coventry, traded likewise with Iceland, using the ships sometimes of East Coast ports, but sometimes of Bristol. For Bristol, though it had no previous dealings in stockfish, rapidly acquired an ascendancy in the Iceland trade. Its name is singled out for mention in the *Libelle of Englyshe Polycye*; its pilots were in demand for the voyage thither; Bristol men, it was persistently rumoured abroad, were responsible for subsequent outrages in Iceland; and an account of Iceland, said to have been written by Columbus after a visit there in 1477, describes how the English came with their merchandise, "especially those of Bristol".[2] The arrival of Bristol merchants is not surprising. For though, unlike the East Coast ports, Bristol had no previous con-

---

[1] *The Heart of Lynn*, ed. H. Ingleby (1925), xvi.
[2] P.R.O., K.R. Customs Accounts, 62/7; Treaty Roll, 1 Edw. IV, m. 10; K.R. Memoranda Roll, Mich. 9 Hen. VI, m. 19; Early Chancery Proceedings, 43/278; *Hansisches Urkundenbuch*, ed. K. Höhlbaum, K. Kunze, W. Stein (Halle and Leipzig, 1876–1907), IX, 467 *et seq.*; B. F. De Costa, "Inventio Fortunata. Arctic Exploration with an account of Nicholas of Lynn" (*Bulletin of the American Geographical Society*, New York, 1881), 14; cf. *Itineraria Symonis Simeonis et Willelmi de Worcestre*, ed. J. Nasmith (1778), 262.

nection with Bergen, Iceland was politically only, and not geographically, an appendage of Norway. Medieval cartographers might indeed depict it clinging close to Scandinavia, but in reality Iceland lies far out to the west in the North Atlantic, and it was Bristol, not Hull or Lynn, which looked out towards the Atlantic and was familiar with its coasts from the west of Ireland to the south of Spain. Like Ireland in early Christian days Bristol now became closely connected with Iceland, while Irish ships also revived their ancient trade to the north-west, taking goods not only of their own countrymen, but of Englishmen such as the merchants of Chester. Indeed the voyage from Ireland to the chief havens of Iceland in the south-west was more direct than that from Hull, and Bristol sailors, in close touch with Ireland, could easily follow it. Most probably they took their customary way to the thriving ports of Western Ireland, and thence directed their course across the ocean to Iceland. It is unlikely that they chose the inner route by the Irish Sea, for here they would have to contend with the perplexing rocks and currents of that "*mare Hybernicum ferocissimum et periculosissimum*", as well as with the Scottish pirates who infested the narrow channel through which their heavily laden ships must pass. On the time spent in the journey no exact evidence is available. "Five days sail" was the mariner's reckoning from Iceland to Ireland in the thirteenth century, before the days of practical compasses. A Bristol ship of the fifteenth century, given a favourable wind, should certainly have reached Iceland within a week.[1]

The cargo carried by these merchant ships was rich and varied, and might be valued by the customers at as much as £500. Its contents appear not only from the customs lists but also from the interesting edict made in Iceland in 1420, soon after the first coming of the English, regulating the "merchant meeting there by law established between

[1] *The Statutes at Large, passed in the Parliaments held in Ireland*, I (Dublin, 1765), 697; *Itineraria Symonis Simeonis, ut supra*, 4; Nordenskiöld, *Periplus, ut supra*, 101.

English and Icelandic men who have come in good peace".[1]
This gives a vivid picture of the trade, for it fixes the price
of each imported commodity in terms of fish. Food in plenty
the English had brought to famished Iceland. Almost at the
head of the list come barrels of wheat and meal, butter,
honey, and wine, malt for the Icelanders' beer, and beer
itself. Minerals also the Icelanders lacked; they had little
iron, and that only of poor quality and, through lack of fuel,
they possessed no smelting furnaces. Hardware was therefore as acceptable as food. Indeed certain Icelanders, like
Pacific Islanders of a later date, were even accused of taking
the nails from the boards of the English ships.[2] Now they
might buy not only nails but iron and manufactured articles,
such as swords and knives, pots and pans, or copper kettles.
There were combs, probably for the weavers, while horse-
shoes must have met a crying need in a country so dependent
on the horse. Wood could also be bought, which Iceland
needed almost as much as iron, also pitch and tar, wax and
salt. Articles of attire were there displayed for the delectation
of both the men and the women of Iceland—hats and caps,
shoes and cheaper shoes for the women, girdles, gloves, and
purses. But the chief business of all was evidently done in
lengths of cloth and linen. These take prior place in the list
of commodities, and the customs show that usually not less
than a third of the value of a ship's cargo was in English or
Welsh cloth, and Irish, Breton or Flemish linen. From this
it is evident that there was some degree of comfort among
certain classes in Iceland, since her land already produced a
coarser cloth of its own, called *vaðmál*. This had been
exported in considerable quantities in earlier days, and had
evidently been one of the country's chief sources of wealth,
since money and taxes were estimated in it.[3] Amongst many
"small wares", trifles whose price could be "according to
agreement", were needles and thread, pins by the thousand,

---

[1] *Diplomatarium Islandicum, ut supra*, IV, No. 337.
[2] *Diplomatarium Norvegicum, ut supra*, XX, pt. 1, No. 784.
[3] Gjerset, *op. cit.*, 206.

lacing points, yarn for the fishermen's nets, and at least one consignment of paper. Thus the English ships were almost universal providers for the Icelanders, and must have stocked many a pedlar's pack.

In contrast to such diversity the Englishman's demands were monotonous. It was fish that he had come to seek, and indeed Iceland had little else with which to tempt him. "For three fish" he would give a pair of women's shoes, "for fifteen fish" a firkin of honey. And though he might occasionally take back *vaðmál* or hides or oil, he left it to the Germans to develop later the export of these and of other lesser products such as falcons, sulphur, and eiderdown. Fish meant principally the hard dried codfish—"*piscis durus vocatus Stockfyssh*"—sometimes alluded to by the Latin *strumulus*. For it was from the cod and his kindred in the extreme north of Europe that fishmongers supplemented their inadequate supplies from nearer waters, in days when, with a strict observance of Lent throughout Western Europe, fish was no luxury but a necessity. There came also in smaller quantities hake, pollack, and salmon, still plentiful in the rivers of Iceland, with herring and unspecified "saltfish". The total value of these return cargoes of fish was, according to the customs valuation, anything up to £600, and, according to the prices they would fetch in England, anything up to £1,000 or more. Aptly does that merchant's handbook, *The Noumbre of Weyghtes*, sum up the variety of Iceland's imports and the sameness of her exports: "The cheffe merchaundyse in Iseland ys Stokefysch and Wodemole and oyle; and good merchaundyse from hens thedyr the course Ynglysche clothe coloured, mele, malte, bere, wyne, Salettes, gauntlettes, longeswerdes, lynon cloth and botounes of sylver, ambyr bedes, knyves and poyntes, Glasses and Combys, etc." [1]

The Iceland trade, unlike most other English enterprise

---

[1] Baasch, *op. cit.*, 78 *et seq.* See Early Chancery Proceedings, 43/278, and J. Thorold Rogers, *A History of Agriculture and Prices in England* (1866–1902), III, 310, IV, 540 *et seq.*; *The Noumbre of Weyghtes* (B.M. MS. Cotton, Vespasian E. ix), f. 99.

of the time, was closely defined by the seasons. In early spring, between February and April, ships usually left England. Throughout the summer they remained in Iceland while the market was open and goods were bought and sold. Between July and September they returned home, making but one voyage thither in the year. Thus John Gough, captain of the *Ive*, was laden ready to leave Bristol on 14th February 1479, and on 18th July arrived home again with his cargo of fish. But this did not complete his work for the year. For as autumn came on the *Ive* set sail again, this time through less inhospitable seas, to reach Bordeaux in time for the vintage. Some merchants attempted to remain in Iceland, thus setting up permanent places of business, but this was forbidden at the outset by the Icelandic authorities, and those who came "in the right merchant manner" disposed of their wares during the summer, and left before winter tempests came on. Now and again, however, when all the wares had not been sold, one or two factors were left behind with them until the following summer. Thus certain merchants from Drogheda left two of their number, Abbot and Wild, behind, promising to fetch them the next year. Abbot complained later in Chancery that no one had come to rescue him, that as a result he had become ill, his servant had died, and his goods had been forfeited "by the rule of that land". It was little wonder that when certain Englishmen began to build themselves houses in the Vestmann Islands the Icelanders renewed their prohibitions against wintering in Iceland, intent on avoiding a permanent colony of such vigorous foreigners in their land.[1]

§ 3

THE DECLINE OF THE TRADE

The commercial dominance of England over Iceland was, however, to proved shortlived. The second half of the

[1] P.R.O., K.R. Customs Accounts, 19/13; *Statutes at Large . . . Ireland, ut supra*, I, 697; *Diplomatarium Norvegicum, ut supra*, XX, pt. 1, No. 789.

fifteenth century witnessed the loss of much that had been gained in the first half, until in the sixteenth century England was to lose her supremacy in the trade, though not in the fisheries.

The distracted condition of English politics, the dynastic struggles which made firm government impossible, proved almost as disastrous to merchants as to barons. Already before 1450 the liberty of sailing to Iceland had become the sport of factions, a mere pawn in the political game. Rival barons, struggling to maintain their ascendancy, used it as a bribe with which to make surer the allegiance of the wealthy middle-class. Just as in 1440 they abolished the privileges of foreigners in England, thus satisfying the clamour of the native merchants, so too they multiplied licences to sail to Iceland, "notwithstanding any Act to the contrary". The Iceland voyage became a reward for political services in the sordid strife at home, so that when in 1461 Edward IV had triumphed at Towton and had been crowned king in London, in the closing months of that year he granted licences for no less than sixteen ships, a record for this century. One was to a servant of his ally the Earl of Warwick, and another for an exceptionally large ship "of 800 tuns or less", to be equipped by supporters of his among the merchants of Bristol. A few years later, after the final victories of Hedgeley and Hexham in the north, Warwick's younger brother received, in addition to his title of Earl of Northumberland, a licence for one of the biggest ships of Hull.[1] Thus England's mercantile policy ceased to be directed by any definite principle save that of political expediency, but was sporadically dictated by the immediate interests of the dominant party of the moment.

But civil strife in England was not the only foe of the Iceland merchants. For just when they were abandoning hope of support at home, their Hanseatic opponents overseas, intent on maintaining the Bergen Staple, were steadily strengthening their influence over Iceland's rulers. Earlier in the century Denmark had been at war with the Hanse,

---

[1] P.R.O., Treaty Roll, 1 Edw. IV, mm. 15, 27; 4 Edw. IV, m. 2.

and had been only too ready to grant privileges to the English in return for their aid, but since 1435 the two powers had been at peace. The Danish kings, destitute themselves of naval strength, henceforth came more and more to rely on the support of the Hanse, especially of the Wendish group which monopolized Bergen, until gradually they were mere pliant instruments in its hands.[1] So close were the connections between the two powers that a rupture with the one almost inevitably involved a rupture with the other, and it is often impossible to distinguish under whose immediate orders ships of the Hanse were acting. Yet the attitude of the Danish kings towards the Icelandic trade was directed not merely by their subservience to the Hanse. Their need of money was as great as their need of the Hanseatic fleet, and even prompted Christian I to pawn the Orkney and Shetland Islands. Hence the Bergen Staple was to them primarily a means of collecting their exorbitant dues, and when it proved impossible thus to confine the trade, their chief concern was to insist on the payment of the dues in Iceland itself. At the same time, like the English kings, they too were readily tempted to make profit out of licences for the evasion of the Staple.

The interaction of these various forces on the progress of the Icelandic trade is clearly apparent in the early years of Christian I's reign. Within a year of his accession in 1448 England resumed her war with France and, since Burgundy was now pro-French, the outlook for trade seemed dark. She was therefore particularly anxious to strengthen her position in Scandinavia and the Baltic, and accordingly in 1449 came to terms with Denmark. The Danish king insisted, in the interests of the Bergen Staple, that she should again renounce the direct voyage to Iceland, as in the treaty of 1432, but promised in return a safe conduct to England's merchants throughout his realms. This truce, which was to last till 1451, was ratified in England in 1450, and commissions were set up

[1] W. Stein, *Die Hanse und England beim Ausgang des hundertjährigen Krieges* (Hansische Geschichtsblätter, Band XXVI, Lübeck, 1921), 94–6.

to inquire into infractions of it. Christian I, on his part, gave effect to it by a decree at his coronation that "all Englishmen and Irishmen who sail to Iceland without our letter and seal shall be outlawed and their goods forfeited". At the same time, despite the Staple regulations, he granted licences to both John Wolffe and William Canynges (in 1449 and 1450) to trade freely to Iceland. That of Canynges at any rate was endorsed by the English king, in consideration of his "notable and faithful services especially when lately Mayor of Bristol, to his great labour and expense".[1]

The settlement, however, was of short duration. The truce was not renewed in 1451; already by a desperate act of piracy England had antagonized the Hanseatics and driven them to reprisals, and by 1452 Denmark had followed their lead, broken with England, and closed the Sound. With the opening of civil war in England any attempt to control the trade was practically abandoned. Merchants seldom troubled to beg a licence from a king over whose custody rival barons were warring, for ships were seldom forfeited. The king of Denmark, meanwhile, was involved in a costly war with Sweden, and could do little beyond publishing a decree to control the affairs of his outlying provinces. The dues that should have been paid in Bergen were not collected in Iceland, and his resentment grew with his losses through the unlicensed trade. Angry with England, he made an alliance with France, and wrote to the king of Aragon of "new dissensions over Iceland with the king of England".[2]

Nor was there much hope of regularizing the trade even when civil war in England was over. For Edward IV was

---

[1] *Foedera, ut supra*, V, ii, 23, 26; P.R.O., Treaty Roll, 28 Hen. VI, m. 2; 29 Hen. VI, mm. 12 14; Macray, W. D., *Report on the Royal Archives of Denmark and Further Report on Libraries in Sweden* (Deputy Keeper of the Public Records, Forty-fifth Annual Report, Appendix 2, No. 1, 1885), 5; *Calendar of Patent Rolls*, 1446–52, 479, 528; *Diplomatarium Islandicum, ut supra*, V, No. 142.

[2] F. Schulz, *Die Hanse und England von Edwards III bis auf Heinrichs VIII* (Zeit. Abhandlungen zur Verkehrs- und Seegeschichte, V, Berlin, 1911), 98; *Diplomatarium Islandicum, ut supra*, V, No. 142.

fatally hampered in his action by his indebtedness to both English merchants and their rivals the Hanseatics, who had helped him to the throne. The Hanseatics and their sub-servient ally Denmark were not likely to consent to any abandonment of the claims of Bergen, while those English merchants who had been to Iceland would not readily submit to a curtailment of their freedom. Hence Edward prevaricated. Just as he renewed the privileges of the Hanseatics in England, so he made also a treaty with Denmark, like those of his predecessors, to the effect that "no English subject should go to Iceland without having asked and obtained the special licence of the king of Norway, on penalty of life and goods, nor to Halgoland or Finmark, unless driven thither by stress of weather". But at the same time he placated the English merchants by granting licences abundantly for the evasion of the Staple. Likewise the Danish king forbade Iceland to English merchants generally, but furtively helped his depleted exchequer by selling licences to individuals to go there.[1]

The continuation of such an anomalous state of affairs, when trade was prohibited but permissible by special licences procured for a consideration from needy kings, inevitably stimulated smuggling. Smuggling, moreover, was comparatively easy in a country such as Iceland, languishing for lack of governance, particularly when the king's repre-sentative was waylaid on the high seas by pirates from Scotland, and for some years held prisoner. But so soon as the Danish king turned his attention seriously to Iceland itself and made a resolute effort to collect his dues and to bridle the interlopers, a clash was bound to come. In 1463 strict in-junctions were sent to Iceland that, since the crown's rights had been much diminished, no trade was to be done with foreigners who did not pay the heavy dues levied on Icelandic goods imported from Norway. The governor, Björn Thorleifsson, now freed from captivity, arrived in Iceland

---

[1] Macray, *op. cit.*, 5; P.R.O., Treaty Roll, 6 Edw. IV, m. 13; 4 Edw. IV, mm. 2, 4, 24; 5 Edw. IV, mm. 4, 7, 8, 19; 6 Edw. IV, mm. 3, 15 *et seq.*

determined to exert his authority. But his activity proved his ruin, and once again, in 1467 as in 1425, the position of the English was jeopardized and odium cast on all their merchants, legitimate or otherwise, by a flagrant act of piracy. For when Björn arrived with a large escort in Rif, where the English were carrying on a brisk trade, there they fell upon him and "Björn the mighty was smitten to death", his body cast into the sea, his house plundered and burnt, and his son taken prisoner and only ransomed for a large sum. But the English had reckoned without his wife. For when Mistress Ólof heard of her husband's fate she cried, "There shall be no weeping but rather gather men." "That she did, and clad herself in a shirt of mail, and a woman's dress over it; so she set out with her men in array. Then they came with craft upon the English, and slew a great company of them, except the cook, who got his life very narrowly for that he had before helped their son." The game was now in the hands of Mistress Ólof. Taking her son, she sailed to Norway, put their case before the king, and is said to have been complimented by him as "a woman pleasant to behold". At last King Christian acted. Not only were the usual letters sent to the new governor, ordering him to outlaw all Englishmen without permits, but four English ships were seized in the Sound in 1468 and sequestered as compensation for the outrage.[1]

Great was the indignation in England. Edward IV wrote haughtily to the King of Denmark that if any offence had been committed he should have been informed, and asking for the restitution of those captured ships which were innocent of any connection with Iceland. But no further satisfaction was forthcoming save that in King Christian's letter to "the mayors and rulers of all cities and towns in England except those of Lynn". Here he declared plainly

---

[1] *Annalar Biørns a Skardsa* (Hrappseyal, 1774–5), I, 50; *Annales Islandici, ut supra*, I, ii, 66–7; *Caspar Weinreich's Danziger Chronik*, ed. T. Hirsch and F. A. Vossberg (Berlin, 1885), 4; *Hansisches Urkundenbuch, ut supra*, IX, 467 *et seq.*, 584; Gjerset, *op. cit.*, 266; *Hanserecesse, ut supra*, II, vi, 97.

that he was keeping certain ships of Lynn which "had fallen into his hands" to satisfy the relatives of the innocent dead; that, not wishing to penalise others, he granted a safe conduct for any that were not of Lynn; but that if any through Lynn's crime had lost their possessions, they must seek damages from Lynn itself. The English merchants, baffled in their appeal to Denmark, and unable to retaliate since no Danish goods came to England, turned to avenge themselves on the Hanse. And since Hanseatic ships had undeniably assisted in the capture, all the Hanseatic merchants in London were arrested and thrown into prison. Vainly King Christian wrote on their behalf to King Edward that he himself had ordered the sequestration because of the outrage in Iceland. Neither party would yield, and though in the spring of 1469 the Hansards were released, in that year a state of war broke out. The contest was but half-hearted, and within two years a truce was concluded. In 1473 it was followed by a second truce renewed in 1476 and in 1479. By these "mutual freedom of trade" was granted—a phrase signifying little, especially when with it was coupled the important exception that the English might still not visit Iceland without special permission.[1]

It was particularly unfortunate for England that she should again have alienated Denmark at that moment and failed to establish a lasting peace. For her prospects in Iceland were less bright than they had been at the opening of the century. At that time not only was the king of Denmark, with his English wife, disposed to be friendly to England and hostile to the Hanse, but in Iceland itself the English merchants were unchallenged by rivals. Now, however, when Denmark was estranged and obedient to the Hanse to the point of excluding the English altogether from Bergen,[2] formidable competitors had appeared, striving to

[1] *Hansisches Urkundenbuch, ut supra,* IX, 476, 468, 478–82; Macray, *op. cit.,* 5.

[2] *Die Lübecker Bergenfahrer und ihre Chronistik,* ed. F. Bruns (Hansische Geschichtsquellen. Neue Folge, Band II. Verein für Hansische Geschichte, Berlin, 1900), 240.

win for themselves the trade of the island. For with the intensification of the Bergen monopoly by the Wendish towns, those Hanseatics who were not of this group had come to follow the example of the English, and to sail direct to Iceland. As early as 1430 some few had broken through the restrictions, but, like the English, they had met with strong opposition, and their venture had been checked by the Hanse League itself. Little was heard of them during the next forty years, but from 1475 evidence of Hanseatic activity in Iceland becomes abundant. The voyage to Iceland was now a regular annual venture on the part of Hamburg, undertaken at the expense of the city. Ships were sent out which belonged wholly or partially to the State, and profits or losses were duly noted in its accounts. Danzigers also now joined the interlopers who, like the English, secured licences from the Danish king. So numerous did these become that the Bergen merchants were moved to make a vigorous protest. On their behalf the Norwegian Reichsrath wrote letters in 1481, and again in 1482, to the meeting of the Hanseatic League at Lübeck. In these they complained that Hamburgers and others of the Hanse had been allowed, contrary to the laws of the realm, to voyage direct to Iceland to the detriment of Norway and the Staple of Bergen, and they asked that the League should prevail upon them to desist. At the same time they induced the new Danish king to forbid the voyage. Meanwhile so much grain was being sent out of Hamburg that the city became alarmed and prohibited the export altogether, though ships continued to load in other places.[1]

Such a rapid advance, when Hanseatics began to compete with the English even in fetching fish from Iceland to London and the Wendish towns too joined in the trade, brought about intense rivalry and, inevitably, friction in Iceland itself where the trade was so little regulated. Clashes ensued both there and on the high seas. The Hanseatics were

---

[1] See above, 124; Baasch, *op. cit.*, 8, 9, 16; *Hanserecesse, ut supra*, III, 1, 350–1, 365; Gjerset, *op. cit.*, 273.

voluble in their complaints. Some reported how their ships
had been robbed in Iceland by men of Bristol or Hull, who
took from them much merchandise including fish, cloth, oil,
tallow, skins, and feathers. Others told how they had been
pillaged on the way to London when by ill-chance they ran
aground off Hartlepool. The English similarly complained
of their treatment at the hands of the Hanse, who were quite
equally guilty of acts of violence. Thus Richard III wrote to
Hamburg of the spoliation of three English ships in Iceland,
and when certain eminent Bristol merchants were accused
by Hanseatics, letters were written by high dignitaries in
Iceland exonerating the English. The original conflict of
Danish officials with lawless interlopers was now inextricably
complicated by the conflict of Englishmen with rival
Germans, and of Hanseatics lawfully trading from Bergen
with other Hanseatics, daringly intruding. In so many-sided
a struggle the various parties could with difficulty be dis-
criminated, and coalitions must have been made and unmade
with bewildering rapidity. When, for instance, the Danish
king's lieutenant in Iceland set forth to attack English ships
from Scarborough, Hanse merchants hastened to his assistance, sending him speedily by horse "3 *armamenta vocata
blankharneys in quadam baga*". Ships of necessity were fully
armed. Sea fights were frequent, and the rights of them it is
impossible now to determine from the fragments of evidence
in records and annals.[1]

Amid the turmoil and confusion of the 'eighties some of
the Icelanders must have looked back almost regretfully to
the time of isolation, even though it had also been a time of
dearth. Seeing their harbours thronged with ships, great
merchantmen and little fishing boats so active that they had
quite outstripped the native fishers; ninety or more German
craft challenging the old-established English ones—they
must have heard almost incredulously of how early in the

[1] *Calendar of Patent Rolls*, 1476–85, 23; *Diplomatarium Islandicum,
ut supra*, VII, 66; *Hanserecesse, ut supra*, II, vii, 348; Baasch, *op. cit.*, 6;
Hansisches Urkundenbuch, ut supra, X, 470, 1201, 489.

century not a single foreign vessel had come near their shores, and of how vainly they had petitioned for six ships from Norway. Now the Icelandic venture was so common a one that Iceland had become too popular a resort; its enfeebled administration was quite unable to cope with the influx of visitors and to adjust the claims of the many disputants. The English had yet more reason to regret the past. Times had indeed changed since the days of those pioneer merchant-men, eagerly welcomed by the Icelanders, duly accredited by English and Danish kings, and unchallenged by rivals, whose advent was of such moment that each was fully recorded in the annals. Now the annals wrote only of tumults and disasters on the sea. Now competition was so keen that Iceland was unpleasantly crowded. Danish kings, dominated by the rival Hanse, were unfriendly if not actively hostile, and English kings, struggling to maintain their power, had long made Iceland the sport of political expediency. Certainly the outlook for the English was less favourable than it had been at the opening of the century. Hence it came about that the more enterprising of them once again sought new fishing grounds. Just as formerly, thrust forth by the Hanse, they had abandoned Bergen for Iceland, so now, when the Hanse had pursued them thither, they were eager to leave Iceland behind, and to push out yet further into the Atlantic, towards fisheries more distant but less frequented. And so it was that when the companions of Cabot, most of whom were from Bristol, returned triumphantly from their quest of the New Found Land, they reported with much satisfaction that "they could bring thence so many fish that they would have no further need of Iceland".[1]

---

[1] *The Reign of Henry VII from Contemporary Sources*, ed. A. F. Pollard (1913–4), II, 333.

III

THE ORIGINS AND EARLY DEVELOPMENT OF THE MERCHANT ADVENTURERS' ORGANIZATION IN LONDON AS SHOWN IN THEIR OWN MEDIEVAL RECORDS[1]

The importance of the Merchant Adventurers' Company has been universally recognized, though variously interpreted. But its inner history remains curiously nebulous. Its evolution and structure seem to have baffled all attempts at clear analysis. Many historians have exercised their ingenuity in unravelling its ultimate origins or expounding the intricacies of a constitution which was probably never static, endeavouring to analyse the life of the now extinct Society by meticulously dissecting a number of charters and letters patent. But these provide merely a bare skeleton, and, as Professor Lingelbach noted: "The one great hiatus in the sources for the history of the Society still exists, for nowhere has there been found a definite clue to the existence or the whereabouts of the private records of the Fellowship."[2] Hence the actual activities of the Society have remained largely a matter for conjecture until now, when such records as Professor Lingelbach sought in vain have come to light and are elucidating the whole matter.

"Merchant Adventurer", a term often loosely used and misinterpreted, must be defined at the outset. It was applied generally in the later Middle Ages to any merchant engaged in trade overseas whose business was not that of the Staplers —the old and carefully regulated export of raw wool—but the newer trade in English cloth. The Adventurer, unlike the Stapler, who went regularly to and fro between England

---

[1] *Economic History Review*, Vol. IV, No. 2, 1933.
[2] W. E. Lingelbach, *The Merchant Adventurers of England: their Laws and Ordinances*, Univ. of Pennsylvania, Translations and Reprints, Second Series, II (1902), viii.

and the English port of Calais, voyaged far afield, east, west, north or south, wherever he could find an opening. Such was William Haryot, "a merchant", says Fabyan, "of wondrous adventures into many and sundry lands".[1] And such were the merchants of the Gild of St. George at Hull, which admitted only those who had no other livelihood "but by grete aventour".[2] The "many and sundry lands" included, at the opening of the fifteenth century, countries as wide apart as Norway, Spain, Prussia and the Netherlands. In three of these regions at any rate there were not merely Adventurers, but organized groups of Adventurers, accustomed to meet together to elect governors and make rules with the consent of the merchants, with authority delegated to them from the King of England. Those trading to Prussia had already secured permission from the King in 1391 so to govern themselves "according to privileges granted to them by the Grand Master of Prussia", while others doing business in Norway, Sweden and Denmark were given similar privileges in 1408. These privileges were based on yet another grant of 1407 to the oldest and most considerable group of Adventurers, that in the Netherlands.[3] With the decline of the two northern groups in the late fifteenth century, this third group became so important that it eclipsed all others [4]; and though originally it was known as "the Company of Merchant Adventurers of England trading to Holland, Zealand, Brabant, Hainault and Flanders", it gradually dropped this cumbersome designation and, since it had absorbed so large a number of Adventurers, virtually arrogated to itself the simple title of

---

[1] A. H. Johnson, *History of the Worshipful Company of Drapers* (1914–22), I, 151.

[2] J. M. Lambert, *Two Thousand Years of Gild Life* (1891), 158.

[3] *Foedera, Conventiones, etc.*, ed. T. Rymer (The Hague, 1739–42), III, iv, 66–7; IV, i, 125, 107; see Cunningham, *Growth of English Industry and Commerce* (1927), 5th ed., I, 415–6.

[4] See M. M. Postan, "The Economic and Political Relations of England and the Hanse", in *Studies in English Trade in the Fifteenth Century*, ed. E. Power and M. M. Postan (1933), 150 *et seq.*

"the Merchant Adventurers of England". Thus the term "Merchant Adventurers' Company", as used by historians, most often denotes the specific company of the Netherlands. It is just as necessary to distinguish this from the other less long-lived groups as it is to distinguish the organized groups from the individual Merchant Adventurer.

It is, then, to the Netherlands group of Adventurers, to which in the later fifteenth century flocked many Adventurers from other regions, that we must look for the origins of the body known as the Company of Merchant Adventurers of England. When we come to examine the existing authorities for its history, their one-sided character is at once obvious. From a long series of charters and letters patent first brought together by Schanz in 1881 in his *Englische Handelspolitik*,[1] and now supplemented by some earlier versions printed by Jansma,[2] an outline narrative has already been compiled of the settlement in the Low Countries and of the privileges of self-government granted there by English kings and foreign princes. The organization by which the merchants managed their affairs in the Netherlands during their visits to the marts in the late sixteenth and seventeenth centuries has also been analysed by Professor Lingelbach, from their own Laws and Ordinances as then recorded by their Secretary.[3]

But though the organization of the Netherland Adventurers abroad has often been dealt with, the English side of their activities during the formative period of the Society's growth has received scant attention. The merchants must have resided in England for a great part of the year, going overseas when they had to attend the marts, yet whether their common interests were reflected in any formal

[1] G. Schanz, *Englische Handelspolitik gegen Ende des Mittelalters* (Leipzig, 1881), I, 332 *et seq.*
[2] T. Sj. Jansma, "De Privileges voor de Engelsche Natie te Bergen-op-Zoom, 1469–1555", *Bijdragen en Mededeelingen van het Historisch Genootschap*, 1929 (Utrecht).
[3] W. E. Lingelbach, "The Internal Organisation of the Merchant Adventurers of England", in *Trans. R. Hist. Soc.*, N.S., XVI, 19 *et seq.* (1901); and *Laws and Ordinances, ut supra.*

MMV—K

association at home has remained entirely unknown. We know so little about what they did here that historians have been deluded into supposing, as van Brakel postulates in *Die Entwicklung und Organisation des Merchant-Adventurers*, that "their organized activities in England were negligible".[1] Van Brakel justifies this negative conclusion by arguing that "since in the Netherlands lay the centre of gravity of their activity, it is self-evident that there also lay the principal seat of government". In actual fact, however, it was not the organization but the evidence of its existence which was lacking, and this gap in the evidence on the English side is now being gradually filled.

While royal charters and letters patent yield no clue, the archives of local gilds have come to shed abundant light on the whole subject. Gross noted as long ago as 1890 the existence of numerous local fellowships of Merchant Adventurers in different towns of England, but was more interested in tracing their relations to the older Gild Merchant than their relation to the whole Company of Merchant Adventurers.[2] Five years after he had written, however, there were published the records of the Merchant Adventurers of Newcastle-on-Tyne.[3] Of these Professor Lingelbach made some use, but he was more concerned with the early seventeenth-century Laws and Ordinances in the British Museum, which he printed. Little fresh evidence was brought to light in the next twenty years, and writers such as van Brakel, Te Lintum,[4] and Sir Charles Lucas, when dealing with the early evolution of the Society, did little else than reinterpret and discuss earlier conclusions. In 1918, however, appeared the still more important records of the York

---

[1] S. van Brakel, "Die Entwicklung und Organisation des Merchant-Adventurers", in *Vierteljahrschrift für Social- und Wirtschaftsgeschichte*, Band V, Heft 3 (1907), 414.

[2] C. Gross, *The Gild Merchant* (1890), I, 151 *et seq*.

[3] *Extracts from the Records of the Merchant Adventurers of Newcastle-upon-Tyne*, ed. F. W. Dendy, Surtees Society, XCIII (1895).

[4] C. te Lintum, *De merchant Adventurers in de Nederlanden* (The Hague, 1905).

Mercers and Merchant Adventurers.[1] Dr. Sellers, in editing them, not only traced the development of the powerful group of Adventurers in York, but did much to elucidate its relations in the Low Countries with the London Adventurers. Yet, though provincial groups had been clearly revealed, the London Adventurers themselves, on whom the whole Company seemed to pivot, still proved entirely elusive. It seemed improbable that they should have been less organized than those of Newcastle or York, but in London there was no Merchant Venturers' Hall as in York, no visible head-quarters of any society. Where the Adventurers' records could be was so baffling an enigma that historians were tempted to deny the existence of any. One clue, however, to their whereabouts had been observed, though not followed up, by several historians. This was the peculiar position of the Adventurers with regard to the Mercers' Company in London. "Modern writers", as Professor Lingelbach says, "accept an intimate relationship between the early Adventurers and the Mercers." [2] So close was this connection that, as Gross wrote: "Down to 1526 the minutes of both Companies were kept in the same book; and the Mercers' Hall was the headquarters of the Merchant Adventurers until the fire of 1666." [3] Again, Schanz called attention to an inventory made in 1547, and now in the British Museum, of privileges, grants, and other records of the Merchant Adventurers at that time preserved in "a cheste of woode bounden with yron bilonginge to the said fellawship of marchauntes adventurers and standing in the inner treasoury in the mercers hall".[4] Schanz, commenting upon this, concludes that "Their whole development up to this time leads one to suppose that the store of records itself

[1] *The York Mercers and Merchant Adventurers*, ed. M. Sellers, Surtees Society, CXXIX (1918).

[2] *Laws and Ordinances, ut supra*, 199, n. 1.

[3] Gross, *op. cit.*, I, 149. See *City of London Livery Companies' Commission, Report and Appendix*, II, 2 (*Parliamentary Papers*, 1884, XXXIX); this seems to be the origin of the oft-quoted statement of Gross.

[4] Schanz, *op. cit.*, I, 335–6, II, 574, quoting B.M. Sloane MS. 2103, f. 2.

could not be great." Professor Lingelbach, on the other hand, was confident that, though he could not locate them, the records were "numerous and very extensive", and that "ere long some at least may be found".[1] Ehrenberg not only believed that they existed, but was firmly convinced, though without proof, that a store of Adventurers' records was still to be found in the Mercers' Hall.[2] In more recent years Jansma, abandoning the optimism of thirty years ago, has summed up the problem in an article putting forward yet a third and catastrophic solution—that they most probably all perished in the Great Fire of London.[3] Yet it is noteworthy that in an old life of William Caxton, though one written long after the Great Fire, there is actually printed, from records in the Mercers' Hall obviously still extant, some correspondence of the Merchant Adventurers. Lucas, who consulted this work during his investigations into the history of the Adventurers,[4] pursued the matter no further. But the author of this life,[5] writing before the days of scientific history and local record societies, had come nearer to giving a true account of the Merchant Adventurers of London than any modern historian. For he had made the acquaintance of the volume wherein are enshrined the minutes of these Adventurers up to 1526, giving the history of their corporate activities on the English side, and revealing step by step the evolution of a group of Adventurers comparable to those of York or Newcastle, and far more important.

This volume, of unique interest among the wealth of Company records in London, does not betray its full significance by its name. It is entitled simply "Acts of Court

---

[1] *Laws and Ordinances, ut supra*, viii.

[2] R. Ehrenberg, *Hamburg und England im Zeitalter der Königin Elisabeth* (Jena, 1896), iv.

[3] T. Sj. Jansma, "Het Archief der Merchants Adventurers en de Groote Brand van Londen", *Tijdschrift voor Geschiedenis* (1929), 282, and "De Privileges voor de Engelsche Natie", etc., *ut supra*, 43.

[4] Sir C. P. Lucas, *The Beginnings of English Overseas Enterprise* (1917), 65, n. 3.

[5] W. Blades, *Life and Typography of William Caxton* (1861).

of the Mercers' Company", and might easily, therefore, elude the seeker after a store of Merchant Adventurers' records. But such an implied separation is most misleading. The charters and privileges might indeed be kept apart (as Schanz observed), but the minutes, up to 1526 (just as Gross stated), were "in the same book as those of the Mercers". The book itself contains over 400 folios in perfect preservation, and was compiled early in the sixteenth century from a number of earlier books, some of which had been mislaid but were found during the process of copying. Hence the entries are not all in chronological order, nor are they a complete series, but, with certain gaps, they report with considerable fulness proceedings in the Mercers' Hall between 1456 and 1526. In addition to these Acts of Court there remains one early volume of Wardens' Accounts. Unfortunately, however, though these begin in the four-teenth century, they stop short in 1464 for over a century. It is these Acts of Court and Wardens' Accounts of the Mercers' Company which, while apparently relating only to the Mercers, in reality fill the most conspicuous gap in the early history of the Merchant Adventurers, and owing to the courtesy of Colonel Watney, Clerk of the Mercers' Company, a full inspection of them has now been possible.

That records of the Merchant Adventurers should be obscured under those of the Mercers will appear only natural when we consider briefly the composition of the Netherlands group. Originally in the thirteenth and four-teenth centuries the English merchants who acquired privileges in the Low Countries from foreign rulers num-bered among them both Staplers and Adventurers. In fact, when the export of cloth was negligible compared with that of wool there was no distinction between Staplers and Adventurers, but one body of "merchants of the realm trading to the parts of Flanders".[1] But in the latter half of

---

[1] Van Brakel, *op. cit.*, 405; E. Lipson, *The Economic History of England*, I (5th ed., 1929), 488; G. Unwin, *Studies in Economic History*, ed. R. H. Tawney (1927), 139, 143.

the fourteenth century, with the tightening control exercised by English kings over the lucrative wool trade, the Staplers became a distinct body, and with the final withdrawal of the wool Staple to Calais those merchants who continued to trade in the foreign towns of the Low Countries, interested in the export of cloth rather than of wool, became clearly differentiated as Merchant Adventurers. Among these cloth merchants in the Low Countries the most influential in the early fifteenth century were those of London. And in the London group itself the dominating influence was that of the Mercers. It was the patron saint of the ancient Fraternity of the Mercers who became the patron saint of all the Adventurers there, and the Adventurers' chapels in Bruges and Middleburg, like the Mercers' chapel in London, were dedicated to St. Thomas à Becket, whose father had probably been a mercer.[1] Indeed, the whole Company of English Adventurers in the Netherlands was commonly known as the "Fraternity of St. Thomas beyond the Sea", even by those who were neither Mercers nor Londoners.[2] Clear evidence of the premier place of the Mercers in the London group comes again from those not of London when they speak of the "Fellowship of Mercers and other Merchants and Adventurers dwelling in and being free within the City of London."[3] Thus the Mercers dominated the London group as the London group dominated the Netherlands group, so that the key to the very core of the Merchant Adventurer problem is to be found in the Mercers' records.

Let us now turn to London itself to trace, with the help of the Mercers' books, the emergence of a new society of Adventurers there.

The first stage in the evolution of the London Merchant Adventurers was the formation of a number of separate groups of Adventurers in several of the great London

[1] R. Hakluyt, *The Principal Navigations, etc.* (Everyman Edition, 1907), I, 203; *The York Mercers and Merchant Adventurers, ut supra,* li; Sir John Watney, *The Hospital of St. Thomas of Acon* (1892), 8.
[2] *The York Mercers and Merchant Adventurers, ut supra,* 121.
[3] Statute 12 Hen. VII, c. 6.

companies whose members exported cloth to the Low Countries, particularly in those of the Mercers, Grocers, Drapers, Haberdashers and Skinners. Each group was a distinct entity with a life of its own, yet not independent but closely bound up with the parent organism within which it had developed. The emergence of these groups may be most clearly perceived in the case of the most important one, that of the Mercers. Here the first hint of such a group is in the Accounts, which, under the year 1443–44, mention an assessment "des Aventurers del Mercery".[1] Later, on the first folio of the Acts of Court, we read of an agreement in 1457 "by the felyship aventurers" to take a levy on every pack of mercery which had just arrived in certain ships.[2] The minutes for the next ten years are very incomplete, but it is plain that by 1465 the Adventurers among the Mercers were holding meetings apart from the rest of the Company. In this year, for instance, a special "Courte of Aventurers" discussed cloth measures, and sent a letter on the subject to William Caxton, "Governour by yonde the see",[3] and from this time on the "Court of Adventurers" often appears in the minutes as distinguished from the "Court of our whole Fellowship", discussing all matters of foreign trade, shipping, customs and subsidies, making and confirming ordinances and corresponding with the Governor overseas. It seems as though the Mercers Adventurers were exclusively concerned at this time with the Low Countries, and it is difficult to determine to what extent they had ever dealt in the trade with the two northern regions of Prussia and Scandinavia, which was now collapsing. If, as seems probable, they had always concentrated on the Netherlands, this may partly have accounted for their ascendancy there, while the irruption of other London Adventurers, with the decline of the northern trade, would create new problems and

[1] Accounts of the Mercers' Company, I, f. 141d.
[2] Acts of Court of the Mercers' Company, f. 1d.
[3] *Ibid.*, f. 140; the entries for 1465–7 are later in the volume and not in their correct place.

stimulate the formation of some common organization among the London Adventurers as a whole.

The growth of an Adventurers' group within the Mercers' Company in the mid-fifteenth century is abundantly clear from their own records. What of Adventurer groups in other companies? Here again it is the Mercers' books from which we derive most of the evidence, since none of these companies themselves possess comparable records. The Drapers and the Haberdashers have each a Book of Ordinances of the fifteenth century, but the Drapers' Court Minutes do not begin until 1515, and neither Haberdashers, Grocers nor Skinners appear to have any Court Books for the fifteenth or early sixteenth centuries. In the Mercers' Acts of Court, however, in the same year (1465) in which the heading "Court of Adventurers" first appears, we read of the Mercers Adventurers and other "divers felyshippes aventerers" making joint representations to the Mayor on a question of diplomatic negotiations with the Low Countries.[1] And three years later two wealthy Mercers caused a scandal in their Company because openly in the hall at St. Thomas they used "divers ungoodly langewage—there beyng present John Middleton and divers other Aventerers as well of the Mercery as of other occupacions", and one broke the head of the other with his dagger.[2] These other "Fellowships Adventurers of the City", to whom frequent reference is made from this time, are not at first more definitely specified, but come gradually to be mentioned by name. In 1489, for instance, we read of a "Courte of the felishippes aventerers" where were assembled "Wardens of drapers, grocers, skynners and other as well as of oure Compeny of the Mercery".[3] Most prominent are the Grocers,[4] Drapers, Haberdashers and Skinners, while less frequently appear the Fishmongers and the Tailors. Yet the proof of the existence

---

[1] *Ibid.*, f. 141.   [2] *Ibid.*, f. 11.   [3] *Ibid.*, f. 89d.
[4] See S. Thrupp, "The Grocers of London", in *English Trade in the Fifteenth Century, ut supra*, 263–5. Dr. Thrupp has here used the Mercers' Acts of Court, and discusses the Grocers' importance as cloth exporters.

of these other Adventurer fellowships does not rest solely on the Mercers' books, for though other court minutes are lacking, account books exist which clearly corroborate our conclusions. Thus, for instance, in the carefully preserved first Account Book of the Skinners' Company, opening in 1492, we come across, though rather later on, a loan for the "Marchauntes adventurers of this Crafte" and the "Skynners Marchauntes Aventurers".[1]

But amongst all these diverse Fellowships of Adventurers that of the Mercers evidently took the lead in London as in the Netherlands. This may be seen from the part they played in procuring the patent of 1462 confirming the right of Adventurers to elect their own Governor in the Low Countries. In this year King Edward IV, contrary to the privileges granted by the charter of 1407, and confirmed in 1413, 1430 and 1437,[2] arbitrarily appointed William Overey Governor "during our pleasure", because of the "good, faithful and acceptable services which he hath done us".[3] But within ten weeks these letters had been annulled, and for a sum of £57, 10s., advanced by the Mercers, the English merchants had secured a patent from the King allowing them to congregate together as before to choose their governors [4]; Overey had been discharged, and Caxton had been elected.[5] The Mercers recovered the money from the whole "Nation" overseas, twice entering the sum in their accounts as owing to them from "The ffelaship by

[1] Accounts of the Skinners' Company (Skinners' Hall), I (unpaged), 1503-4, 1505-6. For permission to consult these I am indebted to Mr. J. J. Lambert, Clerk of the Company.

[2] *Foedera, ut supra*, IV, 107; *Calendar of Patent Rolls*, 1413-5, p. 108; *ibid.*, 1429-36, 81; B.M. Sloane MS. 2103, f. 2, quoted in Schanz, *op. cit.*, II, 575.

[3] *Hakluyt, ut supra*, I, 204. This charter, isolated from its context, has been misinterpreted—e.g., *Transactions of the Royal Historical Society*, New Series, XVI, 45. Its omission from the list of their own charters given by the Merchant Adventurers, which has puzzled historians, now becomes plain. So also does the fact that this charter of 1462 makes no mention of previous charters to the Merchant Adventurers, for it directly contravened them.

[4] *Calendar of Patent Rolls*, 1461-7, 187.

[5] Schanz, *op. cit.*, II, 578.

yende þᵉ See", "for þᵉ sute of þeir pryvelage" or "for þeir patent".[1] The Governor himself at this time was often a mercer, such as Caxton, William Pykering, or John Wendy, and much of the correspondence that passed between the Governor and royal officials at home came through the Mercers. Again, in negotiations to improve trade it was often the Mercers who led the way, and the costs of such negotiations were more than once levied by order of the Mercers "by yonde the see by the hole nacion".[2]

The formation of the separate groups of Adventurers within the various companies soon led to their being drawn towards one another, with the Mercers Adventurers as their centre and focus. The impulse towards such a fusion came both from within and without. In a time of trade crisis, when the Mercers were incurring heavy expenditure on behalf of all the Adventurers, whether in sending deputations to the King, procuring letters patent, or equipping embassies to foreign princes, they were naturally anxious to call on the other Adventurers, who more and more frequented the Low Countries, to assist them. If, on the other hand, the Mercers were planning to suspend all shipments abroad, and were bringing pressure to bear on the Governor to enforce their decision, other Adventurers, disagreeing with their policy, might murmur among themselves and insist on making their voices heard in the councils of the Adventurers, resenting the dictation of the Mercers. Co-operation in their business with the Low Countries was in many ways to their advantage. Shipping in the same vessels to the same marts, it was to the interest of each to devise a common safeguard for the ships, a common system for paying—or evading—customs or subsidies, a common assault upon the vested interests of the foreigner or of the Staple, or on the policy of the cloth manufacturers, often opposed to their own.

[1] Accounts of the Mercers' Company, I, f. 203.
[2] Acts of Court, ff. 6d, 141. The influence of the Mercers is also shown by the removal of Pykering from his office as Governor by the London Adventurers on the advice of the Mercers, whom he had displeased, in 1483. Watney, *op. cit.*, 12.

The gradual fusion of the groups was the result not merely of vital forces at work among the Adventurers themselves, but also of the intervention from above of king and mayor. Just as abroad organized communities of Adventurers had been called into existence by the action of kings of England and local ruling powers, as well as by their own voluntary association, so in England the consolidation of the Adventurers was due to the interaction of various forces—national, civic and individual. The trade of the Adventurers and the political relations of England and the Low Countries were so closely interwoven one with another that during the numerous fluctuations and crises of the later fifteenth century there was much correspondence between the king and the merchants as well as between the king and the ruler of the Netherlands. Edward IV would frequently summon all the adventurers together through the mayor, in default of any organization with which he could deal direct, to hear their wishes or to dictate his own, or to request them to provide an ambassador. When in 1465 he asked them to appoint ambassadors to Burgundy, the Mercers' Wardens and "the Wardens of divers felyshippes aventerers", summoned by the mayor, declined this honour, avowing that "it is not oure parte here in the Citie to take uppon us a mater of so grete weyght", and they begged the mayor to answer the king accordingly "in the most plesaunt wise that he can".[1] But later on, in 1477, when the Duke of Burgundy had been slain in battle and a new treaty was being negotiated with his successor, "certen persones of divers ffelyshipes aventerers had ben befor my lorde Chaunceler & other of the kynges Councell for a communicacion to be had with the dukes Enbassatours for thentercours".[2] And when in 1482 the King of France repudiated the betrothal of the Dauphin to King Edward's daughter and Edward therefore decided to forbid his subjects to trade with those of France, then "the mynde of the kynges grace . . . by the Mayre at the yelde

---

[1] Acts of Court, f. 141.
[2] *Ibid.*, f. 34d.

hall was there shewed unto the Wardens of the felishippes aventerers of the said Citie".[1] The payment of customs and subsidies was of as great import to the king as his diplomatic relations with foreign powers, and on this matter also the Adventurers were continually being drawn together. Thus in 1479 the king, "beyng straungely enformed howe that the marchauntes of this his citie shulde enbesell gretely his subsidie, etc.", ordered the mayor to tell the merchants that he must be paid. For this purpose the mayor assembled at the Guildhall the Wardens of "dyvers felyshippes aventerers".[2]

It must not be supposed that such common assemblies were at first always held in the Guildhall and at the instance of king or mayor. As far back as 1468, as we have seen,[3] Adventurers of more than one company were gathered together "in the halle at St. Thomas", and we come across a similar assembly at the Mercers' Hall in 1481, when it is noted that "alle other felishippes beyng departed" the Mercers' Fellowship voted a special reward of a "gowne clothe of oure lyverey" to Pykering, then Governor in the Netherlands, for his great labours "for the plesour of oure feliship".[4] Nothing further is recorded of the subjects under discussion at these meetings, but it is certain that by this time the London Adventurers were accustomed to charter vessels jointly for the marts, for in 1475 the Wardens of the Mercers wrote to Pykering that "There be divers Shippes here appoynted as well by drapers, grocers, haberdysshers and the assent of the fysshemongers as by oure felyshippe whiche nowe by goddes grace shall come to this Bamas marte."[5] In 1483, while there still seems to be no regular assembly of Merchant Adventurers, comes the first hint of a common fighting fund. The Adventurers contended that by the death of Edward IV the "importable Charges of Subsidie of tonnage and pondage", granted for life to the king,

[1] *Ibid.*, f. 60d.   [2] *Ibid.*, f. 45.
[3] *Supra*, 152.   [4] Acts of Court, f. 58d.
                    [5] *Ibid.*, f. 26d.

became void. The collectors, however, disagreed, and it was said that they "besy them gretely to contynue thexecucion of thoffice". Accordingly there was held in the Mercers' Hall an "Assemble of adventerers of dyvers ffelishippes", the first so headed in the minutes. Here the Adventurers resolved that they would unite to resist the collectors, that they would boldly take up their goods, and that any who were "interupte and lett" should be aided by a common fund, contributed by all the fellowships and repaid ultimately by a levy overseas, since it "apparteyneth to the generaltie of all Merchauntes Aventerers of this londe". Several more meetings were held, legal advice was taken, and a petition presented jointly to the Protector, and by united action the Adventurers won the day.[1]

Although the Adventurers were momentarily united by their hatred of subsidies, there was as yet no recognized or permanent association among them, and it was this very lack of any authorized organization, the need for which had become evident, which was to lead in the next few years, through confusion and quarrelling, to a more formal union. Full particulars of the dispute are not forthcoming, but it appears that a restraint of trade had been determined upon in London at a meeting of Adventurers of various fellowships in 1484, and that the Governor overseas, himself a mercer, had accordingly arrested and imprisoned certain merchants guilty of doing business in Antwerp. These pleaded ignorance, and through their fellowships at home complaint was made early the following year in a General Court of Adventurers. Here "Richard Swan Skynner, William Crell Tayllour, and Robert Boys Cutler of ungoodly demeanour and unfittyng in theire langage", had spoken against certain of the Mercers "so uncurtesly . . . to suche great displeasure of all the Courte for the whiche they alle departed".[2] The matter was investigated and the Governor instructed to let the delinquents off with a small fine, but

[1] *Ibid.*, ff. 62, 63, 64.
[2] *Ibid.*, ff. 66–71.

criticism of the Governor's proceedings was evidently bitter, and perhaps explains the paragraph devoted to the Adventurers in the Chronicles of London for 1485.[1] It would seem as though the other London Adventurers, to whom the trade of the Low Countries was becoming of more and more importance, were coming to challenge the traditional supremacy there of the Mercers, and to claim for themselves a greater share in the control of the Adventurers' affairs.

For over twenty years the Merchant Adventurers of London had been feeling their way towards union. The successful culmination of their efforts towards some new organisation to meet the needs of the time came, perhaps fittingly, with the advent of the Tudor monarchy. At the opening of Henry VII's reign the "merchants adventurers, citizens of the city of London, into the parts of Holland, Seeland, Brabant and Flaundres", united to petition, as at the beginning of Richard III's reign, for a pardon and discharge from all subsidies on goods landed before the first day of the first Parliament. So influential were they that this was granted and instructions sent accordingly to the customs officials (February 4, 1486).[2] Within two months these London Adventurers, who had so strikingly demonstrated their power, were to ask and receive recognition from the city. At the crucial moment there is a gap in their own records, but the records of the city itself, even more important at this point, reveal the essentials of the case. In the Journals of the Guildhall, under the heading, "For the receiving of letters from the parts of the Duke of Burgundy," a decision is recorded for March 22, 1486, to the effect that the mayor and aldermen should every year choose "two lieutenants, one from the craft of the Mercery and the other from one of the other crafts frequenting the parts of the Duke of Burgundy, to receive any letters sent from overseas for any matters concerning merchants frequenting those parts,

---

[1] C. L. Kingsford, *Chronicles of London* (1905), 193.
[2] *Materials for a History of the Reign of Henry VII*, ed. W. Campbell (Rolls Series, 1873), I, 273.

and to write back and make answer". These lieutenants were also to choose a clerk for that purpose "and a place where the said merchants can assemble", and the mayor was to choose servants to warn the merchants to come together at the appointed place.[1] Thus the mayor and alderman set up a special authority over and above that of the Mercers to deal with correspondence which concerned all the Adventurers. Perhaps the Adventurers took courage from this to propose a yet more complete organization. At any rate a fortnight later a petition was presented to the mayor, aldermen and common council "for thencresyng of good and sadde governaunce amonge the merchauntes of London aventurers in to the parties beyonde the see, that is to witte Holand, Seland, Braban and fflaunders", asking them to "enact and graunte unto theym certein liberties, fraunchises and other articles" there specified. An act was accordingly passed in common council which formally created the Merchant Adventurers' organization of London, and apparently rendered obsolete the decree of March. It was enacted that every year the mayor and aldermen should choose two "able persones", one a mercer and the other "of sum other feleaship of the said merchauntes within the Citee of London", to be lieutenants there to the Governor beyond the sea. These lieutenants were given authority to summon assemblies where, by the advice of the merchants and subject to the approval of the mayor, ordinances might be passed for "Imposicions, assembles, shippynges, ffreightes & conductes" and other necessary matters, and where fines might be imposed and levied. Any merchant disobeying the ordinances was to be taken before the mayor and aldermen "and by theym punysshed as a manne disobedient to the Wardeyns of his ffealeshippe".[2] By this act the Fellowship of the Merchant Adventurers of London for the first time received official recognition. Its ostensible purpose as a

[1] London, Guildhall, Journal of the Proceedings of the Court of Common Council, 9, f. 101.
[2] *Ibid.*, 9, f. 102b.

corporate body was to equip and dispatch the fleets from
London to the quarterly marts,[1] and to levy the necessary
money for their safe conveyance thither. Further than this
its exact scope was not defined, but its real functions proved
to be much wider and to include the whole direction of the
Adventurers' mercantile policy and the virtual control of
their finances.

The common assembly of the newly constituted Fellowship had, as we have seen, actually taken place often in
former years, so that the mayor was only setting the seal of
his authority on what was already in existence. This
assembly had at first been called somewhat vaguely an
"Assemble of aventerers of dyvers ffelishippes",[2] but by
1484 it was termed a "Generall Courte of Aventerers," and
after 1486 showed still more clearly the fusion of the various
groups by the title "Generall Courte of the felishipp
aventerers" or "Generall Courte of the felyshipp of this
Citie adventerers".[3] As to its composition there are occasional direct references. Once there were reported to have
been 80 present, and once 93 names of members attending
are given.[4] Membership was drawn largely from the
Mercers, Drapers, Haberdashers, Grocers and Skinners, and
in a lesser degree from the Tailors and Fishmongers and
perhaps other city companies such as the Ironmongers.
Henceforth, therefore, the London Fellowship possessed the
most distinctive feature of the fully developed gild or livery
company—the right to hold a court with power to make
ordinances and to enforce them by fines and punishments.
The jurisdiction of this court, as in the case of other gilds,
was not only supported by the mayor, but, since it was
implicitly delegated by him, was exercised strictly in
subordination to him. All ordinances were subject to his
approval, and in matters of special moment he might himself

[1] The Cold, Pask, Synxon and Balms (Winter, Spring, Summer, Autumn)
marts.
[2] E.g., Acts of Court, f. 62d.
[3] *Ibid.*, ff. 154d, 90d, 93, 356d, 327.
[4] *Ibid.*, ff. 93, 235, and cf. f. 176 for another list of names.

intervene. Thus, in the critical year of 1493, when all intercourse with the Low Countries was suspended, the mayor
saw the Adventurers' correspondence, and on one occasion
told them to keep back their own letter until they could
enclose one from him.[1]

But while in certain essential features the new Fellowship
of the Merchant Adventurers of London resembled the
medieval gild, it was in many respects peculiar. Despite its
importance, it had no meeting-place of its own, as had the
Newcastle Merchant Adventurers,[2] but almost invariably
held its assemblies in the Hall of the Mercers, thus clearly
betraying its origin. Nor had it any regular officials of its own.
Only three officials, "appointers", "conduitors" and auditors, appointed by and responsible to the Fellowship as a
whole, can be discerned in the fifteenth century, and these
were merely chosen for particular tasks at irregular intervals,
with very limited powers. Appointers were chosen when a
fleet was about to sail for a mart, to see to its equipment and
protection, and these were either elected in General Court or
named by the different fellowships.[3] Closely akin to the
appointers, and indeed sometimes identical with them,[4] were
the conduitors, who assessed and levied the necessary rates
to pay for the convoys, and kept accounts of them.[5] These
accounts were checked by auditors.[6] Apart from these
auditors, conduitors and appointers, and many special
committees with both administrative and legislative powers,
the Fellowship used almost entirely the Mercers' officials.
It was the Mercers' Clerk who wrote their letters and kept
their minutes; it was the Mercers who made up their accounts
and looked after the funds in the Mercers' treasure chest.
Correspondence with the Fellowship of the English Nation
overseas was often carried on simply by the Mercers'

[1] Ibid., f. 324.
[2] The Merchant Adventurers of Newcastle-upon-Tyne, ut supra, xlviii.
[3] Acts of Court, ff. 95d, 107.
[4] Ibid., f. 105.
[5] Ibid., ff. 87, 91, 92, 99, etc.
[6] Ibid., f. 87d.

Wardens, who answered letters addressed to the whole
Fellowship and took it on themselves to report to the
Governor decisions of the General Court on which he must
act.[1] Indeed, it would appear as though the Mercers'
Wardens almost considered themselves as Wardens of the
whole Fellowship. More strictly, however, letters were
directed to and from "the Wardens of the Mercery and all
other adventerers of the Citie of London" or "the ffelyshipp
of the Citie of London adventerers."[2] In fact the London
Fellowship had as many Wardens as there were Wardens of
all the companies from which its members were drawn.
When the Lord Chancellor therefore asked to see "the
Wardens of felishippes aventerers," then there were sent
to him "the Wardens of mercers, drapers, ffyshemongers,
haberdisshers, tayllours and other mo."[3] When important
documents, such as the indentures of an agreement between
the Adventurers and Calais, had to be sealed, they were sealed
"with the comen seales of the felishippes of the mercers,
drapers, grocers, haberdisshers and skynners of the Citie
of London."[4]

The new London Fellowship was indeed a complex
organism. For it was not yet completely independent and
detached from the parent companies out of which it had
grown. Its members, while united in the new Fellowship,
were still intimately bound up each with their own original
companies, whether Grocers, Drapers, Haberdashers, Skinners, Mercers or others. Only gradually did the sense of a
new corporate personality emerge. In 1489, for instance, the
ships of the Adventurers were arrested in the Court of
Admiralty by creditors, some of whom were themselves
London Adventurers, to whom the Fellowship owed considerable sums of money. This seemed to the Fellowship
very derogatory to their own Court, and a decree was

[1] E.g., *ibid.*, ff. 358, 362, 366.
[2] E.g., *ibid.*, ff. 324, 345, 368, 331d, 354d.
[3] *Ibid.*, f. 154d.
[4] *Ibid.*, f. 95.

accordingly passed in General Court that no freeman of the English Nation overseas should arrest any ship until the matter was investigated in General Court in London, on pain of 100 marks.[1] Nor were the General Courts always regular or willingly attended. On one occasion two Courts which were summoned "came not," and the Wardens of the Mercers, Drapers, Grocers, and Haberdashers were moved to tell the mayor of the "lachesnes and hurt of the said felishipp for lak and defaute of assemble." So the mayor ordered the Adventurers to appear, reminding them of the decree of 1486.[2] The various groups which made up the London Fellowship were still clearly discernible as distinct entities, and often there was friction between them which seemed as though it would disrupt the Fellowship. More than once the Mercers, when there was "grete variaunce" between them and other fellowships, threatened to secede and to ship independently, not "callyng or requyryng any other felishippes therunto, but and they or any of them wyll desyre to shipp with us."[3]

Of all these groups which made up the London Fellowship and were not yet firmly welded together, that of the Mercers, the nucleus towards which the others had been attracted, predominated. In the General Court they probably did so by sheer weight of numbers and influence, for it is noticeable that when special funds were levied the Mercers often contributed half of the whole sum. In committees and in deputations to the king and his council mercers were again to the fore; sometimes they made up half or more of the number and almost always they had twice as many representatives as any other company.[4] Similarly in the Act of 1486 it was provided that one of the two lieutenants should always be a mercer.[5] Even though the other fellowships had some share in the legislative side of the whole Fellowship's concerns, its executive, as we have seen, was almost entirely

---

[1] *Ibid.*, f. 93.   [2] *Ibid.*, f. 90d.
[3] *Ibid.*, ff. 94, 108.   [4] E.g., *ibid.*, ff. 327, 334.
[5] There is no allusion to these lieutenants in the Mercers' books.

in the hands of the Mercers. And not only was it through
the Mercers' officials that the wishes of the Fellowship were
conveyed to the Governor overseas, but the Governor
himself was almost invariably a mercer. All the important
Governors in the late fifteenth and early sixteenth centuries—
John Pykering, John Wendy, John Etwell, John Sheldon,
John Clifford, John Hewster, and Richard Gresham—
were, as Caxton had been earlier, leading members of the
Mercers' Company.[1] The tendency among outsiders to
identify the Fellowship as a whole with the Mercers'
Company is scarcely surprising. Under its shadow the
Fellowship had grown up, with no separate treasury or
executive, needing no royal charter, much as the earlier
misteries had grown up under the shadow of the
fraternities.

While its constitution was still not clearly defined, the
London Fellowship grew rapidly in corporate strength and
activity. Unlike the medieval English gild, it did not merely
make rules for the conduct of trade, but, like the modern
company, it actively concerned itself in the prosecution of
the trade. It resembled rather a Regulated than a Joint Stock
Company, since each member traded individually, but it
was the Fellowship which chartered the ships, fixed the
freights, determined when the fleet sailed, whither it went or
whether it was despatched at all. Merchants of high repute
were deputed to go down to the docks to see that all was in
order and that "the shippes have theire Complement and
also furnysshed with men, with vitaill, takkle and ablementes
of warr lyke and accordyng to the Charter partie."[2] These
Appointers were sometimes given discretionary power to
procure an extra armed convoy if necessary "for fear of
enemies." Thus in 1489 the "appoynters of shippes nowe
at Gravesend" received a letter reporting how, on the day
of their departure, a Court of Fellowships Adventurers was

---

[1] I have found no reference to any Governor of the period who was not a
Mercer, except the unsuccessful Master Rydon mentioned in 1485.
[2] Acts of Court, f. 88d.

assembled "at Sent Thomas of Acres, where amonge other the Wardens of drapers, grocers, skynners and other as well as of oure compeny of the mercery ben condiscended and agreed to obaye, holde and kepe alle suche direccion for suretie and savegarde by godes grace in sendyng furth of the shippes lyke as by all youre discrecions it shall seme most convenyent & necessarie to be had and don. Wherefore that ye wolle endevoyre you to the most profetable waye for the eas and welfare of us alle." [1] Similarly, when it was rumoured that many enemies were about, especially off Sluys, and three ships had been deputed to sail, the Appointers were told to consider with the masters and pursers "whether they shall departe with suche men as in their Charter partie . . . and for xd. sterling for freight of every clothe or to take yn to them moo men and to gyve and paye unto them xijd. sterling for the freight of every suche clothe." [2] The decision must often have been a difficult one, and masters and owners of ships were sometimes impatient of the delay in receiving final instructions from London. Indeed, it was not surprising that, when there were rumours of hostile fleets in the Channel, of ships being burnt in Seland,[3] or of "a grete armye" rigging out in France,[4] there was sometimes a "dowte of any aventer." [4] The need of a royal navy to protect merchant shipping was very apparent, and the Mercers' books afford interesting evidence of the first attempt made to supply this need by Henry VII. While he was prepared on occasions to allow his formidable new warships to convoy the cloth fleet across the Channel, Henry, with his accustomed caution, would run no unnecessary risks. In 1491, for instance, he insisted that the Adventurers should first send a swift messenger overseas to spy out the state of affairs, and report on the strength of the army and navy of the Archduke Philip. Accordingly a letter was sent from the Fellowships of Adventurers to a mercer at Bruges, and despatched by a messenger who was given £5 for his expenses. Eleven days

[1] *Ibid.*   [2] *Ibid.*, f. 96d.
[3] *Ibid.*, f. 100d.   [4] *Ibid.*, f. 99.

later the answer came. It was read out in a General Court of
Adventurers and sent on to the king with a request that, if
the king agreed to a shipping, the royal ships might accom-
pany those of the Adventurers. The king's reply, read
out in court next day, was scarcely encouraging. He first
advised them not to ship at all as yet, but to await developments, then remarked condescendingly that in any case if
they had only "the iiij shippes spoken of" it were "full
small stryngthe," and that "as for his shippes of warre,"
the presence of English warships in foreign waters might
cause international complications, while, even were he to
send them, his ships were too large to negotiate the shallows
there.[1] The following year, however, the Adventurers' fleet
went out with the king's ships of war, and later on both
Henry VII and Henry VIII more than once lent ships and
soldiers for "wafting the ships of the Merchant Adventurers
into Seland."[2]

On the return voyage the despatch of the ships properly
equipped and protected was entrusted to the Governor, and
he sometimes received special instructions from London.
In 1475, for instance, a letter was written to "John Pekyring,
Governour, and to all the felyshipp Englysshe merchauntes"
at Antwerp, informing him of the names of seven ships
which had been appointed, the number of armed men in
each and the freight to be charged both out and home, and
telling him to see that they were laden before any others and
were well victualled, "tackled and with ablements of warr."
According to the usual custom, Adventurers shipping in any
other vessels before these were fully laden were to pay the
full freight to the owners of these ships.[3]

[1] *Ibid.*, ff. 99–100: "The Cuntrey there will not be content or pleased to se
or suffur any suche shippes of warre withouten licens there to lye withyn their
stremes, for the kynges grace wolde not be pleased that any shipp of warr
estraunger withoute licens shuld so entre and lye withyn any his stremes here."
[2] See, e.g., *Letters and Papers of Henry VIII*, ed. J. S. Brewer, I, pt. i
(2nd ed., 1920), 671; Acts of Court, ff. 106, 107.
[3] Acts of Court, ff. 26d, 27; cf. *The York Mercers and Merchant Adventurers,
ut supra*, 75.

The London Adventurers co-operated not merely in the equipment of their fleets for the marts, but in formulating a common policy and taking common action to secure the most favourable conditions for their trade. During the foreign complications of Henry VII's reign they were continually before the king and his council giving expert evidence or pleading their own cause. Since Henry's adversaries were usually aided and abetted from the Low Countries while the Yorkist Duchess of York lived, he more than once for diplomatic reasons forbade all commercial intercourse, and the trade of the Adventurers seemed threatened with extinction. But money would settle most matters with Henry, as appeared from the events of 1489. After the discomfiture of Lambert Simnel, when Henry had as yet come to no agreement, the Adventurers were sternly upbraided for daring to go to the Low Countries, and were further told that John Wendy, one of their leading merchants, and John Colet, their Clerk, had assisted the rebels. In vain they pleaded a safe-conduct from the King of the Romans; this was not recognized by the King of England, so they sent to him a deputation of a mercer, a grocer, a draper and the Common Sergeant, lent by the mayor, and gave them £20 "for the costs." Nine days later the Mercers invited the Wardens of the Grocers, the Drapers, the Fishmongers, the Skinners, the Haberdashers, the Tailors and the Upholders to come and hear the King's reply. In this they were rebuked not for going to the Netherlands, but for going without a licence, and were informed that any who procured a licence might freely trade as before.[1] There were occasions, however, when even money would not move the king. When, for instance, the Perkin Warbeck expedition was being prepared in the Low Countries, Henry endeavoured to bring pressure to bear on his foes by absolutely prohibiting commercial intercourse. The Merchant Adventurers were recalled and ordered to hold their marts only in the English port of Calais. Reprisals followed in the Low Countries with

[1] Acts of Court, ff. 154–6.

the prohibition of the sale of English cloth there. The Merchant Adventurers petitioned against the restraint,[1] as did the townsmen of Bruges, but the king was adamant, and the Adventurers were compelled to submit.[2] Yet though King Henry, when faced by a serious menace to his throne, compelled the Adventurers to assist him in this way, he was ready to do all in his power to assist them. He would invite their help in council when negotiating a treaty, and would ask them to investigate and report upon such privileges as English merchants had previously possessed in the Low Countries. Accordingly in 1495, when Henry was negotiating the *Intercursus Magnus*, a committee of twelve was appointed in General Court to look up "suche remembrances of Previleges in thys place remaynyng to the Englysshe nacion by fflaunders and other the townshippes in thoos parties of the Duke of Burgoyn."[3]

Despite the *Intercursus* the Adventurers' troubles were not ended. New tolls and taxes were laid upon them in Antwerp. Those who refused to pay had the houses and cellars where they kept their cloth closed violently, with two or three locks put on them, and the collectors threatened that the Governor himself should be "grevously punysshed and corected in body and goodes." To secure the withdrawal of these impositions the Adventurers again united in sending deputations to seek out the king at Windsor, Woodstock and elsewhere, armed with translations of the foreign proclamations. Henry VII proved eager to further the cause of his merchants, ordering them to keep him fully informed of new developments. At the same time he was condescending in his patronage, being careful to tell them that only their own foolishness had led them into the difficulties from which he proposed to extricate them. Sternly he wrote:

[1] *Ibid.*, ff. 324–6.
[2] The predominance of the London Adventurers in the Netherlands is clearly shown on this occasion by their letter dismissing the Governor and ordering him to see to the safe conveyance of their privileges and the jewels and plate in the chapel (*ibid.*, f. 327).
[3] Acts of Court, f. 336d.

"That ye wolde so sone enclyne and conferme you to the said unlaufull ymposicion we marvell gretely and than to call uppon us for Remedye." He went on to advise them, since they had so "encumbered" themselves, to sell their goods as fast as they could and to return in all haste, leaving as little as possible behind them, promising that the Council would then consider the matter. Yet while privately scolding them, he wrote on their behalf what the Adventurers described as "a Sharppe letter from the King to the Duke." [1] Again, therefore, the Adventurers withdrew from Antwerp; again they looked up their previous privileges in the Mercers' Hall; and again, at the king's request, they appointed ambassadors, "two sad discrete persones of the Cite of London adventerers," instructing the Governor abroad to provide "good mannerly lodgeyng" for them all together in one place with their whole delegation to the number of thirty, with bedding and hangings, good wine and horsemeat.[2]

It was at such times, when trade with the Low Countries was forbidden, that the chronic friction between the Merchant Adventurers and their two chief rivals, the Hanseatics and the Staplers, became acute. This common rivalry was yet another incentive towards union among the Adventurers. More than once, when trade was prohibited, they met together to frame a petition to the king that the restraint should apply not only to his own subjects but to the Hanseatics, who would otherwise reap so great an advantage by the Englishman's enforced idleness and might capture the whole trade to the Low Countries. As the Adventurers ominously put it: "whiche if it shulde so any whyle contynue wolde growe to right grete Inconvenyency and distruccion eyther of us the kynges subiettes marchauntes or of the straungers as god forbede and defende." [3] With the Staplers

---

[1] *Ibid.*, ff. 338–54, 363; this letter is perhaps the one printed in *Letters and Papers of the Reigns of Richard III and Henry VII*, ed. J. Gairdner (Rolls Series, 1861–3), II, 69.

[2] *Ibid.*, f. 363.

[3] *Ibid.*, ff. 327–30, 332–4, a commentary upon the violent anti-Hanseatic riots in London this year.

relations were yet more strained, since the more the Adventurers expanded the export of English manufactured cloth, the more the export of raw wool shrank. Hence the irritated Staplers took every opportunity of harassing the Adventurers whenever they were compelled to resort to Calais with their unwelcome bales of English cloth; the Adventurers, on their part, from time to time made life almost intolerable for Staplers who ventured into the cloth trade in the Duke of Burgundy's lands. The story of the long battle between them has often been told,[1] but the Mercers' books afford interesting evidence of how it stimulated co-operation among the Adventurers, of the General Courts called to discuss the matter, and of the committees of Adventurers from various fellowships appointed with power to draw up petitions and conclude agreements.[2] Wise merchants became members of both Companies.

The great expense in which the cessation of trade with the Low Countries and the consequent negotiations with the king, Burgundy, the Staple and Calais involved the Adventurers brought to the fore the question of finance. Two methods of raising funds were employed by the London Fellowship. The regular expenditure on the despatch of the fleets and their safe convoy was met by a levy on all goods in the ships, referred to as the "conduit money." The assessment and collection of this were a frequent source of discord, but after the crisis of 1489 [3] a regular system seems to have been established. The conduitors, who were usually influential merchants from different fellowships, drew up a detailed rate of the amounts to be paid on all goods brought into London in the Adventurers' ships, basing it upon the costs of the particular conduit. Thus for the ships returning from the Synxon mart of 1497, a bale of madder was to be charged 12d., a sack of hops 16d., feathers, balls and glasses

---

[1] E.g., in Schanz, *op. cit.*, I, 344 *et seq.*
[2] Acts of Court, ff. 90, 91, 98, 132, 183d, 212d.
[3] *Supra*, 162.

half the freight, and a hundred bundles of brown paper 30d.[1] Sometimes the support of the custom officials was enlisted to ensure that none carried off their goods without paying. If there was a surplus it was very likely distributed among the various fellowships.[2] While the costs of the return convoy were thus levied in London, those of the outward convoy were levied overseas on all goods arriving there in the Adventurers' ships, or in ships which accompanied them. Instructions were sent from London by the appointers or the Mercers' Wardens to the "Treasurers of the English Nation," telling them of the sums due for the convoy arranged for and asking them to appoint conduitors to collect the amounts and to render an account to London.[3] When the expenses were very great, a loan might be raised first in London and repaid if possible on the return of the ships. This was done in 1492, when, during the perilous times of Henry's war with France, the conduit for the previous Balms and Cold marts was expected to reach the vast sum of £12,000 or £13,000.[2]

Extraordinary expenditure on behalf of the Adventurers in times of crisis was met in a different way. Since the securing of favourable conditions for trade in the Low Countries concerned all the English merchants dealing there, the London Fellowship considered that they should all contribute towards expenses.[4] When, therefore, deputations were sent to the King and his Council provided with funds as well as with new hats and gowns, ambassadors despatched overseas, or bills and petitions drawn up and presented, then loans were raised in London from all the Adventurers' fellowships, to be afterwards refunded from overseas. Thus the Skinners entered in their accounts for 1503–4 that they had "paid to the Wardens of the Mercers for a loan for the marchauntes adventurers of this Craft to be

[1] Acts of Court, f. 356.
[2] Ibid., f. 105.
[3] Ibid., ff. 97, 357, 358.
[4] See supra, 157, and cf. London, Guildhall, Repertory of the Court of Aldermen, i, f. 52b, 55b.

paid again as appeareth by a bill thereof made £4." [1] And
two years later they entered: "Item Receyvid of the Company of Marchauntes Adventurers £4 whiche was lent and
paid byfore owte of the Box of the Craft in aᵒ mvciij ffor
Skynners Marchauntes Aventurers." [2] Overseas the loan was
paid either from the freedom fines or by special impositions.
Not unnaturally the Mercers' Wardens, who transacted
the affair, had often to write to the Treasurers again and
again for the money, threatening to do no more for the
Nation. [3]

A new problem now arises. By what authority, if any, did
the London Fellowship order the taxation of the whole
English Nation overseas? To find an answer to this question
it is necessary to return once more to the Netherlands,
having traced the emergence of the Adventurer groups in
London and their gradual though still incomplete amalgama-
tion. Originally, as has been shown, the Adventurers in the
Netherlands were predominantly Londoners and Mercers,
associated together in the "Fraternity of St. Thomas
beyond the Sea," with its chapels in the mart towns. [4] But
with the increasing difficulties for English trade in the more
northerly regions, Adventurers from other cities flocked to
the Netherlands in ever-increasing numbers, concentrating
their business there and taking advantage of the privileges
granted there to the English. Amongst these newcomers
were many who at home were organized in city Adventurer
fellowships with as venerable and complicated an ancestry as
that of London, though more completely unified. [5] The
Merchant Adventurers of York and of Newcastle, for
instance, regularly equipped fleets for the quarterly marts,

[1] Account Books of the Skinners' Company, I, 1503–4; cf. Registers of the
Ironmongers' Company, I, ff. 91d, 92d, shown to me at Ironmonger Hall by
Mr. J. F. Adams Beck, Clerk of the Company.
[2] *Ibid.*, 1505–6.   [3] Acts of Court, ff. 54, 97, 357–362.   [4] *Supra*, 152.
[5] On the origins of provincial fellowships, see Gross, *op. cit.*; *The York
Mercers and Merchant Adventurers, ut supra*; *The Merchant Adventurers of
Newcastle-upon-Tyne, ut supra*. Among these provincial fellowships there
was no such distinctive gild grouping as still survived into the sixteenth
century among the London Adventurers.

and, with Adventurers from other northern towns, established themselves in the mart towns with their own shops
and stalls well away from those of the Londoners, claiming
the right to be ruled by their own Governors, since royal
charters had empowered the merchants to choose not one
Governor but "Governors." [1] Since trade was legally still
open to all, it seemed for a time as though it would remain
organized on a civic rather than on a national basis, and that
the North and South of England would be as divided
overseas as they sometimes threatened to be at home. But
the London Fellowship, faced with grave financial problems,
alarmed at the prospect of an unregulated trade with
unlimited competition from interlopers, resolved that all
must come within the original Fraternity. This conception
of a single organization with exclusive rights of trade, such
as were usually granted to the later Regulated Companies,
was vigorously challenged by the Northerners. Already in
1478 Pykering, as Governor, had stated the issue, seizing
the contributions of the northern towns, raising the entrance
fee for trading, levying impositions and forcing all to show
their cloth in the same streets. [2] Pykering was on this
occasion rebuked by Edward IV for his arbitrary acts, but
ere long he was to triumph. For when on the conclusion of
the *Intercursus Magnus* he went out as Governor, he took with
him two significant letters. One was from King Henry VII
"to oure trusty and welbeloved subiettes the marchauntes
adventerers that nowe be and hereafter for the tyme shalbe
in the parties under thobeysaunce of our Cosyn tharchduke
of Austriche & Duke of Burgoyn." It told them to follow
in all things "the sad advise and counceill of oure trusty and
welbeloved John Pykering whom at the desyre and nomina-
cion of the most partie of you resydent in our said cite of
London we have ordeigned and assigned to be Governour,

---

[1] See, *e.g.* the charter of 1407, *Foedera, ut supra*, IV, i, 107, and that of
1462 (*Cal. Patent Rolls*, 1461–7, p. 187).
[2] *The York Mercers and Merchant Adventurers, ut supra*, xxxvii–xxxix,
75 *et seq.*

maister and ruler of you all the hole ffelyshipp for the better order to be had amonge you." [1] Probably the troublous times of the Pretenders had shown Henry the advantages of a unified trade which he could use as a diplomatic weapon against his foes. The other letter was from the Mercers' Wardens, who, as has been shown, managed the financial affairs of the London Adventurers, to the Fellowship of the Merchants of the English Nation. It showed how Pykering was sent out for the good of "all" the king's merchants in those parts and asked that he might be paid £40. If this was done, said the Mercers, they and "all other felyshippes" (i.e., of London) would be ready to give further aid to the Nation.[2] Henceforward the king referred to Pykering as the "master of the fellowship of our subjects merchants adventurers" just as foreign princes commonly spoke of the "Governor of the English Nation," showing that there was considered to be but one all-inclusive fellowship. The Northerners did not readily submit, but again petitioned against the "uncharitable and inordinate covetise" of the Londoners, who forbad anyone to buy and sell "except he first compound and make fine with the said fellowship of merchants of London" and raised the entrance fees to the almost prohibitive sum of £20. This time, however, they were less successful. For though the fine was limited by Statute to ten marks, the right of the Fellowship to compel all to join was tacitly admitted.[3] Thus the Adventurers abroad were consolidated into a single gild-like group, with royal authorization and the right to levy fines from all engaging in their trade. At the same time they were now more definitely under state regulation, for the Government had intervened to limit their freedom to take what fines they pleased, and henceforth the entrance fines could only be raised by Act of Parliament.[4]

---

[1] Acts of Court, f. 338d.   [2] *Ibid.*, f. 339.   [3] Statute 12 Hen. VII, c. 6.
[4] Cf. the limitations of fines in the Eastland Company; and see discussions for petitions to raise the entrance fine, Acts of Court, ff. 316, 321; for subsequent changes in the entrance fines see Lipson, *op. cit.*, II, 217.

The newly unified group or "Company" as it now came more often to be called, soon acquired both a coat of arms [1] and a more precise form of government. By the Letters Patent of 1505 it was provided that there should be one Governor for the Merchant Adventurers in the Low Countries and a Court of Assistants of "24 of the most sadd, discreet and honest Persons of divers Fellowships of the said Merchants Adventurers." [2] The Company, like the gilds, had now developed an oligarchic form of government. On this Court of Assistants the Northerners secured at least some representation, as for the first time is made clear in two references in the Mercers' books. In 1517 it was decided at a court in the Low Countries that at every Cold mart there should be chosen as Assistants twelve "wyse, sad, discrete and substanciall persones, viij of dyvers felyshippes of the Cite of London, & iiij of other dyvers good townes in Englonde." The names of those elected follow, and there is a second list for 1522.[3] But though the Northerners had secured some share in the control of the Company in the Netherlands, the Londoners still dominated it. In the General Court they must certainly have been in the majority, and in the Court of Assistants, as shown by the above figures, they had at this time two-thirds of the representation. And since the Governor seems regularly to have been a Londoner, their influence was paramount in the executive also. Hence the whole policy of the Company of Adventurers could be dictated by the Londoners. If the London Adventurers determined that a tax should be taken, the other Adventurers

---

[1] In 1498; Schanz, *op. cit.*, II, 575, from the Merchant Adventurers' Inventory of Privileges (Sloane MS. 2103, f. 2).

[2] Printed in G. Cawston and A. H. Keane, *The Early Chartered Companies* (1896), 249, and Schanz, *op. cit.*, II, 549. This Patent provides for the Adventurers' government in Calais, to which they had temporarily removed.

[3] Acts of Court, f. 263: "Furthwith were chosen for London . . . William Baylly, John Aleyn, aldermen, William Bromewell and Robert Baylly, mercers, Nicholas Lambert, grocer, John Rudston, draper, John Josson, skynner and Polle Wethipolle, tayllour, and for the cuntrey William Cure of York, aldreman, Maister John Blakston of Newe Castell, aldreman, William Hert of Norwiche, aldreman and John Colsell of Excetour."

could be compelled to comply with their wishes.[1] It was not surprising that these other Adventurers resented the paramount influence of the Londoners and their own powerlessness. Thus Norwich members of the "Fellowship called the Fraternity of St. Thomas beyond the Sea in the Archduke's lands" wrote bitterly to the York Adventurers that they found themselves "sore aggrieved and not consent to" acts made "by London merchants" in the courts abroad, and that they had spoken against them in court, "but to no effect."[2] Separatist tendencies were still strong, and merchants still had their roots firmly fixed in their own cities, keenly conscious of the independent origins of their own fellowships and resentful of the ascendancy of London, just as in the London Fellowship the Adventurers were each loyal members of their own original companies and jealous of the Mercers' domination. Hence the Company of Merchant Adventurers in the Netherlands, despite its apparent unity, was in reality as complex an organism as that of the London Fellowship; formed of a variety of groups, with the London group as its nucleus and centre, each group still firmly attached to its parent company.

The London group of Adventurers, with its Fraternity of which all other Adventurers were now members, was not important merely because it carried most weight in the counsels of the Adventurers abroad. It occupied an altogether peculiar position, becoming to the whole Company of Merchant Adventurers very much what the Mercers had become to the London Fellowship, not only dominating its courts and committees, but providing it with a permanent home and a permanent executive, writing and receiving letters on its behalf and keeping its funds. It must be remembered that in the early sixteenth century there was still no security of trade with the Low Countries, particularly before the *Intercursus Malus*. Negotiations were almost continuously in progress, and the Adventurers refused to settle in any one

[1] Cf. *The York Mercers and Merchant Adventurers, ut supra,* 123.
[2] *Ibid.,* 121.

city as a staple, since while they were free they could "dryve the townshippes by feare of theyre withdrawing." [1] Hence it was almost imperative that they should have some headquarters to which they could always resort, where they could keep their charters and treasures, and from which, when they had temporarily withdrawn from the Low Countries, they could carry on negotiations.

In London, therefore, as well as in the Low Countries, courts met, presided over by the Governor, in the customary meeting-place of the London Fellowship. The holding of courts in the Mercers' Hall was indeed expressly sanctioned by the king. In the Letters Patent of 1506, given at a time when the Adventurers had for the moment abandoned the Low Countries, John Sheldon, the Governor, and his deputies or successors are empowered "to call courts and congregations of the said merchants within the City of London at the place of old accustomed or elsewhere as often as shall seem fit," and with "the assistance of twenty-four or at least thirteen of the Company to impose fines upon them." [2] Here as usual the Crown was only officially authorizing an established custom. Theoretically a national court of the whole Company seems to be implied, but it seems extremely improbable that such a court ever met. For the Governor could summon one at any time, and travelling difficulties must have rendered the attendance of the Northerners practically impossible, especially at short notice. There are in the Mercers' books the minutes of many such General Courts in London presided over by the Governor from the beginning of Henry VIII's reign,[3] but there is no clue to representatives of other cities being present, and the names when given can be identified as those of Londoners. Similarly the Court of Assistants in London,

---

[1] *Acts of Court*, f. 357d.

[2] *Calendar of Patent Rolls*, 1494–1509, p. 445, and Schanz, *op. cit.*, p. 553. W. E. Lingelbach seems to have overlooked this when he wrote: "Nowhere in the Letters Patent or Charters is there any mention of a General Court in London."

[3] For the ten years before this the entries are scanty.

which now took the place of the constant committees of earlier days, seems to have consisted exclusively of Londoners.[1] The only hint of a really national court in London being even contemplated was when once a General Court of the London Fellowship, making answer to the Council about a bill of the Shearmen and Fullers, said they thought that "withoute a Generall Assemble as well of the merchauntes of all other Cities, townes and Boroughes withyn the realme of Enlond (*sic*) as of the Citie of London the said bill can not be convenyently aunsward."[2]

Through these General Courts and Courts of Assistants held in London much business was transacted for all the Adventurers, particularly in negotiations with the Low Countries. Letters from the town of Antwerp to the "Governour and other merchauntes of the nation of Englonde" were read and discussed in General Court in London, and ambassadors of Antwerp were received by the Adventurers in the Mercers' Hall. The account of the reception of the Pensionary, Jacob de Witt, sent by Antwerp in 1509, gives a vivid picture of such a General Court: "At whiche courte were aldremen, Wardens and viij persones of the most auncient and discrete of theis Compenyes herafter written—that is to say mercers, grocers, drapers, ffyshemongers, tayllours, skynners and haberdysshers; and the aldermen sittyng uppon the high Bynche a longe maister John Hawes, oure maister, begynnyng to sitt at the south ende of the table, and all thaldermen a bothe syde of hym, and oure other Wardens syttyng uppon the Benche on the South syde in order, and maister Governour satt byfore theym uppon the fourmes ende, and than all other felishippes satt aboute the house every man in his degre, and when the hous was thus ordered Maister John Hawes, oure maister, shewed unto the Compeny the cause of their assembly at

---

[1] Acts of Court, ff. 176, 235d, 250, 300; there seems to have been no provision made for a really national court as was later done in the case of the Eastland Company. See Lucas, *op. cit.*, 177.

[2] *Ibid.*, f. 198d.

that tyme was for that there was comen a Pensonarii from Andewerpe and hath brought with hym lettres of credens from the said towne unto the compeny of merchauntes aventerers of this cite."[1] Naturally the most frequent subjects dealt with in these London courts, besides negotiations with foreign powers and with the Staple, were conduits, times of shipping and the question of which marts, if any, were to be visited. Thus in 1509 at a General Court of Adventurers in London the Governor asked whether they would ship to next Balms mart; there was a difference of opinion, the Governor desired a show of hands, and the majority determined that they would ship.[2]

It may be said that all these matters were the concern of London alone and do not, except for the presence of the Governor, indicate a national court. But there is no doubt that the General Court in London also initiated legislation and confirmed Acts made abroad which applied to the whole Company. Thus in 1526 we read of an Act made by the Governor and the Merchant Adventurers abroad being read in Court in London: "Whereupon by the said assemble here it is thought to be good and profetable for the holle Generaltie with the whiche acte they are right well contented to afferme the same, etc."[3] In London in the same year the Court of Assistants deputed seven Adventurers to draw up articles "for the comen welth of merchauntes adventerers" on a variety of specified topics; it is particularly noticeable that these mainly concerned the conduct of trade abroad, even down to the lodging and apparel of apprentices, and that they included the provision that two Governors should be elected. These articles were then read in a General Court in London and sent out by the Wardens of the Mercers to the Company overseas asking them to "peruse" them and fix the necessary fines for breach of them.[4] So much business

---

[1] *Ibid.*, ff. 172–6. Two of the Mercers' Wardens, one of the Drapers', and one of the Grocers', were sent down to the church below the hall to bring up the Pensionary.

[2] *Ibid.*, f. 172.   [3] *Ibid.*, f. 426.   [4] *Ibid.*, ff. 409 *et seq.*

was now being done in London for all the Merchant
Adventurers that they had now a special Solicitor (first
appointed in 1515) "for the merchauntes adventerers—here
in Englonde." [1] Further, just as the Mercers had originally
kept the treasure of all the London Adventurers, so now the
whole London Fellowship kept that of the national company.
Already by 1510 the Merchant Adventurers had a treasure
chest in the Mercers' Hall, [2] and later it becomes clear that
this was to be controlled by the whole London Fellowship.
For in 1518 it was ordained that a new one of iron should be
bought by the Governor at the cost of the Adventurers; this
was to have three locks and three keys, one to be kept by the
Mercers' Wardens, one by the Grocers', and one, that of the
padlock, by the Drapers'. [3] Into this chest was put the surplus
money belonging to the Company at the end of each mart.
It was the duty of the Treasurer of the Company to deliver
it to the Wardens who had the keeping of the keys, to
receive an acquittance from them, and to deliver this
acquittance "over the other side of the see before the
assistants in the next mart." [4] Similarly the charters and
privileges granted both by English and foreign rulers were,
as has been shown, kept in the Mercers' Hall, and there they
were sometimes consulted on behalf of the Company as a
whole. [5]

Not only did the Adventurers hold courts and keep their
treasures in London, but the Governor himself was continually to and fro, holding his courts either in the Low Countries
or in London; when he was in London he left deputies in the
Low Countries; when he was in the Low Countries he left
deputies in London. [6] The inconvenience to the Company
abroad of his flittings to and fro was at one time (1526)

---

[1] *Ibid.*, f. 217, and see ff. 260d, 409.   [2] *Ibid.*, f. 188.
[3] *Ibid.*, ff. 247, 248, and see ff. 301d.   [4] *Ibid.*, ff. 247–8, 249.
[5] In the Acts of Court, vol. ii, which contains no Merchant Adventurer
minutes, there is a note of a document being sent overseas at the request of
the Company, and returned again, f. 76. There is as yet no trace of the
Company's own minutes for this period.
[6] Acts of Court, ff. 312, 314d.

met by the provision that there should be two Governors, so that one should always be at the mart, but there is no proof that this arrangement lasted.[1] In a similar way the difficulty of his absences from London had once in 1516 been met by the appointment of a separate Governor for the realm of England, but this plan was not permanent, and in 1517 and again in 1518 it was agreed that the Wardens of the Mercers should always be deputies for the Governor in England.[2] Thus the Mercers' Wardens acquired a yet further and national importance. The fact that a special seat for the Governor was appointed in the Mercers' Hall "when Mr. Governor shall keep his courts in this place"[3] makes any attempt at a geographical distinction as to where the seat of government lay seem trivial and unreal; there was a seat for the Governor on both sides of the Channel, but whether he held his courts overseas or at home it was the wishes of the London Adventurers which prevailed. Yet, further, the Londoners evidently had the controlling interest in the election of the Governor, not only through their numerical superiority in the courts abroad, where the elections were held, but through the court at home, which at any rate once acted as a court of appeal in the case of a disputed election.[4] And when in 1526 the Company overseas elected two Governors "folowyng your discrete advise and our auctorities," one of those elected then secured letters from the Mercers' Wardens excusing him on the ground that he "coulde not streyn his body in goyng of borde of the ship, nor in the shipp because of the Wedering."[5]

The London Merchant Adventurers had thus by the time of Henry VIII grown into a body much more important than that envisaged in the Ordinance of 1486. Far removed were the days when they sought civic sanction for their meetings. Now they dared boldly even to defy the mayor. When in 1518 the mayor remonstrated with the Company

---

[1] *Ibid.*, ff. 409 *et seq.*; by the Articles of 1526.
[2] *Ibid.*, ff. 235d, 237, 248, 243d, 250.
[3] *Ibid.*, f. 240d. [4] *Ibid.*, f. 235d. [5] *Ibid.*, ff. 419, 426.

overseas for choosing two aldermen, urgently needed in London, as their assistants and fining them heavily for not being present at the marts, the Governor insisted that by royal charters they were fully at liberty to call London aldermen overseas. In vain the mayor protested that the business of the City of London was "more ponderous and of gretter weight and difficulty then yours." The Court of Assistants in London "all with oon voyce ansueryd: That they wold noon otherwyse do than they had doon." [1] So closely were the London courts and the London treasury now identified with those of the whole Company that the London Fellowship had developed no complete and independent organization of its own, but occupied a peculiar position midway between the Mercers and the national Company of the Merchant Adventurers trading to the Netherlands. Its position reveals clearly the origins and growth of the now unified national Company. Dominating all the Adventurers in the Netherlands, whom they had compelled to come within their Fraternity of St. Thomas, the London Adventurers gave them a permanent home, transacted their business, kept their funds, decided which marts were to be attended and when, and legislated for the whole Company, both through the courts at home and through those abroad in which they could command an easy majority. In the same way the London Adventurers were themselves dominated by the Mercers' Company, whose vigorous Adventurer group was the nucleus round which they had coalesced. Mercers were in the majority both in their General Courts and in the Court of Assistants; the Mercers' Wardens transacted much of their business and presided over their meetings, and thus, in the absence of the Governor, over the meetings of the whole Company; Mercers' Hall was their headquarters, and hence the headquarters of the whole Company and the repository of its treasure and of its private records.

[1] London, Guildhall, Journal, 11, f. 345b, Repertory of the Court of Aldermen, iii, f. 216b, iv, f. 23, v, ff. 147, 149; Acts of Court, ff. 254–63.

IV

AN INDUSTRIAL REVOLUTION OF THE THIRTEENTH CENTURY [1]

It has been commonly supposed that the thirteenth century witnessed a decline in the nascent cloth industry of England, a decline which was only to be checked and converted into renewed advance and yet more spectacular progress under the vigorous patronage of Edward III. We read, for instance, of the "impoverished state" of the industry "on the eve of the great experiment"; of how "something was wrong with the industry, and if it was to be given fresh life something must be done." [2] Such a conception of arrested growth and even of decay is not, however, borne out by a close investigation of the sources. On the contrary, they reveal rather the expansion and rapid development of the industry up to the eve of the accession of Edward III. The reason for this discrepancy is not that the sources themselves have been misinterpreted, but that only one group of them, the urban records, has been hitherto explored in this connection. It has been too readily assumed that the history of industry in England at this time was to be found in the history of her towns and their gilds, and that symptoms of decline evident here signified a decline in the industry as a whole. In reality, however, rural records also throw a flood of light on the industrial history of the time, and when they are considered in conjunction with those of the towns it becomes apparent that the century was one of

[1] *Economic History Review*, XI, No. 1, 1941. Owing to war conditions it proved impossible to check and to complete all the references in this article, particularly those to MS. sources in the custody of the Public Record Office.

[2] E. Lipson, *The History of the English Woollen and Worsted Industries* (1921), 11; cf. E. Lipson, *The Economic History of England*, 7th edition (1937), 449–50; L. F. Salzman, *English Industries of the Middle Ages* (1923), 203.

striking progress industrially, though of equally striking change and upheaval. It witnessed, in fact, an industrial revolution due to scientific discoveries and changes in technique; a revolution which brought poverty, unemployment and discontent to certain old centres of the industry, but wealth, opportunity and prosperity to the country as a whole, and which was destined to alter the face of medieval England.

In the early Middle Ages the various processes of cloth-making were all strictly "handcrafts." The chief processes, apart from dyeing and finishing, were four. First the wool was carded or combed by hand; then it was spun on the rock or distaff. Next the yarn thus prepared was woven on a loom worked by hand and foot, and finally the loose "web" thus made was fulled by hand or foot. The process of fulling, that is to say, of beating or compressing the cloth in water, served first of all to shrink the cloth, reducing it in width by anything from a fifth to a half, and in length to a corresponding extent.[1] This so increased the density and weight per unit of length as to give it much greater resistance to weather and wear. Secondly, it served to "felt" the cloth, so inextricably entangling the fibres that the pattern of the weaving often ceased to be visible. This not only gave the cloth greater fabric strength, but also a smoother and softer surface, and it was an essential preliminary to the finishing processes of raising and shearing applied to the finer cloths. In addition to shrinking and felting the cloth, making it close and firm, the fulling process also scoured it and cleansed it, with the aid of various detergents [2] such as fuller's earth, removing especially the oil with which the wool had been impregnated before spinning. Now the mechanising of

[1] For the purpose and nature of fulling, see J. and J. C. Schofield, *The Finishing of Wool Goods* (1935), and J. Schofield, *The Science and Practice of Scouring and Milling* (1921). The medieval assize of cloth sometimes quoted a different standard for cloth "watered" and cloth "unwatered," *e.g.* Statute 11 Henry VI, c. 9.

[2] Cf. G. Espinas, "Essai sur la Technique de l'Industrie textile à Douai aux xiii et xiv⁰ siècles," *Mémoires de la Société nationale des Antiquaires de France*, LXVIII (1909), 42.

the first three cloth-making processes during the eighteenth and nineteenth centuries is a commonplace of history, but the mechanising of the fourth during the thirteenth century, though it gave rise to an industrial revolution not less remarkable, has attracted scarcely any attention. It is with this that the present article proposes to deal.

Three primitive methods of fulling "by might and strength of man," without any mechanism, have been most commonly used in western Europe: beating with the feet, with the hands, or with clubs wielded by hand. Most suited to long heavy broadcloths is some method of fulling by foot such as is vividly portrayed in the paintings on the piers of the *fullonica* at Pompeii, and in those of the house of the Vettii there. In these we can see the fuller at work, standing almost naked in a trough, trampling the cloth under foot, while his hands rest on low side walls by which he can support and raise himself. Traces of what may have been fulleries such as these in Roman Britain have been revealed in three places: at Titsey and Darenth in Kent, and at Chedworth in Gloucestershire. Here have been found very similar troughs, circular in form, with low side walls and drainage facilities.[1] Their close proximity, in each case, to beds of fuller's earth and to what later became flourishing centres of the industry, would seem to lend some support to the theory that they were fulleries, though the matter cannot be considered as finally determined. From Roman Gaul we have an actual representation of a fuller at work in a trough, carved on the "fuller's tomb" at Sens.[2] So for a thousand years and more fullers trod the cloth underfoot, as indeed they have long continued to do in outlying parts, such as the Hebrides, untouched by the mechanical inventions of the thirteenth or of the eighteenth centuries. The early fourteenth century ordinances of the fullers' gilds both at Lincoln and at

[1] *Archaeologia*, LIX (1904), G. E. Fox, "Notes on some probable traces of Roman Fulling in Britain," 208–9; *Guide to Chedworth Roman Villa* (1926), 12–13.

[2] C. Roach-Smith, *Collectanea Antiqua*, V (1861), plate XX, fig. 1.

Bristol mention this working "in the trough,"[1] and later on in *Piers Plowman* we read of cloth that is "fulled under fote."[2]

Sometimes hands were used instead of, or in addition to, feet. A visitor to Skye in 1774 thus described the Luaghad, or fulling of cloth, there: "Twelve or fourteen women, divided into equal numbers, sit down on each side of a long board ribbed lengthways, placing the cloth on it: first they begin to work it backwards and forwards with their hands, singing at the same time as at the quern: when they have tired their hands, every female uses her feet for the same purpose, and six or seven pairs of naked feet are in the most violent agitation, working one against the other: as by this time they grow very earnest in their labours, the fury of the song rises; at length it arrives to such a pitch that without breach of charity you would imagine a troop of female demoniacs to have been assembled."[3]

Hand fulling alone, or fulling with clubs wielded by hand, has probably always been used for smaller articles. Indeed methods of fulling even in the same locality seem commonly to have varied according to the size and character of the articles to be fulled. A traveller to Iceland in 1814–15 thus describes two different methods in vogue there: "Both ends being knocked out of a barrel, it is filled with articles to be fulled, when it is laid on the side, and two men lie down on their backs, one at either end, with their feet in the barrel, and literally *walk* the cloth, by kicking it against each other. Smaller articles they full by placing them between their knees and breast, and then moving backwards and forwards with the body, turning them always with their hands till ready. This accounts for the very awkward motion which the Icelanders almost always fall into when sitting,

[1] Toulmin Smith, *English Gilds* (1870), 180, "*in alveo*"; *Little Red Book of Bristol*, ed. F. B. Bickley (1900), II, 12, "*ouveraunt en le stok.*"
[2] *Piers Plowman* (B), XV, 445. Angus Pirie, a skilled weaver of Dornoch, used to full his cloth by foot in a trough but has given up this method as too strenuous and too chilling now that he is old.
[3] Quoted in E. Lipson, *History of the English Woollen and Worsted Industries* (1921), 139.

and from which many of them cannot refrain even in church." [1] In France in the eighteenth century fulling by hand was frequently used for hosiery, and fulling with clubs wielded by hand for hats and caps.[2] We may infer a similar use of clubs in Roman times from the account of the martyrdom of Saint James the Less, written in the second century: "*Quidam autem ex eis, accepto fuste ex officina fullonis, quo comprimebat vestes, valide infligit ejus capiti.*"[3] For this reason the fuller's club became the emblem of St. James and is to be seen in many medieval representations of him, as for instance in the east window of Gloucester Cathedral, on the rood screen at Ranworth, on one of the stall panels at Blythburgh, and on the font at Stalham.[4]

In medieval records it is not easy to distinguish this method of using clubs from that of fulling by hand alone, since both could be described as "fulling by hand" in distinction to "fulling by foot." At any rate it seems that in England one or other of these methods of hand fulling was commonly used for hats and caps. Thus in London long after mechanical fulling had commonly been adopted for broadcloths, the Hurers successfully petitioned against this method being allowed for hats and caps, and ordinances were passed to this effect in 1376 [5]; several citizens were fined for breach of the ordinance and, during the hearing of a case against one John Godefray, a jury of cappers and hatters declared that caps could not and ought not to be fulled under the feet or in any other way than by the hands of men.[6] It is clear that the hatters and cappers were as much opposed to fulling by foot as to mechanical fulling; thus again in 1404

[1] E. Henderson, *Iceland* (Edinburgh, 1818), I, 365.
[2] Savary des Bruslons, *Dictionnaire Universel de Commerce*, II, 526; Postlethwayt, *Universal Dictionary of Trade and Commerce* (4th edition, 1774): "Fulling." [3] *Acta Sanctorum*, vol. XIV, 35.
[4] For other examples, see C. Cahier, *Caractéristiques des saints dans l'art populaire* (1867), 547; F. C. Husenbeth, *Emblems of Saints*, 3rd edition, ed. A. Jessopp (1882), 110.
[5] *Memorials of London*, ed. H. T. Riley (1868), 400.
[6] *Calendar of Plea and Memoranda Rolls*, 1364–1381, ed. A. H. Thomas (1929), 230, 233; *Memorials of London, ut supra*, 529.

they petitioned that their work should not be fulled in mills *or by feet*, but only by the hands of men, and again offending citizens were punished.[1] Most probably hand fulling was reserved for small articles such as hats and caps, made usually of felt, while the long, heavy broadcloths which came to form the staple of the English export industry were fulled by foot.

Such were the primitive methods of fulling in use when the English woollen industry was first established. Most important of them is fulling by foot, since this method was applied to the long, heavy broadcloth which came to form the staple of the English export industry.

The mechanical method of fulling invented during the Middle Ages, and in use for many centuries, was evolved from the primitive method of fulling by foot. The invention was a twofold one. In the first place the action of the two feet was replaced by that of two wooden hammers, alternately raised and dropped on the cloth as it lay in the trough, and controlled probably by a revolving drum on the tilt- or lift-hammer system.[2] In the second place this revolving drum was attached to the spindle of a water-wheel, and this supplied the motive power. Thus, by a simple contrivance, water power was made to replace human labour, and a series of hammers could be set to work with but one man standing by to watch the cloth and see that it was kept properly moving in the trough. The whole was then spoken of as a *molendinum fullericum*, or "fulling mill,"[3] since, though it was not strictly a mill (*molendinum*) in that it did

---

[1] *Memorials of London, ut supra*, 667.

[2] This revolving drum could be turned by hand, and such a device may still be seen in use in parts of Scotland to-day, though it is very heavy to work.

[3] While "fulling mill" is the most widely used term, certain parts of England had their own local terms, derived from words of different origins describing the same fulling process. Thus in place of "full," "fuller," "fulling mill," we find "tuck," "tucker," "tucking mill" in the west country, especially in Cornwall, Devon and Somerset; and "walk," "walker," "walking mill" (or "walkmill") in the north, especially in the Lake District, while in Wales a fulling mill becomes a "pandy." Many of the sites of these ancient mills can be identified by the fact that they have one or other of these expressions attached to them.

not grind (*molere*), it bore a resemblance in one part of its mechanism to the water corn mill. Indeed the building itself, down by the water, with its leet and its revolving wheel, would be difficult to distinguish externally from a corn mill. Henceforth, just as there had hitherto been a distinction in rentals, surveys, etc., between the windmill, the watermill and the horsemill (*molendinum ventricum, molendinum aquaticum* and *molendinum ad equos*), so now there appears a further distinction between the water *corn* mill and the water *fulling* mill (*molendinum aquaticum blaericum* and *molendinum aquaticum fullericum*).

The question now arises as to the date of the invention of the water fulling mill. This would seem impossible to fix with any certainty. M. Bloch asserts that there was a fulling mill at Grenoble "about 1050," [1] but the actual evidence does not seem to support his conclusion. The charter to which he refers speaks of certain rights "*in unum quodque molendinum, quando edificatur, et in bateorium, similiter quando edificatur.*" [2] Now a *bateorium, battorium, batatorium* or *baptitorium* is certainly a place where beating or hammering is carried on, but we are not justified in assuming that this beating was done by water power, or that it was necessarily the beating of cloth. Ducange defines *Bateria* as, "*Ars tundendi pannos, terendi cortices et alia similia facienda,*" and in a charter quoted by him there are enumerated "*furnos, torcularia, molendina, baptitoria, et fullonos.*" Clearly, then, a *baptitorium* or *bateorium* is not even synonymous with a fullery, much less with a mechanical fulling *mill*, and there is as yet no evidence that the fulling mill was known on the continent at that date.[3] In England, at any rate, it seems as though water fulling mills were introduced in the latter part of the twelfth century. The earliest reference to one so far discovered is that in the survey of the Templars' lands made

[1] *Annales d'histoire économique et sociale*, No. 36, Nov. 1935, M. Bloch, "Avènement et conquêtes du moulin à eau," 543.

[2] *Cartulaires de l'Église Cathédrale de Grenoble*, ed. M. J. Marion (Paris, 1869), 119.

[3] See note at end, p. 210.

in 1185. This mentions a "*molendinum fulerez*" at Newsham in Yorkshire and another, built by the Templars themselves, at Barton, close to Temple Guiting, in the Cotswolds.[1] Four years later a charter to the Abbey of Stanley in Wilts speaks of the "*molendinum monachorum fullericum.*"[2] The absence so far of any earlier references to fulling mills does not, of course, prove their non-existence, and how far the lack of other evidence for the twelfth and earlier centuries is due to lack of documents comparable to those of later centuries it is impossible to say. But a significant change in nomenclature points also to the change having been introduced in the late twelfth century. For from the opening of the thirteenth century not only do references to such mills increase, but so also does the use of the phrase *corn* mill in distinction to *fulling* mill, while the word *fullonia* disappears, giving place to *molendinum fullericum*. Certainly the fulling mill cannot have been at all widely used until the thirteenth century, and it is in the late thirteenth century that we come across the first evidence of opposition to its use on the part of the handworkers.

The origin of the invention is even more obscure than its date. We know neither in what country, nor by whom, water power was first applied to fulling, nor whether the idea spread from a common source or was evolved independently in different regions. It is conceivable that the Templars may have introduced the fulling mill into England. At any rate the religious orders were among the first to take advantage of it and to develop its possibilities. In monastic cartularies many early references, not all of which can be precisely dated, are to be found to fulling mills. About the year 1200 the

---

[1] R. Dodsworth and Sir W. Dugdale, *Monasticon Anglicanum* (1655–73), II, 540; B. A. Lees, *Records of the Templars in England in the Twelfth Century* (1935), ccxiii, 50, 127, cxxv. There was also a derelict fulling mill at Witham, Essex, in 1308, and this may, it is suggested, represent the "mill" in the survey of 1185, *ibid.*, lxxix.

[2] W. de G. Birch, *Collections towards the history of the Cistercian Abbey of Stanley, Wilts* (1876), 43, quoting Harleian MS. 84, f. 273b; see also pp. 15, 17, 33, for later references.

Abbey of Winchcomb possessed a fulling mill at "Clively," and when the Abbot made a grant of another mill it was on condition that it should not be converted into a fulling mill to compete with his own.[1] The monks of Evesham held a fullers' mill (*molendinum fullonum*) at Bourton-on-the-Water in Gloucestershire in 1206 [2]; the Augustinian friary of St. John the Baptist at Ludlow had one before 1221, probably on the Teme [3]; Newminster had one on the Wansbeck very early in its history [4]; St. Albans had established one by 1274,[5] and in an extent of the Abbey of Kirkstall of 16 Edward I a fulling mill is mentioned as well as a tanning mill.[6]

Nor were the great episcopal estates behind the monastic ones. The earliest Pipe Roll of the Bishop of Winchester (1208–9) shows that he then possessed four fulling mills (described as "*fulleraticum*" and "*foleraticum*"): at Waltham, Sutton, Brightwell and New Alresford; mills to which Dr. Hubert Hall called attention as "perhaps the earliest fulling mills in England of which we have mention." [7] Later rolls show the Bishop possessed of a fulling mill at Downton in Wiltshire by 1215, of two in Oxfordshire, at Witney, by 1223, and of one in Somerset, at Taunton, by 1224.[8] The Bishop of Bath owned a fulling mill at Kidderminster in 1293,[9] while early in the following century the Bishop of

---

[1] *Monasterium Beatae Mariae Virginis et Sancti Cenhelmi: Landboc*, ed. D. Royce (1892), I, 195.

[2] *Chronicon Abbatiae Eveshamensis*, ed. W. D. Macray (Rolls Series, 1863), 213.

[3] British Museum, Harleian MS. 6690, f. 89 ff., quoted in T. Wright, *History of Ludlow* (1852), 98.

[4] *Newminster Cartulary* (Surtees Society, vol. 66, 1878), 3.

[5] *Gesta Abbatum Monasterii Sancti Albani*, ed. H. T. Riley (Rolls Series, 1867), I, 410 ff.

[6] P.R.O. Ancient Extents 86 (1).

[7] *Pipe Roll of the Bishop of Winchester*, ed. Hubert Hall (1903), xxvii, 1, 13, 41, 61.

[8] P.R.O. Ecclesiastical Commission, Various, II, 159273, 159278 ff. References given by Miss M. Wretts-Smith.

[9] *Inquisitions Post Mortem for the County of Worcestershire*, edited for the Worcester Historical Society by J. W. Willis Bund (1894), I, 43; *Calendar of Inquisitions Post Mortem*, III, 45 (21 Edward I).

Exeter agreed to join with the Mayor and Commonalty of Barnstaple in erecting mills, including fulling mills, on the river which divided their property.[1]

It must not, however, be assumed that, since many of the earliest surviving references are to mills on monastic and ecclesiastical estates, laymen lagged behind. Indeed in the monastic cartularies themselves we get glimpses of lay owners of fulling mills, for such mills often happened to be part of endowments bestowed by laymen upon a monastery. About the year 1200, for instance, Robert of Seckworth owned two "myllis fuleree" in Seckworth and granted the tithes of them to the nunnery of Godstow.[2] Godstow also claimed tithes in 1235 of the mill called "pannmylle" (probably a "cloth mill") at Wycombe.[3] Again, when Peter Undergod founded the hospital of St. John the Baptist near the bridge over the Teme at Ludlow, he endowed it, *inter alia*, with the fulling mill which he had bought from Gilbert de Lacy.[4]

The fulling mills on lay estates for which most early records survive are, not unnaturally, those of the king himself. One of the first royal mills was that near Marlborough, at Elcot. This was in existence in the reign of John and was rebuilt by the king's orders in 1237. The task was entrusted to William de Pretsch and Vincent Carpentar', who had workmen under them, and cost altogether £4, 17s. 4d. Most of this money was spent on felling and carting timber from Savernake forest; the rest on remaking the mill-pond, the weir, the mill-wheel and its enclosure, the mill-race and also the "*flagella et baterella*"—probably the hammers for beating the cloth.[5] In 1251 Henry III ordered

---

[1] *Reprint of the Barnstaple Records*, ed. J. A. Chanter and T. Wainwright (1900), I, 110, No. xx.

[2] *The Godstow and Oseney Registers*, ed. A. Clark (Early English Text Society, 1905), I, 43.   [3] *Ibid.*, 89.   [4] Wright, *op. cit.*, 98.

[5] *Calendar of Liberate Rolls*, I, 278; *Great Roll of the Pipe, 1241–2*, 175; *Rotuli Litterarum Clausarum*, ed. T. D. Hardy (Record Commission, 1833–44), II, 23; *Rotuli Chartarum*, ed. J. D. Hardy, I, i (1119–1216), 218, m. 4, 6.

a fulling mill to be built in his park at Guildford [1]; the royal manor of Steeple Langford in Wilts had one in 1294,[2] and by the beginning of the following century there was a royal fulling mill in the West Riding at Knaresborough.[3]

When we turn to trace fulling mills on estates other than monastic, episcopal or royal, there is, unfortunately, no comparable evidence available. The sources are on the whole later in date and different in character. The mandates and instructions on royal Close Rolls and Liberate Rolls have, for instance, no parallel, and in place of the twelfth and early thirteenth century monastic cartularies we have only scattered deeds, scarcely ever so early in date. Nor are there any early consecutive series of manorial accounts such as those enrolled on the great Pipe Rolls of the Bishop of Winchester or on the royal Pipe Rolls, but only separate accounts, surviving in fragments. The principal sources are threefold: first the Inquisitions Post Mortem taken on the death of a supposed tenant-in-chief for the information of the king; secondly, Rentals and Custumals of individual manors drawn up for the information of the lord of the manor and his officials; and, thirdly, year to year Accounts kept of the administration of such manors and records of their Courts. These three sources are extensive from the latter part of the thirteenth century, though not until then. The first is the most accessible in print, through the *Calendars of Inquisitions Post Mortem*, but these are deceptive for the present investigation since they do not always reproduce the detailed extents in which the fulling mills are usually to be found. In these printed calendars, for instance, no fulling mills appear for Wiltshire before the reign of Edward III, but the more detailed *Abstracts of Wiltshire Inquisitions Post-Mortem* (1242–1326) give five.[4] Hence, for

[1] *Calendar of Liberate Rolls*, III, 376; T. H. Turner, *Domestic Architecture in England*, I (1851), 233, II (1853), 149.

[2] P.R.O. Rentals and Surveys, General Series, portf. 16, no. 66.

[3] *Calendar of Close Rolls*, 1302–7, 35.

[4] *Abstracts of Wiltshire Inquisitions Post Mortem*, ed. E. A. Fry, I (1242–1326) (1908), 119, 227, 246, 257, 350.

counties where we have no such thorough survey, the originals must constantly be consulted. It must further be remembered that these inquisitions may not always record the state of affairs at the moment that the return was actually made; they may reproduce earlier surveys. Thus when a fulling mill appears we can only be certain that it existed either at that or at an earlier date. Nor do Rentals and Custumals always give precise dates; often their date can only be inferred from their handwriting, and even then it is possible that they are sometimes copies of earlier surveys. None of these sources are sufficiently comprehensive to form any basis for statistical analysis, but from them and other records we can at least gain an impression of the rapid extension of the fulling mill during the thirteenth century and its widespread distribution at the beginning of the fourteenth century. And it must be borne in mind that the mills of which record has survived can be only a small proportion of the total, and that the present investigation cannot claim in any way to be exhaustive.[1]

The accompanying table attempts to set out geographically the evidence which has so far come to light as to the distribution of fulling mills in England before the reign of Edward III. All the mills noted here date from the thirteenth or early fourteenth centuries (before 1327), except for the three already mentioned as dating from the late twelfth century; most of them belong to the reigns of Edward I or Edward II.[2]

From this survey, inadequate though it must be, it is evident that the use of the fulling mill had become widespread over England and the borders of Wales between the end of the twelfth and the beginning of the fourteenth century. The fulling mill was, indeed, destined to supersede almost entirely the primitive fulling "under the feet of

---

[1] Further evidence is constantly coming to light, and collections of local deeds still have much to yield. The writer would welcome information as to other early mills than those listed below.

[2] For abbreviations used in the references, see list at end of article.

The Pennines

Yorkshire: West Riding

Almondbury	M.A., 29/2 (32–3 Ed. I); 1145/21 (Ed. (II))
Alverthorpe	Yorks Archaeological Soc., Record Series, XXIX, *Wakefield Court Rolls*, I, 250 (1296)
Bradford	M.A., 29/2, 1145/21
Castleford	M.A., 1145/21
Kirkstall	Anc. Ext., 86 (1)
Knaresboro'	*Supra*, p. 193
Leeds	M.A., 1154/21
Newsham	*Supra*, p. 190
Rothwell	M.A., 29/2, 1145/21
Thorpe Arch	*Cal.I.P.M.*,IV,25(29Ed.I)
Wakefield	*Wakefield, ut supra*, I, 176, 252 (1277, 1296); II, 185 (1316)

North Riding

Burton Constable	I.P.M., Ed. II, 63
Masham	*Cal. C.R.*, 1302–7, 164

Lancashire

Burnley	Chetham Soc., CXII, *Two Compoti of the Lancs and Cheshire Manors of Henry de Lacy, 24 and 33 Ed. I*, 4, 8, 15, 16
Colne	*Ibid.*
Manchester	*Ibid.*, p. xxii
Wyresdale	I.P.M., Ed. II, 69

The Lake District

Applethwaite (Windermere)	I.P.M., Ed. II, 81
Brampton	*Cal. I.P.M.*, III, 184 (23 Ed. I)
Carleton	M.A., 824/28 ff. (1 Ed. I ff.)
Carlisle	C. Gross, *Gild Merchant*, II, 39
Clifton	*Cal. I.P.M.*, III, 432 (28 Ed. I)
Cockermouth	Surtees Soc., CXXVI, *Register of St. Bees*, 48, 449 (27 Ed. I); R. & S., 730; M.A., 460/24
Crosthwaite	I.P.M., Ed. I, 32 Ed. II, 81 [1]
Dacre	I.P.M., Ed. II, 82
Egremont	*Cal. C.R.*, 1288–96, 402
Embleton	I.P.M., Ed. II, 75
Glassonby	I.P.M., Ed. II, 76
Grasmere	I.P.M., Ed. I, 5, 32; Ed. II, 81 [2]

The Lake District

Greenriggs	I.P.M., Ed. II, 17
Grizedale	I.P.M., Ed. II, 82
Kendal	P.R.O. Assize Roll, 979, m. 2 (40 Hen. III)
Millom	I.P.M., Ed. II, 50
Penrith	M.A., 824/28 ff. (1 Ed. I ff.)
Sowerby	*Ibid.*
Staveley	Lancs & Cheshire Record Soc., vol. 54, *Lancs Inquests, Extents and Feudal Aids*, II, 148

The Midlands

Derbyshire

Hartington	*Cal. I.P.M.*, III, 300 (26 Ed. I); M.A., 29/3 (7–8 Ed. II)
Wirksworth	*Cal. I.P.M.*, III, 291 (25 Ed. I); M.A., 29/3

Nottinghamshire

Warsop	*Notts I.P.M.*, 128 (1268)

Northamptonshire

Wellingboro'	

Staffordshire

Barton	M.A., 29/3 (7–8 Ed. II)
Himley	*Cal. I.P.M.*, VI, 470 (20 Ed. II)
Rolleston	M.A., 29/3

Worcestershire

Hartlebury	M.A., 1143/18 (30–1 Ed. I)
Kidderminster	*Worc. I.P.M.*, I, 43 (1293); *Cal. I.P.M.*, III, 45
Mitton	J. R. Burton, *Kidderminster*, 21
Overbury (*see* Cotswolds)	
Shelsley (*see* Welsh Marches)	

The Welsh Marches

Alvington	*Tax. Eccl.*, p. 172
Caerleon	M.A.1202/6 ff. (7 Ed. II ff.)
Ludlow	T. Wright, *Ludlow*, 98; Brit. Mus. Harl. MS., 6690 f., 89 ff.
Monmouth	*Tax. Eccl.*, 172
Painscastle	I.P.M., Ed. II, 50
Shelsley	*Worc. I.P.M.*, II, 7
Talgarth	*Cal. C.R.*, 1307–13, 200
Usk	M.A.,1202/6 ff.(7 Ed.II ff.)
Wilton	I.P.M., Ed. II, 82

The West of England

Cornwall

Heskyn	*E.C.H.*, 207 (1307)
Lawhitton	*Mon. Ex.*, 429 (1308)
Legha in Buryan	*E.C.H.*, 208, n. 8 (1316–17)
Penryn	*Mon. Ex.*, 430 (1308)
Sheepstall nr. Ruan	*E.C.H.*, 207 (1260)
Talgarrek in Camborne	*E.C.H.*, 206 (1260)
Treclego	*E.C.H.*, 207 (1291)
Tremodret	*E.C.H.*, 207 (1291)
Trewithian in St. Wenn	*E.C.H.*, 207 (1313)
Tybesta	I.P.M., Ed. I, 95

Devon

Bovey Tracey	I.P.M., Ed. II, 100 (19 Ed. II)[3]
Chudleigh	*Mon. Ex.*, 428
Crediton	*Mon. Ex.*, 427
Harpford	I.P.M., Ed. I, 42 (27 Ed. I)
Hartland	I.P.M., Ed. I, 32 (27 Ed.I)[3]
Molton, North	I.P.M., Ed. II, 36, 59 (7 & 10 Ed. II)[3]
Molton, South	I.P.M., Ed. II, 100 (19 Ed. II)
Moreton Hampstead	*Cal. I.P.M.*, III, 282 (25 Ed. I)
Sampford Courtenay	I.P.M., Ed.I, 21 (23 Ed. I)[3]
Slapton	I.P.M., Ed. I, 32 (35 Ed.I)[3]

Somerset

Cheddar	M.A., 1131/3 (1301)
Dulverton	Brit. Mus. Add. MSS., 16332
Dunster	Maxwell-Lyte, *Dunster*, I, 297
Taunton	Eccl. Com.
Wells	M.A., 1131/4 (1308–9)
Wiveliscombe	*Ibid.*
Wookey	*Ibid.*

The Cotswold District

Barton-on-Windrush	*Supra*, p. 190
Bourton-on-the-Water	*Supra*, p. 191
Hawkesbury	C.R., Gen. Series, 175/41 (19 Ed. (II))
Hinton	*Cartulary of the Monastery of St. Peter of Gloucester* (Rolls Series), III, 60

The Cotswold District

Overbury	*V.C.H., Worc.*, II, 301
Stanway	*Tax. Eccl.*, 234 (1291)
Wheatenhurst	R. & S., 245 (15 Ed. I)
Winchcomb	*Supra*, p. 191

The Middle Thames Region

The Kennet Valley

Benham Valence	*V.C.H., Berks*, I, 198
Burghfield	*Ibid.*, III, 403; Brit. Mus. Harl. MS., 1708, f. 209
Chilton Foliat	*Wilts I.P.M.*, 350 (1307)
Elcot	*Supra*, p. 192
Hampstead Marshall	*V.C.H., Berks*, IV, 182; I.P.M., 54 Hen. III, 25
Newbury	*V.C.H., Berks*, I, 388, IV, 136
Reading	*Ibid.*, III, 344
Speen	*Ibid.*, IV, 107; M.A., 750/23 (5–6 Ed. I)

The Thames Valley

Medmenham	I.P.M., Hen. III, 30 (1263)
Purley	*V.C.H., Berks*, III, 421
Seckworth	*Register of Godstow*, I, 43
Witney	*Supra*, p. 191

The Chilterns

Wendover	Anc. Ext., 79 (2) (24 Ed. I)
Wycombe	*Register of Godstow*, I, 89 (1235)

Wiltshire

North

Chilton Foliat	(*see* Kennet Valley)
Chippenham	*Wilts I.P.M.*, 246, 300 (1300)
Stanley-on-the-Marden	*Supra*, p. 190

South

Downton	Eccl. Com.
Harnham	*Wilts I.P.M.*, 227 (1299)
Mere	*Ibid.* 257; M.A., 1055/21 (1300)
Sarum, Old	*Cal. I.M.*, I, 328 (1277–8)
Steeple Langford	R. & S. Gen. Ser., 16/66 (1294)

Hampshire		The London District	
Alresford,			
New	*Supra*, p. 191 (1208–9)	Stratford	*Cal. Letter Books of London* ed. R. R. Sharpe, C. 51 (1299)
Sutton	*Ibid.*		
Waltham	*Ibid.*		
Winchester	*Infra*, p. 206		
South-Eastern England		**East Anglia**	
Guildford	*Cal. L.R.*, III, 376 (1251)	Lawford, Essex	*Cal. I.P.M.*, II, 380 (15 Ed. I)
Tonbridge	*Hundred Rolls* (Record Comm.), II, 219	Witham, Essex	*Supra*, p. 190 n. 1
The London District		Hadleigh, Suffolk	H. Pigot, *Hadleigh*, 229 (1305)
Enfield	*Cal. I.P.M.*, V, 192 (5 Ed. II)	Aby (*or* Strubby), Lincs	*Cal. I.P.M.*, VI, 158 (1321–2)
		Tothill	*Cal. I.M.*, I, 238 (1264–5)

[1] See also J. Somervell, *Water Power Mills of South Westmorland* (Kendal, 1930), where the probable sites of several of these mills are identified.

[2] Cf. M. L. Armitt, "Fullers and Freeholders of Grasmere," *Westmorland and Cumberland Archaeological Society*, New Series, vol. 8, 139.

[3] See also *Devon Association for the Advancement of Science, Literature and Art*, vol. XLIV (1912), R. Pearse Chope, "The Aulnager in Devon."

men," though its final triumph was not yet assured, and a veritable revolution in one of the chief branches of cloth manufacture was in progress. Foot fulling was giving way to mechanical fulling; human labour was being displaced by water power; the industry was being carried on at the mill rather than in the home; it was dependent as never before upon considerable capital equipment, and was already passing out of the gild system of control. Moreover, changes in technique and organization, striking enough in themselves to warrant the use of the word revolution, were giving rise to changes in location no less striking—changes which were to affect the distribution of the whole English woollen industry. For the survey, it will be seen, reveals remarkable concentrations of mills in the West Riding of Yorkshire, in the Lake District, in Cornwall, Devon, Somerset and the Cotswolds, in Wilts and in the Kennet Valley, with a corresponding dearth of mills in the eastern parts of England. Further, it

shows that the mills were almost entirely in the country
districts rather than in the towns. Now in both these
respects a startling change has taken place since the twelfth
and thirteenth centuries. Then the chief centres of cloth
manufacture were not in the hilly northern and western
regions of England but in the eastern lowlands; not in the
rural districts but in the cities. York, Beverley, Lincoln,
Louth, Stamford and Northampton [1] were then famous for
their fine quality cloth, and next to them in importance came
London, Oxford, Winchester, Leicester and Colchester. In
all these cities there was a large-scale industry supplying
London and, in many instances which we can trace, the
export market, and many have left record of their organized
groups of fullers [2] as well as weavers. Now, however, with
the invention of the fulling mill, water power was becoming
a decisive factor in the location of the industry, and it began
to concentrate on the swift, clear streams of the north and
west, in remote valleys far beyond the bounds of the ancient
chartered cities of the plains.

Hence it comes about that this chapter in the development
of England's woollen industry is written largely in the
records of the manor rather than of the borough. Indeed, in
many instances which we can trace, the initiative in the new
developments was taken by the lord of the manor, and the
capital equipment provided by him. Thus, as we have seen,
King Henry III reconstructed his fulling mill at Elcot, using
timber from his forest at Savernake,[3] at a cost of £4, 17s. 4d.,
while the Bishop of Winchester built a new fulling mill at

[1] See, e.g., Newcastle Records Series, II, *Pleas from Curia Regis and Assize Rolls*, 307; *Calendar of Patent Rolls*, 1247–58, 309; F. D. Swift, *The Life and Times of James the First . . . of Aragon* (1894), 229; *Calendar of Close Rolls*, 1234–7, 73, 301; 1247–51, 154, 157, 301, 375.
[2] E.g., Lincoln, 1200 (*Curia Regis Rolls*, I, 259); Stamford, 1182 (F. Peck, *The Antiquities of Stamford* (1785), 17); Northampton, 1275 (*Hundred Rolls*, II, 3); London, 1298 (*Liber Custumarum*, ed. H. T. Riley, Rolls Series (1860), I, 128); Leicester, 1260 (*Records of the Borough of Leicester*, ed. M. Bateson (1899), I, 89); Winchester, 1130 (*Pipe Roll 31 Henry I*, Record Commission (1833), 37).   [3] *Supra*, 192.

Brightwell costing £9, 4s. 4d.[1] Similarly the fulling mill at Burnley was built anew ("*de novo constructo*") for £2, 12s. 6d. at the expense of the lord of the manor, and money was also spent on the repair of that at Colne.[2] Such instances could be multiplied.

The incentive to such enterprise on the part of the lord of the manor was that the fulling mill was an investment from which considerable profit could be derived. For, like the corn mill, the oven, the wine press, the dye pan, or any other such equipment erected by the lord, it could be made a manorial monopoly, to which the tenants owed suit.[3] Its value varied not only according to its own efficiency, but also according to the size, population and industry of the area it served. Thus, for example, a half share in the fulling mill at Kendal was at one time worth 10 marks a year, but in 1274 its value was considered to have fallen to 8 marks.[4] The reason alleged was that the tenants at Kentmere no longer did suit to it, and probably what had happened was that the mill at Staveley had now been built[5]; and since Staveley is half-way between Kentmere and Kendal, this would mean for the tenants a journey of only about four instead of eight miles down the Kent valley with their cloths. It is perhaps not a mere coincidence that the development of the fulling mill took place during the century which saw the crystallization and culmination of the manorial system with seignurial rights and privileges at their height.

[1] *Pipe Roll of the Bishop of Winchester, ut supra*, 13: "*in uno molendino foleratico facto de novo*" (1208–9).

[2] *Two Compoti of the Lancashire and Cheshire Manors of Henry de Lacy, 24 and 33 Edward I*, Chetham Society, New Series, CXII (1907), 15, 16.

[3] On this subject see *Beitrage zur Geschichte der Technik* (1913), C. Koehne, "Die Mühle im Rechte der Völker"; *Annales d'histoire économique et sociale*, no. 36, *ut supra*, and cf. G. Espinas, *La draperie dans la Flandre française au moyen âge* (Paris, 1923), II, 213, n. 6: the Duke of Burgundy writes to his receiver concerning his corn mills at Bruay, suggesting that for his greater profit one of them should be made into a "molin foleur de draps."

[4] P.R.O. Inquisitions Post Mortem, Edward I, 5.

[5] See Table p. 195.

How eagerly such monopolies were coveted may be seen from Jocelin de Brakelond's story of Herbert the Dean, who thought that "the profit which may come from the wind ought to be denied to no man." When Herbert excused himself thus for erecting his own windmill the Abbot was speechless with rage, and when Herbert pleaded that it was only to grind his own corn and not other men's, he retorted, "I thank you as much as if you had cut off both my feet; by the face of God, I will never eat bread until that building be overturned." [1] If even the wind could be thus monopolized, it was still more easy to enforce control over the water, to insist that the lord alone had the right to use it for profit-making, and that no one else could do so without a licence purchased from him. Even before the introduction of the fulling mill, the lord claimed the right to dispose of the watercourse as he pleased for fulling and dyeing, reserving it wholly to himself, or leasing it out, often as a monopoly, to others. Thus for instance at Hadleigh one John Garleberd was granted for an annual rent ten feet of land along the bank of the mill pond, with permission to wash his dyed wool there and draw out water, on condition that no one else should have access there.[2] Later on two dyers were fined at Hadleigh for washing dyed wool in the lord's pond without licence.[3] Similarly the cellarer of Bury St. Edmunds claimed the right to prohibit the town fullers from using the water. So profitable were such monopolies that frequently when some measure of freedom was granted to tenants the lord expressly reserved the right to maintain them in his hands. So, for instance, in the charter of 1228 granted by the Archbishop of York to Sherburn in Elmet, the "burgesses in our borough of Shireburn" were forbidden on pain of

---

[1] *Chronica Jocelini de Brakelonda*, ed. J. G. Rokewode (Camden Society, Old Series, XIII, 1840), 43. Cf. the dispute at Hesdin-le-Vieux over the fulling mills of the Prior of S. Georges (G. Espinas and H. Pirenne, *Recueil de documents relatifs à l'histoire de l'industrie drapière en Flandre* (Brussels, 1906–23), II, 690).

[2] P.R.O. Ecclesiastical Commission, Various, I, 16/2.

[3] *Ibid.*, 16/9.

forfeiture to have an "oven, dye-pan or fulling stocks."
Those who made use of the Archbishop's dye-pan might
have, in any week they pleased, "a cartload of dead wood
from our wood at Shireburn." [1] Or again, a charter of King
John to Ulverston reserved in the king's hands the oven, dye-
pan and fullery ("*furnum, tinctoriam et fulloniam*").[2]

Nor did the lords of the manor claim merely the exclusive
right of erecting and possessing such fulleries or fulling mills.
They insisted also that all cloth made on the manor must be
brought to the manorial mill and there fulled by the new
mechanical method, and no longer at home "by hand or
foot"; just as they insisted that all corn must be ground in
their wind mills or water mills, and not at home by hand
mills. Such a claim would seem as difficult to justify as it
certainly was to enforce. Never, perhaps, was it wholly con-
ceded, and both manorial court rolls and monastic chronicles
bear witness to the constant opposition it aroused, and to the
hatred which it inspired. At Hawkesbury, for instance, in
1325–6, one Matilda, daughter of Adam the Carter, was
fined for fulling a piece of cloth "*alibi quam ad molendinum
domini.*" [3] Other such cases occur on manorial court rolls, but
most striking is the evidence from monastic sources, and
most vivid of all is the account of the struggle over the
fulling mills at St. Albans in 1274. At this time the abbey
of St. Albans was evidently as proud of its mills as of its
conventual buildings. Abbot John (1235–60) spent, it is
said, no less than £100 on their reconstruction, taking them
back into his own hands after they had been leased out at
farm and allowed to fall into disrepair. His successors were
evidently determined to make a goodly profit out of them

[1] *Old Yorkshire*, 2nd series, 1885, W. Wheater, "The Ancient Cloth
Trade."

[2] T. West, *Antiquities of Furness* (1813), 85, 418; *fulloniam* cannot
strictly be interpreted as fulling *mill* as it is here, and often elsewhere, translated: it would seem to denote almost always the primitive non-mechanized
fullery, and by the fourteenth century the word has virtually disappeared.
Cf. charter, quoted by Ducange, reserving "*furnos, torcularia, molendina, et
fullonos.*"

[3] P.R.O. Court Rolls, General Series, 175/41.

and claimed that no grinding of corn or fulling of cloth, even of small pieces,[1] could be carried out anywhere except at the abbey mills. The people of St. Albans, however, resisted what they considered to be an unwarranted usurpation; they gave the abbey mills a wide berth and preferred to grind and full at home, free of charge, by the primitive old-fashioned methods.[2] In 1274 matters came to a head in what the chronicler describes as a great insurrection, provoked by the zeal of Abbot Roger in enforcing his monopolies by entering the houses of offenders and levying distraint. The people of St. Albans determined to contest the case in the king's court, opened a fighting fund to which rich and poor contributed, and, when Queen Eleanor was passing through St. Albans, staged a great demonstration to enlist her support. The Abbot tried to outwit them by diverting the royal route and taking the Queen by a back way to the abbey, but his stratagem failed, and the Queen was intercepted by an angry crowd consisting mainly of women, whose attack, said the monkish chronicler, was formidable "since it is difficult happily to compose the anger of women." Weeping and lamenting and stretching forth their hands, the women complained bitterly of the Abbot's tyranny, crying "Domina, miserere nobis." It was not easy, however, for an English mob to make their grievances intelligible to a foreign queen and her entourage, and the sympathy aroused by their tears seems quickly to have been dispelled by the assurances of the astute Abbot that the light words of such women were really unworthy of credence. At any rate when the people of St. Albans brought their case into the king's court, judgment was given against them, and, despite an

[1] "*Pannos viles*" in contrast to "*pannos grossos*," i.e. probably small pieces woven for use at home rather than whole broadcloths woven for sale; this restriction would be peculiarly irksome.

[2] One of the fullers, Henry de Porta, living in Fullers Street, was accused of erecting in his house a "*truncum ad fullandum pannos*"; this may perhaps imply some partly mechanized device such as wooden hammers attached to a revolving drum worked by hand. Such a device is still used to-day, e.g. in the "Clansman Mills" at Killin. Cf. *supra*, 188 fn. 2.

appeal, the abbot won the day and the judgment was proudly entered in the chronicle for future reference.[1]

The story of the gradual emancipation of the industry from seignurial control does not concern us here, for it belongs to the later Middle Ages and is part of the larger story of the disintegration of the manor and the transition from medieval to modern. Indeed the development of the cloth industry mirrors the rise and decline of the manor as it does that of the gild. Let us turn rather to consider the effects of the invention of the fulling mill and its extension in rural districts upon the old-established urban centres of the cloth industry.

The development of the fulling mill affected decisively the location of the industry, in that it determined that it should be dispersed over the countryside rather than concentrated in the towns.[2] For though at first these mills, often in remote rural valleys, dealt no doubt with the cloth woven for the needs of the rural population, ultimately they came to cater for the needs of the industrialists. Since cloth could be fulled in the mills mechanically, and therefore more cheaply, inevitably much of the work that had been done in the cities came to be sent out to them, and more and more they took over the fulling branch of the cloth industry, threatening the handcraft fullers in the towns with unemployment and starvation. In London, for instance, so serious was the competition of the country fulling mills that complaint was made to the king in 1298. It was said that certain men of the city had sent cloths "outside the city to the mill of Stratford and elsewhere, and caused them to be fulled

[1] *Gesta Abbatam Monasterii Sancti Albani, ut supra*, I, 323, 410 *et seq.* The struggle continued, here as elsewhere, for more than a century, and was one of the causes contributing towards the Peasants' Revolt. Cf. the struggle at Evesham during the fourteenth and fifteenth centuries over ovens and cornmills; in 1307 a private oven erected in his house by William de Tettebury was thrown down by the Abbey steward with the aid of the town bailiffs, and in 1388 the hand mills of other tenants were destroyed, as was a horse mill in 1430. (G. May, *History of Evesham* (1845), 83.)

[2] In this respect the English industry offers a striking contrast to that of Flanders.

there, to the grave damage of those to whom the cloth belonged and also of the men using this office in the city." [1] Round these mills grew up groups of industrial workers entirely outside the jurisdiction of the urban gilds. In many little rural hamlets in valleys where water power had been turned to account we find colonies of fullers in the late thirteenth century, working evidently to supply no merely local demand. Thus there were fullers scattered throughout the West Riding valleys; at Calverley, for instance, there seem to have been at least five in about 1257.[2] The tendency for one of the chief branches of the woollen industry to shift from the town to the country gave a great stimulus to the development of the industry as a whole there, and doomed to failure the attempt of the cities to concentrate it within their walls to their own profit. To the advantages of water power were added the advantages of freedom from the high taxation in the towns and from the restrictions of the gilds. Colonies of weavers also began to settle round the fulling mills, and, as the industrial population of the rural regions increased, so that of the cities decreased, and the once mighty weavers' gilds sank into insignificance and poverty. The industry, in fact, was deserting the towns for the countryside. There is clear evidence of this decay in the case of at least seven of the leading cloth-producing cities, and others may yet be found to have been in similar case.

Winchester, for instance, in the twelfth century had a considerable number of both weavers and fullers, each organized in their own gild, and each paying £6 yearly to the crown in the time of Henry I.[3] But by the time of Edward I it was becoming increasingly difficult to collect the money, and the reason given for this was that large numbers of the

[1] *Liber Custumarum, ut supra,* I, 127; *Calendar of Letter Books of the City of London; Letter Book C,* ed. R. R. Sharpe (1901), 51.

[2] H. Heaton, *The Yorkshire Woollen and Worsted Industries* (Oxford Historical and Literary Studies, vol. 10, 1920), 5, quoting *Calverley Charters,* Thoresby Society Publications, vol. VI, 8–55.

[3] *Pipe Roll 31 Henry I,* 37.

clothworkers had left the town.[1] At Oxford also there was a weavers' gild paying £6 to the crown in the twelfth century.[2] But in the reign of Edward I they successfully petitioned that the sum should be reduced to 42s. on the ground that, while there used to be sixty or more weavers in the town, there were now only fifteen. Later they asked for a further reduction to 6s. 8d., since there were only seven weavers left, and those were poor; finally, in 1323, they pleaded that all these were dead and had no successors.[3] The Lincoln weavers also were finding difficulties about paying their annual £6 to the crown in the early fourteenth century and alleged the same reasons, stating that there were no weavers left in Lincoln between 1321 and 1331 and from then until 1345 only a very few, though when Henry II granted their gild there were more than two hundred.[4] In London the number of looms was said to have fallen from 380 to 80 early in the fourteenth century.[5] York was in very similar difficulties. In the twelfth century its weavers' gild had paid a larger sum than any other—£10 annually, but during the thirteenth century it fell into more and more serious arrears, pleading in excuse that "divers men in divers places in the country, elsewhere than in the city or in the other towns and demesne boroughs—make dyed and rayed cloths." [6]

The decline of the industry in all these five boroughs is easily apparent, since each had an old-established weavers'

[1] *Victoria County History, Hampshire*, V (1912), 477. Complaints of financial stringency are, of course, a commonplace of the public records, but the reason here given for the difficulty, read in conjunction with the Bishop of Winchester's records, seems to bear the stamp of truth.

[2] *Pipe Roll 31 Henry I*, 2; see also *Victoria County History, Oxfordshire*, II (1907), for an account of the fluctuations of the weavers' gild (p. 242 ff.).

[3] *Oxford Historical Society*, XXXII (1896), 99, 123–4; P.R.O. Ancient Petitions, 132/6569.

[4] *Calendar of Close Rolls*, 1348–50, 120 (Petition of 1348); *Telariorum*, given as "spinners" in the calendar, is a synonym for *Textorum*, i.e. weavers.

[5] Lipson, *Economic History of England, ut supra*, 450, quoting *Liber Custumarum, ut supra*, I, 416–425. Other versions give the original number as 280.

[6] Heaton, *op. cit.*, 29 (Petition of 1304).

gild, paying annually to the crown as lord of the borough. It is less easy to trace developments in the six other leading cloth-making cities, for four at least of these were not royal boroughs, none of them had privileged early gilds, so far as can be discovered, and comparable evidence is not therefore available. Yet here too we can find signs of decay. Northampton, for instance, complained in 1334 that formerly 300 clothmakers had worked there, but that now the houses where they used to live had all fallen down.[1] Leicester in 1322 declared that there was only one fuller left in the town "and he a poor man,"[2] and it is significant that from the end of the thirteenth century the very extensive Leicester records contain less and less about the cloth industry and more about the marketing of raw wool.

Competition from the country districts was not, of course, entirely new. Some clothmaking had always been carried on in the villages. But hitherto the "great industry" for export had been to a marked extent concentrated in the cities and controlled by them; there lived the capitalist entrepreneurs, carrying on the dyeing and finishing processes, often in their own houses, and employing the colonies of skilled weavers and fullers settled within the walls, though they would also buy the rough unfinished webs brought in for sale by the country people. Now, with the invention of the fulling mill, the balance was tilted in favour of the country districts, and the cities were faced with constantly intensified competition. How then did they strive to maintain or recapture their supremacy?

Where circumstances were favourable some set up their own mills, as did Winchester in 1269, when the town granted permission to nine fullers to construct a fullers' mill.[3] But the slow-moving courses of the rivers on which most of these towns lay were less adapted to mills than were

---

[1] *Rotuli Parliamentorum ut et Petitiones et Placita in Parliamento* (Record Commission, 1767-77), II, 85.

[2] *Calendar of Inquisitions Miscellaneous*, II, 138.

[3] *The Black Book of Winchester*, ed. W. H. Bird (1925), 190.

their swift upper courses, nor can the requisite space for the diversion of the watercourse have been always readily available. Moreover, there would tend to be strong opposition to an innovation which would throw so many out of work, and all the forces of conservatism would be arrayed against it.

Other towns therefore resisted the adoption of the new methods, urging the inferiority of machine work as well as the unemployment it caused. Thus a complaint from certain Londoners to the king in 1298 declared that, according to the accepted custom, cloths should be "fulled under the feet of men of this office, or their servants, in their houses in the city and not elsewhere," but that certain fullers had sent such cloths "outside the city to the mill of Stratford and elsewhere and caused them to be fulled there, to the grave damage of those to whom the cloth belonged and also of the men using this office in the city." [1] The petitioners did not, however, secure the prohibition of fulling at mills, but only an ordinance that no cloth should be sent outside the city to be fulled at mills ("*pur foller as molins*") except by those who actually owned the cloth, and that six men should watch at the city gates, arrest the cloths, and keep them until the owners came and avowed them as theirs.[2] Twelve years later one Godfrey de Loveyne was heavily fined for sending three cloths outside the city to be fulled at mills.[3]

Most towns, however, concerned themselves primarily with confining the industry within the city walls. Their own civic ordinances could at least compel clothmakers in the city to employ city labour only and thus to maintain the wealth and prosperity of the city. Thus when the craft ordinances of Bristol were written down in the city's Little Red Book, that of the fullers decreed "*qe nul hom face amesner*

[1] *Liber Custumarum, ut supra,* I, 127.
[2] *Ibid.,* I, 127, 128; *Calendar of Letter Book C, ut supra,* 51.
[3] *Calendar of Letter Books of the City of London, Letter Book D,* ed. R. R. Sharpe (1902), 239 ("*pannos crudos*" is probably raw, i.e. unfulled, cloth, not "undyed").

hors de ceste ville nule manere drap a foler qe home appele raucloth sur peyne de perdre xld. pur chescun drap." [1] In the same ordinance there is mention of cloth being sent "to the mill" ("*al molyn*"), so that clearly the opposition was not to milling as such but to the work going out of the city. Such resistance to the competition of country fullers is very evident in the ordinances of other towns also. At Winchester, for instance, in 1402, clothmakers of the town were forbidden to employ either fullers or weavers outside the town.[2] A somewhat similar ordinance seems to have been made at Leicester in 1260, and citizens were punished for breach of it.[3]

Such ordinances might do something to prevent city manufacturers from having dealings with workers outside, but they could not prevent an independent industry from flourishing in the country districts. Some cities therefore turned to an authority higher than that of the city and prayed the king to aid them in securing the monopoly they coveted. The York weavers, with those of other royal boroughs in Yorkshire, had already, by their charter of 1164, been granted a monopoly of making dyed and rayed cloth in all Yorkshire. At the end of the thirteenth century their monopoly was, as we have seen, being seriously infringed, so in 1304 they petitioned the king and he ordered the Exchequer to have enquiries made and to compel all found plying the craft in illegal places to refrain.[4] We do not know what effect, if any, was given to this order, but we do know that it did not, any more than did the cities' own ordinances, succeed in the impossible task of confining the cloth industry within urban walls.

The decline of the industry in the thirteenth century in what had been its most flourishing urban centres is as striking as is its expansion in rural regions during the same

---

[1] *Little Red Book of Bristol*, ed. F. B. Bickley (1900), II, 7.
[2] *Black Book of Winchester, ut supra*, 8.
[3] *Records of the Borough of Leicester, ut supra*, I, 91, 347.
[4] Heaton, *op. cit.*, 28–9.

period, but it is the urban side of the matter which has hitherto attracted the attention of historians, and from it they have falsely deduced a decline in the industry as a whole. The real significance of this decline now becomes clear. The industry was developing, and developing rapidly, but outside the jurisdiction of those cities that had once taken the lead in it. The decay of the once famous cloth-making cities of the eastern plain and the rise of the country fulling mills shows not only that the rural industry was gaining over the urban, but also, when we consider the preponderance of fulling mills in the north and west of England, that the broadcloth industry as a whole was tending to shift from east to west, to new centres in the West Riding, the Lake District and the West of England. For here were to be found ample supplies not only of fine wool but also of water power. In the twelfth and early thirteenth centuries the fine quality English cloths specially in demand abroad were cloths "of Stamford," "of Lincoln," "of Louth," "of Beverley," "of York"; but in the fourteenth and fifteenth centuries there was no demand at all for these cloths, but much for "Kendals," "Ludlows," "Cotswolds," "Mendips," "Castlecombes," "Stroudwaters," or "Westerns," and the primary, though not the only, factor in this change was the invention of the fulling mill.

ABBREVIATIONS IN TABLE OF MILLS

M.A.	= Public Record Office, Ministers Accounts.
C.R.	= ,, ,, ,, Court Rolls.
R. & S.	= ,, ,, ,, Rentals and Surveys.
Anc. Ext.	= ,, ,, ,, Ancient Extents.
Eccl. Com.	= ,, ,, ,, Ecclesiastical Commission, Various, II, 159273 ff.
I.P.M.	= ,, ,, ,, Inquisitions Post Mortem.
Cal. I.P.M.	= *Calendar of Inquisitions Post Mortem.*
Cal. I.M.	= ,, ,, *Inquisitions Miscellaneous.*
Cal. C.R.	= ,, ,, *Close Rolls.*
Cal. L.R.	= ,, ,, *Liberate Rolls.*
V.C.H.	= *Victoria County History.*
Tax. Eccl.	= *Taxatio Ecclesiastica, circa* 1291 (Record Commission 1802).
Mon. Ex.	= Oliver, *Monasticon Exoniensis* (1846–54).
Wilts I.P.M.	= *Abstracts of Wiltshire Inquisitions Post Mortem*, ed. E. A. Fry (1908), 1242–1326.
Worc. I.P.M.	= *Inquisitions Post Mortem for the County of Worcestershire*, ed. for the Worcester Historical Society by J. W. Willis Bund (1894).

Notts I.P.M. = Thoroton Society, Record Series, Vol. IV, *Inquisitions Post Mortem for Nottinghamshire*, Vol. II (1279–1321), ed. J. Standish (1914).

E.C.H.   = Charles Henderson, *Essays in Cornish History* (1935), p. 206, "Cornish Tucking Mills and Windmills." [1]

[1] This gives no references, but is based mainly on the author's own extensive collection of Cornish deeds, now in the Truro Museum.

Note.—Since this article was written some 30 additional early English fulling mills (pre-1327) have come to light, and I am much indebted to those correspondents who have kindly brought a number of these to my notice. In addition, Mr. R. V. Lennard has called attention in the *Economic History Review*, XVII, No. 2 (1947), to the mention of a fulling mill in a charter of the Abbey of St. Wandrille in Normandy calendared by J. H. Round (*Calendar of Documents preserved in France*, No. 166, p. 58). This document is a seventeenth-century version, in the Bibliothèque Nationale, of a charter ascribed by Round to the years 1060–80. The original charter is in the Archives départementales de la Seine-Inférieure at Rouen (Série H, non coté) and has been published by Ferdinand Lot, who dates it at about 1086–87 (*Etudes critiques sur l'abbaye de Saint-Wandrille*, Bibliothèque de l'Ecole des Hautes Etudes, 204ᵉ fascicule, Paris 1913, pp. 96–7). Even though this too speaks of a "*molendino fullonario*" and thus seems to prove the fulling mill to have been in existence in the late eleventh century, it in no way invalidates the general conclusions on p. 190.

V

THE ENGLISH CLOTH INDUSTRY IN THE LATE TWELFTH AND EARLY THIRTEENTH CENTURIES [1]

The late twelfth and early thirteenth centuries saw the zenith of the urban cloth industry in England. The "great industry" for export was then centred in the towns, as never again, and the cloth, when marketed, took its name from a city, not from a district. Very different was the state of affairs by the fifteenth century, when the revolution brought about by the introduction of the fulling mill, as described in a previous article,[2] had caused the industry as a whole to migrate from the urban centres into the country districts and to shift from the East Anglian plain to the upland valleys of the west; then the trade names in vogue were such as "Mendips", "West of Englands", "Cotswolds", "Essex Straits" or "West Ridings".

Pre-eminent among these urban industrial centres were four clothing towns not far apart on the East Anglian plain, specializing in fine-quality cloths, and then at the height of their fame and prosperity: Beverley, Lincoln, Stamford and Northampton. Not far off were York, Louth and Leicester, dealing more often in slightly cheaper cloths. These were the towns above all which provided fine cloth to replenish the royal wardrobe,[3] in so far as this was not purchased from abroad, and in each there was a large-scale industry supplying not only the home but also the foreign market. In 1204,

---

[1] *Economic History Review*, XIV, No. 1, 1944. As this article was compiled while the writer was on war service without ready access to sources, it proved impossible to check and complete all the references. In almost every case, however, the source is given, if not the precise reference.

[2] "An Industrial Revolution of the Thirteenth Century", *Economic History Review*, XI, 39–60.

[3] See, e.g., *Calendar of Patent Rolls*, 1232–47, 23; *Calendar of Close Rolls*, 1234–7, 73, 301, 375; 1247–51, 154, 157; *Calendar of Liberate Rolls*, III, 1245–51, 194, and I, 1226–40, 493 (scarlets of Lincoln purchased as a present for the Queen of Norway).

for instance, John of Beverley loaded "scarlet of Stamford" in a London ship,[1] and in the mid-thirteenth century it is evident that clothmakers of Stamford must have had constant dealings with Italy. For when certain Lucca merchants carried away Stamford cloths worth £102 without paying for them, the matter was considered so serious for the reputation of other Lucca merchants that they agreed that the Stamford citizens might recoup themselves by taking $1\frac{1}{2}d$. in the mark on the goods of all Lucca merchants until the whole had been paid.[2] Later in the century we read of cloths of a Lincoln man on a ship chartered by Lucca merchants,[3] and of certain Spanish merchants who, when robbed by pirates off the coast of Norfolk, had on board "cloths of scarlet and other cloths from Stamford, Beverley, York, Lincoln, Northampton and Louth".[4]

The reputation of Lincoln, Stamford and Beverley as cloth-making centres is borne out by a metrical list of English towns and their characteristic products, compiled almost certainly in the mid-thirteenth century.[5] "Escarlet de Nichole" is the entry descriptive of Lincoln,[6] and Beverley too is characterized by its cloth—burnet of Beverley.[7] "Hauberge de Estamford" tells equally of Stamford's skill in cloth-making for, though this has usually been translated

[1] W. Wheater, "The Ancient Cloth Trade" in *Old Yorkshire* (2nd Series, 1885), 262.   [2] *Calendar of Patent Rolls*, 1247–58, 309 (1254).
[3] *Calendar of Letter Books of the City of London, Letter Book A*, ed. R. R. Sharpe (1899), 138.
[4] *Newcastle-upon-Tyne Records Committee. Publications, II: Northumberland Pleas from the Curia Regis and Assize Rolls*, 1198–1272, ed. A. Hamilton Thompson (1922), 307.
[5] Bodleian, Douce MS. 98, f. 194; see *Notes and Queries*, IVth Series, VIII, 223 (1883), and J. Thorold Rogers, *Six Centuries of Work and Wages* (1884), 105. Rogers here considers the list to have been drawn up "a little after the middle of the century" but the MS. to be of the close of the century, though the Bodleian Catalogue of Western MSS. dates the MS. 1320–30. Cf. *English Historical Review*, XVI, 501.
[6] "Lincoln scarlets" are the only ones to be specially listed in the royal wardrobe accounts of the thirteenth century.
[7] Cf. purchases of burnets at Beverley by Henry III, e.g. *Calendar of Close Rolls*, 1234–7, 301; 1253–4, 46. Henry III also ordered burnets from Northampton and Stamford (*ibid.* and 1247–51, 154).

"inns of Stamford", it clearly refers to the cloth known as "hauberge", "haubergett" or "halbergett"; indeed, King Henry III himself once ordered three good "haubergettos" to be made and dyed in grain for him at Stamford.[1]

Beyond this group of cities on the eastern plain lay others also notable for their cloth industry, but producing mainly cheap varieties, the russets and burels that were purchased by the king not for his own apparel but as alms for the poor. Most famous of these was Colchester. The king bought "russet of Colchester" in 1252 and ordered russets there also in 1249 and 1254,[2] and "Russet de Colcestr'" is the one mention of the cheaper cloths in the list which signalized Lincoln, Stamford and Beverley for the more expensive ones. With Colchester may be grouped Oxford, London and Winchester. The king ordered "russet of Oxford and burel of London" in 1232 and sent to Oxford for more cheap cloth for a Christmas gift to the poor in 1233.[3] In London he was constantly purchasing burel or other cheap cloth for his almsgiving,[4] often from the London burellers, to some of

[1] *Calendar of Close Rolls*, 1234–7, 73. No satisfactory explanation has yet been found of the meaning of this term. It is used only in the first half of the thirteenth century. Magna Carta lays down a particular width (2 yards between the lists) *pannorum tinctorum et russetorum et halbergettorum*. The word perhaps refers to texture rather than colour. We read, for instance, in the Northamptonshire Assize Rolls (1202–3) of a *pallium hauberget' tinctum in burneto*; King John ordered many yards of white "halberg'" together with a large quantity of dyed cloth and scarlet (M. Bateson, *Medieval England* (1903), 147); and Henry III, as shown above, ordered three haubergets to be made and dyed in grain for him. The "Stamforts" so popular on the continent in the thirteenth century have been thought to be either cloths made at Stamford or imitations of them, but it seems very probable that this word is actually derived from *stamen forte* ("of strong warp thread", i.e. a species of worsted). See S. W. Beck, *The Drapers' Dictionary* (n.d.).

[2] P.R.O., Exchequer K.R. Accounts Various, Wardrobe, 349/18; *Calendar of Liberate Rolls*, III, 1245–51, 254; *Calendar of Close Rolls*, 1247–51, 198; 1251–3, 135; 1254–6, 8.

[3] *Calendar of Close Rolls*, 1231–4, 41; *Calendar of Liberate Rolls*, I, 1226–40, 191, 208.

[4] E.g. *Calendar of Liberate Rolls*, I, 1226–40, 259, 233, 159; III, 1245–51, 39, 318. It is impossible to be certain of the precise meaning of "burel" in the thirteenth century or of the origin of the term; several derivations seem all equally probable.

whom he was in debt to the extent of £155 in 1250,[1] and from the early thirteenth century there are frequent references to burel manufacture in London, as, for example, in special concessions by the crown to those who "cause burels to be made", or to the "weavers of burels".[2] Similarly the mid-thirteenth century records of Winchester have much to say about the makers of burels and the looms for weaving burels.[3] While Colchester, London, Winchester and Oxford were clearly the most important sources for the cheaper cloths, other lesser centres of manufacture can be distinguished, such as Marlborough and Bedwyn, whose burels are included with those made at London in the special concession of 1218 with regard to the Assize.[4]

Thus in all these towns there was a large-scale industry, supplying London and probably the export market as well as local customers. But scattered all over England there were other towns with organized groups of craftsmen engaged in cloth-making, even if their cloth had not yet, so far as we know, acquired a wide reputation outside its own district. In the north country there were groups of dyers, for instance, at Newcastle[5] and Darlington[6] in the twelfth century, and of weavers, fullers and dyers at Egremont.[7] In the midlands and eastern counties there were weavers' gilds at Nottingham and Huntingdon.[8] In the west country we know of weavers at Gloucester,[9] dyers at Worcester,[10] a "Fullers' Street" at

---

[1] *Calendar of Liberate Rolls*, III, 1245–51, quoted in L. F. Salzman, *English Industries of the Middle Ages* (1913), 198.

[2] *Calendar of Patent Rolls*, 1216–25, 155; *ibid.*, 523; *Calendar of Close Rolls*, 1251–3, 206.

[3] *Victoria County History, Hampshire*, V (1912), 478 (quoting rent roll of the Bishop of Winchester of 1251); *Archaeological Journal*, IX, 69 ff.

[4] *Calendar of Patent Rolls*, 1216–25, 155.

[5] C. Gross, *The Gild Merchant* (1890), II, 182, quoting charter of Henry I.

[6] *Victoria County History, Durham*, I (1905), 338. The dyers paid a separate rent of 6s. 8d. when the borough as a whole paid £5.

[7] "assessum tinctorii, textorii, fullonii". *Cumberland and Westmorland Archaeological Society Transactions*, I, 284.   [8] P.R.O., Pipe Roll 31 Hen. I.

[9] *Calendar of Charter Rolls*, III, 378; cf. Bailiffs Accounts No. 1356 (at Gloucester) temp. Edward I: *de textoribus eiusdem ville* 20s.

[10] *Pipe Roll 19 Henry II* (1172–3), Pipe Roll Society, xix (1895).

Tewkesbury [1] and a "Dyers' Street" at Cirencester,[2] and of a russet manufacture at Totnes which provided a cover for the king's bed in 1253.[3]

The raw materials for England's cloth industry at this time were drawn from all parts of Europe. Wool came principally from the extensive local supplies, unrivalled elsewhere in Europe, which not only fostered the native industry but also fed those of Italy and the Low Countries, then at the height of their prosperity, thus providing England's principal export. There was also, however, some import from Spain of both wool and yarn, at any rate by the mid-thirteenth century. These were amongst the goods for which tolls were fixed at London in 1257 and 1279,[4] at Winchester in 1264 [5] and at Southampton about 1300, and in London there was a special ordinance of the weavers prohibiting the mixture of Spanish and English wool.[6] Fuller's earth also was in abundant supply in this country, and there is no trace of any import. Nor is there any evidence that teasles for the use of the cloth finishers were brought from abroad at this period to supplement those grown in this country. Rather it seems likely that there may have been an export trade in these, as in wool. At any rate early in the fourteenth century the Flemings were said to be buying up all the *cardones qui Tasles vulgariter nuncupantur*, so that there was a shortage in this country and Edward II was persuaded to prohibit their export.[7] With dyestuffs, however, the case

[1] *Victoria County History, Gloucester*, II (1907), 154 (1257).
[2] *vicus tinctorius*, E. A. Fuller, *Ancient Cirencester* (1874), 5, quoting deeds in the Abbey Registers.   [3] *Calendar of Close Rolls*, 1253–4, 176.
[4] Public Record Office, Close Rolls; grants of murage to London in these years. The printed *Calendars of Close Rolls* in almost every case omit the detailed lists of goods on which tolls were to be taken, but these lists throw a most interesting light on the trade and industry of the towns at this time, and are well worth study.   [5] *Ibid.*, grant to Winchester of 1264.
[6] F. Consitt, *The London Weavers' Company* (1933), 11, 12, quoting Letter Book C, f. 42, and *Liber Custumarum*, ed. H. T. Riley (Rolls Series, 1860), I, 122–6.
[7] W. Cunningham, *Growth of English Industry and Commerce* (5th ed. 1927), I, 656. Customs Accounts show that by the fifteenth century, at any rate, they were being imported into this country.

was very different. Though many of the dyes then used were produced in England, local supplies were insufficient in quantity and variety to meet the growing demand. Even those native to this country were supplemented by additional supplies from other parts of north-western Europe, while other different varieties of dyes were imported from the north of Europe, the Mediterranean and even tropical lands.

Woad (*waida, gaida*) was the most important of all dyestuffs. It was used not only for blue cloth, but as a foundation for other colours too. The best deep blue, perse, was properly dyed in woad alone, on white wool, mordanted with ashes, though some dyers, not succeeding in this way, tried to achieve the correct shade by putting "wool dyed in woad into madder and *bultura* to make the colour darker of the likeness of perse colour", and others used "black and grey wool or madder and alum". Both practices were condemned at Leicester.[1] The woad plant has been cultivated in this country from the days of the Saxons, if not earlier, until quite recent times, and eleventh-century instructions for its planting are still extant.[2] But by the twelfth century at least there were very considerable imports from other parts of western Europe, more especially of Picardy woad from Amiens, Corbie, Nesle and the whole Somme region[3]; here the importance of the medieval industry was long commemorated in Amiens cathedral by the thirteenth-century inscriptions to several "maieurs des waidiers", as it still is by the life-like sculpture of two woad-men standing with a bulging sack of woad balls between

[1] *Records of the Borough of Leicester*, ed. Mary Bateson, I (1899), 84, 102 (1259, 1264). Perse was a high-quality cloth, fetching up to 6s. a yard in the late thirteenth century; see, e.g., P.R.O., Exchequer K.R. Accounts Various, Wardrobe, 353/8. For the mixing of madder and woad cf. the London ordinance of 1300 (F. Consitt, *op. cit.*, 12).

[2] W. Cunningham, *op. cit.*, I, 572, § 10, 12, 15; J. B. Hurry, *The Woad Plant and its Dye* (1930), unreliable historically, gives a full account of the cultivation and processing of woad.

[3] The Toulouse district became more important as a source of supply for England in the later Middle Ages. See *supra*, 36–7.

them.[1] In 1194 the Chamberlain of London accounted for £96, 6s. 8d. in fines paid by merchants for leave to import woad into England,[2] while in the early thirteenth century there were evidently extensive imports all round the south and east coasts, for the duties paid on woad there in 1213 amounted to nearly £600.[3] The importance of the early thirteenth-century trade is again shown by the agreement made in 1237 between the Picardy merchants and the City of London. At this time foreigners bringing woad to London were not allowed to stow it in houses or cellars or to trade through the country with it, but only to land it on the quay, enclose it with hurdles and hatches, and sell it on the spot. In 1237, however, the Picardy merchants secured a convention with the City giving them liberty to warehouse within the City, to sell in the City to citizens or strangers, and to carry their woad out of the City to such parts of the country as they pleased. In return for this concession they agreed to pay the Sheriffs fifty marks sterling a year at the times of the great fairs of St. Ives, Winchester and Boston.[4] To confirm the compact the Picardy merchants paid a round sum of £100 towards the cost of the conduit for bringing water into the city from Tyburn spring; from the size of this sum it is clear that the business must have been a very considerable one. A later agreement made between the woad merchants of Amiens and Corbie and the town of Norwich in 1286 fixed the duties which were to be paid there and permitted the merchants to stay as long as they pleased.[5] How widespread

---

[1] See Hurry, op. cit., Plate XVII. For the inscriptions in the windows see A. Thierry, Recueil des monuments inédits de l'histoire du Tiers Etat. Première série: chartes, coutumes, actes municipaux, statuts des corporations d'arts et métiers des villes et communes de France. (Paris 1850–70), II, 25, 94. The inscriptions were read and noted by Ducange in 1667.

[2] F. Madox, History of the Exchequer (1769), I, 775.

[3] Hurry, op. cit., 55; see Madox, op. cit. Hurry seems incorrect in stating that this sum included only the duties on imports entering by a certain number of ports, and he is in error in attributing a mention of woad imports to FitzStephen. [4] Liber Custumarum, ut supra, I, xlii, 64, 68–9.

[5] Records of the City of Norwich, ed. W. Hudson and J. C. Tingey (1906–10), II, 209 et seq.

the trade in woad was throughout the country at this time is incidentally shown by the grants of murage enrolled on the Close Rolls.[1] In the grant to London of 1233 dues are fixed for every frail of woad brought in by foreign merchants. In 1251 they were payable on woad sold at York, and in 1253 at Lincoln. Later on they appear in grants of murage in all parts of England.

While woad was, so far as we know, the only blue dye, a number of different dyes were used for red shades. The commonest of these was madder (*garancia, warancia*) which, when mordanted with alum, gives a kind of tomato red. Like woad it was grown in this country as well as in many other parts of western and southern Europe, and it too is mentioned in eleventh-century planting instructions.[2] Besides being used for red cloth it was also sometimes used with woad, as shown above, to give different shades of blue. It, too, appears in the murage grants,[3] but there is no definite trace of its import from abroad at this time, so that home-grown supplies may have proved sufficient.

The rarer red dyes, brasil, vermilion and grain, must have been wholly imported. The terms "brasil" and "vermilion" were used in the Middle Ages both for the dyestuffs themselves and for the bright red colour they yielded, but by the sixteenth century the second usage tended to disappear and the term scarlet, which originally implied a particularly fine type of *cloth* but was then coming to be used for a *colour* only, was used for any brilliant red, though especially for that yielded by grain.[4] Brasil and vermilion are both mentioned

[1] See *supra*, 215, note 4.

[2] See *supra*, 216, note 2; cf. J. S. Furley, *The Ancient Usages of the City of Winchester* (1927), 41, para. 56, where there is mention of tolls on madder brought to Winchester in carts.

[3] E.g. for Stamford in 1267.

[4] For a full discussion of the meaning of the term "scarlet" in the Middle Ages see J. B. Weckerlin, *Le Drap Escarlate au moyen âge* (Lyons, 1905). That scarlet did not at first denote a colour is shown by such passages as Froissart's description of the King of Portugal dressed in a white scarlet with a vermilion cross of St. George. Scarlet was very much more costly than any other cloth, commanding a price unknown to the tailors of to-day. King John,

in thirteenth-century dyeing regulations, such as those of Northampton, which prohibit the use of either brasil or vermilion in the dyeing of "cloth imperial".[1] The Leicester records of the same period, using the word for a colour, speak of "vermilion" cloths being made at Leicester and sold at Lynn.[2] Both dyes must have been imported from long distances. Brasil (*brasillum*, *bresil*, *brisell*) may have come from the East Indies, for it was derived from the red wood of the East Indian tree *Caesalpina Sappau*, much used for its dye by the Indians and Persians. Vermilion (*vermilio*, *verme*, or *worme*), though popularly supposed to be the blood of a little worm, was actually a mineral dye derived from a crystalline substance said to have been found on the shores of the Red Sea. Brasil, imported by aliens, is mentioned in the London murage grant of 1233, and both brasil and vermilion appear in the London grant of 1257 and in Ipswich and Fordwich grants of about the same time.

Most rare and costly of all red dyes was grain (*granum*), which yields a peculiarly brilliant and lasting scarlet colour. It acquired its name from the fact that it was derived from the dried bodies of the grain-like insect *Coccus Ilicis*, found on a species of oak which flourishes in Mediterranean lands,

---

for instance, paid 8s. a yard, and Edward I also paid 8s. or 7s. 6d. for Lincoln scarlets a century later, spending on them sometimes as much as £30 or £40 a year (P.R.O., Exchequer Accounts Various, Wardrobe, 359/18, 360/22, 363/21; *Rotuli Litterarum Clausarum*, ed. T. D. Hardy (Record Commission, 1833–4), I, 104). Presents of it went from Henry III's court to his wife's French relations, to the King and Queen of Norway and to the Sultan of Damascus (*Calendar of Liberate Rolls*, I, 1226–40, 341, 493, 71; *Calendar of Close Rolls*, 1242–7, 145). It would seem that since scarlets were most often dyed red with the most costly of all dyes, grain, it gradually became the custom to apply the name scarlet to fine cloths dyed in grain to the exclusion of all others, and finally to the colour alone. This change of usage may be illustrated by comparing the Authorised Version (1611) of Exodus xxxv, 25, "that which they had spun of blue, purple and scarlet", with the version of Wyclif, who uses "vermilion" in place of scarlet. See also the two versions of Revelation xviii, 16.

[1] *Records of the Borough of Northampton*, ed. C. A. Markham and J. C. Cox (1898), I, 229.

[2] *Records of the Borough of Leicester, ut supra*, I, 68–9, 86.

particularly in Portugal. The first distinct reference to its import into this country is in the murage grants where, in that to London of 1233, there is mention of tolls on *grana* imported by aliens. It was clearly used for dyeing cloth at this time in England, since we read in 1235 of cloth which was to be made for the king at Stamford and well dyed in grain;[1] in 1251–2 of Irish mantles for the royal wardrobe which were to be dyed in grain,[2] and again in 1249 of the payment of £7, 10s. to one Bernard Curuzan for *grana* for dyeing cloth.[3]

Little evidence has survived as to the yellow dyes used at this period. Saffron, much grown in England, particularly in East Anglia, may have been used in the cloth industry as well as for culinary purposes; so also, no doubt, were other native plants such as woadwaxen or "dyer's weed" (*Genista Tinctoria*), commonly used for many centuries in the Lake District, together with woad, for the dyeing of "Kendal green". Weld (*gualda*, *waald*), though a native of southern Europe, has been naturalized in the north, and in the later Middle Ages much was imported into England.[4] Sumach (*symak*, *cymak*) was certainly imported in the thirteenth century,[5] but there is no clear evidence of its having been used for cloth dyeing.

Many varieties of lichens and barks were probably used, and it seems likely that there was already an import of these from northern Europe. At any rate orchil or archil (also called "cork"), a lichen dye which gave a purplish red, was being imported from Norway by the early fourteenth century.

Almost more important than the import of the actual dyes was the import of the mordants for fixing them. For scarcely any of these dyes will take satisfactorily without a mordant, and the colour ultimately produced varies according to the particular mordant used.

[1] *Calendar of Close Rolls*, 1234–7, 73, "*in grana*".
[2] P.R.O., Wardrobe Accounts, 349/18, "*mantell' hibernici tingendis in grana*".
[3] *Calendar of Liberate Rolls*, III, 1245–51, 216.
[4] Tolls were paid on it at Dunwich in the fifteenth century.
[5] Tolls were paid on it at London in 1279.

Potash (*cineres* or "woad-ashen"), produced from wood ashes by leaching, was the commonest of these and the easiest to apply. It formed part of the stock in trade of most dyers and was so generally used with woad that the term "woad ashes" or "ashes which pertain to woad" was frequently applied to it.[1] Thirteenth-century regulations at Leicester stipulated that ashes only, and not alum, should be used for dyeing perse.[2] Tolls were levied at Northampton on casks of ashes in 1251. Though these ashes could be produced in England, both from wood fires and from the burning of whole trees, they were also imported from abroad, especially from the Baltic, by the mid-thirteenth century.[3]

Alum was the mordant most used after potash, and the sole mordant used for scarlet. It was imported from southern Europe in bags. The finest quality was said to come from the shores of the Black Sea. An almost equally fine quality came from the coasts of Asia Minor, and in 1275 a Genoese obtained from the Emperor Michael Palaeologus the lease of a mountain in the Gulf of Smyrna where were alum mines already exploited by the Greeks. Here he built and fortified the town of New Phocaea, secured also a monopoly of importing alum from the Black Sea, and made a large fortune. The mines remained in Genoese hands until 1459. It is just possible that English merchants may themselves have visited New Phocaea in the thirteenth century.[4] At any rate the Genoese were importing alum into England at the opening of the fourteenth century.[5] From early in the thirteenth century tolls were being paid on alum at the ports,[6]

---

[1] E.g. ashes "ke afferte a weide" in a thirteenth-century list of tolls at Winchester. J. S. Furley, *op. cit.*, 58. Ashes were also used for soap making.

[2] *Records of the Borough of Leicester, ut supra,* I, 102.

[3] E.g. the ship of a Hamburg merchant, attacked off Dunwich in 1260, was laden with ashes, pitch, etc.

[4] If Gibbon's conjecture is correct in thus interpreting Ducas's mention of Ἰγγληνοι as visiting New Phocaea. Alum was produced to some extent in this country, e.g. in the Isle of Wight, but this may have been an inferior quality. See references in *The Little Red Book of Bristol,* ed. F. B. Bickley (1900).

[5] N. S. B. Gras, *Early English Customs System* (Cambridge, Mass., 1918), 269. [6] E.g. at Torksey (1228), London (1233, 1257), Gloucester (1260).

and amongst several cargoes loaded by a Dunwich merchant at Bordeaux in 1275 there were 50 bales of alum claimed by a Barcelona merchant.[1]

Verdigris and copperas also appear in many of the murage grants, as for instance at London in 1257 and 1279 and at York in 1284, and it is probable that both were used as mordants, though they were certainly also in demand for sheep-dressing.[2] Verdigris is most often used after dyeing to fix the colour, while copperas tends to deepen the colour as well as fixing it. Argol (crude cream of tartar), not strictly a mordant but useful with other mordants for brightening the colour, appears later in the century amongst the goods for which tolls were to be paid at London and York.[3] Since this is prepared from the hard crust on the sides of vessels in which wine has fermented, most of it, at any rate, must have been imported.

It is clear from this brief survey of raw materials that the dyers were dependent upon imports as was no other branch of the cloth industry. The weavers had abundant supplies of home-grown wool, unsurpassed anywhere in Europe, to draw upon. For the fullers, England was rich in fuller's earth, and to this and to her fine pastures and clear streams she was largely to owe her supremacy in the industry. For the cloth finishers, again, there were as yet ample supplies of home-grown teasles. Only in dyestuffs was there any considerable trade with other lands. Thus dyeing involved not only much technical skill and scientific knowledge but dealings with foreign markets, and it is not surprising to find that those responsible for this stage of the cloth-making industry were men of substance and influence, closely in touch with foreign merchants, buying dyes from them, selling cloth to them, and often organizing the whole production of the finished material. They were in fact merchants and entrepreneurs rather than artisans, leaving the actual labour of dyeing to their own hired servants.

[1] *Calendar of Patent Rolls*, 1272–81, 117.
[2] *Victoria County History, Essex*, II (1907), 330, note 4.
[3] London, 1279; York, 1284.

The dyers of Worcester, for instance, were evidently dealing with Flemish merchants in the time of Henry II, possibly purchasing woad from them, for we read that on one occasion they owed £12 to "the King's enemies of Flanders".[1] Thus closely concerned with foreign trade, inevitably in each city the dyers drew together with others who were buying and selling, in order to protect and regulate their trade, and from the earliest times of which we have record we find dyers as members of the merchant gilds.

One of the earliest gild merchant membership rolls still extant is that of Leicester for 1196. Here the first admission is that of a dyer, "Nicholas Tinctor", and later on in the same year another dyer is admitted—"Galfridus de Eitona, teintor", with a dyer, "Radulfus francus, tinctor", as one of his pledges.[2] A number of dyers occur on subsequent rolls of the thirteenth century, and it is probable that there were many others not specifically mentioned as such. For occupations are not invariably given. They seem only to be added for greater precision where the gild member would otherwise be designated merely by a Christian name or by a Christian name and a place-name. Those with sufficiently distinctive surnames needed no further description.

Now it is significant that among the many different trades which do appear on the gild merchant membership rolls, those of weaver and fuller are conspicuous by their absence. Miss Bateson, indeed, finds a weaver on the Leicester gild roll in the early thirteenth century,[3] but in fact he appears only as the father of a new member who is described as "Ricardus filius Adam' Tixtoris".[4] Gross, too, when urging that "craftsmen as a rule were freely allowed to enter the gild merchant and to enjoy the other burghal franchises", states that rolls of gild merchant members mention weavers and fullers as well as dyers. The bulk of his evidence, however,

---

[1] *Pipe Roll 19 Henry II* (1172–3) (Pipe Roll Society, XIX, 1895), 165, "*de xii li. quas tinctores de Wirec. debuerant inimicis Regis de Flandr.*").

[2] *Records of the Borough of Leicester, ut supra,* I, 12, 13.

[3] *Ibid.,* I, xxix.   [4] *Ibid.,* 28.

refers to dyers, whom he finds as members of gild merchants at Leicester, Barnstaple and Andover. Those few weavers of the twelfth and thirteenth centuries whom he quotes as evidence actually appear in the records not as gild merchant members, but merely as paying a tax.[1] Cunningham, again, though arguing that the gild merchant of Shrewsbury "must have had nearly every householder, poor or rich, as a member", finds dyers upon its roll of 1209, but not weavers or fullers.[2] Thus while there were many dyers in the merchant gilds of the twelfth and thirteenth centuries, there seems at present no evidence of weavers and fullers being members. Craftsmen as such were not necessarily excluded, but it is important to differentiate among craftsmen, and not to generalize that all were admitted.

But not only have we negative evidence of the lack of weavers and fullers on the gild merchant membership rolls. There is also positive evidence that they were deliberately

---

[1] Gross, *op. cit.*, I, 108, note 3. The references here to vol. II, 14, 313, 378, and to Rep. MSS. Com. 1881, 404 (Leicester), all concern *dyers*; those to J. Thompson, *History of Leicester to the end of the seventeenth century* (1849), 87 and vol. II, 246 are to *assessment rolls* of Leicester and Wallingford; those to vol. II, 60, 210, concern other craftsmen unconnected with the cloth industry. It is rash to assume that in 1305 "Walter le Webbe" is necessarily a weaver himself and not taking his surname from his forbears, though "Willelmus Scot, tinctor" is certainly a dyer (Sir R. C. Hoare and others, *The History of Modern Wiltshire* (1822–44), VI, 742). Even if, as seems doubtful, the Andover ordinance of 1338 implies that weavers and fullers could be members of Andover's merchant gild in 1338, it does not imply that such was the rule throughout England a century and a half earlier. The Wycombe ordinance of 1316 does not necessarily mean that weavers were members of its gild merchant, for it says only that weavers wishing to work within the liberty of the borough must give the *gildam* yearly 1s. for each *argoys* (? loom) and that they should thereby be quit of all things touching the gild of merchants such as stallage, etc. (*quietus quilibet eorum de omnibus rebus Gildam mercator' tangentibus tanquam stallagius etc.*), thus implying only that the gild merchant exercised the right to tax them and that they each compounded for the tax by a single payment. See the original Leger Book No. 1 at High Wycombe; the rendering of *quietus* as "free" in the Report of the Historical Manuscripts Commission has perhaps led to a misconception of the meaning of the ordinance.

[2] W. Cunningham, "The Gild Merchant of Shrewsbury", *Transactions Royal Historical Society*, New Series, IX (1895).

excluded. At Leicester, for instance, Nicholas the Chaloner
was attainted and expelled from the gild in 1276 because he
kept weaver's work in his house after entering the gild.[1] It
is interesting to compare with this the early thirteenth-
century charters to Aberdeen and Perth. William the
Lion's charter to Perth in 1210 permitted the citizens to
have their merchant gild, "with the exception of the fullers
and weavers", and so did that of Alexander II to Aberdeen
in 1222.[2]

The difference between the position of the dyers and of
the weavers and fullers is further emphasized by the fact
that the dyers, bound together in the merchant gilds with
other traders, had apparently no gilds of their own, as had
the weavers and fullers. It is remarkable that no mention of
any dyers' gild seems to have survived for the twelfth or
thirteenth centuries. Weavers and fullers, on the other hand,
while entirely outside the merchant gilds, were closely
united in gilds of their own, and had been from the earliest
days of which records survive. Neither weavers' nor fullers'
gilds can be traced back with certainty beyond the reign of
Henry I, but both existed in this reign and both may have
existed earlier. Five weavers' gilds and one fullers' gild were
certainly in being at the time of the first extant Pipe Roll in
1130. The most important of them was the London weavers'
gild (*Gilda Telariorum*), which paid £16 into the Exchequer
that year. Next in importance came the weavers' gilds of
Winchester, Lincoln and Oxford and the fullers' gild of
Winchester, which each paid £6. The weavers' gild of
Huntingdon was probably smaller and had perhaps only
recently come into existence, since its payment of £2 was
recorded under the heading "New Agreements" (*Novae
Conventiones*).[3] That of Nottingham is recorded as having
paid nothing, so that it had probably been in existence earlier

[1] *Records of the Borough of Leicester, ut supra*, I, 169.
[2] Scottish *Leges Burgorum*, quoted in Gross, *op. cit.*, II, 213, note 4:
ut habeant gildam suam mercatoriam exceptis fullonibus et telariis; W. Kennedy,
Annals of Aberdeen, I (1818), 11.
[3] *Pipe Roll 31 Henry I*, Record Commission (1833).

MMV—P

and failed to pay up this year; later it was paying £2 a year. The York weavers' gild, later on a very important one, first appears on the Pipe Rolls in 1165, paying £10. Other such gilds existed which made no payments direct into the Exchequer and which therefore do not appear on the Pipe Rolls. The weavers of Gloucester, for instance, owed 20s. annually to the king, but since this was granted by charter in the time of Stephen to the Abbot and Convent of St. Augustine's at Bristol, it is not mentioned on the Pipe Rolls.[1] Yet others again existed which, since they were not in towns on royal demesne, had no need to seek royal sanction.

The first distinct references to the merchant gilds are almost contemporary with those to the weavers' and fullers' gilds. The two earliest date probably from the early years of the reign of Henry I, and "soon after", as Gross says, "during the reign of Henry I, the Gild Merchant appears in various municipal charters and, as the latter multiply, under Henry II, Richard I and John, it is mentioned more frequently among the burghal franchises".[2] The first mention of Lincoln's weavers' gild is in 1130, of its merchant gild in 1157.[3] Winchester's weavers' and fullers' gilds are first heard of in 1130, its merchant gild in 1155–8.[4] At York the merchant gild appears on the Pipe Roll of 1130, the weavers' gild not till 1165. At Nottingham the weavers' gild first appears on the Pipe Roll of 1155, but there is no mention of the merchant gild in the charter of this year and it first appears in the charter of 1189.[5]

Thus in the late twelfth and early thirteenth centuries we find the weavers and fullers each united in gilds of their own, while the dyers have no gilds of their own but are united

---

[1] *Calendar of Charter Rolls*, III, 378; cf. Bailiffs Accounts, no. 1356 (at Gloucester) temp. Edward I: *de textoribus eiusdem ville* 20s.
[2] Gross, *op. cit.*, I, 5.
[3] W. de G. Birch, *The Royal Charters of the City of Lincoln* (1911), 1.
[4] J. S. Furley, *op. cit.*
[5] *Records of the Borough of Nottingham*, I (1882), 3, 7.

together in the merchant gilds. And while the weavers and fullers were actively securing privileges from the crown for themselves, the dyers, with other members of the merchant gilds, were securing charters of wider scope for their town as a whole. That the dyers, with other members of the merchant gilds, where such existed, were largely instrumental in obtaining these civic charters is very clear from the many grants of privileges in the charters themselves concerning dyeing as well as merchant gilds. Those who drew up the charters were eager to exploit every opportunity for monopoly, and amongst the monopolies they coveted were those of dyeing cloth and of buying cloth for dyeing. Henry II's charter to Lincoln restricted the dyeing of cloth to burgesses and members of the merchant gild,[1] and his charter to Newcastle decreed that only burgesses might purchase webs for dyeing (*telas ad tingendas*),[2] while Nottingham's charter of 1200 restricted the dyeing of cloth within ten leagues' radius of Nottingham entirely to the borough.[3] Similarly, later on in the thirteenth century the burgesses of Shrewsbury secured by their charter of 1227 that they alone might buy raw cloth (*pannum crudum*), thus keeping for themselves control over the dyeing and finishing processes,[4] while in Chesterfield by the charter of Edward I only burgesses might be dyers.[5]

The dyers, in fact, unlike the weavers and fullers, were among the ruling class of the rapidly growing towns at this time, assisting in directing civic policy as a whole and in protecting and regulating the trade of the towns. Not only, however, did they restrict the dyeing industry within each

[1] *Calendar of Charter Rolls*, III, 7.
[2] W. Stubbs, *Select Charters*, ed. H. W. C. Davis (1913), 134. W. J. Ashley (*An Introduction to English Economic History and Theory*, I, i (1893), 74) renders this "could buy, make (i.e. finish) or cut cloth for dyeing", but the Latin clearly has "could *buy for dyeing*" (*Nullus nisi burgensis poterit emere telas ad tingendas nec facere nec secare*).
[3] *Records of the Borough of Nottingham*, I, 11.
[4] Gross, *op. cit.*, II, 211.
[5] *Records of the Borough of Chesterfield*, ed. P. Yeatman (1884), 36.

town to those who were burgesses. So great was their influence that the crown was prevailed upon to confine the making of dyed cloth to the towns, prohibiting any dyeing in the country except such as was done for people's own use and not for sale. Richard I's famous Assize of Measures (1197), in addition to fixing a uniform width of two yards for all woollen cloth, decreed that no dyeing for sale, except only in black, should be carried on anywhere in the kingdom except in the cities and capital boroughs.[1] Thus it extended to all cities and boroughs the monopoly that Nottingham had achieved over her immediate neighbourhood.

What then was the relationship between the dyers and the weavers and fullers? Evidence for the early and mid-thirteenth century is slight, but for one at least of the towns specializing in cloth-making—Leicester, some court rolls of great interest have survived from the year 1253. These tend clearly to show that by then there had emerged, probably from among the dyers, a class of entrepreneurs employing weavers and fullers, controlling the whole production of the cloth, and selling it at the great East Anglian fairs.

Let us take, for example, two important Leicester citizens, Henry Houhil and Richard of Shilton, whose names frequently appear upon the rolls between 1253 and 1263. Henry Houhil was a burgess with considerable property in Leicester and was one of thirty-five gildsmen bound under a heavier penalty than others to come at all summonses of the Alderman to all councils of the community of the gild.[2] He was himself concerned in the dyeing of wool, for in 1259 he was fined for putting wool dyed in woad into madder to make it darker like perse colour.[3] He must also have been responsible for the making of the wool into cloth, for in the same year he was fined for putting black

---

[1] Roger of Hovenden, *Chronica*, ed. Stubbs (Rolls Series, 1871), IV, 33: *Nulla tinctura vendenda, nisi solummodo nigra, fiat alicubi in regno nisi in civitatibus aut capitalibus burgis.* This clause of the Assize seems to have received little, if any, attention.

[2] *Records of the Borough of Leicester, ut supra*, I, 76.

[3] *Ibid.*, 84.

wool into woad to make it blacker and for using this wool later on in perse cloth (*quod posuit nigram lanam in wayda ad eam faciendam nigriorem et postea eam posuit ad pannum persum*).[1] From this it would seem clear that he was employing weavers to make up his own wool into cloth. He was also employing fullers for scouring and felting the raw web. In 1256, for instance, he brought a suit against one of these fullers, Roger of Ketton, who was convicted of "fulling the coloured cloths of Henry Houhil" by a prohibited method.[2] Finally, we know that he was trading at Boston Fair, for he complained in 1259 that Peter Blund' and Richard of Shilton refused him entrance to the shop there which ought to have been his by lot.[3] A special row was assigned to Leicester at this fair. The cloth merchants (described as *Draparii*) had their stalls on the south side of it, and the wool merchants (*Lanarii*) on the north. At night, if they wished, they might take the cloth to their lodgings both for safe keeping and to fold and dress it, but it might only be sold in the row.[4]

Richard of Shilton who, like Houhil, was one of Leicester's leading citizens,[5] was also producing as well as selling cloth. Like Houhil he was fined for dipping wool dyed in woad into madder,[6] and he too sued a fuller for defective fulling of a blue cloth of his.[7] He was evidently trading at Boston. Peter Blund', reeve of Leicester, who was concerned with him in the dispute over Houhil's stall at Boston, was also engaged in dyeing, for he was amongst those fined in 1259 for using illegal processes. That he was dealing in cloth is also shown by the purchase from him of russet worth £6 on the occasion of the Earl of Leicester's visit to the town in

---

[1] *Ibid.*, 85. The list of those fined is not given in the printed version but is to be found in the MS. at Leicester.
[2] *Ibid.*, 71: *quod fullavit pannos coloratos Henrici Houhil. . . .*
[3] *Ibid.*, 83.
[4] *Ibid.*, 84, 95.
[5] *Ibid.*, 45, 77.
[6] *Ibid.*, 85 (MS. version).
[7] *Ibid.*, 101.

(?) 1270.[1] The lists of those fined for contravention of the dyeing regulations also include [2] "Adam de Welton, dyer", who entered the gild merchant in 1254, and Henry of Ruddington who was mayor of Leicester from 1259 to 1270.

The extent to which capitalist employers such as Houhil and Shilton organized the industry under their control is further revealed by such ordinances concerning the industry as have been preserved on the Leicester gild rolls. Ordinances for the weavers and fullers, including the fixing of wage rates, were made by the merchant gild on which, as we have seen, the dyers were represented but not the weavers and fullers. Such were the customs agreed to in the gild of merchants with the consent of the weavers and fullers in 1260.[3] The weavers swore that they would not weave at night, that they would use three shuttles, and that they would conceal no infidelity in their work. In 1264 it was "provided and agreed" in the merchant gild that the weavers should be paid at the rate of $\frac{3}{4}d.$ a yard for russets and $\frac{1}{2}d.$ a yard for all other cloth, and they were allowed to work at night so long as their work was not defective. At the same time they were forbidden to weave for the country villages while the men of Leicester had sufficient work for them. If they were short of work this was to be pointed out to two specially appointed members of the gild who might then, if they thought fit, permit weaving to be done for the villages.[4] Defective weaving was punished by the merchant gild.[5]

The fullers' ordinances of 1260, like those of the weavers,

[1] *Records of the Borough of Leicester, ut supra*, I, 127.
[2] As shown in the MS. version.
[3] *Ibid.*, 89: *constitute fuerunt hee consuetudines in Gilda mercatorum cum consensu mercatorum et textorum et fullonum.* Cf. the reference on p. 106 to certain weavers and fullers who made an ordinance by themselves against the community of the gild merchant.
[4] *Ibid.*, 105. The weaver was thus not yet wholly dependent upon the entrepreneur.
[5] *Ibid.*, 105: *Rog. de Kildesby textor pro defectu texture unius panni Marie le Stabler.*

are partly concerned with technical regulations. Imperfect cloths must not be fulled without reference to the mayor and bailiffs; certain detergents must not be used for coloured cloths [1]; backhandles [2] must not be put on to dry cloth. This last prohibition shows that the fullers were also engaged in the raising of the nap on the cloth in preparation for the final process of shearing. The backhandle was a wooden frame consisting of a handle and central upright about a foot long in all, with two cross-pieces, one about a foot long between handle and upright and a second shorter one higher up, on which teasles were set; when this was passed over the cloth the sharp hooks of the teasles fluffed up the surface, drawing out the fibres. It was important that the cloth should be wet during this process, or the hooks would scratch away the fibres altogether, robbing the surface. For this reason raising was often carried out while the cloth was still wet from the fuller's hands, [3] and references to it frequently appear in the ordinances of fullers' gilds. The only fullers' ordinances we have for the thirteenth century are those of Leicester, but the first extant ordinances of the fullers' gild at Bristol, enrolled in the Little Red Book in 1346, clearly distinguish between two classes of craftsmen, prescribing different wages for those who work in the stocks at the actual labour of fulling and for those who work on dry land at the

[1] *Ibid.*, 89: *in arzilio et fecibus*; cf. the conviction of Roger of Ketton in 1256 for fulling *in glire et fecibus* (71); the meaning is uncertain.

[2] *quod non ponent Bachandle super siccum pannum.* The Editor prints *Bathandle*, adding a note to the effect that "Bac" not "Bat" is clearly written, but that the reading must be *Bat*, i.e. a small mallet for beating the cloth. The word has not been met with elsewhere than in the Leicester records, but taking this reference in conjunction with that of 1343 it seems clear that the instrument referred to is not that used for pounding the cloth in the stocks, but that for raising the nap. The 1343 ordinance forbids the use of iron "bachandles", "cardes" or "skrattes" instead of teasles. The substitution of metal hooks for teasles may be connected with the shortage of teasles mentioned above (35). It was strenuously resisted throughout the Middle Ages (see, e.g., Statute 4 Ed. IV).

[3] See M. Postlethwayt, *Universal Dictionary of Trade and Commerce* (4th edition, 1774), under "Cloth", and *A Visit to Hunt and Company's Lodgemore and Frome Hall Cloth Mills*, ed. H. Mayhew (n.d.), 21.

perch, i.e., the wooden bar or frame, over which the cloth was hung during the raising.[1] The earliest extant ordinances of the fullers' gild at Lincoln, made probably in 1337, also refer to this process, forbidding any member of the gild to work at the perch (*ad perticam*) with a woman, except with his own wife or her servant.[2] We read elsewhere of cloth being "drawn on the perch" and the process itself is sometimes called "perching". It is vividly depicted in the late medieval window of the clothworkers at Semur cathedral, where the backhandle itself, set with teasles, is clearly shown, and we see the craftsman drawing it down over the cloth, which is hung for the purpose on a horizontal bar rather longer than the width of the cloth.

The Leicester fullers were forbidden to fix their own rates of pay, nor might they hold any meeting among themselves unless two members of the merchant gild, nominated for the purpose, were present.[3] It was also laid down that if the owners found any defect in the cloths after they had been raised,[4] they should show them to four members of the merchant gild who should present the defects to the mayor and commonalty. Two of the leading cloth entrepreneurs were among those chosen for this purpose. Defective fulling was punished by the gild.[5]

There is a very significant difference between the procedure for making ordinances for the weavers and fullers and for the dyers. Whereas in the former case rules were

---

[1] *Little Red Book of Bristol, ut supra*, II, 12: *en le Stokkes al overagne qest appelee fullyng* and *sur terre cest a savoyr a la perche*. For a description of the actual fulling process at this time see previous article, *Economic History Review*, XI, No. 1, 40 *et seq., supra*, Ch. IV.

[2] J. Toulmin Smith, *English Gilds* (1870), 179. These ordinances are first recorded in 1389, but are stated to have been made in 1337. Salzman would not seem to be justified in identifying the perch (*pertica*) with the wooden rod with which the cloth was beaten (*Medieval English Industries*, 221–2).

[3] In 1275 the fullers were fined for contravening this order.

[4] *Brochiati et cotunati*.

[5] *Records of the Borough of Leicester, ut supra*, I, 109, William Pennyfoot, fuller (1269), 71, Roger of Ketton (1256), 101, William of Shilton, fuller (1264).

made by the merchant gild and imposed upon the weavers
and fullers, who then agreed to them by oath, in the latter
case they were made by the members of the merchant gild
for themselves. Thus in 1263, "on the Thursday next before
Candlemas, in full morning speech, it was provided and
agreed in common by the community of the Gild of Merchants of Leicester that henceforth none *of them* shall make
any perse coloured cloth except with white wool and woad
and ashes,[1] and without any admixture of black wool or
grey wool, or madder or alum".[2] Anyone contravening this
rule was to forfeit both his cloth and his wool and to lose the
liberties of the gild for a year and a day. This seems to have
been a reiteration of an earlier rule which, as we have seen
above, a number of important members of the merchant gild
were fined for breaking.

The Leicester records throw no light on the preliminary
processes of carding and spinning, carried on no doubt by
women throughout Leicester and beyond, nor on the final
process of shearing after the raising of the nap. Nevertheless
they give us a vivid picture, if not complete in all its details,
of an industry highly organized on a capitalist basis in a
town specializing in cloth-making. Many of the leading
citizens are capitalist entrepreneurs, purchasing wool, having
it washed and dyed in blue, vermilion or other colours,
probably on their own premises, giving it out to carders
and spinners, employing weavers and fullers throughout the
town,[3] under stringent supervision, at piece-work rates fixed
by themselves, and marketing the finished cloth from their
own stalls at the great East Anglian fairs of Boston, St. Ives [4]

---

[1] Translated "crude tartar" in the printed volume.

[2] *Records of the Borough of Leicester, ut supra*, I, 101–2: *In pleno morspechio,
per communitatem Gilde mercatorum Leycestrie communiter fuit provisum et
concessum quod de cetero nullus eorum faciet pannos persos nisi de Lana alba et
Wayda et Cineribus et sine aliqua admixtione Lane nigre seu grise lane, seu
Warancie seu alume.*

[3] When the process of fulling became mechanized by the invention of the
fulling mill, fulling, like dyeing, was often carried on by the entrepreneur
himself, who invested some of his capital in a mill.

[4] *Records of the Borough of Leicester, ut supra*, I, 95.

or Stamford.[1] Alongside of this great industry for export there must have remained a small industry working for purely local demand. Weavers, no doubt, were not wholly dependent upon the large entrepreneurs, and must have continued to weave cloth for their customers' own personal use.

It would be unwise to assume that in every case it was from among the dyers that this capitalist class emerged. Weavers and other craftsmen may by skill or good fortune have grown richer than their fellows, abjured the practice of their craft with their own hands, like Nicholas the Chaloner,[2] and entered the merchant gild to organize the production of cloth. So also woolmongers and other traders who had acquired even a small amount of capital may have invested it in what was becoming an increasingly profitable enterprise. But that dyers very often became responsible for organizing the whole process elsewhere than at Leicester is borne out by the wealth and importance of dyers in many places[3] and also by the list of fines paid in Yorkshire by those making cloth of the wrong width, as given on the Hundred Rolls. Here almost the only trade name by which any of the makers are designated is that of dyer.[4]

No records comparable to those of Leicester are known still to exist for the other great cloth-making cities for the mid-thirteenth century, so that we cannot trace with any certainty the organization of their industry. Stray indications of its capitalist nature appear, however, here and there. In London, which produced mainly coarse burel rather than fine dyed cloth, control of the industry was in the hands of entrepreneurs who were called "burellers". Thus in 1225 we read of the "men of London who cause burels to be made",[5] who were evidently employing workers under them. From

---

[1] *Ibid.*, 79.

[2] *Ibid.*, 104. Nicholas the Chaloner (coverlet maker) was fined "because he wove fullable cloth against the liberty of the Gild and against his oath made when he entered the Gild".

[3] E.g. Philip' Tinctor who was mayor of Exeter in 1259. See also *Victoria County History, Hants*, for references to several wealthy dyers in the thirteenth century.   [4] Hundred Rolls for 1275.   [5] See above, 213–4.

the middle of the century we find "burellers" selling cloth to the king, and from 1275, when the Letter Books begin, there are frequent references to other activities of theirs, such as the buying of yarn and the control of the assay of woad. The disputes between burellers and weavers at the close of the century [1] clearly reveal a capitalist organization in which the burellers are putting out yarn to the weavers. They would seem to indicate, however, that in London the weavers had so far retained a somewhat more independent position than at Leicester. They were not allowed, for instance, to fix their own rates of pay, but neither were these to be fixed by the burellers; they were to be a matter of agreement between the weaver and the entrepreneur who "caused the cloth to be made". At Winchester, as at London, we find references to those who "cause burels to be made". In its thirteenth-century Consuetudinary, for instance, it is laid down that only burgesses could *fere uverer bureaus ne chaluns*. This has been erroneously quoted as showing that *weavers* were allowed to enjoy the municipal franchise. It shows rather that the control of cloth production was in the hands of entrepreneurs and that it could be undertaken only by burgesses. The making of cloth, indeed, did not imply simply its weaving, but a whole series of successive processes, and the very variety of these processes, and the many different craftsmen involved, led inevitably to its early organization on a capitalist basis.

Once it has been accepted that capitalism in the English cloth industry dates not, as is often supposed, from the late fourteenth and fifteenth centuries but that it was in existence two centuries earlier, a flood of light is thrown on many records which have hitherto puzzled historians, particularly on the laws of the weavers and fullers of Beverley, Winchester, Oxford and Marlborough. These laws are said to have been derived from similar laws of London. The earliest extant version of them is to be found in a collection of documents on the laws and customs of London dating,

---

[1] Fully related in Consitt, *op. cit.*

apparently, from the end of the twelfth century,[1] and they are also recorded in the London *Liber Custumarum* of the fourteenth century.[2] First and fullest comes the law of the weavers and fullers of Winchester, then that of Marlborough, and finally those of Oxford and Beverley. Hitherto commentators have been almost entirely preoccupied with the legal and constitutional aspect of these laws. Attention has been directed principally to the provision that weavers and fullers might not attaint a freeman nor bear witness against him, and discussion has centred mainly on the reason for this prohibition, which has been explained by supposing that all weavers and fullers in these towns were foreigners or that they were all landless, or, more logically, by pointing out that the feudal immunities they had won by their charters set up rival jurisdictions to those of the towns.[3]

A close analysis of these laws shows, however, that the majority of the clauses (six out of seven in the case of Winchester) refer not to the legal but to the industrial status of the weavers and fullers, and that they are primarily concerned with the economic organization of the industry and reflect the subservience of the wage-earning craftsman to the capitalistic entrepreneur.

One group of clauses, restricting the business dealings of the weavers and fullers, shows clearly that they could not take their own cloth to the fairs and that they were virtually dependent upon the entrepreneur, at any rate so far as cloth for a wide market was concerned, though they might weave individual pieces for other citizens. At Winchester they might not go out of the town to do any business, nor might

[1] British Museum Add. MSS. 14252, f. 111. The writing is late twelfth century and none of the dates mentioned are later than 9 John. The MS. concludes with "*E ceste lai unt il en la franchise de Lundres, si cum il dient*".

[2] *Liber Custumarum, ut supra*, I, 130. Printed also in *Beverley Town Documents*, ed. A. F. Leach (Selden Society Publications, XIV, 1900), 134.

[3] For the most recent discussion of this question see E. Lipson, *Economic History of England* (7th ed. 1937), I, 367 *et seq.* Lipson follows Leach in rejecting the suggestion of Riley, followed by Gross and Cunningham, that the weavers and fullers were all aliens, but he disposes of Leach's suggestion that they were landless.

they sell their cloth to any outsider but only to merchants of the city. At Beverley likewise they might not go out of the town to do any business. At Marlborough they might not weave [1] nor work except for the townsmen, and at Oxford they might not weave nor full any cloth of their own without permission.

A second group of clauses limits the weavers and fullers entirely to their own crafts and prevents them from usurping the privileges of members of the merchant gild by venturing either to dye or to cut cloth. At Winchester they might not dye nor cut [2] cloth, and at Beverley they might not cut cloth. Further, at Marlborough they might have nothing pertaining to the making of cloth worth a penny except 5 ells a year to clothe themselves.[3] Very similar to this last clause is one at Winchester, prohibiting the weavers and fullers from buying anything pertaining to their craft unless they made agreement with the sheriff each year.[4]

Further, the laws confirm that weavers and fullers generally were excluded from the ranks of the burgesses, and thus sharply differentiated from the class of entrepreneurs whose employees they were,[5] though, should they become rich, they might abjure their craft and themselves become burgesses and producers of cloth. At Winchester it

---

[1] *tistre*, erroneously translated *dye* in *Beverley Town Documents, ut supra*, xlvi. Cf. the similar prohibition at Leicester, *supra*, 230.

[2] *sechir*. This should probably be translated *cut* rather than *dry*; cf. charters to Chesterfield and Newcastle stating that no one is to be a dyer or to cut (*secare*) cloth unless he is a burgess. At Leicester also only members of the merchant gild could cut cloth. (See *Records of the Borough of Leicester, ut supra*, I, 63.)

[3] *ne avoir rien del suen ke aprendre a dras faire vaillant un dener, fors a tant cum amunte a cinc alnes de drap a soi vestir par an.*

[4] *Ne le teler ne fulun ne poet achater neis ceo ke apent a sun mester, kil ne face le gre al viconte chascuntan.*

[5] Cf. also the case at Lincoln in 1200 in which it was stated that the fullers had no community with the citizens (*Curia Regis Rolls of the Reigns of Richard I and John*, I (1922), 259). This case would seem to refer to dyers working as craftsmen for entrepreneurs who were trying to prevent them from trading on their own. With this may be compared the ruling in the Scottish *Leges Burgorum* that no dyer could be in the merchant gild unless he abjured the exercise of his craft by his own hand (Gross, *op. cit.*, I, 213). See W. J. Ashley, *An Introduction to English Economic History and Theory* (1901), I, 83.

is laid down that if one of them enriches himself and wishes to give up his craft he must forswear it, put out of his house the instruments of his craft, and pay for the freedom of the city. The Beverley provision was almost exactly similar. That of Marlborough was stricter still; if a weaver or fuller so enriched himself that he coveted the franchise of the town, two years must pass during which he must see if he could live without his craft, and the third year he must forswear his craft and turn all his tools out of his house. The law of Oxford adds that if a weaver dies and his widow still wishes to follow the craft, she can be married only to a weaver. The Leicester records, as we have seen, provide actual illustrations of the working out of such a law in practice. Nicholas the Chaloner, for instance, though he had forsworn his craft when he entered the gild merchant, continued to practise weaving and as a result was first fined and later expelled from the gild.[1]

Our evidence for the English cloth industry in the late twelfth and early thirteenth centuries is slight. Both central and local records are scanty compared with those for the fourteenth and fifteenth centuries. We have neither aulnage nor customs accounts from which to make any quantitative or qualitative analysis of the cloth produced in different parts of the country or exported abroad, nor can we tell to what extent it had yet ousted foreign cloth from the English market. Few court rolls survive to record particular transactions which might throw light on the technique and structure of the industry, while neither the houses, wills nor tombstones of the great cloth-makers, much less any of their letters, still exist to show us what manner of men they were. Nevertheless, from such evidence as we have we can catch a glimpse of the long-departed glory of the great East Anglian cloth-making towns, Beverley, Lincoln, Stamford and others, a glory still reflected in the wealth of Early English building that has there survived, recalling the days when their cloth was sought by merchants of Italy and Spain and rivalled the fine cloths of Flanders for the king's own use.

[1] *Records of the Borough of Leicester, ut supra*, I, 104, 169.

VI

TRENDS IN THE EXPORT OF ENGLISH WOOLLENS IN THE FOURTEENTH CENTURY [1]

In the industrial society of to-day the historian, seeking to trace the progress of industrialization in centuries past, finds himself continually thwarted by the lack of that quantitative data without which he must ever grope in darkness. Most of all is he baffled when he attempts to probe beyond the sixteenth century into the middle ages. The great textile industries of Flanders and Italy, with their many thousands of workers living wholly by the manufacture of woollens for export, have left no continuous records from which the course of their trade can year by year be determined in the formative period of the twelfth and thirteenth centuries; even for the two succeeding centuries there survive only spasmodic figures, difficult of interpretation, and those but for a few individual cities. The lesser manufacturing industries are still more sparsely documented. In one case, however, and that fortunately no unimportant one, we are better served. That is in the case of the export industry in English woollens in that critical early period of expansion when it was overtaking the industries of Flanders and Italy and transforming England from an exporter primarily of raw materials into an exporter primarily of manufactured products.

Now the crucial period of this transformation, it has long been realized, was in the fourteenth century—roughly from the outbreak of the Hundred Years War in 1337, and it is this period with which I propose here to deal. A close investigation of the quantitative data relating to the English woollen export industry at this time has a double interest;

[1] *Economic History Review*, Second Series, III, No. 2, 1950. Paper read on 15th April 1950 before the annual conference of the Economic History Society.

not only does it enable us to trace year by year the trends in the development of an infant industry on the way towards a position of supremacy in the markets of Europe, but it is, so far as I am aware, the only industry whose development can thus be traced in the medieval world.

The data for such a study are to be found, as is well known, in the returns of the royal customs officials concerning the duties on cloth, enrolled year by year on the Exchequer Customs Accounts.[1] These accounts are unusually comprehensive. From the date of the first taxes on cloth exports, viz. those on alien exports from 1303 and on native exports from 1347, they cover all English ports, except a few unimportant ones,[2] all English woollens, except a few cheap varieties (I do not propose here to consider worsteds), and all exporting merchants, without any of the exemptions which vitiate so many customs accounts, especially local ones. The series is a magnificent one, without parallel elsewhere in Europe, and it survives intact in the Public Record Office. It was first systematically examined by the late Professor H. L. Gray, whose pioneer article in the *English Historical Review* for 1924 [3] remains to this day the standard authority for the history of the development of the export trade in English woollens in the fourteenth century. Valuable as Gray's work has been, its usefulness is impaired by two serious drawbacks. In the first place, Gray attempts to relate exports to total production by quoting the returns of the Ulnager, which purport to give statistics of the quantities of cloth manufactured for sale throughout the country. These returns, even for the fourteenth century, are a highly

---

[1] Public Record Office: Exchequer L.T.R. Customs Accounts.

[2] The royal customs officials normally did not collect in the following regions: the county of Durham, Cornwall, Cheshire, Lancashire, Wales (beyond Chepstow in the south and Chester in the north). Surviving accounts of the Palatinates of Durham and Chester, of the Duchies of Cornwall and Lancaster, and of the Principalities of Wales show, however, that export of cloth from these regions was slight.

[3] H. L. Gray, "The Production and Export of English Woollens in the Fourteenth Century", *English Historical Review*, xxxix (1924).

unsatisfactory source, as I have shown elsewhere [1]; neither the totals for the country as a whole nor the details for particular persons and places can be accepted without most careful scrutiny in each instance. In the second place, and more germane to our present inquiry, Gray has proceeded on a selective basis, taking only figures for specimen years, or averages over certain short periods.[2] This haphazard and piecemeal method, while giving a rough impression of the net results of the century's development, has concealed many interesting and significant fluctuations and given no real picture of the movement of trade during the century. It seems therefore worth while to extract the whole of the evidence, and thereby to discover not only the general trend of the trade over the century, but certain medium- and short-term trends. These trends may perhaps be of interest not only to the medievalist, by helping to illuminate the history of England in that restless age, the later fourteenth century, but also to the student of industrial development in any age.

A year by year scrutiny of the customs accounts shows at once that the transformation of England's trade by which she became primarily an exporter of manufactured woollens rather than of raw wool was no steady forward movement, nor one interrupted solely by the Black Death. In the fourteenth century we can in fact discern three marked periods of expansion, each of some fifteen years or so, separated by two sharp setbacks. The first phase of expansion, in the 1330's and 1340's, roughly from the outbreak of the Hundred Years War to the eve of the Black Death, can only be dimly perceived, for it came at a time when none but alien shipments of cloth were subject to customs duty. So, too, when we come to the first setback; this lack of quantitative data on the previous advance makes it impossible

[1] E. M. Carus-Wilson, "The Aulnage Accounts: a Criticism", *Economic History Review* (1929), II, No. 1, *infra*, Ch. VIII.

[2] All told, Gray has used figures for only 22 of the 53 years with which he deals. In some cases he has generalized, dangerously, from the figures of a single port, see *infra*, 255, n. 1.

to measure the extent of the depression. Nevertheless a word or two must be said about these two periods before proceeding to firmer ground.

In the first phase of expansion, in the 1330's and 1340's, the most striking feature that can be quantitatively demonstrated is the capture of the home market by English manufacturers. Early in the century English woollens already had a high reputation both in England and on the continent, where many of them fetched a high price.[1] But the volume of exports was comparatively small, and England herself was a heavy buyer of foreign cloth, principally of cloth imported by Flemings, and made by Flemings from English wool. In the 1320's these imports of foreign cloth were still considerable, but in the 1330's they fell with catastrophic suddenness, and by 1340 they had virtually ceased: for the remainder of the century they remained a mere trickle, chiefly of certain speciality cloths.[2] This much is clear from the figures of alien imports, taxed since 1303. It is clear also from records of cloth purchases, such as those for the royal Wardrobe.[3] War, as so often, had been the forcing

[1] Lincoln scarlets were bought for the royal Wardrobe in England at the opening of the fourteenth century at £8 and £7, 10s. for a cloth of 20 yards (P.R.O. Exchequer K.R. Accounts Various, Wardrobe, 359/18, 360/22, 363/21); this price of 8s. or 7s. 6d. per yard seems to have been the top price of any in England at this time. For sales abroad see R. Doehaerd, *Les relations commerciales entre Gênes, la Belgique et l'Outremont d'après les archives notariales génoises aux xiiie et xive siècles*, Institut Historique Belge de Rome, Etudes d'Histoire Economique et Sociale, II–IV, Brussels 1941; E. M. Carus-Wilson, "The English Cloth Industry in the late Twelfth and Early Thirteenth Centuries", *Economic History Review*, XIV, No. 1 (1944), 32, 33, supra 211, 2; and H. Laurent, *Un grand commerce d'exportation au moyen âge: la draperie des Pays-Bas en France et dans les pays méditerranéens (xiie–xve siècle)* (Paris, 1935), 76, for a reference to cloth of Lincoln (*de Nicola*), in a Venetian tariff of 1265.

[2] Alien imports averaged some 12,000 cloths per annum in 1303–11, and only some 2000 cloths per annum in the late 1330's (P.R.O. Exchequer L.T.R. Customs Accounts 356/2). Precise figures for each year are not available owing to gaps in these import accounts. In the 1360's it was much the same; in the 1380's the amount was considerably reduced.

[3] In the time of Edward II and in the early years of Edward III, royal purchases were made mainly at the great fairs and to some extent overseas, and

house for industry. The temporary closing of the English market to Flemish cloth and the prohibition of the export of English wool to Flanders, to bring pressure to bear upon Flanders, had given (not for the first time in history)[1] a momentary advantage to the English producer; his was now a protected industry. Yet more important, when these extreme measures were withdrawn and export of raw wool to Flanders was again allowed, the heavily increased export duties, amounting to some 33 per cent., burdened the foreign producer with greatly increased costs, and thereby again provided the infant English industry with such a measure of protection as enabled it to surmount even a comparatively high-cost period of initial development.[2] At the same time, large government orders for the clothing of the armed forces —2000 pieces of cloth were bought for the navy alone in 1337[3]—acted as a further stimulus to the home industry. War-time needs, war-time diplomatic policy, and war-time fiscal policy, had together given an immense impetus to the development of England's woollen industry.

they were predominantly of foreign cloth, especially cloth of Douai, Ghent, Bruges, Louvain, Malines. In the late 1330's the Flemish cloth had largely disappeared, though there were extensive purchases of Brabantine cloth, chiefly from Brussels. By the time of Richard II there is little mention of any cloth of foreign origin, while purchases were made no longer at the great fairs or from foreign merchants, but mainly from English cloth dealers in London and in provincial centres such as Coventry. (P.R.O. Exchequer K.R. Accounts Various, Wardrobe).

[1] The export of wool was prohibited, for example, in 1244 and in 1258, and in 1258 it was ordained that all should use woollen cloths made within the realm. *Annales Monastici*, III, *Annales Prioratus de Dunstaplia*, ed. H. R. Luard (Rolls Series, 1866), 163; *Chron. Domini Walteri de Hemingburgh*, ed. H. C. Hamilton, I, 306 (English Historical Society, 1848). There were many subsequent embargoes (e.g. 1270 and 1295) as relations between France, England and Flanders became more and more strained. On the unemployment caused in Flanders by that of 1337, see H. Pirenne, *Histoire de Belgique* (Brussels, 1922), II, 109.

[2] Cf. Eileen Power, *The Wool Trade in English Medieval History* (1941), 101. This continuous measure of protection was no doubt ultimately more effective than the sporadic embargoes, which in any event were evaded by licence.

[3] P.R.O. Exchequer L.T.R. Wardrobe Accounts 361/3 m. 30.

The force of this impetus can be precisely estimated only by the measure of the English producer's advance in the home market. But of the expansion of the industry at this time there is ample supporting evidence, if only in the number of foreign textile workers that it was able to absorb.[1] And there now seems no doubt that this was the time of a sharp contraction of production in the Flemish cities—a contraction of at least 50 per cent. at Ypres, as van Werveke, rightly correcting previous interpretations of the Ypres figures, has shown.[2]

How far the English export trade, as well as the home trade, expanded at this time must remain a matter of conjecture. The retaliatory measures by which Flanders forbade the import of English cloth [3] imply that some English cloth, at least, must have been reaching the marts of the Low Countries, but we still have figures only for alien shipments. Not until April 1347 were native merchants also taxed. Hence we have full export returns for little more than a year before the catastrophe of the Black Death. These first returns give an export of 3202 cloths (reckoned in terms of standard "cloths of assise")[4] for the five months up to

[1] There is no comprehensive study of this immigration, but see H. de Sagher, "L'immigration des tisserands flamands et brabançons en Angleterre sous Edward III", *Mélanges d'histoire offerts à Henri Pirenne* (Brussels, 1926). Immigration into the midlands and west country appears, however, to have been more considerable than has hitherto been supposed, and in addition to the Flemings and Brabantines there were large numbers of skilled artisans from Ireland. See, for example, P.R.O. Assize Roll 971, f. 1; *Rolls of Warwick and Coventry Sessions of the Peace*, ed. E. G. Kimball (1939), 27, 28, 46, 85; P.R.O. Exchequer Lay Subsidies 113/31.

[2] H. van Werveke, "De Omvang van de Ieperse Lakenproductie in de veertiende eeuw", *Mededelingen van de Koninklijke Vlaamse Academie voor Wetenschappen, Letteren en Schone Kunsten van Belgie, Klasse der Letteren* IX, 2 (Antwerp, 1947).

[3] These measures become frequent in the second half of the century but are to be found at Bruges by 1346. Pirenne, *op. cit.*, 196.

[4] The standard whole "cloth of assise" (*pannus integrus de assisa*), in terms of which the customs were reckoned, was 26 yards long by $6\frac{1}{2}$ or 6 quarters wide before fulling (*Statutes of the Realm*, I, 260, 395; II, 60). Other cloths, larger or smaller, paid customs proportionally (*Cal. Patent Rolls*, 1345-8, 276).

Michaelmas 1347, and an export of 4422 cloths for the following complete year, from Michaelmas to Michaelmas, with which the chart below begins. This second figure most probably already shows the effects of the plague, which reached England in July 1348 and had been ravaging the continent some months earlier, so that it would be dangerous to generalize as to the level of exports at this time, though we may hazard a guess at an annual export approaching 6000 cloths.

England's Exports of Woollen Cloth, 1347–99 [1]

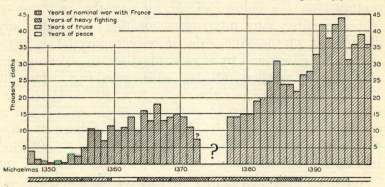

It is, however, clear that the five years succeeding the outbreak of the Black Death were years of depression for the growing English industry. Never does the annual export total reach 2000 cloths; once it sinks beneath 700. Such a depression is scarcely surprising. Pestilence—probably the most severe and widespread of the many pestilences of the century—raged through Europe from 1347 to 1349, taking heavy toll of producers as well as consumers of cloth. To pestilence succeeded dearth. In England grain prices rose steeply in the harvest year 1350–1, and again in the following year, reaching in 1352 one of the highest levels of the century.[2] City dwellers, purchasing foodstuffs, can have had

[1] See note on p. 262 on the method by which this chart has been compiled.
[2] J. E. Thorold Rogers, *A History of Agriculture and Prices in England*, I (1866), 209, 232.

little to spare for buying cloth, unless indeed they were speculators in grain. It was not to be wondered at if cloth sales remained low.

But the causes of the depression are to be found not only in pestilence and dearth. We must look more closely into the state of the foreign market. The principal market for England's cloth at this time was Gascony. Gascony, a part of the realm of the King of England, was bound to England as much by economic as by political ties, thriving by the exchange of her wines for English cloth and foodstuffs—an exchange upon which her life depended, so far had she concentrated on the culture of the vine to the exclusion of other pursuits.[1] Any interruption of the wine trade, any disturbance of the vineyards, at once reduced Gascony's purchasing power and by so doing had severe repercussions on England's woollen industry. Now three years before the Black Death appeared war had again struck deep into Gascony, after five years of respite from 1340 to 1345. The contending French and English armies had been at grips with each other in the very heart of the wine-producing region, the hinterland of Bordeaux up the valleys of the Garonne and the Dordogne. And there, when a truce was made in the autumn of 1347, abbeys, castles and cottages lay ruined, vineyards desolated and trampled down, their cultivators slain or driven into hiding, whether by the armies of Derby or by those of the Duke of Normandy.[2] Production and export of wine were inevitably at a low ebb, and the trouble was only intensified by the ravages of the Black Death in the following year. The returns of wine exports from the Gironde estuary for 1348–9 give the measure of the calamity, and vividly reveal the afflicted state into which the country had fallen. Whereas at the beginning of the century over 90,000 tons of wine had been laden

[1] E. M. Carus-Wilson, "The Effects of the Acquisition and of the Loss of Gascony on the English Wine Trade", *Bulletin of the Institute of Historical Research*, (1948), XXI, No. 63, 148–9, *infra*, Ch. VII, 269–70.

[2] R. Boutruche, *La crise d'une société; seigneurs et paysans du Bordelais pendant la Guerre de Cent Ans* (Paris, 1947), 198–9.

annually, this year shipments had dropped to scarcely 6000 tons. There was some recovery in the following year, but exports remained for some time at a much reduced level. [1]

To the twofold scourge of war and plague that smote Gascony there was added yet another, that of famine, even before the arrival of the Black Death. The harvest that was being gathered while the truce of 1347 was being negotiated was a disastrous one, coming as it did, said the chronicler, after floods worse than any since the Deluge. There followed the great dearth, when the price of corn reached famine level and many died of starvation.[2] If the devastations of war and pestilence combined to reduce Gascony's purchasing power by curtailing the supplies of wine available for export, so also must the great dearth have done by raising the cost of the bare necessaries of life. England's chief market had, for the moment, collapsed. So too it must have been with other subsidiary markets, if in a lesser degree where the devastations of war were not added to those of dearth and plague.

By 1353 there were signs of recovery, and in the late 1350's and through towards the end of the 1360's, as the chart makes plain, England's woollen export trade advanced with great rapidity. In this, the first phase of expansion which can be quantitatively measured with some precision, exports rose from less than 2000 cloths per annum (taking the average of the six years up to 1353), to almost 16,000 cloths per annum in the years 1366–8.[3] During these fifteen years (1353–68) the annual rate of growth averaged 18 per cent.—no mean achievement. Everything favoured an expansion of trade. Food prices, while not unduly

[1] These and later data on the wine trade are from the researches of Miss M. K. James, unpublished at the time this was written, but since published in *Economic History Review*, 2nd Series, IV, No. 2, 1951, "The Fluctuations of the Anglo-Gascon Wine Trade during the Fourteenth Century."

[2] *Petite chronique de Guyenne jusqu'à l'an 1442*, ed. Lefèvre-Pontalis (Bibliothèque de l'Ecole des Chartes, XLVII, 1886), 61.

[3] I.e. to 15,826 cloths. Gray's average of 14,593 for these years is the result of his omission of the returns for Melcombe, Poole and Newcastle.

depressed, were never at famine levels. Moreover the English manufacturer still had an immense advantage over his Flemish and Italian rivals in the comparatively low cost of his raw material. And while the export duty on wool remained high, amounting still to some 33 per cent., the new export duty on cloth, imposed in 1347, was trivial, amounting only to some 2 per cent.[1] Thus English cloth could still be sold abroad, as well as at home, much more cheaply than foreign cloth made of English wool. Yet more, the foreign markets were reviving, particularly that of Gascony, still principal purchaser of England's cloth. Bristol, chief port for the Gascon trade and herself concerned mainly with Gascony, was taking throughout this period some half or more of all England's shipments of cloth, and it is very significant that her annual exports mounted at this time from 1300 cloths (in 1353–5) to over 6000 in 1361–3, while in 1367 they reached almost 8000. Already by 1353 the chief wine-growing regions of Gascony were showing signs of recuperating from the effects of battle, plague and hunger. The war had receded, not to return thither for fifteen years. Peasants ventured back to their holdings; new immigrants arrived; houses were rebuilt; lands were granted out on condition that fresh vines were planted and old ones restored within a few years. The task of re-peopling and re-planting went on apace: well-tended vineyards again covered the countryside. Yet more, the labour of clearance and settlement of virgin land, interrupted early in the fourteenth century, was resumed, for the sowing of corn or the planting of vines. This great work of reconstruction, as the researches of Boutruche have recently shown, is very apparent in the records from 1355; it becomes greatly intensified after 1363, and it reaches its climax in 1368.[2] Its progress, in fact, coincides exactly with the upward trend of England's cloth

---

[1] The rate was 1s. 2d. for native merchants, 1s. for Hanseatics, and 21d. for other aliens, per standard cloth of assise other than scarlet cloth and cloth dyed partly in scarlet, which paid at higher rates. The average value of standard sized cloths then exported was in the region of £3.

[2] Boutruche, op. cit., 207.

exports. Inevitably the port of Bordeaux sprang into renewed activity. Between 1363 and 1369 wine exports thence, which had averaged 14,000 tons per annum between 1348 and 1356, rose to 39,000 tons (1364–7).[1] The Archbishop of Bordeaux, with his receipts from the sale of his wines trebling in the course of these fifteen years, and his total revenues in the 1360's approaching the level of the years before the outbreak of war,[2] had money and to spare for new clothing from England for himself and his household, as indeed must his tenants have had.

Moreover, during all these fifteen years there was no severe fighting in any theatre of the war, except for two brief spells in 1355–6 and 1358–60, and in 1360 the truce of 1356–8 was succeeded by the peace of Brétigny, giving a short respite in which foreign trade could pursue its way wholly unhampered by the commandeering of merchants' ships or by constant fighting on the high seas. Insecurity there was, but less than in times of actual war. And even though war broke out again in 1363, it was carried on for some years in but half-hearted fashion, so that though shipments might sometimes be interrupted, they would usually get through in the end, while markets were little disturbed.

These then are some of the factors favouring a vigorous upward trend of England's cloth exports. That she was gaining over Flanders is shown by the evident distress of the Flemish textile cities in the 1360's, by the continuing low level of Ypres production,[3] and by appeals such as that of the weavers of Ghent to their Count, in 1367, revealing the desperate crisis of their industry.[4]

Indeed England's foreign trade as a whole was evidently enjoying a boom. Wool exports were lower, but only very slightly lower, than at the peak point the close of the thirteenth and the opening of the fourteenth century (when

[1] See *supra*, p. 247, n. 1. [2] Boutruche, *op. cit.*, 251–2, 257–8.
[3] Van Werveke, *op. cit.*, 9; cf. also van Werveke, "Essor et déclin de la Flandre", *Studi in onore di Gino Luzzatto* (Milan, 1949), 158.
[4] G. Espinas and H. Pirenne, *Recueil de documents relatifs à l'histoire de l'industrie drapière en Flandre* (Brussels, 1906–23), II, 399–400.

they reached some 35,000 sacks per annum),[1] and their decline was almost compensated for by the export of wool made up into cloth, and more than compensated for if we take account also of the wool which must have been used for the home-manufactured cloth which now took the place of imported cloth. Exports of raw wool and exports of manufactured wool (even considering only woollens and not worsteds), together with wool used to replace foreign cloth on the home market, averaged some 37,000 sacks annually between 1353 and 1368.[2] Clearly there was no decline of wool production while, since some of this wool was made up into cloth, the employment it gave and the profit it brought must surely have been greater than before. The late 1350's and early 1360's, despite a second outbreak of plague in 1361, were evidently a time of prosperity for many classes of the community, not merely for cloth merchants like Robert Cheddar, reputedly the richest man ever known in Bristol until William Canynges a century later. Cheddar's wealth was proverbial. When Canynges, after the death of his son and heir, gave more and more of his money away to

[1] Eileen Power, *The Wool Trade in English Medieval History* (1941), 102.

[2] Cloth exports from Exch. L.T.R., Customs Accounts (see chart); wool exports from A. Beardwood, *Alien Merchants in England, 1350–1377* (Medieval Academy of America, Cambridge, Massachusetts, 1931), Appendix C; wool used to replace foreign cloth on the home market reckoned on the basis of a foreign importation early in the century of 12,000 cloths (see p. 242, n. 2 *supra*). It is clearly impossible to estimate precisely how much wool went into any given number of cloths of assise, particularly in view of the scarcity of information on this point for the fourteenth century. But the figure of 81 lb. of wool per cloth, used by Gray in *Studies in English Trade in the Fifteenth Century* (ed. E. Power and M. Postan, 1933, 362, n. 27), and used here, though it is derived from a document of the time of Edward VI, is more satisfactory than the figure of 38 lb. used by Gray in his article in the *English Historical Review* (*ut supra*, 25), for this last figure, from a Statute of 1468, relates to the light East Anglian cloths (cf. a passage in the City of London Journals, temp. Edward IV (Journal 8, f. 180), reckoning 760 lb. wool to 20 *kerseys*, i.e. 38 lb. per *kersey*). At Coventry in 1451 not less than 30 lb. yarn were to be used for a "dozen" (i.e. half a cloth of assise), while in 1525 cloths were distinguished as those containing under 88 lb., 88–96 lb., and over 96 lb. of wool (*Coventry Leet Book*, ed. M. Dormer Harris, Early English Text Society, 1907–13, 262, 689). Worcester cloths, temp. Henry VII, contained 84–90 lb. yarn (V. Green, *Worcester*, 1796, II, App. LVIII).

the church, the family of his widowed daughter-in-law brought a suit against him in Chancery on the ground that she was without clothing and other necessaries suitable to her degree, although Canynges had promised to provide handsomely for the couple and to leave his son as well off "as any man left his son in Bristowe within a hundred yere . . . savynge only Robert Chedder".[1] Peasants and artisans also prospered, and the prosperity of both may in part be attributed to the expansion of the cloth industry. For this, in addition to giving employment to many whole-time artisans, gave also employment part-time to many agricultural workers, especially to small-holders such as cottars,[2] and to those wives and daughters everywhere who made up that vast army of spinners needed to keep the weavers supplied: thus it put money into the pockets of almost every family in the cloth-making regions—and cloth-making was then widespread over many parts of the countryside. It was little wonder that William Langland, composing the first part of *Piers Plowman* in 1362 (if scholars are right in thus dating Text A), wrote of those choosy labourers who grumbled if they were not offered high wages, who deigned not to dine on last night's stale vegetables and refused to accept penny ale and a piece of bacon, insisting on fresh meat or fried fish, hot or very hot.[3]

But hunger and pestilence were never far from medieval man. Langland's warning, at the close of this part of his poem, was timely. Make money while you can, he concluded:

For hunger hitherward hasteth him fast,
He shall awake with water wasters to chastise;
Ere five years be fulfilled such famine shall arise,
Through floods and through foul weathers fruits shall fail.[4]

---

[1] E. M. Carus-Wilson, *The Overseas Trade of Bristol in the later Middle Ages*, Bristol Record Society Publications (1937), VII, 141.
[2] See, for examples of this, H. Heaton, *The Yorkshire Woollen and Worsted Industries* (1920), 21–5.
[3] *Piers Plowman*, ed. W. Skeat, Early English Text Society (1886), I, 222. Langland's poem does not reflect merely provincial conditions, for he was very familiar with London.   [4] *Ibid.*, I, 223 (spelling modernized).

At the end of the 1360's there occurred a succession of disasters and a slump in England's foreign trade in many ways comparable to that at the end of the 1340's. In 1368 pestilence again appeared, ravaging England and many other lands, and lasting for two years.[1] In England it was followed by floods so severe that, as Fabyan puts it, "the corn was drowned in the earth". As a result, the harvest of 1369 was the worst known since that calamitous one of 1316, and in 1370 there was such a scarcity of grain that prices rose to famine level, wheat reaching 3s. a bushel, the peak price of the century—even in 1352 it had not been as high as this.[2] The great dearth made a profound impression. Long afterwards 1370 was known as "the great dear year". And Langland, continuing his poem some seven years later, in this less happy period, wrote of a time "not long y-passed" when the commons of London were harassed with anxiety because no carts came to town from the Stratford bakeries, when beggars began to weep and workmen were aghast—

> In the date of our drought: in a dry April
> A thousand and three hundred: twice thirty and ten.[3]

Very different is the tone of this part of his poem from that of the first: it is to this section that there belongs that grim vision of Antichrist, when disease and death assailed all mankind, laying low kings and popes, great and poor, until Conscience begged nature to cease her plagues. Plague was indeed endemic in these years. It raged again through western Europe in 1373-5, appearing in 1373 in

---

[1] *The Anonimalle Chronicle*, ed. V. H. Galbraith (1927), 58; Walsingham, *Chronicon Anglie*, ed. E. Maunde Thompson, Rolls Series (1874), 65; Walsingham, *Historia Anglicana*, ed. H. T. Riley, Rolls Series (1863-4), I, 309; *Chron. Mon. de Melsa*, ed. E. A. Bond, Rolls Series (1868), III, 170; Otterbourne, *Chron. Regum Anglie*, ed. T. Hearne (1732), 133; Fabyan, *New Chronicles of England and France*, ed. Henry Ellis (1811), 480.

[2] Walsingham, *Historia Anglicana* and *Chron. Anglie*, *ut supra*; Fabyan, *ut supra*; *A Short English Chronicle* (*Three Fifteenth Century Chronicles*, ed. J. Gairdner, Camden Society, 1880), 21-4; J. E. Thorold Rogers, *op. cit.*, 213-32 (barley, oats and beans also reached higher prices than at any time in the century except 1315-16 and 1321-2).

[3] *Piers Plowman*, *ut supra*, I, 402.

France, where it was "grievous and hideous", in Italy and many other lands. In 1374 it was in southern England, described as the "fourth pest", and in 1375 in the north; the English chroniclers record that it endured a great while, carrying off many of the richest and most substantial folk, such as citizens of London, clerks of the Exchequer and of Chancery. In 1378 it appeared again in Yorkshire, continuing all the year beyond. In Gascony it was followed in 1373 by so bad a harvest that once more there was scarcity, "great dearness of corn", and "great famine throughout the Bordelais".[1]

To the evils of plague and famine there was once again, as in the late 1340's, added the evils of heavy fighting, with its consequent devastation and disturbance of trade. The conflict between England and France, which had smouldered since 1363, now broke out, in 1369, into a savage combat which raged unchecked until the patching up of a truce in 1375. Gascony was engulfed. Conquering French armies, penetrating further and further into the English territories, reached in 1374 the very heart of the country, the immediate hinterland of Bordeaux. In 1377, when on the expiry of a brief truce the onslaught was renewed, Bordeaux itself was threatened; French armies encamped within half a day's march of the city, and the peasants, panic-stricken, fled, leaving their grapes ripe, we are told, to perish on the vines.[2] Evidence is abundant of the havoc wrought by these campaigns. Far and wide through Gascony lands lay waste and abandoned, emptied of inhabitants, but invaded by "thickets and brambles".[3] Except for the city of Bordeaux itself the country was in ruins; the Gascon market for English cloth vanished for the time being almost completely.

The collapse of the Gascon market is very evident from

[1] Walsingham, *Historia Anglicana, ut supra*, I, 319; *Anonimalle Chronicle, ut supra*, 77, 79; Otterbourne, *ut supra*, 133; Fabyan, *ut supra*, 485; *Petite chronique de Guyenne, ut supra*, 63; *Chronique bourdelaise*, ed. G. de Lurbe (1703), 22.

[2] Boutruche, *op. cit.*, 212, quoting *Archives Historiques du Département de la Gironde*, XXII, 370.   [3] *Ibid.*, 214.

the Customs Accounts. Exports of cloth from Bristol, concerned chiefly with the Gascon trade, dropped catastrophically in 1371–2 from the very high level maintained throughout the 1360's. In the next year they would seem again to have been low, but unfortunately figures are available only for the autumn shipments, and after this they cease altogether for four years, for Bristol and for all other ports, while the customs were put out to farm.

If the sudden slump in Bristol's exports with the collapse of the Gascon market is the most striking feature of the early 1370's, only less striking is the reversal of the upward trend of cloth exports as a whole, at least until the figures temporarily cease in 1374. We have here a depression of no mean sort. Such data as exist for the wine trade tell the same tale. Imports of wine into England, which at the beginning of the century had probably been in the region of 14,000 tons per annum, and in one year (1350) even shortly after the Black Death were about 8800 tons, were in 1371–2 less than 6000 tons. The more complete record of Bordeaux exports show total shipments there contracting sharply on the outbreak of war in 1369, sinking to under 8000 tons in 1374–5, and remaining at a very low level throughout the 1370's, despite a partial restoration in time of truce.[1] England's exports of raw wool were also declining at this time, though less markedly, and if we make the same calculation as for the 1360's, then we find that the total of raw wool and manufactured wool exported, plus the wool that might have been used to replace foreign cloth on the home market (supposing home consumption to have remained the same as early in the century) now averaged only 30,000 sacks per annum (1368–73) as compared with 37,000 sacks during the fifteen years' upward trend, and 39,000 sacks in 1360–67.[2]

It is, I think, plain that from 1369 and on at least into

---

[1] Data from the researches of Miss M. K. James, *ut supra*. Records of wine imports into England are few and far between until the end of the century.

[2] Data, *ut supra*, 250, n. 2.

the early 1370's—how much longer we cannot unfortunately tell—English trade was suffering from a severe depression, a depression which has not, perhaps, hitherto been recognized.[1] Is it wholly a coincidence that it was at this moment that the finances of some of the great estates which had weathered the storms earlier in the century now showed signs of severe strain, as did those of Canterbury?

Historians of these later years of Edward III, discerning there a certain gloom and disillusionment, have sought to find a reason for this in the decline of England's fortunes in the war and in the favours lavished upon Alice Perrers. But Englishmen have not always been utterly cast down by the defeat of their armies on foreign soil, nor by the influence of a royal mistress over an ageing monarch. And it is at least arguable that at the root of the gloom and discontents of those years lay, together with the maintenance of high taxation, and attempts, albeit in vain, to freeze wages, a trade depression reducing the income of rich and poor alike.[2]

What then, briefly, of the years that follow. When customs returns are again available at the opening of Richard II's reign, in 1377, there has already, it is evident, been a certain measure of recovery; and from 1379 the cloth export trade resumes its upward trend, at first somewhat

[1] Gray, jumping straight from 1368 to 1377 in his examination of the cloth customs figures, concludes that after 1368 there was "little change for another twenty years". He finds "stagnation for a decade" before 1380, and *after* 1380 "a depression for two or three years". His depression is the result of generalizing from the money totals of cloth customs receipts in London, and comparing those for 1380–4 with those of 1377–80. This leads him into error, not only because he has misread the figure for 1382–3 (it should be £258 not £151) but because the figures for those years include payments for a much greater number of the cheaply rated Hanse cloths than previously, and because the big increase of these years was not in London.

[2] The account of the "Good Parliament" of 1376 given in Fabyan suggests that the Commons were well aware that the country was suffering from an economic depression, even if they could not correctly diagnose its cause. For they complain that as a result of the incompetence of the government "the lande myght not be plentuously of chafre, marchaundyse or rychesse", and that this and high taxation had impoverished the people. (Fabyan, *ut supra*, 486.)

hesitatingly, then vigorously, except for a slight depression in 1385–8, until almost the close of the reign, reaching its zenith between 1390 and 1395 with a total export in three of these years of over 40,000 cloths.[1] The pace of advance is, however, less rapid than in the previous period of expansion, the annual rate of growth averaging only 8 per cent. (1380–95) instead of 18 per cent. (1353–68), but this is in accordance with what we should expect. Nor at the close of the period was England yet transformed, as she was to be in the succeeding century, into an exporter primarily of manufactured products, for she was still shipping abroad each year sufficient wool to make more than 80,000 cloths. Nevertheless the trend was unmistakable. The export industry in English woollens had witnessed a remarkable development, and it was now a formidable rival to the once paramount industries of Italy and Flanders, whose history at this time, in striking contrast, tells not of progress but of decline.

Now nominally England and France were at war through all these years, for peace was not signed until 1396. But in fact fighting was only sporadic, so that France was not devastated by campaigning, and there were two intervals of truce (1383–5 and 1388–96), intervals which, it is worth noting, coincide with the most marked increases in cloth shipments. The only period of serious warfare was that of 1385–8, coinciding precisely with the slight depression. These were years of panic and confusion in England, with much calling out of ships and local levies, for French armies were landing at Leith to march with the Scots across the border, and a French invasion fleet was twice prepared across the Straits of Dover, with shipping gathered from

---

[1] During this period (for 1380–8 and for 1391–9) certain arbitrary adjustments are necessary in order to arrive at annual totals, since returns for some ports do not always coincide with the normal Exchequer years (Michaelmas to Michaelmas); e.g. for Bristol in 1394–9 an average over the five years has been taken, and for London in 1391–3 an average over the two years. This results here and there in a slight levelling out of fluctuations. See note on chart, *infra* 262–3.

the Baltic to the Mediterranean, and vast quantities of stores—including ready-made hutments in sections for setting up as a fortified base camp on English soil.[1] At such a time all shipping was disorganized, both by the commandeering of merchant vessels and by the hazards at sea, and stocks may well have piled up at home, awaiting a more favourable opportunity.

Gascony, throughout these years, enjoyed a long period of slow but sure recovery, and there was much replanting of vineyards, especially in 1391–5. But even though "those great days of reconstruction", as Boutruche calls the early 1390's,[2] coincide with the zenith of England's cloth trade in the fourteenth century, the recovery of Gascony does not alone account for its immense expansion. It is very noticeable that Bristol's trade shows at this time but a slight increase over that of the 1360's, an increase not at all in proportion to the total expansion,[3] and Bristol was still carrying the greater part of the Gascon cloth exports. Moreover the growth in Bristol's shipments is to be accounted for to a considerable extent by the development of an active business with Portugal, now at peace after years of civil war and in close alliance with England, and with the Toulouse region, whence English dyers were now drawing the bulk of their woad, instead of from war-ravaged Picardy.[4] The really striking advance was not in the west, but in the northern and Mediterranean markets. It is at this moment that English producers were invading in force the marts of the Baltic, the

[1] J. H. Ramsay, *The Genesis of Lancaster* (1913), II, 221 *et seq*. Much shipping was also requisitioned in these years for John of Gaunt's Castilian expedition. See *Calendars of Patent Rolls* for these years, *passim*, for the calling up of ships and men. [2] Boutruche, *op. cit.*, 218.

[3] Whereas England's cloth trade as a whole is treble that of the 1360's, Bristol's has only increased by 16 per cent. Bristol in the 1390's was carrying only one-sixth of England's cloth exports, as compared with nearly one-half in the 1360's.

[4] It seems to have been at this time that the Tolosane market was virtually lost by the Flemish and Brabantine cloth manufacturers, their place being taken by the English above all others. See Ph. Wolff, "Un chemin de Flandre", *Le Moyen Age* (1946), Nos. 3–4, 271.

North Sea and the Low Countries, and also of the Mediterranean, gaining in these regions a decisive advantage over their Flemish and Italian competitors. That this was so is shewn by the mounting cloth exports of the Italian merchants, especially in the 1380's, and of the Hanseatics, especially in the 1390's. Whereas in the 1360's they took between them only some 23 per cent. of England's exports (some 3000 cloths), in the early 1390's they took 42 per cent. (some 16,000 cloths).[1] In addition to these foreign shipments, English merchants themselves were vigorously penetrating the northern markets, particularly the great distributive marts of the Low Countries and of Prussia. The drapers of Coventry, for instance, whose business was rapidly growing, were not only finding new outlets through Bristol to Portugal, sometimes in their own ships, but were also sending large consignments of cloth from east-coast ports to the Baltic.[2] The extent of the Englishmen's trade in these northern lands cannot be quantitatively measured, but that it was very considerable we can see from the constant complaints about them by the Hanse, from the numbers of their ships and cloths which were seized when an open clash occurred, and from the fact that they already had a privileged organization of their own in Danzig by 1391, and in the Low Countries shortly afterwards.[3] Henceforward events in these regions were to affect England's textile exports even more than events in Gascony.

These developments were accompanied by a marked expansion of the cloth trade of Hull, which had increased

[1] Shipments by aliens other than Hanseatics were at this time mainly Italian; they averaged some 5600 cloths in the early 1380's and some 9700 cloths in the early 1390's. Those of the Hanse, still only some 2700 in the early 1380's, reached 6300 in the early 1390's.

[2] E. M. Carus-Wilson, *The Overseas Trade of Bristol in the Later Middle Ages*, Bristol Record Society Publications (1937), VII, 193; *Literae Cantuarienses*, ed. J. B. Sheppard, Rolls Series (1889), III, 79 *et seq.*

[3] *Supra*, 144; *Literae Cantuarienses, ut supra*; M. Postan, "The Economic and Political Relations of England and the Hanse (1400–1475)", *Studies in English Trade in the Fifteenth Century*, ed. Eileen Power and M. M. Postan (1933), 96 *et seq.*

nearly fourfold since the 1360's, of Southampton, whence Italians were now taking almost as much cloth as at any time in the middle ages,[1] and still more of London, whose trade had increased tenfold. An analysis of individual sailings in the early 1390's [2] shows that it was London and Hull which were carrying the greater part of the Baltic, North Sea and Low Countries trade, and that their other shipments, such as those to Gascony, were very small in comparison; while Southampton was carrying the greater part of the Mediterranean trade, and little else besides. It enables us further, if we try to measure the relative importance of the various markets, to reach the tentative conclusion that the principal outlet for England's cloth at this time was in the Baltic and in the great distributive marts of the Low Countries; that Gascony now came second, and together with Portugal and to a much lesser degree Spain provided an equally important outlet; and that the Italian market came third, being more important than Portugal but less important than Gascony.

The advance of the English industry at this time on the markets of Europe is thrown into sharp relief by the distresses of its principal rivals, the once mighty textile cities of Flanders and Italy. The dissensions between masters and men, between city and city, between town and country, between craft and craft, that fill the pages of the chroniclers, if in part the cause, are in part also the symptoms of their industrial decline. And these dissensions reached a climax in the last quarter of the century. In Flanders the employers were faced with growing wage demands at the very time when, faced also with growing English competition, they

[1] The level of Southampton's cloth exports for the years 1391–6 (5971 cloths per annum alien, and 8301 alien and native together) was exceeded, scarcely perceptibly, between 1430 and 1440, and by some 25 per cent. between 1440 and 1450, but at no other time until the close of the fifteenth century.

[2] From the detailed customs returns from individual ports (P.R.O. Exch. K.R. Customs Accounts); these are fragmentary, seldom covering a complete year, and only in the case of Bristol do they actually specify whence or whither a ship is sailing. Hence an analysis of them is difficult, and can yield only tentative conclusions.

were least able to meet them [1]; the rise in the cost of living
was not compensated by an adequate rise in wages, and
while some of the workers turned for consolation to those
strange mystical sects like the *Danseurs* which flourished in
time of adversity, more sought a remedy in revolution. In
1379 the storm broke in full fury. The cities of Ypres,
Ghent and Bruges passed into the hands of the weavers, and
Flanders was plunged into five years of sanguinary civil war,
a war in which many thousands of textile employees were
slain.[2] Thus the tribulations of Flanders were but intensified,
and it was scarcely surprising that the English industry,
pursuing its uneventful way, leapt ahead, while cloth production at Ypres was no greater in the 1380's than in the
post Black Death depression.[3] The Florentine industry, too,
had reached a crisis; 1378 saw the mass rising of the wool-
carders, and the brutal severity of their repression did
nothing to solve the mortal malady from which the industry
suffered.[4] The few isolated figures that survive for Florentine
output, whatever the difficulties of their interpretation, point
assuredly to a serious decline.[5]

[1] Their situation was slightly ameliorated by the currency manipulations
of the time. While the progressive debasement of the Flemish *gros* raised the
cost of living and thus depressed the condition of the wage-earner—for wages
lagged much behind prices—it also, by reducing real wages and selling prices
on the foreign market, gave a measure of assistance to the Flemish export
industry and temporarily somewhat retarded its decline. For the latest discussion of this phenomenon see H. van Werveke, "Currency Manipulation
in the Middle Ages, the case of Louis de Male", *Transactions Royal Historical
Society*, 4th ser. (1949), XXXI.
[2] H. Pirenne, *Histoire de Belgique* (Brussels, 1922), II, 199 *et seq.*
[3] H. van Werveke, "De Omvang van de Ieperse Lakenproductie in de
veertiende eeuw", *ut supra*. Contraction of production in the Flemish cities,
and in Florence, was to some extent compensated for by increase of production
in smaller centres. This cannot be measured, but the impression remains of an
overall decline, cf. Laurent, *op. cit.* 205; Van Werveke, "Essor et déclin de la
Flandre", *ut supra*, 159; C. Cippola, "Trends in Italian Economic History in
the later Middle Ages", *Economic History Review*, 2nd ser. (1949), II, 181.
[4] N. Rodolico, *I Ciompi, Una pagina di storia del proletario operario*
(Florence, 1945).
[5] R. Davidsohn, "Blüte und Niedergang der Florentiner Tuchindustrie",
Zeitschrift für die gesamte Staatswissenschaft (Tübingen, 1928), LXXXV,
225.

Our study of England's cloth exports from 1347 to the end of the century has shown us two periods of rapid advance—the first more rapid than the second—separated by a marked depression. It has pointed also to two periods of notable prosperity for England's foreign trade. In the second period, as in the first, wine imports were high—standing at about the same level as at the beginning of the century.[1] Wool exports, it is true, had substantially declined, and even if we make the same allowances as before for wool exported as cloth and for wool that was probably used at home to supply cloth formerly imported, we have a somewhat diminished total.[2] It must, however, be borne in mind that manufactured woollens were a more valuable export than raw wool, though they of course involved imports of certain raw materials such as dyestuffs. Moreover, since so large a portion of it was now manufactured at home, England's wool must have given much more employment to the country than at the beginning of the century,[3] and this at a time when the population was reduced, perhaps, by one-third. This

[1] Data from Miss James, *ut supra*.

[2] Some 33,000 sacks. Annual exports of raw wool averaged some 21,000 sacks in 1390–5.

[3] The English woollen industry probably employed somewhere in the region of 17,000–20,000 people at the end of the fourteenth century *on the export trade only*, reckoning on the basis of full-time workers; in practice, of course, the work was more widely spread. Taking into account the cessation of foreign imports, and supposing home demand to have remained the same, it was probably employing some 23,000–26,000 more people than at the beginning of the century, reckoning again on the basis of full-time workers. The *total* number employed was of course larger than this, but cannot be estimated as we have no means of ascertaining total production for home consumption as well as for export. The figure suggested above for the export trade alone is larger, it will be observed, than that suggested for the industry as a whole by Professor Postan in his article "Some Economic Evidence of Declining Population in the later Middle Ages" (*Economic History Review*, 2nd Ser., II, 1950, 232), published since the writing of this paper. This is due principally to the fact that in making the estimate given above a substantial proportion (over a third) of the labour costs was attributed to the cost of carding and spinning—work which commanded a much lower wage rate than that of the master weaver or fuller; Professor Postan's estimate, on the other hand, was based on a uniform wage rate comparable with theirs.

suggests a high level of productivity for the country as a whole and, still more, a high level of productivity *per capita*. If the rural industry of the late fourteenth century was in some ways less efficient than the urban industry of the late thirteenth,[1] it certainly enabled many peasant families to supplement their earnings from the land, while at the same time they could live more cheaply than the urban workers. Wages were high; there would seem to have been full employment; and after the revolt of 1381—aftermath perhaps of the years of depression—there was little sign of labour unrest. Cloth prices, too, were high. Chaucer's weaver and dyer were prosperous folk: their knives, belts and pouches were set not with brass but with silver; so too was his west-country clothier, that redoubtable goodwife living near Bath, who yielded precedence in church to none. The late 1380's and 1390's, when Coventry citizens were completing the matchless tower of St Michael's and Chaucer was creating his more imperishable masterpiece, have long been acclaimed as a time of high achievement for England in architecture, literature and the arts, and as a time of luxury and extravagant fashions comparable perhaps only to the 1360's. Ostentatious spending, whether on clothes or on cathedrals, is not necessarily a sign of a sound and flourishing economy. Yet I venture to think that a study of its trade returns shows that this period was also, like the late 1350's and 1360's, a time of high achievement for England in the economic sphere, more particularly for her merchants and clothmakers.

NOTE ON CHART OF ENGLAND'S EXPORTS OF WOOLLEN CLOTH, 1347-99

This chart is based upon the Exchequer L.T.R. Enrolled Customs Accounts which record port by port the totals of customs paid on cloth for each Exchequer year running from Michaelmas to Michaelmas; here and there use has also been made of the Exchequer K.R.

---

[1] Though fulling costs should have been lower than in the urban industry of the thirteenth century, because of the use of the fulling mill.

Customs Accounts, i.e. of the detailed particulars sent up from individual ports. Four circumstances make it impossible in every case to ascertain precise annual export totals, especially in the latter part of the century, though the margin of error probably never exceeds some 8 per cent. and is seldom likely to be so much. The following points should therefore be borne in mind when the chart is being consulted, in addition to points mentioned in the article itself (e.g. on pp. 240, n. 2; 244, n. 4; 250, n. 2; 256, n. 1).

(i) *Kerseys*, whose manufacture appears to have developed rapidly in the latter part of the century, at first apparently evaded custom. They were made chiefly in Essex and other counties within easy reach of London, where their export was largely concentrated and was mainly in the hands of the Hanseatics. At Michaelmas 1388 they were first customed, at the rate of three kerseys to one cloth of assise, and from then until 25 May 1389 (when the custom was discontinued) they are separately detailed for London where they amount to 2039½ cloths of assise exported by the Hanse, and 486 cloths by other aliens and by denizens. From Michaelmas 1389 to February 1390 they were again customed and separately detailed in London, where they amount to 1108 cloths of assise exported by the Hanse and 46 by other aliens and by denizens. After 12 November 1390 they are permanently subjected to customs. They are separately detailed for London up to Michaelmas 1391 (amounting to 2826 cloths of assise "alien and denizen"; whether this includes Hanseatic shipments is not clear). From Michaelmas 1391 they appear to be merged among the ordinary cloths of assise. Thus the total shown in the chart for 1388–9 includes eight months' kerseys shipments (some 2500 cloths of assise), and that for 1389–90 four months' shipments (some 1000 cloths of assise), while after this kersey shipments are regularly included.

(ii) In some cases the accounts do not cover exactly an Exchequer year from Michaelmas to Michaelmas. Annual totals have then been estimated (unless they can be discovered from Particular Accounts) by taking the monthly average over the longer of two adjacent accounts and using it to adjust both accounts. This affects particularly: Boston, 1386–8; Bristol, 1385–7 and 1395–9; London, 1383–5, 1388–90 and 1391–3; Sandwich, 1397–9; Southampton, 1380–3 and 1384–7. Thus there is some levelling out of fluctuations in these years.

(iii) At some ports the customs were farmed in years other than 1373–7 when they were farmed for England as a whole. In such cases, unless Particular Accounts survive, there is no record of the annual amounts shipped. Export totals have therefore been arbitrarily determined by taking into account the average percentage of England's total cloth exports which such ports carried in the years immediately before and after the gaps. Fortunately none of the major woollen ports are affected. The gaps in question are:

(a) *Yarmouth* (including Ipswich) 1362–99. This gap fortunately affects chiefly worsted exports; exports of woollens from these ports averaged only 716 cloths annually in 1356–62 (some 8 per cent. of England's total export), and 1117 cloths in 1401–4 (some 4 per cent. of England's total export).

(b) *Sandwich* 1369–73. Exports thence averaged 59 cloths in 1360–8 (some 0·5 per cent. of England's total export), and 243 cloths in 1401–5 (some 0·8 per cent. of England's total export).

(c) *Exeter* 1371–99. Exports thence averaged 983 cloths in 1359–76 (some 8 per cent. of England's total export) and 269 cloths in 1401–5 (some 0·9 per cent. of the total).

(iv) Sometimes at London, Sandwich and Southampton, only the amount of customs duty paid is recorded, not the number of cloths on which it was paid. In such cases the number of cloths can, however, be satisfactorily estimated with considerable precision, though not with absolute certainty, because of the different rates paid according to whether merchants were denizens, Hanseatics, or other aliens, and according to whether cloths were in grain (i.e. scarlets), without grain (i.e. dyed in other colours or white), or worsted. In making estimates for the chart the following procedure has been adopted: for *London* (1377–99) the amount of money which probably represents customs on cloth in grain and worsteds has first been deducted from the total, after being estimated on the basis of average exports in the years immediately preceding the gap, viz. cloth in grain *c.* £3 (20 cloths), worsteds *c.* £20 (2800 cloths, 38 double beds, and 100 single beds). It should be noted that even a large fluctuation in worsted exports would not greatly affect the issue since they were customed at so low a rate, i.e. worsted cloths at $1\frac{1}{2}d.$ alien and $1d.$ native. From the remaining money total the export of cloth without grain has been calculated. Up to 1380 money totals are given separately for denizens and aliens; after that the proportion of the two has been determined from the average up to 1380, the known totals of 1383–4 and the totals of the early fifteenth century. Totals of the Hanse are stated separately throughout and they have therefore been disregarded for the purposes of the above calculation. For *Sandwich* and *Southampton* a similar method has been used, except that it has not been necessary to eliminate worsted totals, since none were exported thence. In Sandwich denizen exports have been reckoned as 6 times as great as those of aliens, and in Southampton the alien exports as $2\frac{1}{2}$ times as great as those of denizens.

VII

THE EFFECTS OF THE ACQUISITION AND OF THE LOSS OF GASCONY ON THE ENGLISH WINE TRADE [1]

The export trade in wine, as Pirenne once remarked, is one of the most important, but one of the least studied, branches of European commerce in the middle ages.[2] For France it played a part comparable to that of the wool trade in England, yet no historian has yet taken it for his theme. This may be due, as Pirenne suggested, to the fact that for three hundred years the great wine-growing region of Gascony was part of the realm not of France but of England. At any rate a very large part of the relevant records, both legislative and administrative, is to be found in the national archives in London.[3] Here, as well as in the French national archives and in local archives at London, Southampton, Hull and elsewhere, much research remains to be done. The present paper attempts no more than to consider very briefly a single aspect of the matter especially pertinent to the subject of this conference,[4] namely, the effects on the English wine trade of the union of Gascony and England in 1152 and, three centuries later, the disruption of this union.

Already before the union, in Norman as in Saxon times,

[1] *Bulletin of the Institute of Historical Research*, XXI, No. 63, 1947. Paper read in French at the Anglo-French Conference of the International Congress of Historical Sciences at Paris, September 1946. The term Gascony is here used in the sense in which it was used in medieval English official documents, i.e. to denote the territory held by the English in south-west France. While the boundaries of this territory were constantly shifting, it always included Bordeaux and the Bordelais.

[2] H. Pirenne, "Un grand commerce d'exportation au moyen âge: les vins de France", *Annales d'histoire économique et sociale*, V (1933), 225.

[3] E.g. all the extant customs accounts of Bordeaux during the period of English rule (P.R.O., Exchequer K.R. Accounts Various, France), in addition to the accounts of English ports.

[4] The relation of politics and economics, with special reference to England and France.

England's demand for wine had been considerable. It was a common daily drink in great households such as the king's, in monastic establishments, and also, most probably, among the middle and upper ranks of society generally. The demand was met partly by home-produced supplies, partly by gifts of wine from northern France or by wine from estates held there, but also, to no negligible extent, by regular commercial imports of wine much superior to that produced at home. Thus the typical English merchant of late Saxon days, as depicted in Aelfric's *Colloquy*, mentions wine as among the goods he commonly imports, while the laws of some of the later Saxon kings concern themselves with regulating the sale of wine brought in by foreigners. Particularly interesting is a decree of Ethelred II fixing the tolls to be paid in London "by the men of Rouen who come with wine ".[1] This, with later confirmations of their privileges in the port of London, would seem to indicate that merchants of Rouen were at least among the principal wine importers in late Saxon and in Norman days; and it is probable that the wines they brought were mostly those of the Seine basin or of Burgundy, for it is these which would naturally find an outlet by the Seine, over which Rouen then reigned undisputed. Some wine also no doubt came from the Rhineland through the "men of the Emperor". But there is little if any mention at this time of wines of south-west France, or of merchants thence. After the establishment of the Angevin Empire, however, and the union of Gascony with England, Gascon wines came more and more to the fore, until in the course of the thirteenth century, profiting perhaps by the collapse of English power in Normandy and the abolition of Rouen's privileges in London, they virtually captured the English market. Gascon merchants too were now much in evidence in England, where they were given special privileges and were soon financing the Crown out of the profits of the wine trade.[2]

---

[1] F. Liebermann, *Die Gesetze der Angelsachsen* (1903), I, 232.
[2] F. Michel, *Histoire du Commerce et de la Navigation à Bordeaux* (1867–70), I, 38–39; Stow, *Annals* (1615), 207; *Calendar of Close Rolls*,

Thus came about a complete change in the source from which England drew her supplies of imported wine: Bordeaux had taken the place of Rouen. Moreover the English were so sure of supplies from this source that they came wholly to rely upon imports, abandoning the attempt to produce wine in their own country, and ceasing to drink such miserable concoctions as those described by Peter of Blois, which with eyes closed and teeth clenched *cribrari oportebat potius quam potari*.[1] From the late twelfth century it is possible to discern traces of a general decline of viticulture in England, in marked contrast to the continuing progress shown by most branches of agriculture, though before this period it had clearly been increasing, stimulated perhaps by the coming of the Normans. Thus in the Domesday Survey 40 vineyards are specifically mentioned, and four of these are noted as having been recently planted.[2] Later on in the monastic records of the first half of the twelfth century there are numerous references to new plantings, such as that at Peterborough,[3] while the abundance of wine-producing vines at this time is shown both by Henry of Huntingdon [4] and by William of Malmesbury; William, when describing the vale of Gloucester, does not say that it is unusual in possessing vines but that it has "a greater number of vines than other parts of England, yielding abundant crops of good

I *et seq. passim*; *Calendar of Liberate Rolls*, I *et seq. passim*; *Calendars of Letter Books of the City of London, passim.*

[1] *Petri Blesensis Epistolae*, Ep. xiv, ed. J. P. Migne, *Patrologiae Cursus Completus*, ccvii (1855), 47ᵃ.

[2] H. Ellis, *Introduction to Domesday Book* (1833), I, 117; *Domesday Book* (Record Commission, 1783–1816), for Dorset, I, 83 (*bis*); Wilts, I, 67b, 69 (*bis*), 73; Somerset, I, 86b, 90 (3), 91; Gloucester, I, 166b; Worcester, I, 175b; Berks, I, 60b; Beds, I, 212; Herts, I, 136b, 138b, 142b; Cambridge, I, 192; Middlesex, I, 128, 128b (*bis*), 129 (*bis*), 130b; Kent, I, 7b, 8, 12; Essex, II, 43b (*bis*), 55b, 58, 71, 73, 74, 77; Suffolk, II, 382, 389, 418, 438. For vineyards newly planted see I, 128, 129, 138b, 175b.

[3] S. Gunton, *Peterborough* (1686), 23.

[4] *Henrici Huntendunensis Historia Anglorum*, ed. T. Arnold (Rolls Series, 1879), 10.

quality ".[1] If his assertion that the local wines will almost bear comparison with those of France is unlikely to find credence here to-day, it at least suggests that they were still being drunk, if not by the most discriminating. Very different was the state of affairs in the thirteenth and fourteenth centuries. Then we find many references to vineyards which had been allowed to fall into decay and few to the drinking of English wine, though many to the purchase of Gascon wine. To illustrate the decay of viticulture let us take for example the county of Worcester. Here Domesday records one vineyard, newly planted, and we know of others in the twelfth century like the royal vineyard at Severn Stoke. In the middle of the thirteenth century, however, the Priory of Worcester, surveying its estates, noted two extant vineyards but implied that there had once been others by references to land "where vines once grew" and to certain vineyard services elsewhere which were still being exacted though the vineyard had disappeared. The royal vineyard too vanished during the thirteenth century, surviving only in the name of a close, and by the end of the middle ages the Domesday one also had gone.[2] Very similar was the course of events in other counties. A great estate like that of the Earl of Lincoln might still have its vineyards at the opening of the fourteenth century, and even produce from them a small quantity of wine,[3] but much more important in the

---

[1] *Willelmi Malmesbiriensis Gesta Pontificum Anglorum*, ed. N. E. S. A. Hamilton (Rolls Series, 1870), 282; cf. reference to the vines of Evesham Abbey in *Rôles Gascons*, ed. C. Bémont (Paris, 1885–1906), I, 192, and to the Earl of Gloucester's vineyard at Tewkesbury in the Pipe Roll for 1183–4.

[2] *Domesday Book, ut supra*, I, 175b; *Victoria History of the Counties of England: Worcestershire* (1907–26), IV, 192; III, 293, 352, 364 n., 367; II, 404. For vineyard services see monastic cartularies, *passim*, and for the customary rent of Winyardsilver or Wynsilver in commutation of them see N. Neilson, *Customary Rents* (1910). The fortunes of royal vineyards in many parts of the country (e.g. in Surrey, Hants, Hereford, Bucks, Hunts, and Staffordshire) may be traced upon the Pipe Rolls.

[3] P.R.O., Ministers' Accounts, Duchy of Lancaster 28, 1/2, 1/3. The Earl had vineyards in Yorks at Cridling and Pontefract, in Dorset at Canford and Coleham, in Cambridgeshire at Grantchester, and on his London estate at Holborn. (I am indebted to Dr. Oschinsky for these references.)

Earl's household economy at this time were the purchases of foreign wine—a little from the Rhineland, a little from Rochelle, and much from Gascony,[1] and before long all references to his vineyards disappear. The royal household too now relied on Gascon wines rather than on its own vineyards or the wines of northern France, just as the monks of Canterbury scorned the French king's annual gift of wine from certain vineyards near Paris, preferring to sell this on the spot and import from Gascony.[2]

While viticulture was declining in England, in the much more favourable climate of Gascony it was steadily increasing, stimulated by the growth of trade with England and by the privileges granted by English kings to their Gascon subjects. Particularly remarkable, though by no means unique, was its development in the Bordelais. Here in the late twelfth and thirteenth centuries vineyards multiplied, spreading over more and more of the countryside.[3] Forests were cleared to make way for them.[4] The "palus" were for the first time brought under cultivation that they might be planted with them.[5] Vineyards came close up to the very walls of Bordeaux, extending even into the city itself. Everyone, high and low, whatever his rank or profession, possessed vines (the great abbeys of St. Seurin and of St. Croix planted their lands with little else),[6] and for all, from the archbishop downwards, the sale of their wines to the English became the dominant

[1] *Ibid.*

[2] Historical MSS. Commission, *5th Report* (1876), 460; *Literae Cantuarienses*, ed. J. B. Sheppard (Rolls Series, 1887), I, lxxvii *et seq.*

[3] J. Barennes, *Viticulture et Vinification en Bordelais au moyen âge* (1912), 21 *et seq.*

[4] Barennes, *op. cit.*, and see, e.g., *Rôles Gascons, ut supra*, II, No. 751, grant (1283) of the royal forest "*que est prope Burdegalam ad excolendam per diversas partes, tam ad vineas, quam ad aliam agriculturam*"; and grant (1289) of royal forest land on condition that, when planted with vines, it shall be worked "*de marra et cultello et omnibus aliis que necessaria fuerint vinee supradicte*".

[5] Barennes, *op. cit.*, e.g. grant of the palus of Cadaujac to certain men "*à condition que ces hommes plantent ces palus en vignes*".

[6] Barennes, *op. cit.*; *Inventaire sommaire des archives départementales antérieures à 1790: Gironde H*, 2, 249.

business of life.[1] Bordeaux, which was to this region what Rouen was to the Seine basin, doubled in size in the first half of the thirteenth century—eloquent witness to the expansion of the trade with England.[2] So profitable was the trade, and so certain seemed the market, that no restriction was placed on the growing of vines in favour of corn, as elsewhere in France.

The legend of a subsistence economy prevailing through Europe in the middle ages is amply refuted, if such refutation is still necessary, by a study of Gascon agrarian development. Specialising in viticulture, Gascony looked to other countries for the supply of those basic foodstuffs which she could no longer produce in sufficient abundance for her own people. In particular she looked to England, who sent her grain, fish and dairy produce and, no doubt because of the union of the two lands, gave her specially favoured treatment in the matter of food imports. Even when export of grain from England was forbidden because of dearth, exception was almost always made in the case of Gascony.[3] And as England developed her manufacture of cloth so this too found one of its principal markets among the Gascon wine-growers.[4] The close economic dependence of Gascony upon England was aptly summed up by a fourteenth-century Bordelais. "How", he remarked, "could our poor people subsist when they could not sell their wines or procure English merchandise?"

[1] For the cultivation of vines by the Archbishop and for his sales of wine to the English, see e.g., *Inventaire sommaire, ut supra, Gironde G,* 90, 93, 100, 116, 117, 122, 128, and cf. *Archives Historiques du Département de la Gironde* (Société des Archives Historiques du Département de la Gironde), XLVII, 190, 325.

[2] C. Jullian, *Histoire de Bordeaux* (1895), 139.

[3] T. Malvézin, *Histoire du Commerce de Bordeaux* (1892), I, 297–9.

[4] P.R.O., Exchequer K.R. Customs Accounts, *passim,* and see the accounts of the Archbishop of Bordeaux in *Inventaire sommaire, ut supra, passim.* On one occasion, for example, the Archbishop bought Colchester cloth to make suits for members of his family; on another he bought an English cheese weighing 35 lb. and 1000 herrings, exchanged wines for dried fish from Cornwall, and sold other wines to English merchants whom he dined in his palace. For fifteenth-century imports of food and clothing see E. M. Carus-Wilson, "The Overseas Trade of Bristol", *supra,* 38–9.

What then happened to this flourishing trade[1] when, at the close of the Hundred Years War, the political link between England and Gascony was snapped? It has often been supposed that for a time at least the commercial connection too was broken, but so far no close examination has been made of all the available evidence. So abundant is this evidence that it is possible to follow the course of events in considerable detail and to trace the fluctuations of the trade with a precision impossible for the twelfth and thirteenth centuries. I propose therefore to-day to confine myself to the years immediately before and after the collapse of English rule, attempting to elucidate only the short-term effects of the break.

It is at once apparent from a study of the English customs accounts that war was more calamitous for the wine trade than actual surrender. During the five years of truce from 1444 to 1449 England's imports of wine—the great bulk of them from Gascony—reached their highest level for the whole of the fifteenth century, totalling some 12,000 tuns in the season September 1447 to September 1448, and some 13,000 tuns in 1448–9.[2] This was in part no doubt due to

[1] The importance of the wine trade in medieval England is sometimes under-estimated. Wine played a much larger part in this country's economy in the middle ages than it does now. Average *per capita* consumption in the fifteenth century must have been some three times that of the twentieth century; supposing a population of 3 million in the mid-fifteenth century it would have averaged 8 pints per head per annum, as compared with 2·8 pints in 1935–8. Annual imports in 1446–8, averaging some 3 million gallons, were worth some £46,000—roughly the same amount as the market value in England of the wool purchased for export abroad at that time; they represented nearly one-third of the value of England's whole import trade, as compared with less than 1 per cent. of it to-day.

[2] See tables of L.T.R. Enrolled Customs Accounts printed in *Studies in English Trade in the Fifteenth Century*, ed. E. Power and M. Postan (1933), and *supra*, 41–3. The total annual wine imports, though they do not distinguish the origin of the wine, may reasonably be taken as a rough indication of the fluctuations of the Gascon trade since all the evidence tends to show that the bulk (probably 85 to 90 per cent.) of the wine imported through the years in question was Gascon. Since the accounts run usually, though not invariably, from Michaelmas to Michaelmas they are particularly valuable for the wine trade. For wine was almost always shipped between December and March. The shipments from each vintage season are therefore clearly separated and there is little chance of any of them slipping from one account into the next.

high crop yields as the result of a succession of good seasons,[1] but it was also the result of the political situation. For the suspension of active hostilities meant not only that the Gascon vineyards were able to recover somewhat from the ravages of war, but that wine ships were less in peril both from pirates and from organized attacks of the enemy, and that they were less liable to be diverted from their business by being commandeered for the king's service.[2]

With the renewal of war in 1449 the whole situation deteriorated. Gascony was attacked at the very moment of the vintage; Guiche, close to Bayonne (the principal wine port after Bordeaux), fell to the French, together with some fifteen other Gascon towns. Exports dropped catastrophically. Less than 6000 tuns of wine reached England in the season 1449–50. Next autumn (1450) the attack was renewed. The French swept down in full force on the rich wine-producing valleys of the Dordogne and the Garonne, defeating the English within five miles of Bordeaux. Ships were commandeered in England for a relieving force, and collected off Plymouth, but there they were kept month after month. Meanwhile the French, the following spring, captured the fortresses guarding the sea approach to Bordeaux and sealed the Gironde with their fleet. At last Bordeaux itself, blockaded by sea and surrounded by French troops on land, sued for peace. On 12th June its citizens promised to surrender by the 23rd if still no help had come from England. It was little wonder that English wine imports for that season (1450–1) were below 6000 tuns.

But the surrender of Bordeaux in June 1451 by no means put an end to the trade on which its very livelihood depended. So important was it for the Bordelais that they should still be able to sell their wines to the English that the continuance of the trade was ensured by the actual terms of the

---

[1] Miss M. K. James has called my attention to the coincidence of the years of truce with a succession of good seasons.

[2] In both the two years preceding the truce ships had been requisitioned in England's chief wine ports for the transport of troops.

surrender. It was agreed by the French king not only that those wishing to leave the city should be allowed six months in which to collect their property and depart, but also that all merchants might bring their merchandise into Bordeaux as before, and that they might come safely by land and sea, paying only the accustomed dues.[1] Even so it was clearly inadvisable for Englishmen, now enemy aliens, to attempt to do business in Bordeaux without special permission. Such permission was not, however, impossible to obtain, and English firms engaged in the wine trade were quick to secure their position. On the very day that Bordeaux surrendered, and on the next day, safe-conducts valid throughout the following season were acquired from the French king at St. Jean d'Angeli for at least ten English ships.[2] A month later licences for some twenty ships, including some of the largest commonly engaged in the wine trade, were similarly procured in England, ostensibly for the purpose of fetching wine and other goods in Bordeaux at the time of its fall.[3] Merchants were evidently confident of a good reception in Gascony, for it would seem as though many of them did not trouble to seek permission from the French authorities until their ships had actually arrived in the Gironde; they then secured safe-conducts from the Admiral at Bordeaux, a few days before they docked and unloaded their cargoes there.[4] The total number of English

[1] *Ordonnances des Rois de France de la Troisième Race*, XIV, ed. L. G. Oudart Feudrix de Bréquigny (1790), 139.

[2] *Archives Historiques, ut supra*, XXXVIII, 223: a note of English ships arriving in Bordeaux in January 1452, visited by Guill. de Rouille by command of the Seneschal of Guienne. This document, preserved among the archives of M. le duc de la Trémoille, is of great value for it gives detailed particulars of safe-conducts carried by each ship, where, by whom, to whom, and on what day they were issued, together with the numbers of crew and merchants on board.

[3] P.R.O., Treaty Roll 134, *passim*, calendared in *Reports of the Deputy Keeper of the Public Records*, xlviii (1887). For examples of these licences *in extenso* see E. M. Carus-Wilson, *The Overseas Trade of Bristol in the Later Middle Ages* (Bristol Record Society, VII, 1937), No. 104 *et seq*.

[4] *Archives Historiques, ut supra*. Eight of the English ships are noted as having received their safe-conducts at Bordeaux between 11th and 19th January.

ships that made the voyage that season cannot be precisely ascertained, but we do know that in January alone no fewer than twenty-six were in Bordeaux, with over a thousand men on board, including some forty or more merchants.[1] In addition to using such English ships, English firms continued as before to load on foreign ships, such as those of Bayonne, and to import through Gascon merchants.[2] Altogether England's imports of wine from all sources during the first year of French rule in Bordeaux exceeded those of the last two years of English rule, reaching 7000 tuns.[3]

With the short-lived restoration of English rule in the autumn of 1452, when citizens of Bordeaux joined with the English to chase the French from the valleys of the Garonne and Dordogne and English ships commanded the Gironde, trade prospered, unhampered by the need for licences or safe-conducts.[4] Regular wine ships were engaged, and fully loaded, like the *Trinity* of Dartmouth which came into Hull in April 1453 with 354 tuns,[5] and England's total wine imports that season rose to close on 10,000 tuns.

When Bordeaux finally surrendered to the French in July 1453, this time on much less favourable terms,[6] some dislocation of trade was inevitable. Even then, however, shipments to England cannot have ceased altogether, for England's total imports of wine that season (1453–4) reached as much as 6000 tuns. By the following season the trade had recovered to such an extent as to assume proportions as great as during some of the years of truce. Total

---

[1] *Ibid.*

[2] P.R.O., Treaty Roll 134 m. 10; *Calendar of Patent Rolls*, 1448–52, 540; P.R.O., Early Chancery Proceedings 26/403, 27/412, 413, printed in C. L. Kingsford, *Prejudice and Promise in Fifteenth Century England* (1925), 194 *et seq.*

[3] P.R.O., Exchequer L.T.R. Enrolled Customs Accounts, *ut supra.*

[4] On Treaty Roll 135, covering 1st September 1452 to 1st September 1453, there are no licences for trade to Gascony.

[5] P.R.O., Exch. K.R. Customs Accounts 61/71.

[6] *Ordonnances des Rois de France de la Troisième Race*, XV, ed. C. E. J. P. de Pastoret, 373; cf. Malvézin, *op. cit.*, II, 17 *et seq.*

imports for 1454–5 were 9500 tuns. That the bulk of this was Gascon wine imported by English merchants and in English ships is confirmed by a detailed Southampton account for the season. This shows, it is true, no sign of the regular wine fleet of previous years—arrivals are scattered— but it does show four English ships arriving with little else than wine, and the total of all wine imports (other than those of sweet wine) is significantly headed "Gascon wine imported by native merchants".[1] Nor was the trade an illicit one. Licences to trade with Gascony were again being granted extensively, both in England and in Gascony. The English licences, enrolled on the Treaty and Gascon Rolls, are themselves further confirmation of the extent of the direct trade still continuing with Gascony. No less than 58 were granted in 1454, and 32 in 1455 [2]; they were made out chiefly to English merchants but also to Gascons, some of whom had left Bordeaux to settle in England, where they carried on business as wine importers from London, Southampton, Bristol and elsewhere.[3]

In the autumn of 1455, however, the whole direct trade was threatened with extinction. England and France were still at war with one another and the economic weapon was a tempting one. The English government had already granted a number of licences to trade with Gascony that winter, and many of the ships were preparing to sail, if indeed they had not already sailed,[4] when on 27th October Charles VII suddenly forbade his officials to give any safe- conducts to the English, his "ancient enemies". Such a decree, however much it might embarrass his enemies, would have gone far to ruin his own subjects in Gascony, and

---

[1] P.R.O., Exchequer K.R. Customs Accounts 141/35.

[2] P.R.O., Treaty Rolls and Gascon Rolls covering these years, *passim*.

[3] There is a noticeable increase in the number of Gascons acting as wine importers at this time, and many were doubtless Gascons who had settled in England; see, e.g., E. M. Carus-Wilson, "The Overseas Trade of Bristol", *supra*, 45–6.

[4] See many licences granted in August, September and October, enrolled on Treaty Roll 137, m. 3, 9, 11, 12, 13, and cf. safe-conduct granted in July by the Admiral of France to William Baldry (see following footnote).

so great was the opposition to it that Charles was almost immediately persuaded to agree that 80 safe-conducts might be granted each year, though only by himself or his Admiral. Shortly afterwards he yielded still further, conceding that they might be granted on the spot by his lieutenant in Gascony.[1] On the strength of this a number of ships arrived and did business, but the quantities they brought back were small.[2] Many were doubtless deterred by the October decree, and the total amount of wine reaching England that season was less than 5000 tuns. The following year it sank still further to below 3000 tuns.

In such a fashion the trade continued for another six years—still in the hands of English and Gascons, but limited, closely regulated, and much diminished in volume. This diminution was due partly, no doubt, to the general uncertainty and to the difficulty and expense of securing licences and safe-conducts (merchants once paid 40 marks for one of these).[3] But it was also due to the insecurity that prevailed upon the high seas and in the Gironde so long as England and France remained officially at war. French ships, bringing wines of English as well as French merchants, or returning with cloth, were captured off the coasts of England by English ships, regardless of safe-conducts.[4] English ships and English ports were plundered by the French, who in 1457, for instance, pillaged in the Channel and attacked both Sandwich and Fowey. The *Anne* of Southampton, regularly

[1] *Archives Historiques, ut supra,* IX, Registers of the Grands Jours of Bordeaux for 1456 and 1459 (from a transcript in the archives of the parlement in Paris), 447–50: evidence put forward in the case of William Baldry *v.* Jean Baudry, Procurator-General of the King in Guienne, concerning the *Margaret* of Orwell; cf. 464: evidence in the case concerning the *Warry* of Sandwich, the *Ghost* of London, and the *Anne* of Southampton.

[2] Archives of Southampton, Port Books: the *Kathrine* of Hampton arrived on 24th December with 18 tuns, the *Christopher* of Hook on 18th January with 46 tuns. (I am indebted to Miss M. K. James for this information.) Cf. P.R.O., Exchequer K.R. Customs Accounts 203/4 (London imports 1456–7), and see *Calendar of Patent Rolls* 1452–61, 302.

[3] P.R.O., Early Chancery Proceedings 27/383, printed in E. M. Carus-Wilson, *The Overseas Trade of Bristol in the Later Middle Ages,* No. 143.

[4] See *Calendars of Patent Rolls,* e.g. 1452–61, 347, 608, 614; 1461–7, 36.

engaged in the wine trade, was once out of action for two years, undergoing repairs as the result of an incident in the Gironde.[1] The *Margaret* of Orwell, when laden with wine in Bordeaux, was held up many months over a dispute about the validity of a safe-conduct.[2]

Trivial in comparison with such risks were the routine restrictions on the activities of English merchants doing business in Gascony and, conversely, of Gascon merchants doing business in England. Each English ship had to stop twice on her way down the Gironde to Bordeaux, first at Soulac to fetch her permit and then at Blaye to deposit her arms, in each case paying a fee. At Bordeaux merchants had to obtain a special licence, lasting only a month, for permission to stay in the city; they might lodge only in specified houses, and might not emerge thence before 7 A.M. or after 5 P.M.; they might buy wines in the country round Bordeaux only if accompanied by a Bordeaux merchant or a special official, and for this too they must purchase a licence. To the expense of all these permits was added the expense of greatly increased custom dues.[3]

This period of restricted and much regulated trade lasted until the summer of 1462. Then once again resort to economic warfare threatened a complete interruption. Louis XI, the declared enemy of Edward IV by his pact with Margaret of Anjou, forbade the export of any merchandise to England; Edward IV, in retaliation, forbade the import into England of any Gascon wines, even with safe-conduct.[4]

Such a stoppage could not, however, be enforced for long. The economic link between England and Gascony, well

[1] See licence to Sir John Lisle (April 1457) for his ship the *Anne* of Southampton, which had been on the stocks for two years as a result of damage by the enemy, Treaty Roll, 139, m. 21; and cf. Early Chancery Proceedings 26/300 and *supra*, 276, n. 1.

[2] *Archives Historiques, ut supra*, IX, 447 *et seq.*

[3] Malvézin, *op. cit.*, II, 23 *et seq.*; for the very similar restrictions on the Bordelais in England see ordinances made for the supervision of the French in Bristol in 1462–3, *Great Red Book of Bristol*, ed. E. W. W. Veale, Text Part ii, 62 (Bristol Record Society, VIII, 1938).

[4] *Calendar of Patent Rolls*, 1461–7, 234.

and truly forged during three centuries of political union, was now too strong to be lightly broken. By the following spring negotiations had begun, the English were again allowed in Bordeaux, and by the autumn of 1463 a truce had been agreed—the first since that of 1444–1449.[1] Difficulties still lay ahead, but the wine trade was well on the way to a very considerable measure of recovery. For Louis XI had wisely rejected the advice of those who would persuade him that he could never be sure of Bordeaux unless he garrisoned the city, rased its walls to the ground and forbade all intercourse with the English. Rather he had come to agree with his Counsellor, M. Regnault Girard, that to impoverish one of his richest cities would gravely menace the peace and the prosperity of his realm, that the whole basis of Bordeaux's wealth was the isle of England, that no other country could take England's place as purchaser of its wines and supplier of its needs, and that the English should therefore be allowed to trade once again as freely as they would.[2]

[1] Rymer, *Foedera* (The Hague, 1739–42), V, ii, 117; Jullian, *op. cit.*, 307.

[2] *Archives Historiques, ut supra,* LVI, 34: memorandum addressed to Louis XI by his Counsellor M. Regnault Girard on "La question si est comme le Roy porra entretenir sa ville de Bordeaux en l'estat qu'elle est et en sécurité." The precise extent of the recovery and the long-term results of the political change are questions which cannot be considered within the limits of this brief paper; ample material exists for their study.

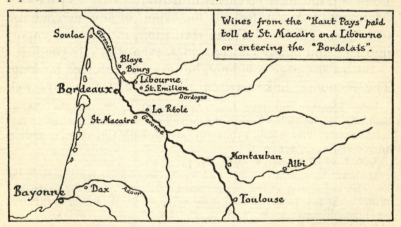

South-west France, illustrating Chapters VII and I §3

VIII

THE AULNAGE ACCOUNTS: A CRITICISM[1]

To those who, eager for scientific precision, seek a sound statistical basis for their economics, the following investigations into documents concerning the cloth industry may be of interest.[2] Historians have hitherto found a useful ally in the medieval aulnager. For his elaborate accounts of taxes paid on cloth produced for sale seem at first sight to reveal much as to the extent, locality, and organization of what was to become, by the end of the Middle Ages, England's leading manufacture and export. Yet ultimately many of his statements prove to be as barren of information as were the conventional medieval "proofs of age."

Table I gives the accounts rendered by Richard More for 1467–1478 of the total number of cloths of assise aulnaged in Bristol, Wilts, Somerset and Dorset.[3] More's methods are of special importance, for from 4 Henry IV to 4 Edward IV, and again from 18 Edward IV, the aulnage was farmed, and accounts of the actual numbers of cloths sealed were not usually returned. The only long series available, therefore, for the fifteenth century is that from 1465–1478, and during this time More was aulnager in Bristol, Wilts, Oxford, and Berks from 1467–1478; in Somerset and Dorset from 1471–1478; and in Worcester, Hants, Gloucester, Hereford, Devon and Cornwall, Surrey and Sussex from 1474–1478. Before 1402 the only accounts useful for comparison, owing to exemptions of kerseys, are a less complete series from 1394–1399. In this table it is evident that exactly the same number of cloths is more than once repeated, and that the

---

[1] *Economic History Review*, II, No. 1, 1929.
[2] These investigations concerned primarily the West of England industry, and for this reason examples are chiefly drawn thence.
[3] P.R.O., Exchequer L.T.R. Enrolled Accounts, Miscellaneous 9. In this and subsequent tables, unless otherwise stated, the year is from Michaelmas to Michaelmas, and the numbers refer to cloths of assise.

last two sets of figures, for two years and one and a half years, are contrived by a very simple calculation. Similarly for Devon and Cornwall, More's predecessor gave the same total in two successive years ($1,066\frac{1}{2}$ cloths); More, for a two years' return, doubled it ($2,033\frac{1}{2}$ cloths), and then by a simple sum reduced it to 1,600 cloths for one and a half

TABLE I

Date	Bristol	Wilts	Somerset and Dorset
7–8 Ed. IV.	3579	$4302\frac{1}{2}$	—
8–9 ,, ...	$3586\frac{1}{2}$	$4302\frac{1}{2}$	—
9–10 ,, ...	3579	4310	—
10–11 ,, ...	2563 [1]	4233 [2]	—
11–12 ,, ...	3579	$4303\frac{1}{2}$	5618
12–13 [3] ,, ...	3384	3953	5619
13 [3]–14 ,, ...	3307	3894	5618
14–16 ,, ...	6614	7788	11236
16–18 [4] ,, ...	4960	$5841\frac{1}{2}$	8427

years.[5] Further inquiry shows that such a ready reckoning was made in most of the counties for which More was responsible,[6] and that a repetition of totals was no uncommon device of other aulnagers, as may be illustrated by four accounts for the West Riding of Yorkshire, given in Table II.[7]

Treygot comes very near to duplicating his first list, and Birnand uses almost the same set of numbers for two and a half as for two years. Nor does each aulnager's original return seem always to have been based on fact. In Devon and Cornwall, as shown above, it was once derived from the previous collector's account. In Bristol it is perhaps not a

[1] Michaelmas–14 Apr. $1067\frac{1}{2}$; 14 Apr.–Michaelmas $1495\frac{1}{2}$.
[2] Mich.–14 Apr. (Thomas Gybbes) 1883; 14 Apr.–Mich. (R. More) 2350.
[3] 29 Oct.   [4] Mich. a. 16–Easter a. 18, i.e. $1\frac{1}{2}$ years.
[5] P.R.O., Exchequer K.R. Various Accounts, Aulnage, 338/18, 20.
[6] E.g., Hants, Gloucester, Worcester, Aulnage, *ut supra*, 347/10, 11.
[7] *Ibid.*, 345/24, 346/22B (places are not in each case given in the same order). Cf. 344/7, where William Kerver gives in three successive years for Somerset and Dorset the same list of places and numbers.

coincidence that in More's account it corresponds closely to the £60 (representing about 3,600 cloths) fixed when the subsidy was farmed. Hence the total returns for each county cannot be regarded as in any way reliable, and a general survey of all the preceding figures suggests that many of them are fictitious and that their evidence as to progress or decline in the cloth industry is far from convincing.

TABLE II

Aulnager	T. Treygot		R. Birnand	
Date	12 Nov. 1468–Mich. 1469 (46 weeks)	Mich. 1469–Mich. 1470 (1 year)	Mich. 1473–Mich. 1475 (2 years)	Mich. 1475–22 Mar. 1478 (2½ years)
Doncaster . .	35½	35½	35½	35½
Barnsley . .	88¾	88¾	142½	142½
Wakefield . .	231	249	160	160
Halifax . .	853	853¼	1493½	1493½
Leeds . .	176¾	177½	320	321
Almondbury .	160	160	427	427
Bradford . .	88½	—	178½	214
Pontefract . .	106	106½	214½	213½
Ripon . .	888	889	1386½	1385½

In addition to the totals for each district and to the account of forfeitures,[1] both enrolled in the Exchequer L.T.R. Enrolled Accounts, the aulnager was required to furnish a schedule of particulars giving, as alleged on the enrolment, the names of all individuals who had paid aulnage, followed by the number of their cloths to which the aulnager's seal had been attached, thus making them current merchandise. Many of these detailed lists survive, and they appear at first to abound in valuable evidence as to the rise of the clothier. Examination, however, shows many of them to be not ordered statements of actual transactions, but a fortuitous concourse of names and numbers recurring at random.

[1] From 1474–8 More declared that there were no forfeitures to report, but it seems from many instances in the Exchequer K.R. Memoranda Rolls that some must have taken place.

Table III tabulates the accounts of Richard More for Wiltshire throughout his term of office, from 1467–1478.[1]

In this table lists (2) and (3) are identical except for one figure. Save for one omission, one new name, and two

TABLE III

	(1)	(2)	(3)	(4)	(5)	(6)	(7)	(8)
Date	1467–8	'68–9	'69–'70	'71–2	'72–3 [2]	'73²–4	'74–6	'76–8 [3]
William Taverner	400	660	660	400	400	320	320	250
William Somer .	87	416	416	96	96	80	80	60
William Henlow .	280	50	57½	280	280	200	200	170
William Dyer .	80	175	175	80	80	80	80	60
Thomas Hille .	87	122	122	87	87	87	87	61
William Stowford	450	220	220	450	450	400	400	300
Laurence de Cule	93	219½	219½	93	93	93	93	68
John Berbor .	80	98	98	80	80	80	80	60
William Henlow .	200	400	400	200	200	200	200	170½
John Hamersmyth	300	260	260	300	300	290	290	220
Rawlyn Hayn .	73	80	80	—	—	73	73	54
William Ersden .	135	112	112	135	135	130	130	80
William Swayn .	250½	100	100	250	250	260	260	215
John Frye . .	301	261	261	301	301	202	202	170
John Halle . .	221	150	150	221	221	201	201	169
Thomas Barbour .	80	160	160	80	80	80	80	60
John Gulluk .	370	69	69	370	370	310	310	250
John Clyff . .	300	387	387	300	300	300	300	260
William White .	350	213	213	350	—	321	321	261
John Weste .	165	150	150	165	165	187	187	130
Thomas Hill .	—	—	—	65	65	—	and others	and others

slightly different figures, (4) is a copy of (1), and is exactly repeated in (5) except for one omission. (7) accounts for two years, yet its first twenty names and numbers are a precise counterpart of the previous one year's list, the total, exactly double that of the previous year, being made up

[1] Aulnage, *ut supra*, 346/23, 347/5, 8, 9, 10, 11. The names do not always appear in the same order. The account for 1470–1, confused by the appointment of different officials by Henry VI, is here omitted.

[2] 29 October.

[3] Mich. '76–Easter '78, i.e. 1½ years.

by the addition of further names (cf. *infra*, Table VI). Column (8) accounts for one and a half years, and its figures are accordingly about three-quarters those of (7).[1] From this constant reiteration it is evident that the same sets of numbers were used again and again, and that they cannot represent the actual number of cloths produced by each individual. Nor can we be certain that they give even an approximately correct yearly average for each name. Table IV places side by side four accounts returned for Bristol.[2]

TABLE IV

(1)		(2)		(3)		(4)	
1467–8		1468–9		1469–70		1471–2	
Haskerd	. 500	Spycer	. 97	Spycer .	. 97	Haskerd	. 500
Jaye	. 49	Dedhouse	. 49	Dedhouse	. 49	Jaye	. 49
Bisshop .	. 90	Dyer	. 500	Dyer .	. 500	Bisshop .	. 90
Gorney .	. 47	Newe .	. 90	Newe .	. 90	Gorney .	. 47
Goddard	. 65	Duffeld	. 47	Duffeld	. 47	Goddard	. 65
Davy .	. 31	Wilkham	. 65	Wilkham	. 65	Davy .	. 31
Morso .	. 100	Ashwode	. 31	Ashwode	. 31	Morso .	. 100
Haywode	. 210	Saywode	. 107½	Saywode	. 100	Haywode	. 210
Kempson	. 152	Gayton	. 210	Gayton .	. 210	Kempson	. 152
Shippard	. 87	Sayer .	. 152	Sayer .	. 152	Shippard	. 87
Witman	. 72	Witman	. 87	Witman .	. 87	Witman	. 72
Sayer .	. 108	Shippard	. 72	Shippard	. 72	Sayer .	. 108
Gayton .	. 114	Kempson	. 108	Kempson	. 108	Gayton .	. 114
Saywode	. 105	Haywode	. 114	Haywode	. 114	Saywode	. 105
Ashwode	. 604	Morso	. 105	Morso .	. 105	Ashwode	. 604
Wilkham	. 516	Davy .	. 604	Davy .	. 604	Wilkham	. 516
Duffeld	. 89	Goddard	. 516	Goddard	. 516	Duffeld	. 89
Newe .	. 184	Gorney	. 89	Gorney .	. 89	Newe .	. 184
Dyer .	. 164	Bisshop	. 184	Bisshop	. 184	Dyer .	. 164
Dedhouse	. 195	Jaye .	. 164	Jaye .	. 164	Dedhouse	. 195
Spycer .	. 97	Haskerd	. 195	Haskerd	. 195	Spycer .	. 97

[1] Cf. two identical lists for Somerset and Dorset, Aulnage, *ut supra*, 347/5, 6, also the close agreement between Elwyn's account for Devon and Cornwall for two years with that of Rowland and Henstecote for one year; *ibid.*, 338/14 and 338/17.

[2] *Ibid.*, 346/23, 347/8. Christian names, here omitted, correspond throughout. Variations in spelling are not reproduced.

Here, except in one case shown in italics, precisely the same series of numbers recurs four times. Unlike those in the Wiltshire accounts, however, these do not always fit the same names. For, though the same series of names also recurs, this series is sometimes reversed, giving a deceptive impression of variety. Witman remains a pivot in the centre round which the others revolve in ordered sequence, so that Haskerd may be found sometimes at the top and sometimes at the bottom. The series of numbers also moves, but on a different principle, to give greater diversity to the kaleido-scope; in (2) and (3) it is shifted one name down, 97 coming to the top, and 500 and 49 are reversed. Hence Davy, for instance, who is opposite the smallest number in (1) and (4), would appear from (2) and (3) to be Bristol's most important cloth producer, and it becomes plain that even less confidence can be placed in the ordered array of numbers allotted to individuals than to the totals for each district.

What then of the individuals themselves? The capricious arrangement of figures makes it impossible to determine which among them were the most important, but have we in these accounts a trustworthy guide as to the numbers actually paying aulnage in any district, and thus as to the extent to which the industry was concentrated in the hands of capitalists? The constant recurrence of the same series of names as shown above suggests a certain artificiality; this is borne out by finding that in some accounts where a county is divided into regions, one name only is recorded for each region—an improbable unification.[1] Even more conclusive evidence is to be found in the marked increase or decrease of names in the same districts, especially when a new aulnager was appointed. Richard More recorded but twenty-one names for Bristol in 1467–8; but an aulnage book of 1–2 Richard III gives forty pages of them,[2] and More's predecessor, John Peke, from Michaelmas to Easter, 1466–7, noted 224.[3] In Peke's list Thomas Ashwode,

---

[1] E.g., Aulnage, *ut supra*, 344/7, 345/24.
[2] *Ibid.*, 339/12.   [3] *Ibid.*, 339/11.

who according to More accounted one year for 604 cloths,[1] does not appear at all; Haskerd has but nineteen cloths to his credit, and Haywode but sixteen (cf. *supra*, Table IV). A similar discrepancy occurs in John Coplestone's accounts for Devon and Cornwall. In 1395–6 [2] he divided his account under the names of towns, which probably included the surrounding districts, and under Barnstaple recorded 3,908 cloths. In 1396–7 [3] he divided it under districts, grouped round the chief towns, and that which includes Barnstaple has 4,307 cloths. In the first account the 3,908 cloths are distributed among twelve persons, of whom John Parman has 1,080 and Richard Burnard 1,005. In the second account the 4,307 cloths are distributed among no less than 109 persons; among these "John Parkman" (the nearest name to "Parman") has only twelve and "Richard Bernard" only twenty-four.[4] Even supposing this change to be accounted for by a different method of aulnage collection, we could only deduce that Parman and Burnard were merchants buying the cloth probably for export, and not that they were clothiers organizing its production. In later "particular accounts" available for Devon and Cornwall, that of 1467–9 gives 248 names for the whole district, including thirty-one for Barnstaple [5]; these numbers are gradually diminished by successive aulnagers until finally More gives in both his accounts but forty-three names for both counties.[6] Similarly John Farley for Hampshire (1467–9) reduced his predecessor's 214 names to eighteen,[7] while in Gloucestershire he made eight names do duty for the whole county.[8]

[1] *Supra*, Table IV.
[2] Aulnage, *ut supra*, 338/11, Michaelmas to All Saints. The cloths in these lists are dozens.
[3] *Ibid.*, 338/2, All Saints to Michaelmas.
[4] Cf. similar discrepancies in two Essex accounts, *ibid.*, 342/9, the shorter of which has been quoted as evidence for the early appearance of "capitalism" in Essex.
[5] Aulnage, *ut supra*, 338/14.
[6] *Ibid.*, 347/10, 11.
[7] *Ibid.*, 344/17, 346/22A.
[8] *Ibid.*, 346/22A.

Such rapid fluctuations can scarcely indicate changes in the organization of the industry. A change in the method of marketing the cloth or of collecting the aulnage might in some cases account for them. Considering them, however, in conjunction with the frequent repetition of precisely the same short lists of names, and the mechanical redistribution of the numbers among them as shown in Table IV, must we not infer that lists were often arbitrarily compressed or abbreviated, and that these formal summaries served conveniently again and again?

The further question now arises as to whether the actual names themselves can be relied upon any more than the numbers. Have we always a list of real men connected with the industry?

Table V gives, in columns 1 and 3, the whole list of names for Somerset and Dorset for 1474–6 as More arranged them, with the number of cloths credited to each.[1] In columns 2 and 4 are given selections from Thomas Elyot's return for Devon and Cornwall for 1472–3 [2]; each bracket marks a complete sequence from the Devon list in its correct order. In 1474 More took over the aulnage of Devon and Cornwall, and with it presumably his predecessor's documents, and the table demonstrates that all the fifty-six Somerset and Dorset names were subsequently drawn from an old Devon list. Reference to Table I will show that the total number of cloths selected by More for Somerset and Dorset was exactly twice the previous one year's total for these counties, the detailed numbers being adjusted to complete this amount. Thus the apparent migration of fifty-six cloth producers from Devon eastwards, and the sudden disappearance of those they supplanted, would seem to have had happy results for themselves. The timely note appended to some of the names—"et sociis suis"—wards off incredulity when numbers are unusually large. Russell, for instance, producing for sale in Devon or Cornwall one

[1] *Ibid.*, 347/10.
[2] *Ibid.*, 338/18. The sign + indicates "et sociis suis."

TABLE V

SOMERSET AND DORSET, 1474–6 | **DEVON, 1472–3**

Name	No.	Name	No.
Parker +	165	Parker	8
Symon	180	Symon	7
Folde	150	Flode	5
Grabbeham	192	Grabbeham	10
Denys	142	Denys	4
Mannyng +	300	Mannyng	7
Chanon +	500	Chanon	7
Broke	80	Broke	5
Tanner	120	Tanner	19
Toker	95	Toker	7
Knoll	167	Knoll	5
Browne	110	Browne	9
Horn	113	Horn	11
Daly	159	Daly	3
Pope	160	Pope	6½
Corton	104	Corton	7
Murleys	109	Murleys	10
Cope	115	Cope	4
Cloteworthi, J.	80	Cloteworthy, J.	7
„ W.	120	„ W.	5
Reede	95	Reede	10
Gregon	160	Gregon	4
Smyth	155	Smyth	7
Swytton	180	Swytton	6
Croker	103	Crocker	8
Eston	160	Eston	11
Thornedon	146	Thornedon	3
Lyveton	123	Lyveton	3
Ryggeway +	360	Ryggeway	11
Jagowe +	215	Jagowe	7
Menyfe	106	Menyfe	6
Eliot	118	Elyot	8
Smyth	130	Smyth	13
Drake, J.	180	Drake, J.	5
„ W.	160	„ W.	3
Coke	153	Coke	7
Rawlyn +	400	Rawlyn	16
Torner +	260	Torner	3
Betty +	356	Betty	10
Herry	103	Harry	11
Bonefaunte	197	Bonefaunte	16

SOMERSET AND DORSET—Cont. | **DEVON—Cont.**

Name	No.	Name	No.
Eliot +	395	Elyot	10
Hunte	260	Hunte	10
Melforde, J.	240	Melford, J.	4
		„ T.	7
		Athole	9
Ascote	257	Ascote	4½
Mollys	243	Mollys	6
Lune	300	Lume	8
Hayle	400	Hayle	7
Russell +	499	Russell	5
Medwill	260	Medwyll	6
Age	240	Age	7
Smyth	260	Smyth	11
Lewys	240	Lewys	3
Arnott	256	Arnott	7
Byne	244	Byne	6
		With 84 others totalling	·743
Total	11236	*Total*	1066½

year only five cloths, prospered exceedingly in his new sphere of action and in two years produced no less than 499 cloths. In the following year and a half the immigrants, with no new recruits, continued to flourish.[1] More must have made up his accounts for Worcestershire for 1474–6 and 1476–8 by a similar resuscitation of bygone records, for eleven out of the thirteen names given may be found in previous lists of Oxford and Berks.[2]

Further evidence of haphazard and meaningless choice of names may be found in More's account for Wiltshire for 1474–6, given in Table VI.[3]

TABLE VI

William Swan	 260	John Wodhouse	
William Ersden	 130	et sociis suis 560	
Rawlyn Hayn	 73	William Johnson	
John Hamersmyth	. . . 290	et sociis suis 440	
William Henlow	 200	Robert Clyff 300	
John Barbour	 80	Henry White 321	
John Frye	 202	William Weste 379	
John Halle	 201	Andrea Gorney 260	
William Taverner	. . . 320	John Godard 240	
William Somer	 80	John Kempson 156	
Thomas Hill	 87	Thomas Shippard . . . 344	
William Dyer	 80	William Gullok 300	
William Stafford	. . . 400	William Clyff 240	
Laurence Cule	 93	William Frye 260	
Thomas Barbour	 80	Thomas Somer 94	
William Henlowe	. . . 200		
John Gullok	 310	Total 7788	
John Clyff	 300		
William White	 321		
John Weste	 187		

The first twenty persons are the same as in previous single years, as are the numbers.[4] Thirteen fresh names and numbers are added in order to bring the total for two years

[1] Aulnage, *ut supra*, 347/11.
[2] *Ibid.*, 347/10, 11, and 346/23.
[3] *Ibid.*, 347/10.
[4] *Supra*, Table III, p. 282.

up to exactly twice that of the last single year.[1] Seven of these
thirteen persons seem to be relatives of the old-established
aulnage payers, now engaging in the business for the first
time, for seven surnames re-appear with new Christian
names. Four are apparently kinsfolk of certain well-known
Bristol merchants (whose names occur in Bristol aulnage
accounts) [2]; for in Bristol we find John Gorney, Andrea
Godard, Thomas Kempson and John Shippard, and here we
have Andrea Gorney, John Godard, John Kempson and
Thomas Shippard. Surely this neat transposition was the
aulnager's own workmanship? [3] Hence of the fair-seeming
show of names and numbers before us, we can only say that
some may, but that all cannot possibly be genuine.

The whole system is as unsatisfactory to the historian now
as it was to the Crown then, if we may judge by the complaint of the King's losses in the Act of 17 Edward IV, empowering the Treasurer once more to let the aulnage to
farm.[4] On at least one occasion Richard More's accounts
seem to have roused misgivings in the minds of the authorities
—though on what particular ground we know not.[5] Yet in
spite of this he survived to farm the aulnage for most of the
south-west of England. We are thus driven to conclude that
aulnagers could and often did with impunity fake their
accounts. It looks as if the return of "particulars" at least
had degenerated into a mere form—for surely even More's
ingenious variations could not have deceived the auditors?

At any rate, it is clear that the greater part of the documents now in our hands cannot be treated as strictly
"original" sources, but as compilations, sufficiently accurate
perhaps to placate the medieval Exchequer, though not
to satisfy posterity. The aulnager commonly sent in the

[1] *Supra*, Table I.
[2] *Supra*, Table IV.
[3] Cf. Aulnage, *ut supra*, 347/10, for suspicion of a similar device in Bristol.
[4] *Statutes of the Realm*, II, 465; cf. *Calendar of Patent Rolls*, 1399–1401,
348, 413, 517, 520, and *Statutes of the Realm*, II, 140.
[5] Exchequer K.R. Memoranda Rolls, 14 Edward IV, Mich. rot. 12,
Hillary rot. 1.

particulars for all the counties for which he was responsible on the same roll in the same handwriting. At best, therefore, these returns are copies of accounts kept, more or less thoroughly, by local deputies. At worst they are imitations of old accounts or pure invention. Usually they seem to be formal abstracts or summaries of the originals, prepared with no pretence of tedious addition of each individual's true total, and varying in form according to the mood of the aulnager or his clerk. Indeed, the aulnager himself often admits this. Thus in Colwyke's first list for Worcestershire (1467–9) there are sixty-two names.[1] In his second list there are only four names, but beside each appears "et aliis." [2] Richard More, however, in his first list, gives twelve names and omits "et aliis." [3] The true original records, where such existed, seldom reached the safe keeping of the Exchequer. But these actual records of payments to the aulnager are of an entirely different character from most of the "particulars" returned by him. Thus *A Boke of the Aunage of Bristow*, dated 1–2 Richard III, containing forty pages on paper, notes day by day in minute detail the number of cloths sealed.[4] John Henlove, for instance, appears during one year twenty-one times, with anything from one to thirteen cloths, and a total, one of the largest in the book, of 111 cloths. The value of these records is inevitably minimized by the apparently frequent evasions of the much hated subsidy,[5] and in any case they are too rare and isolated to furnish material for any safe generalizations.

We have, then, among the whole series of accounts a few which are, strictly speaking, originals, but a great number

[1] Aulnage, *ut supra*, 346/21.
[2] *Ibid.*, 346/24.
[3] *Ibid.*, 347/10. Cf. two York accounts, 345/24. Other stages through which these accounts passed are illustrated by the corrected rough draft of a final list, *ibid.*, 347/3, 346/25.
[4] *Ibid.*, 339/12, and cf. 339/7.
[5] Exchequer K.R. Memoranda Rolls, *passim. Calendar of Patent Rolls*, 1399–1401, 517. Confiscated cloth seems frequently to have been recovered forcibly by its owners.

of second-hand compilations of doubtful veracity, often abbreviated, distorted, and repeated again and again. These can scarcely form a secure foundation for statistics. Rather do they afford an example of how the medieval official may prove as misleading an authority as the litigant or the chronicler. For the aulnager was no mere machine automatically registering payments; he also was influenced by personal inclinations, love of ease, perhaps, or of gain, or by conventions of his day unknown to us. The chronicler has often been censured for seeking in fable or in his own fancy matter for his narrative. The aulnager, less imaginative, dealing in a mass of hard figures and formal details, has hitherto escaped serious criticism; yet for the unwary he has woven an intricate web, well-nigh impossible to disentangle; ingeniously cooking his accounts, devising new patterns from old materials, and leaving behind him works of art rather than transcripts of fact.

SUBJECT INDEX

Aelfric's *Colloquy*, xii, 266

alabaster, exports of, carved, 5, 52, 60, 93

alien immigrants, from Flanders and Brabant, 244 n. 1; Gascony, 45, 80, 275; Iceland, 117; Ireland, 20, 80, 244 n. 1; Italy, 80; Spain, 80; Wales, 80

—— merchants in England; Flemish, xiii, xxi, xxii; French in Bristol, 48, 80; Gascon, xxi–xxii, 45, 80, 275; German *see* "Easter-lings", Hanse; Irish, 19 *et seq.*, 80; Italian, xi, xxi, xxii, xxv, 55, 80, 258; Genoese arrested in London, 71; Picard, xiii, xxii, 217; Portuguese, 59; Spanish, 55, 80; Welsh, 80

almonds, 27, 37, 50, 65

alum, 8, 27, 37, 51, 221–2

anchors, 51

anise, 27

"appointers" (of ships), 161, 165, 171

apprenticeship, to Bristol merchants, 81–2; to Bristol weavers, 20; to merchant adventurers, 179

archil, 220

argol, 222

arms and armour, 8, 26, 47, 51, 60, 62, 64, 113, 126, 131, 132, 138, 141, 164, 166

assize of cloth, xviii, 184 n. 1, 214, 228, 244 n. 4

attorneys, 83

auditors, 161

aulnage and aulnagers, 84 n. 1, 85, 240–1, 279–91

backhandle, 231, 232

bacon, 24, 126

balls, 170; for tennis, 10

barrel staves, 60

bastard (sweet Spanish wine), 52

beadles, xxviii

beans, 52

beaver, 37, 51

beef, 126

beer, 21, 27, 121, 122, 126, 131, 132

bells, 1, 9, 99

"Berkeley wood", 5

Black Death, 241, 244–7, 254, 260; in Iceland, 104

boards, 25, 51

books, owned by merchants, 95; stolen, 54

bowstaves, 25, 37, 51

brasil, 218–9

bream, 23

Brétigny, peace of, 249

bridges, 5, 11, 19

brokers, xxviii; of woad, 36

burel and burellers, 213–4, 234

butter, 21, 24, 126, 131

carcases from Ireland, 24

cards. *See* wool-cards

cattle, Icelandic, 103, 109; Irish, 23; Welsh, 7

cheese, 270 n. 4

cloth, English, *passim*

—— of assize, xviii, 184 n. 1, 244 n. 4

—— customs, xvii–xviii, 248 n. 1, 262–4

—— exports, introd. *passim*, 211–2, 239–64; to Gascony, 4, 10, 13, 38, 270 n. 4, 276; Iceland, 119, 131; Ireland, 27; Low Countries, 143 *et seq.*; Mediterranean, xviii, 64–5, 70; Portugal, 60; Spain, 52

—— industry, 4–9, 49, 184–246 *passim*; capitalist organization, 233–6; change of location, 198, 203–9; evidence

293

cloth, industry—contd.
    for twelfth and thirteenth centuries, 238, 251; handcraft processes, 184; manpower, 251, 261 n. 3; production costs, xx n. 2; raw materials, 215–22, 250 n. 1. *See also* aulnage and aulnager, clothiers, fulling
—— prohibited in Low Countries, 168, 244
—— types, of Beverley, 209, 212; burnets, 212 n. 7; Castlecombes, 209; Cotswolds, 209, 211; Essex straits, 211; Kendals, 209; kersey, 52, 263, 280; of Lincoln, 209; of Louth, 209; Ludlows, 209; Mendips, 209, 211; *pannos crudos*, 207; *pannos grossos*, 202 n. 1; *pannos viles*, 202 n. 1; ray, 208; russets, 7, 213, 215, 229, 230; scarlet, xvii, 27, 69, 212 n. 6, 218 n. 4, 242 n. 1; of Stamford, Stamforts, 209, 212, 213 n. 1; Stroudwaters, 209; West of Englands, 211; West Ridings, 211; Westerns, 209; Worsteds, 27, 264; in grain, without grain, defined, 27. *See also* burel and burellers, hauberge.
cloth, foreign, Flemish, xvi, xxii, 242–3, 244, 249, 257 n. 4, 259; Icelandic, *vaðmal*, 103, 131, 132; Irish, Drap d'Irland, 26; faldynges, 25; frieze, 26; whittles, 26; Italian, 258, 260; Welsh, 7, 52
"cloth mill", 192
clothiers, 9, 85, 262
coal, 5, 8, 11, 38
cocket, 26
cod, 22, 132
combs. *See* wool-combs

Companies of London
    Drapers, 151, 152, 160, 162, 163, 167, 178, 179 n. 1, 180
    Fishmongers, 152, 160, 162, 167, 178
    Grocers, 151, 152, 152 n. 4, 160, 162, 163, 167, 178, 179 n. 1, 180
    Haberdashers, 151, 152, 160, 162, 163, 167, 178
    Ironmongers, 160
    Mercers, xxvi, xxix, xxx, 10, 147–82 *passim*; clerk of, 161; hall of, 147–9, 156–7, 161, 169, 177, 180, 182
    Skinners, 151, 152, 153, 160, 162, 167, 171–2, 178
    Tailors, 152, 160, 162, 167, 178
    Upholders, 167
compass, 106–7, 107 n. 1
"conduit money", 161, 170–1
"conduitors", 161, 170
conger, 23
convoys, 33, 35, 165–6, 170, 179. *See also* "conduit money", "conduitors"
copperas, 222
cordovan, 37, 51
cork, 51, 60
customs accounts, xi, xvii–xviii, xix n. 1, 22, 25, 26, 56–7, 66, 83, 93, 240, 242 n. 2, 248 n. 1, 254, 259 n. 2, 262–4, 271, 275; of Bordeaux, 30, 34 *et seq.*, 246 *et seq.*, 265

dairy produce. *See* butter, cheese
damask, 64
Danish officials in Iceland, 114, 141
Danseurs, 260
Danzigers, licensed to trade with Iceland, 140
dates (fruit), 50, 52
discovery, voyages of, 97, 100, 127, 142
Domesday survey, 267, 286

drapers, 5, 71, 85, 167, 175 n. 3;
    Draparii, 229. *See also*
    Companies of London
dyers, 8, 9, 51, 214, 222–4, 226–8,
    234, 237 n. 5, 262
dyes and dyeing, 216–22; regulations,
    219, 227–9; dye pans, mono-
    poly of, 199–201. *See also*
    names of dyestuffs

"Easterlings", xiii, 10
Eastland Company, 174 n. 4

factors, 55, 82–3, 92
fairs, East Anglian; sales of cloth at,
    229, 233, 242 n. 3
famine, 39, 104, 245–7, 251–3
feathers, 141, 170
figs, 50, 52, 65
fish, xxv, 7, 8, 11, 29, 251, 270
—— Bristol's trade, 21, 38–9, 60
—— imports from Iceland, 102,
    119–20, 132; Ireland, 21–3;
    Newfoundland, 142; Nor-
    way, 105; Spain, 50
—— Royal prise in Bristol, 22–3.
    See also names of fish
fish-hooks, 10, 125, 126
fishing, 15; off Iceland, 108–9, 125;
    off Ireland, 21; off Norway
    and Denmark, 105
—— vessels, 87, 109, 125–6, 127–8
fishmongers, 11, 121, 122, 123, 129.
    See also Companies of London
flax, 25
flock, 26, 77
Fraternity, for Mariners, Bristol, 12
—— of St. Thomas à Becket, 150;
    in London, 150; "beyond
    the sea", 150, 172, 176, 182
freight rates, 87, 164–6
fruit, 8, 27, 50, 60, 62, 64. *See also*
    dates, figs, raisins
fulleries in Roman Britain, 185
fullers (tuckers), 9–10, 178, 204,
    214, 223–4, 225–7; as wage-
    earners, 231–2, 236. *See also*
    fulling, fulling mills, gilds

fuller's earth, 184, 185, 215, 222
fulling, 184 *et seq.*, 233 n. 3; in
    France, 187; Iceland, 186–7;
    Scotland, 186; in Roman
    times, 185, 187; early
    methods, 185–8; mechanisa-
    tion, 188 *et seq.*; terminology,
    188 n. 3, 201 n. 2
fulling mills (tucking mills, walk
    mills), 9, 188 *et seq.*; opposi-
    tion to use of, 203, 207–8
furs, 69, 74. *See also* hides and skins

gild merchant, xxv, 146, 233 *et seq.*,
    230, 232–4, 237 n. 2, 5;
    date of earliest, 226; exclusion
    of weavers and fullers from,
    223–4, 238; industrial
    monopoly of, 227–8, 237;
    wages fixed by, 230, 232–3;
gilds: of fullers, 204, 207, 225–6,
    231–5; of weavers, 204, 208,
    225–6, 235; of English Mer-
    chants in Ireland, 19; of the
    Holy Trinity, Coventry, 5;
    of St. George, Hull, xxix, 144
glasses, 132, 170
goldsmiths' work, 1, 64, 69, 74, 78,
    94, 132, 262
"Good Parliament", 255 n. 2
grain (corn), 2, 5
—— civic provision of, 5, 38
—— exports, to Gascony, 38, 270;
    Iceland, 103, 122, 131;
    Ireland, 25; Portugal, 60;
    Spain, 52; Wales, 8
—— imports, from Ireland, 25
—— prices, 39, 245, 247, 252. *See
    also* rice
grain (scarlet dye), 27, 51, 52, 60,
    218, 219, 220
Great Red Book of Bristol, 9, 46, 88,
    89
grenefish (ling), 22
grindstones, 51
Grocers. *See* Companies of London
gurnard, 23

Haberdashers. *See* Companies of London
haburden (cod), 22
haddock, 23
hake, 16, 22, 23, 38, 52, 132
"halbergett", 213
"hanse", xiii–xiv; of Flemish merchants in London, xiii; of German merchants, *see* Hanse; of Picard merchants, xiii
Hanse, Hanseatic League, xiii, 1, 10, 65, 66, 80, 96, 102, 103, 112, 116, 124, 134–5, 136–7, 140–1, 169, 258; in Bergen, 108, 112; in London, arrested, 139. *See also* " Easterlings "
hats and caps, 60, 131, 187
"hauberge", 213
"haubergett", 213
hawks, 24
herring, exported to Gascony, 38, 270 n. 4; to Spain, 52
—— from Iceland, 132; from Ireland, 21, 23; Norfolk and Suffolk, 21
—— prices, 22
—— salt, 22, 23
hides and skins, 7, 11, 29, 38, 46, 51, 52, 65, 132, 141; Irish, 17, 23–4. *See also* leather and leather goods
honey, 17, 37, 50, 131, 132
hops, 46, 53, 170
horses, Irish, 24
horse-shoes, 131
hound fish, 22
household effects in fifteenth century, 77–8
houses, merchants', xxvii, 69, 73, 75 *et seq.*, 93
Hundred Years War, xxii, 43, 56, 239, 241, 271; effect on Anglo-Gascon trade, 40–1, 246–9, 271; in Gascony, 241–9, 253, 272

industrial disputes, 69, 235, 259–60
Intercursus Magnus, 168, 173
—— *Malus*, 176
iron, xxviii, 5, 8, 15, 16, 26, 37, 51, 52, 80, 93, 131. *See also* metal-ware
Ironmongers. *See* Companies of London
Issak (petty custom at Bordeaux), 30

Kalmar, Union of (1397), 104
kettles, copper, 131
knives, 26, 131, 132

laces, 51. *See also* points
land, merchants' investments in, 79, 80
lard, 24, 50
lead, xxv, 52, 60, 70
leather and leather goods, 2, 23, 26–7, 51, 131. *See also* cordovan
leather workers, 7, 24
licences, to buy wines, 277; to catch salmon, 23; to export corn, 39, 70; to ship staple goods elsewhere than Calais, 67, 70; to ship customs free, 83, 90; to stay in Bordeaux, 48, 277; to Frenchmen to stay in England, 48
—— to trade, to Bordeaux, 273–7; to Iceland, 109, 120–3, 135–7; to Low Countries, 167
licorice, 37, 50, 52
linen, 4, 25–6, 131, 132
ling, 22, 23
lodestone, 106–7

mackerel, 23
madder, 10, 46, 53, 170, 216, 218
malt, 5, 122, 131, 132
mantles, Irish, 26, 52, 220
mariners, Fraternity for, 12; masses for, 13; payment of, 87; Breton, 46; Spanish, 53, 55, 63; Welsh, 97
meal, 126, 131

Measures, Assize of (1197), 228
meat, 24, 39, 251. *See also* bacon, beef
Mercers. *See* Companies of London
"merchant", significance of term, xxv, 84–5
Merchant Adventurers, Merchant Venturers, *passim*, xi–xvii, xxvi–xxx, 10, 143–182
—— chapels, 150; coat of arms, 175; court of assistants, 175, 177; definition of term, xi–xiii, xxvi–xxviii, 143; entry fines, xxix, 174; financial affairs, 170–2, 180; general court of, 160 *et seq.*; governor of, 164 *et seq.*; origin of Company, 143–82; relations with Hanse and Staplers, 169–70; solicitor, 180; treasurer, 180
—— of Bristol, xxvii–xxviii, 73; of Exeter, xxviii n. 3; of London, xxvi–xxvii, xxx, 143–82; of Newcastle, 146–7, 161, 172; of Norwich, 176; of York, xxix, 146–7, 172, 176
Merchant Staplers, xv, xxv, xxvi, xxx, 143, 149, 150, 169–70
—— Venturers. *See* Merchant Adventurers
merchants, alien. *See* alien merchants
merchants' marks, 90
merchants, women, 93–4
metal-ware, exports, to Ireland, 26; Iceland, 131; imports, from Gascony, 37; Spain, 51. *See also* anchors; arms and armour; fish-hooks; horseshoes; kettles; knives; nails; needles; pins; pots and pans; wool-cards; wool-combs
mills, 16, 23, 200, 201. *See also* "cloth mill", fulling mills, tanning mill
milwell (cod), 22, 23
monopolies, burghal, of making dyed cloth, 208, 227–8

monopolies, manorial, 199–203
—— of trade, in alum, 221; in wool, xxv; to France, Spain and Portugal from Bristol, xxviii; to the Low Countries, 173–4
mordants, 37, 220–2. *See also* alum, potash
murage, 218, 220, 222

nails, 26, 51, 131
needles, 131
Noumbre of Weyghtes, The, 132

oars, 25
oil, xxviii, 27, 51, 52, 55, 60, 92, 132, 141, 184; edible, xviii n. 1, 60; medicinal, 60; wool oil, xxviii n. 1, 60, 184
orchil, 220

"pannmylle". *See* "cloth mill"
paper, 132; brown, 171
Peasants' Revolt, 203 n. 1
pepper, 67, 71. *See also* spices
perch (cloth frame), 232
perry, 27
perse, 216 n. 1
pewter, xxv, 26
Picquigny, Treaty of (1475), 48
Piers Plowman, 186, 251
pilgrims, 16, 67–69, 154
pins, 131
piracy and pirates, 2, 15–8, 35, 44, 46, 48, 53, 56–7, 62, 69, 71, 90, 91, 114, 116, 119, 130, 136–8, 212, 276
pitch, 27, 37, 131
plague, 82, 252–3. *See also* Black Death
plaice, 23
points (laces), 27, 132; pointmakers, 52
pollack, 22, 132
porpoise, 22
potash, 37, 221
pots and pans, 27, 131

quays, at Bordeaux, 11; at Bristol, 11, 93
quicksilver, 52

raising the nap, 184, 231
raisins, 50, 52, 65
ray (fish), 23
records, of London Companies, 152; of Merchant Adventurers, 143–9
Ricart's Calendar, 20
rice, 50
rosin, 37, 51
rugs, 23, 26

safe conducts, 46–8, 57, 61, 89, 91, 167, 273, 276–7
saffron, 37, 50, 52, 220
salmon, 18, 21, 23, 26, 132
salt, 16, 17, 126; Bourgneuf, 46, 51, 60; Portuguese, 60; Spanish, 15, 51; to Iceland, 126, 131; to Ireland, 16, 17, 23, 26
—— fish, 21, 22, 23, 126, 132
scalpin (whiting), 22
seals (fish), 22
sea-shanties, 12
shearmen, 178
shipbuilding, 105–6; at Bristol, 13, 86–90
shipowners, 84–7
ships, capacities, 88, 274; crews, 89–90; types of, 87–8, 105–6, 166; warships, 43, 69, 165–6
shipwreck, xii, 12, 68, 91, 110
silk, 10, 64–5
Skinners. *See* Companies of London
skins. *See* hides and skins
"smigmates", 51
soap, 27, 51, 52
spices, 27, 37, 50, 64–8, 71, 78
sprats, 21
staple, for fish at Bergen, 108 *et seq.*; for wool, etc. at Calais, xv, xxv, xxx, 64, 67

Staplers. *See* Merchant Staplers
steel, 37, 60, 62
stockfish, 98, 119, 123, 132
sugar, 37, 60, 92
sumach, 220

Tailors. *See* Companies of London
tallow, 24, 51, 141
tanning mill, 191
tar, 46, 51, 131
teasles, 10, 26, 215, 216, 222, 231, 232
Templars, 189–90
Teutonic Order, xvii
timber, 5, 11, 99, 104, 131, 192, 198; Irish, 24–5
tin, xxv, 7, 11, 52, 64, 67, 70
tolls, 7, 9, 15, 17, 24, 30–2, 37, 40, 109, 168, 215, 221, 266
Tolsey Court, Bristol, 12, 50, 69, 87, 95
trowes, 5
tucking mills, 188 n. 3. *See also* fulling mills
tunny-fish, 50
Turks, 67, 70, 72

ulnage. *See* aulnage
Upholders. *See* Companies of London

velvet, 74
verdigris, 222
vermilion, 218–9
vinegar, 50
viticulture, in England, 267–9; in Gascony, 28, 248, 267 *et seq.*; in Portugal, 62

wages, 251, 255, 259–60, 262; of fullers, 231–2; of weavers, 229–30, 235
wainscots, 46, 53, 77
walk mills, 188 n. 3. *See also* fulling mills
Wardrobe, Royal, 242
Wars of the Roses, 96

wax, xxviii, 8, 24, 37, 51, 52, 60, 92, 131

weavers, 4, 9, 10, 20, 214, 223–4, 235, 260, 262; as wage earners, 229–30, 236. *See also* gilds

weld, 220

whale, 22

whiting, 22, 23

Windsor, Treaty of (1386), 59

wine, xxi–xxii, 8, 15, 27, 92; consumption in England, 266, 271 n. 1, 2; freight rates, 87
—— trade, Gascon, 28–49 *passim*, 246, 254, 265–78 *passim*; Portuguese, 17, 59–60, 62; Spanish, 50, 52, 55; Rhineland, 268–9; from Rouen, 266; export to Iceland, 122, 131–2, to Ireland, 14, 27. *See also* viticulture

Winyardsilver, 268 n. 2

woad, 5, 8, 9, 36, 47, 51, 216–8, 257

woad, assay, in Bristol, 36, in London, 235; brokers of, 36
—— imports in Bristol, 36–7, 51, 80, 92; from Caen, 47
—— of Picardy, xiii, xxii, 216–18; of Toulouse, xxviii, 37, 257

women merchants, 93–4

wool, 2, 5, 9, and *passim*
—— export, xiii–xvi, xix–xxvi, 64, 67, 70, 149–50, 243, 249–50, 254–6, 261 n. 2; duty on, xvii–xviii, 243, 248; prohibitions of, xvi, 243
—— per cloth, xx, 250 n. 2
—— Spanish, 52, 215

wool-cards, 10, 26

wool-combs, 26, 37, 51, 131, 132

woolfells, xviii

woolsacks, size of, xviii

Wynsilver, 268 n. 2

yarn, 235; linen, 25; for nets, 132; woollen, from Spain, 215

INDEX OF PERSONS, PLACES AND SHIPS

Abbot, —, 133
Aberdeen, 225
Aby, fulling mill, 197
Adam of York, 35
Adam the Carter, of Hawkesbury, 201; Matilda, his daughter, 201
Adour, river, 29
Alberton, John, 62
Albi, 37
Alexander II, King of Scotland, 225
Aleyn, John, 175 n. 3
Alfonso of Naples, 72
Alford, Piers, 63
Algarve, 62
Alison, 53
Almondbury, fulling mill, 195
Alverthorpe, fulling mill, 195
Alvington, fulling mill, 195
Amiens, "Amyas", xiii, 216, 217
—— Cathedral, 216
Amondbury, 280
Amsterdam, *Marie Knight* of, 124
Andover, 224
Andrew, 65
Anjou, Margaret of, 74, 277
Anne of Southampton, 276 n. 1, 277, 277 n. 1
Anthony of Faro, 62–3
Antina, Petrus de, 65
Antony, 91
Antwerp, xiv, 157, 166, 168, 169, 178–9
Applethwaite (Windermere), fulling mill, 195
Aquitaine, Eleanor of, 28
Aragon, 53, 136
—— Katherine of, 58
—— Simon, 80
Arthur, Prince, 58
Atlantic Ocean, 1, 61, 96, 97, 100
Avon, river (Somerset), 2, 4, 8, 9, 11, 12

Ayleward, John, 20
Ayr, 18

Bacon, Robert, 127
Bagot, Clement, 18, 87
Baldry, William, 275 n. 4, 276 n. 1
Baltic, xvi, xvii, xxiii, xxvii, 13, 81, 96, 102, 135, 144, 221, 257–9
Bann, river, 23
Bannebury, John, 16
Barcelona, merchant of, 222
Barnsley, 280
Barnstaple, 7, 8, 192, 224, 285
Baron, —, 83
Bartholomew, 122
Barton (Staffs.), fulling mill, 195
Barton-on-Windrush, fulling mill, 190, 196
Bath, Bishop of, 191
Baudry, Jean, 276
Baylly, Robert, 175 n. 3
—— William, 175 n. 3
Bayonne, 29 *et seq.*, 44–5, 51, 57, 80, 82, 87, 92, 272, 274; exports, 37; grain imports, 39; privileges suspended, 44; shipping of, 34
Beauchamp, Richard. *See* Warwick, Earls of
Bedford, John, Duke of, 110
Bedwyn, 214
Behaim, 117
Beirut. *See* Beyrout
Benham Valence, fulling mill, 196
Bensyn, Barnard, 45, 80
Bergen, xxiii, 66, 98, 111, 116, 117, 119, 129, 130, 135, 137, 139, 140, 141, 142; English merchants excluded, 139; forsaken by English merchants, 111; monopoly, 104, 140; plundered by pirates, 116; staple at, 102, 104, 108, 109,

Bergen—contd.
110, 116, 118, 124, 134, 135, 140
Berkeley, 19
—— Sir Maurice, Lord of Beverston, 79
Berkshire, aulnage, 280, 288
Beverley, 198, 209, 211, 212, 213, 238; laws of the weavers and fullers, 235–8
—— John of, 212
Bewdley, 8
Beyrout, 73
Bilbao, 53
Bird, William, 78
Birmingham, 8
Birnand, R., 280, 281
Biscay, 53
Bishopsgate, xxvii
Black Prince, 59
Black Sea, 70, 221
Blakeney, 101 n. 1, 126, 127
Blakston, John, 175 n. 3
Blaye, 32, 33–4, 44, 47, 277
Blois, Peter of, 267
Bloxwich, John, Bishop of Hólar, 123
Blund', Peter, 229
Blythburgh church, 187
Bonyfaunt, John, 19
Bordeaux, xii, 10, 11, 13, 14, 29, 31, 37, 38, 39, 40, 43, 45, 49, 82, 84, 87, 92, 133, 222, 246, 249, 253, 254, 269–70, 272, 278; abbeys of S. Seurin and S. Croix, 269; accounts, 30, 34 et seq., 246 et seq., 265; advantages as a port, 30; capitulates to French (1451), 44, 272–4; constable of, 34, 35; English shipping in, 34 et seq.; privileges of citizens, 30–1, 44; renewal of trade (1463), 47, 278; restrictions on English merchants in, 47, 48, 277; St. Peter's church, 87; supplants Rouen in wine trade, 267. See also wine trade

Bordeaux, Archbishop of, 38, 41, 249, 270 n. 1 and 4
Bordelais, 30–1, 34, 45, 253, 269, 270, 272
Boston, 8, 119, 263; fair 217, 229, 233
Bourg, 32, 44
Bourgneuf, Bay of, salt from, 46, 51, 60
Bourton-on-the-Water, fulling mill, 191, 196
Bovey Tracey, fulling mill, 196
Boys, Robert, 157
Brabant, "Braband", xiv, xvi, xxvi, xxvii, xxix, xxx, 144, 159
—— Duke of, xiii, xiv
Bradford, 280; fulling mill, 195
Brakelond, Jocelin de, 200
Brampton, fulling mill, 195
"Brasile", "Brasylle", island of, 97
Bridgenorth, 8 n. 1
Brightwell, fulling mill, 191, 199
Bristol, xi, xxvii, xxviii, xxix, 1–97 passim, 114, 116, 119, 128, 141, 207, 275, 280
—— aulnage, 280, 281, 283, 285, 289, 289 n. 3, 290
—— churches: All Saints, 54, 76, 93–4; St. Augustine, priory, 226; St. Ewen, 5; St. John the Evangelist, 12; St. Mary Redcliffe, 11, 36, 94; St. Nicholas, 46, 70; St. Peter, 20; St. Stephen, 94; St. Werburgh, 36; Trinity, 14, 62–4
—— clothmaking in, 4, 49–50
—— cloth exports, xviii, 27, 254, 256 n. 1, 257, 263
—— description, 1–13 passim
—— foreign merchants in, 19–21, 48, 80, 275
—— fullers' gild, 185–6, 207–8, 231
—— geographical advantages, 2
—— merchant class, 73–97
—— overseas trade, with Brittany, 46–7; Gascony, 28–49, 254, 257; Iceland, 129–30; Ireland, 14–28; Mediterranean,

Bristol, overseas—contd.
    64–73; Portugal, 58–64, 257, 258; Spain, 49–58; Toulouse region, 257
—— shipowners and shipping, 55–6, 84, 86–92
—— streets, etc.: Baldwin Street, 12; "the Bull", 76; High Street, 75, 79, 93; "Irish Mead", 20; "Key", 11, 12; "le Cok in the Hope", 76, 79; "le Grene Latyce", 76; Llafford's Gate, 79; Marsh Gate, 93; Marsh Street, 12; Old Corn Street, 36; Redcliffe Mead, 79; Redcliffe Street, 4, 77; St. Nicholas Street, 79; St. Thomas' Street, 4; Temple Street, 4, 79; Touker Street, 4; "Welsh Back", 11, 12, 79; Winch Street, 79
—— Tolsey Court, 12, 50, 69, 88, 95
Bristol Channel, 2, 7, 11
Brittany, 13, 17, 24, 29, 36, 47, 60, 63, 64. See also Bristol, overseas trade
Bromewell, William, 175 n. 3
Bruay, 199 n. 3
Bruges, xiv, 150, 165, 242 (243) n. 3, 244 n. 3, 260
Brussels, 242 (243) n. 3
Buckingham, 7
Bullok, John, 19
Burgh, Sir William de, 17
Burghfield, fulling mill, 196
Burgundy, 135, 155, 170, 266
—— Dukes of, 155, 158, 168, 170, 173, 199 n. 3
Burnham, 127
Burnley, fulling mill, 195, 199
Burrishoole, 17
Burton Constable, fulling mill, 195
Bury St. Edmunds, 200

Cabot, John, 97, 142
Caen, 47
Caerleon, 7; fulling mill, 195

Calais, xv, xxv, xxx, 67, 144, 150, 162, 167, 170, 175 n. 2. See also staple
Calverley, 204
Candia, 73
Canning, George, 81
Cantabrian mountains, 37, 51
Canterbury, 255, 269
Canynges, John (son of William, d. 1474), 79
—— John (mayor of Bristol, d. 1405), 80–1, 85
—— Simon, 80
—— Thomas, 92
—— Thomas (mayor of London), 81
—— William (mayor of Bristol, d. 1396), 80, 84, 85
—— William (mayor of Bristol, d. 1474), 4, 11, 55, 62, 66, 72, 75, 77, 79, 81, 83–4, 85, 86–7, 89, 94, 120, 136, 250
Cardiff, 7
Carleton, fulling mill, 195
Carlisle, fulling mill, 195
Carmarthen, 7
Carpentar', Vincent, 192
Carrickfergus, 17, 24
Carveule of Vermewe, 15
Castile, 62; relations with England, 56–8; trade with Bristol, 49–58, 59
—— Isabella of, 58
Castleford, fulling mill, 195
Castro, 53
Caxton, William, xxvi, 148, 151, 153, 154, 164
Chapman, Richard, 18
Charles VII, King of France, 47, 72, 275–6
Chaucer, xii, xiii, 262
Cheddar, fulling mill, 196
Cheddar, Robert, 79, 250–1
Chedworth, 185
Chelsea, xxvii
Chepstow, 7, 19, 34, 119, 240 n. 2
Cheshire, 240 n. 2
Chester, 4, 5, 14, 18, 19, 130
—— Palatinate, 240 n. 2

Chester, Henry, 93
—— Alice, his widow, 76, 93–4
—— John, his son, 92, 93
Chesterfield, 237 n. 2; dyers in, 227
Chilterns, fulling mills, 196
Chilton Foliat, fulling mill, 196
Chippenham, 10; fulling mill, 196
Chirche, John, 63
Chok, Richard, 72
Christ Church, Canterbury, Prior of, 14
Christian I, King of Denmark, 135–6, 138, 139
Christopher of Hook, 276 n. 2
—— of Hull, 35
Chudleigh, fulling mill, 196
Cinque ports, 2
Cirencester, "Dyers' Street", 215
Cley, 127
Clifford, John, 164
Clifton, fulling mill, 195
"Clively", fulling mill, 191
Cockermouth, fulling mill, 195
Coder, William, 72, 95
Cog Anne, 67–8, 88
Cog Joan, 86
Coke, Philip, 85
Cokkes, James, 78
Colchester, 198, 213, 214, 270 n. 4
Colet, John, 167
Colne, fulling mill, 195, 199
Colsell, John, 175 n. 3
Columbus, Christopher, 129
Colwyke, ——, 290
Commines, 48
Compostella, 16, 69; shrine of Saint James, 54
Compton, John, 76
Concarneau, 46
Conquet, 46
Constantinople, fall of, 70
Conterayn, Moses, 45, 50, 80
Copenhagen, 111
Coplestone, John, 285
Corbie, "Corby", xiii, 216, 217
Cordova, 51
Cork, 15
—— John de, 76

Cornwall, 7, 9, 38, 53, 119, 240 n. 2; aulnage, 280, 281, 283 n. 1, 285, 286, 288; fulling mills, 196, 197
—— Duchy of, 240 n. 2
Cotswolds, 9; fulling mills, 196, 197
Coventry, 5, 7, 8, 119, 121, 129, 242 (243) n. 3, 250 n. 2; "blue", 5; drapers, 258; Guild of Holy Trinity, 5; St. Michael's church, 262
Crediton, fulling mill, 196
Crell, William, 157
Croft, Thomas, 97
Cromer, 119, 121, 126, 127
Crosby, Sir John, xxvii
Crosthwaite, fulling mill, 195
Crozon, 46
Cure, William, 175 n. 3
Curteys, ——, stockfishmonger of London, 121
Curuzan, Bernard, 220
Cypressat, lord of, 31
Cyprus, 73

Dacre, fulling mill, 195
Dalrymple, John. *See* de Rumpyll, John
Dam, Damme, Roger of, 92
Damascus, Sultan of, 218 (219), n. 4
Damme, 93; St. Mary's church, 92
Dammin, Balthasar van, 112, 113
Daramayo, Ochoa, 52
Danzig, xvi, xxiii, 13, 258
Darenth, 185
Darlington, 214
Dartmouth, 24, 34, 121; *Trinity* of, 274
Davy, Patrick, 39
—— Richard, 84
Dawes, Edward, 36
Dax, fortress of, 41
Dean, Forest of, 5
de Burgh, Sir William, 17
Dee, river, 14
de Lacy, Gilbert, 192
de la Founte, William, 90
de Loveyne, Godfrey, 207

Denmark, xvii, 110, 134, 135, 139, 144

de Porta, Henry, 202 n. 2

de Pretsch, William, 192

De Puebla, Spanish Ambassador in England, 58

Derby, Walter, 86

Derbyshire, fulling mills, 195

Dersingham, 127

de Rumpyll, John, 18

de Tettebury, William, 203 n. 1

Deva, 53, 57

Devenysh, Nicholas, 20

Devon, 7, 9, 119; aulnage, 280, 281, 283 n. 1, 285, 286, 287, 288; fulling mills, 196, 197

de Welton, Adam, 230

Dickinson, John, 126

Diniz, King of Portugal, 61

Domingo de Fuenterrabia, 53

Doncaster, 280

Dordogne, 32, 45, 246, 272, 274

Dorset, aulnage, 280, 281 n. 3, 283 n. 1, 286, 287

Douai, 242 (243) n. 3

Douro valley, 62

Dover, Straits of, 18, 256

Downton, fulling mill, 191, 196

Drayton, Michael, 11

Drogheda, 18; merchants of, 24, 133

Dublin, 18, 19; Guild of English Merchants in, 19; privileges of English merchants in, 19

Ducastet, John, 46

Dulverton, fulling mill, 196

Dunster, fulling mill, 196

Dunwich, 128, 222

Durham, 51

—— county, 240 n. 2

—— palatinate, 240 n. 2

Dyrholm, 108

East Indies, 219

Edward I, King of England, xiii, 218 (219) n. 4

—— II, King of England, 215

—— III, King of England, 183, 255

Edward IV, King of England, xix, 15, 47, 49, 53, 57, 74, 90, 134, 136–7, 138, 139, 153, 155, 156, 173, 277

Egremont, fullers and dyers, 214; fulling mill, 195

Egypt, 67

Eitona, Galfridus de, 223

Elcot, fulling mill, 192, 196, 198

Eleanor, Queen of Edward I, 202

—— of Aquitaine, 28

Elmet, 200

Elyot, Thomas, 286

Enfield, fulling mill, 197

Eric, King of Denmark, Norway and Sweden, 109, 110, 111, 113, 115

Erlandsson, Hank, 106

Erlyngham, Thomas, 126–7

Essey, John, 84

Esterfield, Esterfeld, John, 78, 95

Ethelred II, 266

Etwell, John, 164

Evesham, 191, 268 n. 1

Eyton, John, 70, 72

Excestre, Philip, 80

Exeter, cloth exports, xviii, 264

—— Bishop of, 191–2

—— Thomas, Duke of, 115

Fabyan, Robert, xxvii, 71, 144, 252, 255 n. 2

Farley, John, 286

Faro, Anthony of, 62–3

Faroë Islands, 128

Fastolf, Sir John, 23, n. 1

Faunt, Philip, 20

Ferdinand of Castile, 58

Finmark, 117, 118, 119, 128, 137

Flanders, "Flaunders", xiv, xvi, xxvi, xxvii, xxix, xxx, 10, 13, 24, 38, 49, 53, 76, 96, 144, 149, 159, 168, 223, 238, 243; textile industry, 239, 242 (243) n. 3, 243 n. 1, 244, 249, 256, 259–60; trade with Bristol, 46

Flanders, Count of, xiv
Fleming, John, 63
Florence, 67; textile industry depressed, 260
Flowre of Minehead, 18
Fordwich, 219
Forster, Stephen, 10–11, 120
Foster, John, 91
Fouler, Roger, 127
Founte, William de la, 90
Fowey, 34, 63, 72, 119, 277; *Julian* of, 91
Freme, John, 46
Froissart, 39
Frome, river, 2, 11
Fuenterrabia, 53
—— Domingo de, 53

Galfridus de Eitona, 223
Galicia, 53, 54
Galway, 16, 17
Galwey, Patrick, 15
Gardner, Thomas, 128
Garleberd, John, 200
Garonne, 32, 40, 41, 45, 246, 272, 274
Gascony, xvii, 28–49, 253, 257, 258, 265–78; definition of medieval Gascony, 265 n. 1; imports, 29, 270; market for English cloth, 246, 248, 253–4, 259, 270; privileges of English merchants in, 32–3. *See also* Bristol, overseas trade; wine trade
Gawge, John, 82
Gaynard, Robert, 82
Gaywode, John, 77, 78, 83
Genoa, 59, 67, 70, 72; ships of 64, 65.
Gentilis, Balthasar, 65
George, 90, 97
George, John, 57
George Heron, 63
Geriksen, John, Archbishop of Upsala, afterwards Bishop of Skálholt, 123

Ghent, 242 (243) n. 3, 249, 260
Ghost of London, 276 n. 1
Gibraltar, 1, 65
Gile, Alfonso, 62
—— Gunsallo, 62
Gironde, 28, 29, 31, 32, 44, 246, 272, 273, 276, 277
Glassonby, fulling mill, 195
Glastonbury, George Inn, 75
Gloucester, 58, 267; cathedral, 187; weavers, 214, 226
—— William, Earl of, 268 n. 1
Gloucestershire, 9; aulnage, 280, 281 n. 2, 286
Godfrey de Loveyne, 207
Godric, St., xii, xiii
Godstow, nunnery, 192
Goldhap, 65
Grasmere, fulling mill, 195
Gravesend, 164
Greece, 68
Greenland, 100, 102
Greenriggs, fulling mill, 195
Grenoble, 189
Grimsby, 13, 128
Grizedale, fulling mill, 195
Guérande, 46
Guetaria, 53; *Mary* of, 52; *San Sebastien* of, 53
Guiche, 33, 272
Guienne, 40
Guildford, fulling mill, 193, 197
Guipuscoa, 53, 57; *James* of, 54, 55; *Mary* of, 52

Hadleigh, 200; fulling mill, 197
Hafnarfjördur, 109, 122
Hainault, 144
Halifax, 280
Hamburg, 141; annual voyage to Iceland from, 140; export of grain, 140
Hampshire, aulnage, 280, 281 n. 2, 286; fulling mills, 197
Hampstead Marshall, fulling mill, 196
Harnham, fulling mill, 196

Harpford, fulling mill, 196
Hartington, fulling mill, 195
Hartland, fulling mill, 196
Hartlebury, fulling mill, 195
Hartlepool, 141
Haryot, Sir William, xxvii
Haut Pays, 38, 39, 43; wines and vineyards of, 30 *et seq.*
Haverford West, 7
Hawkesbury, 201; fulling mill, 196
Hebrides, 185
—— Bishop Patrick of, 99
Hedgely, 134
Helgafell, 114
Henry I, King of England, 22, 204, 225, 226
—— II, King of England, 19, 28, 205, 223, 226, 227
—— III, King of England, 192, 198, 213, 218 (219) n. 4
—— IV, King of England, xvi, 31
—— V, King of England, 15, 109, 110
—— VI, King of England, 74, 85, 117, 282 n. 1
—— VII, King of England, xix, xxvi, 73, 127, 158, 165, 166, 167, 168, 173–4
—— VIII, King of England, xix, xx, xxiv, 166, 177, 181
Henry of Huntingdon, 267
Henry of Ruddington, 230
Hereford, 7
Herefordshire, 280
Heskyn, fulling mill, 196
Hexham, 134
Himley, fulling mill, 195
Hinton, fulling mill, 196
Hólar, 122; Bishops of: Bloxwich, John, 123; Johnson, John, 121–2; Williamson, John, 122–3
Holland, xiv, xvii, xxvi, xxvii, xxix, xxx, 144, 159
Holy Ghost of Schiedam, 124
Hook, *Christopher* of, 276 n. 2
Horn, 109
Huelva, 53

Hull, 1, 13, 34, 35, 66, 265; Bench books, 114; *Christopher* of, 35; expansion of cloth trade, 258–9; harbour, 2; trade with Iceland, 116 *et seq.*
Humber, 2, 128
Hunt, John, 77
Huntingdon, weavers' gild, 214, 225
—— Henry of, 267

Iceland, xvii, xxviii, 1, 5, 8, 11, 13, 14, 66, 73, 81, 89, 91, 96, 98–142 *passim*, 186; children sold, 117; emigrants to England, 117; fulling in, 186–7
—— trade with, 98–142 *passim*; commodities of, 131–2; decline of, 132–42
—— union with Norway (1262), 101, 102. *See also* Bristol, overseas trade; fishing; Lynn, trade with Iceland
Ilfracombe, 7
"Insula Humana" (Isle of Man), 7
Ipswich, 219
Ireland, xxviii, 4, 13–28 *passim*, 38, 65, 87, 99, 124; trade with Bristol, 13–28; with Iceland, 130; exports, 23 *et seq.*; imports, 25–7
Irishman, Patrick, 20
Irish Sea, 130
Isabella of Castile, 58
Isle of Man, 7
Isle of Wight, 35
Italy, Bristol's trade with, 64–73 *passim*; English cloth trade to, 212; English wool in, 215; textile industry, 239, 256
Ivarsson, Vigfus, 110
Ive, 133

Jakes, Elizabeth, 93
—— Robert, 79
James II, King of England, 28

James of Bristol, 61
James of Guipuscoa, 54, 55
James, Saint, shrine of, 54
—— the Less, Saint, 187
Jay, John, 97
Jerusalem, xvii, 102
Jocelin de Brakelond, 200
John, Abbot of St. Albans, 201
John de Cork, 76
John de la Passage, 50
John, King of England, 2, 192,
    201, 213 n. 1, 218 n. 4, 226
—— of Beverley, 212
John of Waterford, 14
John I, King of Portugal, 59
Jonet, John, 21
Joppa, 68, 96
Jorsalafari, 102
Josson, John, 175 n. 3
Julian, 55, 87
—— of Bristol, 17
—— of Fowey, 91

Katharine Sturmy, 69–71
Katherine, 11, 53
Katherine of Aragon, 58
Katherine of Bristol, 120
Kathrine of Hampton, 276 n. 2
Kendal, 7, 52; fulling mill, 195, 199;
    "green", 220
Kennet Valley, fulling mills, 196, 197
Kent, 185
Kentmere, 199
Ketton, Roger of, 229
Kidderminster, fulling mill, 191, 195
Kidwelly, 7
Kilkenny, 23, 25
Kilmainham, Prior of, 15
Kingrode, 2, 21, 48, 67, 91
Kinsale, 15, 16
Kirkjubaer, 124
Kirkstall, fulling mill, 191, 195
Knappe, Thomas, 12
Knaresborough, fulling mill, 193,
    195
Kyle, Edward, 78
—— Joan, 78

Lacy, Gilbert de, 192
Lake District, 209, 220, fulling
    mills, 195, 197
Lambert, Nicholas, 175 n. 3
Lancashire, 240 n. 2; fulling mills, 195
Lancaster, Duchy of, 240 n. 2
Landes, 37
Langland, William, xii, xiii, 251, 252
Languedoc, 37
La Redo, 53
La Réole, 32, 40, 41
La Rochelle, 34, 35, 64, 269
Laugharne (?), 7
Lawford, fulling mill, 197
"Lawgher Havyn" (Laugharne?), 7
Lawhitton, fulling mill, 196
Lawless, Patrick, 20
Leeds, 280; fulling mill, 195
Legha in Buryan, fulling mill, 196
Leicester, 198, 206, 208, 211, 216,
    219, 228, 229, 235; mer-
    chant gild, 222–3, 224, 225,
    230, 233, 238; organisation
    of cloth industry in, 233–4;
    regulations for dyers and
    dyeing, 221, 233; regulations
    for weavers and fullers, 230–
    1, 232
—— Edmund, Earl of, 229
Leicestershire, 79
Leith, 256
Leominster, 7
Levant, 64, 66 n. 1, 67, 70, 71,
    96; Italian merchants lose
    supremacy, 70
Lewys, William, 85
Libourne, 31–2, 44
Limerick, 16, 17, 23; St. Mary's
    church, 16
Lincoln, 99, 198, 209, 211, 212,
    213, 218, 237 n. 5, 238;
    fullers' gild, 185–6, 232;
    merchant gild, 226, 227;
    weavers' gild, 205, 225, 226
—— Earl of, 268–9
Lisbon, 13, 16, 17, 59, 61–2, 63, 64,
    80, 87, 92, 93
Lisle, Sir John, 277 n. 1

Liverpool, 14
Llanstephan, 7
Lloyd, —, 97
Lofoten Isles, 128
Loire, river, 41
Lombard, John, 80
—— William, 46
l'Ombrière, castle of, 31
Londe, Robert, 20
London, *passim*; agreement with Picard merchants, 217–8; burellers, 234–5; cloth exports, xviii, 259, 263, 264; *Liber Custumarum*, 236; looms in, 205; murage grants, 218, 220, 222; ordinances for fulling, 187; weavers, 225, 235; wool exports, xviii. *See also* Companies of London; Merchant Adventurers
—— Bishop of, 22
Lopt, Thorvard, 124
Louis XI, King of France, 47, 49, 277, 278
Louth, 198, 209, 211, 212
Louvain, 242 (243) n. 3
Loveyne, Godfrey de, 207
Low Countries (Netherlands) *passim*; Bristol's connections with, 17, 81; organization of English merchants in, xiv, xv, xvi, xxix, 143–82 *passim*; trade with, English, 143–82 *passim*; Irish, 25; Gascon, 29; Spanish, 49. *See also* Brabant, Flanders, Holland, Zeeland
Lübeck, 14, 140
Lucca, 14; merchants of, 212
Ludlow, drapers, 5; fulling mill, 191, 192, 195; merchant of, 8
Lunaris of York, xii
Lusk, 21
Lynn, 34, 219; church of St. Nicholas, 105; trade with Iceland, 111 *et seq.*; ships of, seized by Denmark, 139

Madeira, 60, 61
Magnus, 123
Malahide, 21
Malines, 242 (243) n. 3
Malmesbury, William of, 267
Malta, 65, 71
Man, Isle of, 7
Manchester, fulling mill, 195
Margaret of Anjou, 74, 277
Margaret of Orwell, 276 n. 1, 277
Margaret Cely, 87 n. 1
Marie, 86, 87
—— of Bristol, 58
—— of Motrico, 57
—— of Navarre, 55
Marie Knight of Amsterdam, 124
Marie de Wilshore, 43
Marlborough, 192, 214; laws of weavers and fullers, 235–8
Marrok, Straits of. *See* Morocco, Straits of
Martyn, Patrick, 15
—— Philip, 15
Mary, 53, 120
—— of Bristol, 15–16
—— of Guetaria, 52
—— of Guipuscoa, 52
Mary and John, 89
Mary Bird, 90 n. 1
Mary Canynges, 89
Mary Redcliffe, 11, 61, 62 n. 1, 89, 120
Maryot, John, 120
Masham, fulling mill, 195
Mauléon, 33
Mauro, Fra, 107
May, Harry, Henry, 20, 39, 62–3, 80
—— Richard, 63–4
Mede, Philip, 72, 79
Medmenham, fulling mill, 196
Mediterranean, xxiii, 1, 64, 66, 67, 68, 70, 71, 88, 96, 102, 216, 257, 208; Italian monopoly of, 65, 73
Melcombe, xviii, 247 n. 3
Mendips, 9
Mere, fulling mill, 196

Meryell, William, 7
Michael Palaeologus, Emperor, 221
Middleburg, 150
Middleton, Elizabeth, 79
—— John, 152
—— Thomas, 79
Milford Haven, 4, 7, 19, 34
Millom, fulling mill, 195
Minehead, 18; ships trading to Ireland, 19
Mitton, fulling mill, 195
Modon, island of, 68
Mold, John, 21
Molton, North, fulling mill, 196
—— South, fulling mill, 196
Monmouth, 7; fulling mill, 195
Montauban, 37, 38
Montferrant, Bertram de, 46
—— Petronilla de, 46
More, Richard, 279–81, 281 n. 4, 282, 285, 286, 288, 289, 290
Moreton Hampstead, fulling mill, 196
Morgan, Stephen, 76
Morocco, Marrok, Straits of, 66, 67, 70, 73
Mors, Ludovic, 36
Motrico, 53, 57; *Marie* of, 57
Munster (Ireland), 15, 16

Nadale, Nicholas, 65
Nantes, 46
Naples, Alfonso of, 72
Napton, Thomas, 121, 129
Narbonne, 37
Neckam, Alexander, 106
Nesle, "Nelle", xiii, 216
Netherlands. *See* Low Countries
Neville, Richard. *See* Warwick, Earls of
New Alresford, fulling mill, 191, 197
Newbury, 10; fulling mill, 196
Newcastle-on-Tyne, xxii, 34, 119, 121, 122, 128, 129, 214, 227, 237 n. 1, 247 n. 3; Merchant Adventurers, 146–7, 148, 161, 172

New Found Land, 142
Newminster, fulling mill, 191
New Phocaea, 221
Newport, 7
Nicholas, 86
—— of Saltash, 128
Nicholas de la Tour, 90
Nicholas the Chaloner, 225, 234, 238
Norfolk, 21, 212
Normandy, 17, 29, 44, 46, 47, 266
North Sea, 1, 65, 102, 258
Northampton, 198, 206, 211, 212; regulation of dyeing, 219; tolls, 221
Northamptonshire, fulling mills, 195
Northumberland, Earl of, 134
Norton, Thomas, 56
Norway, xvii, 96, 98, 99, 137, 142, 144, 220; trade and relations with Iceland, 100 *et seq.*
Norwich, 175 n. 3, 176, 217
Newsham, fulling mill, 190, 195
Nottingham, 5; dyeing in, 227, 228; merchant gild, 226; weavers' gild, 214, 225, 226
Nottinghamshire, fulling mills, 195

Old Sarum, fulling mill, 196
Ólof, mistress, 138
Oporto, 59, 62
Orkney Islands, 135
Örlyg, 99
Orwell, 128; *Margaret* of, 276 n. 1, 277
Oswestry, 79
Overey, William, 153
Oxford, 198, 205, 213, 214; laws of the weavers and fullers, 235–8; weavers' gild, 205, 225
Oxfordshire, aulnage, 280, 288; fulling mills, 191
Overbury, fulling mill, 195, 196
Ozerio, Jerome de, 61

Padstow, 7
Painscastle, fulling mill, 195

Pale, the, 18, 28
Palmer, Nicholas, 50
Pálsson, Hannes, 112, 113, 115;
    his indictment of English in
    Iceland, 113–14
Paris, 269
Passage, 53
Paston, Margaret, 21
—— family, 22
Patrick, Bishop of the Hebrides, 99
Paul, Bishop, 100
Pavy, John, 92
—— William, 95
Payn, John, 57
Peke, John, 285
Penmarch, 46
Penrith, fulling mill, 195
Penryn, fulling mill, 196
Pera, 70
Percy, John, 114
—— family, regulations for break-
    fast, 21, 22
Perrers, Alice, 255
Perth, 225
Peterborough, 267
Petre of Bristol, 57
Petrus de Antina, 65
Philip, Archduke, 165
Picardy, 216, 257
Picquigny, Treaty of, 48
Pillars of Hercules, 65
Pisa, 59, 67, 73
Plymouth, 4, 7, 17, 34, 65, 272;
    pilgrims embarking at, 54, 69
Pompeii, 185
Pontefract, 280
Poole, 247 n. 3
Porta, Henry de, 202 n. 2
Porter, William, 18
Portugal, xxviii, 4, 5, 8, 17, 29, 53,
    56, 65, 81, 90, 96, 220, 257;
    shipping and navigation, 61;
    trade with Bristol, 58–64,
    257, 258. See also wine
    trade
Portugalete, 53
Pretsch, William de, 192
"Prikkingham, Pryor of", 12

Prussia, 90, 116, 144, 151, 258;
    merchants of, 112
Purley, fulling mill, 196
Pykering, Pekyring, John, 156, 164,
    166, 173, 174
—— William, 154, 154 n. 2

Quimper, 46
Quimperle, 46, 61
Quyrke, John, 18

Ranworth, 187
Reading, fulling mill, 196
Red Sea, 219
Regnault Girard, 278
Renamond, John, 54
Renteria, 53
Rhineland, 266, 269
Richard I, King of England, 226, 228
—— II, King of England, xix, 27,
    35, 59
—— III, King of England, 141
Richard of Shilton, 228–30
Richards, Alice, 10
Richeman, John, 122
Ríf, 138
Ripon, 280
Robert of Seckworth, 192
Rodecog, 80
Roger, Abbot of St. Albans, 202
Roger of Ketton, 229
Roger, William, 82–3
Rolleston, fulling mill, 195
Ross, 15
Rothwell, fulling mill, 195
Rouen, 270; wine trade, 266, 267
Rouille, Guillaume de, 273 n. 2
Rowley, Thomas, 92
—— Margaret, his widow, 92
—— William, junior, 92
—— William, senior, 92
—— Joanna, his widow, 92
Ruddington, Henry of, 230
Rudston, John, 175 n. 3
Rumpyll, John de, 18
Russell, Margery, 93
—— Robert, 82
Rydon, Master, 164 n. 1

St. Albans, fulling mill, 191, 201; mills, 201–2
St. Croix, Abbey of, 269
St. Emilion, 32, 44
St. Ives, 7, 217, 233
St. Jean d'Angeli, 273
St. Jean de Luz, 34
St. John the Baptist, Friary, Ludlow, 191, 192
St. Macaire, 32, 41
St. Pol de Léon, 46
St. Seurin, Abbey of, 269
St. Wandrille, Abbey of, 210
Salimbene, 28
Salisbury, 77
Saltash, 119; *Nicholas* of, 128
Saltes, 53
Salva Deo, 65
Sampford Courtenay, fulling mill, 196
Sampson, Thomas, 86
—— Joan, 86
Sandwich, "Sandwyche", 13, 54, 64, 72, 121, 277; cloth exports, 263, 264; *Warry* of, 276 n. 1
San Lucar Barrameda, 53
San Sebastian, 53
San Sebastien, of Guetaria, 53
Santander, 53, 93
Sasiola, Godfred de, 55
Savernake forest, timber from, 192, 198
Scarborough, 119, 128, 141
Schellendorp, Stephen, 113, 115, 125
Schiedam, *Holy Ghost* of, 124
Scotland, 17, 186
Scrope, Sir Stephen, 14
Seckworth, fulling mills, 192, 196
—— Robert of, 192
Seglysthorn, John, 92
Seine, river, 41, 266, 270
Selander, Hankyn, 62–4
Selly, David, 39
Semur cathedral, 232
Sens, 185
Severn, river, 2, 4, 11, 65
Seville, 16, 51, 53, 68, 92

Shannon, river, 16; salmon in, 23
Sheepstall, fulling mill, 196
Sheldon, John, 164, 177
Shelsley, fulling mill, 195
Sherburn, "Shireburn" (in Elmet), 200–1
Shetland Islands, 135
Shilton, Richard of, 228–30
Shipward, John, 55, 79, 83, 94
Shirburn (Somerset), 9
Shrewsbury, 5, 18; dyeing in, 227; merchant gild, 224
Shrewsbury, Earl of, 45
Shropshire, 8
Sierra de Marao, 62
Simnel, Lambert, 167
Skagafjörd, 122
Skálholt, 99, 109; Bishops of: Geriksen, John, 123; William, 98; Williamson, John, 122
Skye, 186
Skyrmot, William, 57
Slapton, fulling mill, 196
Sligo, "Slegothe", 17, 21
Sluys, 165
Smyrna, Gulf of, 221
Snaefellness, 99
Somerset, 9, 79, 119; aulnage, 280, 281 n. 3, 283 n. 1, 286, 287; fulling mills, 191, 196, 197
Somme, river, 41, 216
Soulac, 47, 277
Sound, the, 136
Southampton, xxii, 2, 35, 55, 64, 73, 263, 264, 265, 275; *Anne* of, 276 n. 1, 277, 277 n. 1; expansion of cloth trade, 259; Italian galleys at, 10; overland trade to Bristol, 65; tolls at, 9, 215
Southwold, 128
Sowerby, fulling mill, 195
Spain, xxvii, 37, 65, 89, 96, 130, 144, 259; oil, iron and wax from, xxviii; trade of Bristol with, 4, 21, 36, 49–58 *passim*, 76, 80, 81, 90;

Spain—contd.
    trade with Gascony, 29; with Ireland, 14, 17; wool and yarn from, 215
Spaynell, William, 86
—— Soneta, 86
Speed, John, 2
Speen, fulling mill, 196
Spenser, Edmund, 26
Spryng, Jordan, 55
Stalham, 187
Staffordshire, fulling mills, 195
Stamford, 198, 209, 211, 212, 213, 220, 234, 238
Stanley-on-the-Marden, fulling mill, 190, 196
Stanton Drew, 79
Stanway, fulling mill, 196
Stavely, fulling mill, 195, 199
Steeple Langford, fulling mill, 193, 196
Stephen, King of England, 2, 226
Stone, John, 20
Stonor, Elizabeth, 77
Stourton, Sir John, 72
Strange, Thomas, 86, 89
Stratford (Middlesex), fulling mill, 197, 203, 207
Strubby, fulling mill, 197
Sturmy, Ellen, 69, 72–3
—— Robert, 66–73, 88; will of, 71, 72
Stychemersh, Stephen, 63
Suffolk, 21, 128
—— William, Duke of, 43, 90
Surrey, aulnage, 280
Sussex, aulnage, 280
Sutton (Hants), fulling mill, 191, 197
Swan, Richard, 157
Swansea, 121
Sweden, xvii, 144
Symondes, William, 84

Tagus, river, 61
Talgarrek in Camborne, fulling mill, 196
Talgarth, fulling mill, 195
Talmont, 35

Taunton, fulling mill, 191, 196
—— Prior of, 93
Taverner, John, 66, 89
Teme, river, 191, 192
Tenby, 7, 34
Tettebury, William de, 203 n. 1
Tewkesbury, 5, 215, 268 n. 1; "Fullers' Street", 214
Thames Valley, fulling mills, 196
Thorgunna, 99
Thorlak, Saint, 99
Thorleifsson, Björn, 137–8
Thorpe Arch, fulling mill, 195
Tinctor, Nicholas, 223
—— Philip, 234 n. 3
Tintern, 7
—— Abbot of, 7
Titsey, 185
Tonbridge, fulling mill, 197
Tooley, Henry, 126
Tothill, fulling mill, 197
Totnes, 215
Toulouse, 37, 216 n. 3, 257
Towton, 1, 134
Treclego, fulling mill, 196
Tremodret, fulling mill, 196
Trewithian in St. Wenn, fulling mill, 196
Treygot, T., 280, 281
Trinity, 53, 86, 97
—— of Bristol, 14, 62–4
—— of Dartmouth, 274
Tybesta, fulling mill, 196

Ulster, 17, 18
Ulverston, 201
Undergod, Peter, 192
Upsala, Geriksen, John, Archbishop of, afterwards bishop of Skálholt, 123
Usk, 7; fulling mill, 195

Vache, John, 115–6
van Dammin, Balthasar, 112, 113
Vannes, 46
Varrole, John de, 55
Vasqueannus, —, 62
Vasquez, Sir John, 60

Vaughan, Henry, 52, 53
Veilho, John, 62–4
Venice, 64, 65, 67, 70
Vermewe, *Carveule* of, 15
Vestmann Isles, 108, 109, 112, 113, 125, 133
Viana, 62
Vigfusson, Ivar, 124; Margaret, his sister, 123
Voet, Bartholomew, 116
Vyell Place, 75

Wakefield, 280; fulling mill, 195
Walberswick, 128
Wales, 7, 9, 11, 65, 119, 194, 240 n. 2
—— South, 9
Wallingford, 224 n. 1
Waltham, fulling mill, 191, 197
Walton, 19
Wansbeck, river, 191
Warbeck, Perkin, 167
Warsop, fulling mill, 195
Warry of Sandwich, 276 n. 1
Warwick, 8; castle, 8
—— Earls of: Richard Beauchamp, xvii, 8; Richard Neville, 72, 89, 91, 134
Waterford, 14, 15, 20; *John* of, 14
Wellingborough (Northants), fulling mill, 195
Wells, 79; fulling mill, 196
Welsh Marches, fulling mills, 195
Welton, Adam de, 230
Wendish towns, 140
Wendover, fulling mill, 196
Wendy, John, 154, 164, 167
Westbury on Trym, 79, 94
Weston, Robert, 121, 123
Wethipolle, Polle, 175 n. 3
Wheatenhurst, fulling mill, 196
Whitby, 128
Wight, Isle of, 35
Wild, ——, 133
William, Bishop of Skálholt, 98
—— of Malmesbury, 267
—— of Worcester, 68, 75, 86–7, 89, 90, 95

William, Richard, 61
—— the Lion, King of Scotland, 225
Williamson, John, Bishop of Skálholt, 122
Wilton, fulling mill, 195
Wiltshire, 9; aulnage, 280, 282, 288; fulling mills, 191, 193, 196, 197
Wiltshire, Clement, 76, 79
Winchcomb, fulling mill, 191, 196
Winchester, 198, 208, 213, 214, 215, 217, 235; fullers' gild, 204, 225, 226; fulling mill, 197, 206; laws of weavers and fullers, 235–8; merchant gild, 226; tolls, 215; weavers' gild, 204, 225, 226
—— Bishop of, 191, 193, 198, 217
Windsor, 168
Wirksworth, fulling mill, 195
Witham, fulling mill, 190 n. 1, 197
Withiford, Hugh, 79
Witney, fulling mills, 191, 196
Witt, Jacob de, 178
Wiveliscombe, fulling mill, 196
Wode, John, 92
—— Thomas, 92
Wolffe, John, 136
Woodstock, 168
Wookey, fulling mill, 196
Worcester, 5, 8; dyers in, 214, 223
—— William of, 68, 75, 86–7, 89, 90, 95
Worcestershire, 82; aulnage, 280, 281 n. 2, 288; fulling mills, 195; vineyards, 268
Wyche, John, 16, 120
Wycombe, 192, 196, 224 n. 1
Wylly, John, 91
"Wynchylsee", 54
Wynne, John, 86
Wyresdale, fulling mill, 195

Yarmouth, cloth exports, 264
Yonge, Thomas, the elder, 81
—— the younger, 81, 95

York, 1, 14, 118, 198, 209, 211, 212, 218, 222; merchant gild, 226; weavers, 208; weavers' gild, 205, 226. *See also* Merchant Adventurers.
—— Adam of, 35
—— Archbishop of, 200–1
—— Duchess of, 167
—— Richard, Duke of, 81, 91
—— Lunaris of, xii

Yorkshire, 190, 204, 208, 209, 253; aulnage, 281; fulling mills, 193, 195, 197
Youghal, 15
Ypres, 244, 249, 260

Zeeland, "Seeland", xiv, xvi, xxvi, xxvii, xxix, xxx, 92, 144, 159